HEROES OR VILLAINS?

the blair government reconsidered

JON **DAVIS**   JOHN **RENTOUL**

OXFORD
UNIVERSITY PRESS

Great Clarendon Street, Oxford, OX2 6DP,
United Kingdom

Oxford University Press is a department of the University of Oxford.
It furthers the University's objective of excellence in research, scholarship,
and education by publishing worldwide. Oxford is a registered trade mark of
Oxford University Press in the UK and in certain other countries

© Jon Davis and John Rentoul 2019

The moral rights of the authors have been asserted

First Edition published in 2019

Impression: 1

Published in the United States of America by Oxford University Press
198 Madison Avenue, New York, NY 10016, United States of America

British Library Cataloguing in Publication Data

Data available

Library of Congress Control Number: 2018960601

ISBN 978–0–19–960885–0

Printed and bound in Great Britain by
Clays Ltd, Elcograf S.p.A.

Links to third party websites are provided by Oxford in good faith and
for information only. Oxford disclaims any responsibility for the materials
contained in any third party website referenced in this work.

For Lord Hennessy, godfather of contemporary British government history

Acknowledgements

The prologue explains the genesis of this book. There are so many to thank for what is our very own 'Journey':

It has been an honour and a privilege to lead first 'The Blair Government', then 'New Labour in Government', and now 'The Blair Years' classes—our thanks to all students and guests.

Next, a heartfelt appreciation to the mighty Strand Group team of Michelle Clement, Dr Jack Brown, Ashley Sweetman, Martin Stolliday, and Eleanor Hallam for all the support, energy, inspiration, niceness, and general fun. Our gratitude also goes to Kamile Stankute, Jan Gökçen, Jamie Sweeney, and Matt Corden for their hard work and good spirits over the past few years.

Special mention must go to all of the Strand Group's Visiting Fellows, who contribute so much by way of teaching and general goodwill—we simply could not do it without them: Lord Adonis, Ed Balls, Alun Evans, Baroness Jay, William Keegan, Jimmy Leach, Sir Iain Lobban, Clare Lombardelli, Catherine MacLeod, Lord Macpherson, Baroness Morgan, Mario Pisani, Sir Dave Ramsden, and Sir Kevin Tebbit—and our old friend, fellow Mile End Groupee from the first days, Dr Simon Case.

We are also grateful to all at King's including Professors Frans Berkhout, Ed Byrne, Bobby Duffy, Jeremy Jennings, Mark Pennington, Evelyn Welch, and Sir Christopher Geidt.

For the Mile End Group years, thanks must go to the visionary Fearghal McGoveran for helping raise the ambition of the early days, Chetun Patel for great companionship from the J. P. Morgan days to QM and beyond, and Dr James Jinks for helping keep the flame alive through tough times. And great respect to Dr Peter Davies, Kat Brown, Morgan Daniels, Abdul Hamid Sheikh Mohamood, Sophie Kimber, Will Gunn, Richard Balmer, Charlene Brennan, Michelle Mansfield, Sarah Taylor, Marie Kemplay, Matthew Jackson, Phil Horscroft, Ben Draper, Jon Bolton, Sian Cleary, and Tom Robinson for their past efforts and current friendship. Among some great QM Professors we pay tribute to the late John Ramsden, Mark White, and Jim Bolton, while Professor Francesco Guidi Bruscoli, first of QM, then of the University of Florence, has always provided great friendship and Italian influence over the years.

A very special note of gratitude must be given to the Cabinet Secretaries who have supported us over the years: Lords Armstrong, Butler, Wilson, Turnbull, and O'Donnell, and the late Lord Heywood. Many serving officials, past and present, deserve our thanks, including Peter Hill, Ed Whiting, and John Tolson.

Special thanks go to the late Charles Cox, Craig Wilson, Mal George, Jacqui Ferguson, and especially James Johns, who found the MEG intriguing and valuable, supporting it over fifteen years to the tune of £2m through first Electronic Data Systems, then Hewlett Packard, Hewlett Packard Enterprise, and finally DXC Technology— without which we could not have achieved what we have.

From Jon, all his love for the support and encouragement from the wife, Mum and Dad, and all the family.

From John, all his love and thanks to his family.

And finally, thanks beyond measure to Peter Hennessy, without whom this simply would not have happened.

Table of Contents

Prologue

The genesis of this book took place in John Rentoul's doorway in the spring of 2008. I had first met John at one of the first Mile End Group (MEG) political and government seminars at Queen Mary University of London in 2004, when I was an organizer of the MEG whilst studying for a doctorate, and he was respondent to Dianne Hayter (now Baroness, and Chair of Labour's National Executive 2007–8). Dianne's lecture was on how the Labour right wing saved the party in the 1980s—'history walking', as an early sponsor used to call the events. Two years later, John kindly allowed me to shadow him for a few days and we kept in touch, charting the end of Tony Blair's government. He was chief political commentator of the *Independent on Sunday*, biographer of Blair, and the go-to person for a media requiring balance—but finding ever fewer supporters of the prime minister as familiarity and the Iraq operation bred contempt. Dislike of Blair, and demand for John, grew and grew.

As I left after one of John's fine lunchtime fry-ups, I mentioned that I was about to inherit the undergraduate lecturing that my mentor, the doyen of contemporary British government history, Professor Peter Hennessy (now Lord Hennessy of Nympsfield) was retiring from. I added that the Queen Mary History Department had called for new 'special subjects', twenty-week-long undergraduate modules with essays, an exam, and a 10,000-word dissertation—truly rigorous history.

The publishing sensation of 2007 was *The Blair Years*, Alastair Campbell's first volume of extracts from his diaries, an edited 600 pages of the most comprehensive daily downloading of a prime minister's brain ever. Professor Hennessy had always been an energetic advocate to his students of extensive primary sources for British Government, including inviting some great practitioners to share their experiences, something wonderfully brought to life through his mighty publications. My thinking was that the Campbell diaries would allow us to do something extraordinary and base new teaching upon the study of a remarkable prime minister only just over a year after he had retired. (When the current director of the Victoria and Albert Museum, former Labour Shadow Education Secretary, Dr Tristram Hunt, in 2008 a colleague in QM's History Department and another in daily media demand, was asked a snap question in reference to our initiative at the end of a *Today* programme interview if he thought the Campbell *Diaries* were a suitable historical resource and he replied, 'Er, no', we gave a collective wry smile.)

I asked John if he would be up for doing something radical and he replied: 'I've always wanted to be professor of Blair studies.' We began to build. We reasoned that, though we had the Campbell *Diaries* and, what with Blair being essentially the first Internet-era prime minister, access to a mass of material previously difficult to corral, we needed further primary material to really bolster the credibility of the module.

Through my apprenticeship under Professor Hennessy, I got to know several of the present and retired senior civil servants, while John had New Labour on proverbial speed dial. If we couldn't have declassified government files, such as Professor Hennessy had used extensively (since 2010 we have the twenty-years rule but it is running slightly behind and the first Blair-era minutes are expected in 2020), we could build upon Hennessy's approach and invite to the classroom on a weekly basis those who took part in the highest levels of government decision-making—and others who actually wrote the minutes. So began a rich seam of classes which often had an air of the select committee hearing about them, paving the way for the current Number Ten Downing Street and HM Treasury-partnered modules I now run at King's College London, following my move in 2014.

The classes began in the autumn of 2008 and quickly attracted media attention, with perhaps the highlight of the first year being Alastair Campbell's appearance in January 2009 accompanied by a *Newsnight* camera team. The students, thankfully, loved the class, really got into the swing of grilling the special guests, and many superb dissertations were written. The *Times Higher Education* shortlisted me for Most Innovative Teacher in 2010. And, in 2011, after letting us know he was 'intrigued', Tony Blair himself took the class in his Grosvenor Square office. In 2012, the teaching moved to a postgraduate setting and was renamed 'New Labour in Government' and then, in 2016, became 'The Blair Years'.

John, now a Visiting Professor, and I began to discuss aping Prof. Hennessy once again, and writing the book of the class (as *The Hidden Wiring*, *The Prime Minister*, and *The Secret State* were).[1] Oxford University Press contracted us and we began. It has taken a long time: partly because we thought that we needed the Chilcot inquiry to report before we did; partly because John's profile grew and grew as he took to Twitter like Ed Balls to primetime TV, and I spent much of my time teaching and institution building. But mostly because contemporary history moved so fast—it has a habit of doing that—the analytical framework we were using kept moving. First, we attempted to construct an all-encompassing tome, but as the unprecedented flood of memoirs and diaries piled up, this became increasingly unwieldy. Then, as the New Labour era truly ended and the Conservative-Liberal Democrat coalition captured the imagination, our friend Lord Adonis suggested we work on the basis that you could look at the years after 1997 as a coalition between the Blairites and the Brownites. Finally, we decided that we would simply work on providing a counterbalance to the vast array of negativity that began around Blair before he even became prime minister, gathered pace throughout his incumbency, and then consumed almost all before it in the years after his retirement. We would demonstrate that so much of the criticism was hyperbolic, unfounded or simply wrong-headed by way of our research. Where our findings demonstrated that the

Blair government was not held in contempt, by nor had it politicized, the Civil Service, but had conducted a brilliant reform of public services and, crucially, had not lied over Iraq, we would say so. But we would also provide new criticism where we discovered it was appropriate. Truly, an attempt to find a new balance.

Moreover, when Prof. Hennessy wrote his huge and hugely influential books *Whitehall* (published in 1989)[2] and *The Prime Minister* (2000), government was different. Secrecy abounded. The consequence was that so many of his footnotes were categorized as 'private information'. The years since have seen a revolution in transparency, not least with the Freedom of Information Act which came fully into force in 2005, but also with the very real need for government to open up and give a sense of what it is taxpayers are getting for their money and how these institutions serve the public. It means that only a handful of the references in this book are unavoidably secret. It also means that there is little need for paraphrasing to protect anonymity and so we have decided to quote at length, which brings the added benefit of reading the first-hand testimony of the senior protagonists.

John and I have always attempted to convey the complexity of governing. The following pages contain an account of highly intelligent and committed men and women who operated in the—sometimes conflicting—belief that what they were trying to do was to make a positive difference to their country, and the world a better place.

We hope you enjoy it.

Jon Davis

Introduction

Tony Blair was *the* political colossus in Britain for thirteen years after he became leader of the Labour Party in 1994. He was prime minister for ten years, second only in length of service since 1900 to Margaret Thatcher (11½ years). This was longer than prime ministers H. H. Asquith (8½ years), Winston Churchill (8½), Harold Wilson (7½), Stanley Baldwin (7), Ramsay MacDonald (7), John Major (6½), David Lloyd George (6), Clement Attlee (6), Harold Macmillan and David Cameron (both 6).

Blair bequeathed a significant domestic legacy, including a settlement in Northern Ireland, revived public services, and a changed society. He was globally influential, a persuasive and activist leader who may prove to be the last British prime minister to bestride the globe. Yet he will always be associated with his decision to join US President George W. Bush in the 2003 invasion of Iraq. Most prime ministers are unpopular when they leave office, but his reputation continued to decline in the years after. Iraq was clearly one of the most important reasons for this, but it was only part of a progression by which Blair went from Olympian heights of popularity and electoral success, privately referred to by David Cameron and George Osborne, respectively prime minister and Chancellor 2010–16, as 'the Master', to becoming toxic for many in the UK.[1] Although he won three elections in a row for Labour, two of them by huge margins, he was disowned by many in his own party, and the term 'Blairite' became an insult of choice. The election of the hard-left Jeremy Corbyn as Labour leader in 2015 seemed to be, if not an equal, at least an opposite reaction to Blair's long dominance from the centre of British politics.

The purpose of this book is to assess the criticisms of him and his government in a dispassionate way, drawing upon our 'Blair Government' and related teaching modules, first at Queen Mary University of London, during 2008–14, and then at King's College London, since 2016.[2] Each year, the students on the modules have been addressed by politicians, civil servants, and special advisers who worked in that government, as well as by Tony Blair himself. This range of guest speakers has provided us with a treasure trove of first-hand testimony. Imagine if the same had happened, capturing a wide range of memories before the passage of time could affect them after Attlee's government fell or, indeed, after the Second World War. As Peggy Noonan, former speechwriter to Ronald Reagan, once said: 'History needs data, detail, portraits, information; it needs eyewitness. "I was there, this is what I saw."'[3] Within the thirty-year rule—currently being reduced to twenty years—under which official papers remain confidential, the only way to get to the heart of government through primary sources is by oral evidence and memoirs of those who were there. (In fact, with Blair, the first prime minister of the Internet age, these sources became much more important, as the shift from paper to electronic record will have lost much correspondence.) The transcripts of our teaching sessions provided a lot of the raw material for this book, and we carried out further interviews, in addition to our own research. Many of our conclusions were shaped by class discussions and we are grateful to all those who took part. It has been fascinating to observe the changing perceptions of the Blair government that students have brought to the course over the years. In the earlier ones, there was a particular interest in, and admiration for, the professionalism of New Labour's media operation; in later years, the negative associations of Iraq have been more evident.

Because the focus of our teaching has been on how government works, the core of the book—chapters 2 and 3—is an assessment of the criticisms of how Blair ran his administration. New Labour was activist and in a hurry. It was criticized in unprecedented fashion from its first days for the *way* it governed. This means a focus on the machinery of government and on the criticisms of decision-making at the centre— in particular of prime-ministerial rather than Cabinet government (the accusation of presidentialism), of excessive informality ('sofa' government), of an unhealthy obsession with media management ('spin'), and of politicizing the Civil Service through the empowering of special advisers ('spads', referred to early on as 'spin doctors'). We consider and evaluate the practice and impact of the markedly aggressive government presentation led by Alastair Campbell, Blair's press secretary and later director of communications and strategy, as he tried to meet the pro-Conservative bias of the British print media, and control the revolution unleashed by 24-hour news TV, and the mass adoption of mobile phones and the Internet. He was the best known of the special advisers, those political appointees who are neither elected politicians nor civil servants, who became such focus of attention and who, according to critics, smashed the ideal of considered, collegiate, and impartial public service. New Labour's activism meant competition with the Civil Service to be managers of an enlarged state, so different from the traditional Conservative approach—often to set a course and let the civil servants get on with it (while cutting activities, numbers, and therefore capability).

Many of these questions return repeatedly to the central political relationship of the period, that between Blair and Gordon Brown, who was Chancellor of the Exchequer throughout. For example, while we found that collective Cabinet government was weak in this period, this was not so much because all power was taken to a 'president' Blair, but because it was drawn to the two-person axis at the head of government. The book starts, therefore, with a chapter devoted to the conceit of treating the Blair government as if it had been a coalition between the Blairite and Brownite parties. We believe that this model helps to understand how the Blair government worked, with its decision-making core being the 'duumvirate' of the two former friends and allies—an unequal and complex relationship that was nevertheless the engine room of what they called their New Labour 'project'.

We are aware, though, that seeing the Blair government as a coalition risks adopting the viewpoint primarily of the dominant party, namely Blair and his Blairites. For them, the relationship with Brown and his supporters was one that had to be managed (or simply tolerated) in order to preserve the supremacy of their man and their faction. It is also true that most of our witnesses were drawn from the Blairite wing of the coalition. Hence the importance of the contributions of Ed Balls, who spoke to our students, was interviewed for this book, and also teaches, as a Visiting Professor at King's College London, the associated course 'The Treasury and Economic History since 1945'. Given that Brown himself has rarely spoken about the inner workings of his time in Blair's government, and only latterly published his autobiography,[4] the testimony of his principal adviser and strategist throughout this period is highly valuable. Balls is perhaps the most important witness in chapter 4, devoted to the workings of the Treasury under Brown, and therefore under Blair, but we were also fortunate to be able to draw on the extensive accounts of former long-serving senior Treasury officials, Lord Macpherson of Earl's Court and Sir Dave Ramsden. We were also fortunate to be able to include the exclusive thoughts of Sir Jeremy Heywood, who served as Secretary to the Cabinet from 2012 until shortly before his death in 2018.

In this book we are interested in the Blair government 1997–2007. Although we obviously have to touch on the Brown administration that followed it, and indeed on the Coalition and Conservative governments that came afterwards, we have not sought to assess Brown as prime minister, either for his handling of the machinery of government or for his broader record, which was dominated by his handling of the financial crisis.

Instead, we close our assessment of the Blair government with Iraq. Because the war is such an important part of the legacy, and is so closely associated with the machinery-of-government criticisms—indeed the phrase 'sofa government' arose from the commentary on the Butler report of 2004 into the intelligence on Iraq's weapons of mass destruction—we devote an entire chapter to it. This relies heavily on the 2016 *Report of the Iraq Inquiry*, chaired by Sir John Chilcot, although we draw on our guest speakers to expand on the politics of the decision. Sally Morgan, who was Blair's Director of Government Relations, for example, offered a remarkable view of Blair's attitude to the House of Commons vote on Iraq on 18 March 2003: that if the Commons had voted in favour of military action but a majority of Labour MPs had voted against, Blair would have seen through the invasion, 'as Prime Minister but not as Labour Prime Minister', and would have stepped down as soon as the initial operation was over.[5]

This book is not an attempt at a comprehensive assessment of Blair's record, but our concluding chapter tries to pull together the strands of our analysis of his government's decision-making. We do not try to assess all the results of all policies: that would require a social and economic history of the period of the kind produced by Polly Toynbee and David Walker.[6] But while our main focus is on the workings of government, the conclusion attempts an overview of the effects of the Blair government's policies in order to assess the quality of decision-making in that period.

Blair's place in the pantheon of prime ministers

To govern is to choose, and to choose is often to divide and disappoint. History tells us that every significant prime minister of the modern age has had a chequered reputation as they depart the stage. The interesting point is how reputations are then sometimes repaired and enhanced, often in light of contemporary mores. The lot of a prime minister who does *anything* is usually a much-criticized one. The opprobrium directed at Blair is much the same as it ever was.

A century on, David Lloyd George is remembered for presiding over the eclipse of the Liberal Party and a cash-for-honours scandal as much as his strong war leadership and pre-war welfare reforms. Winston Churchill is remembered as arguably the greatest ever Briton because of his leadership during the Second World War, which stands high above the many controversies of his long life—crossing the floor of the House of Commons not once but twice, the Dardanelles campaign, going back on the gold standard, standing against both Indian independence and Edward VIII's abdication, and generally being 'gloriously unfit for office',[7] in Roy Jenkins's equally glorious phrase, during his second 'Indian summer' premiership. Attlee's reputation has risen in recent decades, focused upon his quiet and calm, yet determined demeanour which got Britain through the Second World War when he was deputy prime minister from 1942, and then as prime minister creating the modern welfare state, most notably the National Health Service. This hero-worship largely avoided awkward questions about his secret acquisition of British nuclear weapons (not even his Cabinet knew), and the troubled legacies of withdrawal from Palestine and India. Attlee was remembered for several decades by many as a 'mouse' whose inability to campaign led to the squandering of the 1945 landslide within six years, a deeply divided party of Gaitskellites and Bevanites, and thirteen subsequent years of Conservative rule. Not until several decades later did supportive books help to turn the tide.

Anthony Eden's premiership, 1955–7, will forever be synonymous with prime-ministerial hubris culminating in national humiliation when perhaps *the* global foreign policy expert launched the Suez invasion—which managed the almost impossible by alienating not only Egypt but France, Israel, the USA, the USSR, much of the Arab world, and most of the Commonwealth. Mention Harold Macmillan and one may think of his presiding over the building of 300,000 homes a year, his end-of-empire 'Wind of Change' speech, and possibly his poor handling of the Profumo affair, a complicated scandal involving the Secretary of State for War, a model, and a Soviet naval attaché. Harold Wilson is remembered mostly for winning, often by narrow margins, four out of five general elections, but also for a slipperiness exemplified by his ill-judged post-devaluation comment 'It does not mean that the pound here in Britain, in your pocket or purse or in your bank, has been devalued',[8] his keeping out of the Vietnam war despite heavy American pressure, and a general air of paranoia about security service plots against him. Edward Heath's time as prime minister, 1970–4, ended in humiliation after an early election, called on the question 'Who governs Britain?' The electorate, impatient with his failure to resolve a dispute with the miners, gave an equivocal answer, returning Wilson at the head of a minority government. Whereas James Callaghan 1976–9, will always be synonymous with going 'cap in hand' to the International Monetary Fund to rescue the public finances and the Winter of Discontent public sector strikes. The *Sun* headline 'Crisis? What Crisis?' may have been words he did not actually utter, but they captured a feeling that he was out of touch and had lost control of events.[9] The legacy of Margaret Thatcher, on the other hand, is one of strength, clarity, divisiveness, and callousness—for some, she saved Britain from malaise and ungovernability; for others, she tore to shreds the existing social fabric; in fact, she did a bit of both. And the John Major years are remembered for the coming together of two themes of twentieth- and twenty-first-century British history: difficult European relations and devaluation. After the pound crashed out of the European exchange rate mechanism, taking the Conservatives' reputation for economic competence with it, a disintegrating governing party foundered on the question of European integration, which contributed to an historic electoral defeat. Gordon Brown may well be remembered by history for his recapitalization of the banks that prevented an economic depression, but his fag-end New Labour years resulted in 2010's electoral defeat, following a tired-looking and accident-prone three years. David Cameron's six years were abruptly ended when he lost the Brexit vote in 2016. The point is that no prime minister, certainly since 1945, has left office to widespread acclaim. This is the context in which the historian should judge Tony Blair.

With his entire record taken into account, Blair invites comparison with twentieth-century prime-ministerial giants Lloyd George, Churchill, Attlee, and Thatcher. From 1994, Blair looked, sounded, and acted like an unusual politician. But it was not until the 'new dawn' election landslide of 2 May 1997 that his exceptionalism was cemented. Labour's failure to win the previous election under Neil Kinnock, when opinion polls suggested he would, had ingrained a deep pessimism about the party's prospects among its leaders and supporters. Blair's electoral success was important not in its own right but because it permitted the longest period of Labour government in history. No previous Labour government had lasted more than six years. Yet it was significant that Blair's triumph, winning 419 seats and a majority of 179 out of 659 contested (beating even the Labour majority of 145 in 1945), on a post-war record swing of 10 per cent and a 71 per cent turnout, came after four Conservative victories stretching back eighteen years.[10] One simply could not argue with these facts, unless one was Neal Lawson, who wrote in 2015 that 'in hindsight the wrong people were voting Labour'.[11] For the idea quickly gained ground that Blair had stolen the 'left-wing' victory for which Labour was on course when its former leader John Smith died in 1994. Whereas many thought that Britain was a naturally conservative country which voted Labour only when the party was centrist, and that the 'hard' left, which Blair opposed, was unelectable.

Blair's victory allowed him and Brown to make and embed change. In their first weekend they granted the Bank of England operational independence in setting interest rates, thereby helping to underpin strong and continuous economic growth, which provided, after a two-year delay inserted in the Labour manifesto to reassure voters, for large increases in public spending. Early on, Blair legislated for trade union recognition and a national minimum wage. Above all, he brought peace to Northern Ireland by concluding the 'Good Friday' agreement on 10 April 1998, less than a year after becoming prime minister. A decade after his retirement there was undeniably broad support regarding this historic success, at least. For over a century, prime ministers had sought in vain to resolve the Irish question, in the euphemistically modern phrase 'the Troubles' since the late 1960s, which after three decades of limited, yet brutal civil unrest and terrorism had claimed three thousand lives. Blair was tireless on this issue throughout his decade in Downing Street, facing real risks and demonstrating extraordinary negotiating skill. The agreement required persistence in implementation, reaching another milestone with the restoration of devolved administration in the St Andrews agreement in 2007. Though noise was occasionally heard afterwards about some unavoidable sleight-of-hand negotiating tactics, and Britain's 2016 decision to leave the European Union has placed pressure on relations with the Republic of Ireland, Blair achieved a settlement that mostly ended the political violence. His leadership was a demonstration of true statesmanship, globally acknowledged—so much so that even Jeremy Corbyn noted the achievement in 2017, though he would not credit Blair by name: 'We went through all the horrors of Northern Ireland . . . and now relative peace and stability. And actually, you know, Northern Ireland has been a bit of a model around the world.'[12] Jonathan Powell, Blair's Chief of Staff, who was so central to the search for peace, gave us the definitive insider's account in his 2008 book *Great Hatred, Little Room*, and came to speak to our students the following year.[13]

The Blair government also oversaw the creation of a Scottish Parliament, a Welsh Assembly, and a London Assembly and mayor. He removed most of the hereditary peers from the House of Lords, although reform stalled after the initial phase. All these changes were contested and difficult, but they did command popular support and were delivered—by contrast with the 1960s and 1970s Labour governments which tried to deliver Lords reform and devolution to Edinburgh and Cardiff but failed.

Investment in public services, especially the National Health Service, was another clear success story for Blair. The NHS has become a touchstone of many Britons' rights. Danny Boyle's opening ceremony for the 2012 London Olympics made that clear to the world. Woe betide anyone who dared to question its founding principles, as Thatcher discovered. In 1997, the cumulative squeeze on funding over nearly two decades made New Labour's somewhat histrionic

'24 hours to save the NHS' a powerful attack. Blair's government delivered unprecedented increases in health spending alongside reform and, bearing in mind the time lags, by 2011 NHS approval ratings were at an all-time high.[14] Though fear and misunderstanding always bred the idea that the NHS was under threat of privatization—it was, after all, Hugh Gaitskell, a Labour Chancellor, who introduced charges for false teeth and spectacles in 1951, just four years after its creation— Blair always believed in the vast bulk of health services being free at the point of delivery. A decade on from Blair's departure, amid widening concern over the NHS's future funding, the New Labour years were seen as a high point.

In foreign affairs, Blair won acclaim in his first term for principled stands against oppression, notably against Slobodan Milosevic in the former Yugoslavia. His partnership and friendship with US President Bill Clinton brought clarity and leadership to the world's centre-left. Of course, the 9/11 attacks on America 'changed everything'.[15] Where Thatcher came to Number Ten a self-confessed 'conviction politician', someone who divided opinion throughout, Blair was initially all things to all people, seemingly in thrall to polling and focus groups and too eager to please—'Bambi' was an early epithet. By the middle of his second term, Blair had become every bit as 'conviction' as Thatcher, and powerfully so on foreign affairs. For many, the decision of a Labour prime minister to back a Republican US president in a pre-emptive war was, and always will be, unfathomable and unforgivable. In fact, the British decision not to engage in the Syrian civil war after 2011 could be seen as the other side of the intervention argument, showing that there are no easy answers, and that intervening and not intervening both have consequences. But undoubtedly Iraq clings to Blair, and in part because of his insistence on taking full responsibility, even though no one person can take the UK to war.

Though Blair had warned about Iraq soon after becoming prime minister in 1997, and joined the US in limited air attacks on Iraqi military installations in 1998, the invasion in 2003 was of a different magnitude. Blair did not seek it. The choice was imposed upon him.

Yet he embraced it: 'It's worse than you think,' he told his aides in July 2002. 'I actually believe in doing this.'[16] Not supporting the US would have upended the US–UK 'special relationship' as it had operated since the Second World War—with interruptions for Suez and Vietnam—based as it was upon the closest military and intelligence partnership perhaps in history. As Blair himself put it, 'Does Britain back the US or France and Russia?'[17] The unarguable reality is that the US was going to invade with or without Blair's backing and rhetoric. Deciding to back the US-led invasion was, however, for many millions in the UK and especially in Labour, ineffective at best and counterproductive at worst in curbing global Islamist terrorism. For them it was an invasion made possible only through the dark arts of propaganda practised by Blair and Alastair Campbell, his Director of Communications and Strategy.

Blair's changing reputation after 2007

Two years after the Iraq invasion, Blair won a third general election in 2005, with a reduced but still historically strong majority of 66. On 27 June 2007, after taking questions for the last time in the Commons and occasioning a never-before-seen standing ovation from both sides of the House, he resigned at the relatively young age of 54. Blair continued his involvement in world affairs, especially in trying to build a state for the Palestinians as envoy of the Quartet (of the UN, US, EU, and Russia) and in trying to improve governance in Africa. Staying out of domestic politics was intended to avoid the charge that he was working against Gordon Brown's government (2007–10), thereby avoiding comparisons with Margaret Thatcher's claim to be 'a very good back-seat driver', which John Major later said he found 'intolerable'.[18] Blair's conscious retreat from the domestic arena lasted until the leftward shift of Labour under Corbyn in 2015 and, even more so, the EU referendum vote in 2016.

Blair left office with an attack on the media, which he described as a 'feral beast tearing people and reputations to bits' in a speech at

Reuters in Canary Wharf on 12 June 2007. The *Mail* and *Telegraph* newspapers, along with the *Guardian*, repaid the insult over the next few years by reporting his money-making activities as 'enriching himself working for dictators', although Blair himself took no money from his foundation's controversial consultancy contracts with the governments of Kazakhstan and Rwanda. Journalists also continued the campaign against the Iraq war at a high pitch. Brown set up the Chilcot inquiry in 2009, when the last UK combat troops were withdrawn, which fed a cycle of reporting based on an ever more simplified popular version of the conflict—'Blair lied, thousands died,' as some of the protesters had it—for the next seven years, reinforcing negative perceptions of Blair with every turn. By the time of the publication of the Chilcot report in 2016, it no longer mattered that, while it levelled many criticisms at Blair, it made no claim that he had lied or that he had improperly used intelligence. Yet much of the media reported the findings as if he had, reinforcing widespread belief in the worst interpretations of Blair's conduct.

While the post-prime-ministerial Blair was routinely portrayed in a bad light by the mainstream press, the period also coincided with the expansion of anonymous, rapidly disseminated, and rabidly opin- ionated social media. Facebook opened itself to everyone in 2006 and Twitter was created the same year. Despite Blair's disdain for, and refusal to join, 'the Establishment'—no seat in the House of Lords and no honours, though he could naturally expect them—the Corbyn move- ment was built on a story, constantly repeating itself on social media, about him as a member of the elite, a Conservative (a 'neo-liberal') in Labour clothing, and, above all, as a warmonger.

This book seeks to take unfounded emotion out of the story.

What is good government anyway?

The first shock in trying to understand British government is the realization, not that the whole process is a mess, which it often is, but that anything gets done at all. The competing structures, agendas, and egos, the conventions and traditions, not to mention the growing importance of regulation and law, all conspire to thwart the reformer. The second shock is that it has been generally accepted over the years (though not recently) that British government has in many ways been the envy of the world. It is almost singularly uncorrupt, as Lord Wilson of Dinton, who was Cabinet Secretary 1998–2002, always points out.[19] While there is always a great debate regarding the overall quality of our elected politicians, the calibre of Whitehall's top rung remains strong, even in an era when pay differentials have widened markedly between highly able individuals in the public and private sectors.

The modern state ushered in by William Gladstone is about 150 years old. Ever seen the clock showing life on Earth in relation to the history of the planet? It begins a fraction before midnight. Now do that for British democracy in relation to the one-million-year history of humanity. It's about the same. And the invention of the National Health Service is even later. The very touchstones of our lives are, in this perspective, really very recent. As a civilization, we seem to have fallen into a trap of having little concept of the past, yet bemoaning the passing of a golden age.

A lot of the criticism of Blair seems to be a demand for an ahistorical perfection. Our analysis is that he was on balance a good prime minister, and certainly better than most of those seeking public office in the modern age, leading a government that delivered as best it could the contradictory demands of the electorate. But the Blair government was far from perfect. Politics and government, let alone a fallible person, can never expect to be. In fact, what does perfection look like in government?

Our hope is that time will eventually see Blair's reputation in some way repaired. Too much of the criticism is simply incorrect. It is our contention that Blair's New Labour government was one of the better administrations to have held office in the UK. Its ministers, advisers, and officials had huge ambition; many of them were highly capable, imbued with a driving sense of public purpose. Especially from 2000,

New Labour developed new thinking about public services which combined high civic ambition with huge resources. In Blair the government had a leader willing to listen, to learn, and to lead his country with verve and authority. Historic victories were achieved, mistakes were made, but overall we believe that the condition of the country improved.

This book is an attempt to answer some of the most contentious, complicated, and unanswered questions of the Blair government. We hope that this reconsideration is a fair account of how it worked, giving due weight to the testimony of the very people who operated within it, and allowing its reputation to be reconsidered—and eventually rebalanced.

I

The Blair-Brown Coalition

One question that kept recurring as we studied the New Labour governments was: should Tony Blair have allowed Gordon Brown so much power? We found ourselves returning again and again to the relationship between the prime minister and his Chancellor. It dominated our understanding of the machinery of government, reshaping the Cabinet structure towards a bipolar model. It determined the rise and fall of lesser ministers. And it was the most important question in assessing policy: had Brown prevented Blair from achieving more in reforming the public services?

In one of our discussions with him about this book in its early stages, Andrew Adonis, who had been Secretary of State for Transport and one of Labour's negotiators in talks with the Liberal Democrats after the 2010 election, drew an analogy between the Conservative-Liberal Democrat coalition and the way that the Blair and Brown governments worked. His insight helped us to approach the question in a fresh way. In this chapter we try to assess whether Blair should have tried to curb Brown by seeing them not as individuals who worked in increasingly dysfunctional partnership, but as the leaders of rival parties who governed in coalition for some of that time.

The Blair-Brown relationship was more than a mere personal rivalry over the right to the top job. It was more, too, than simply the latest manifestation of the historical tension between Numbers Ten and 11 Downing Street—a tension that usually takes time to develop. And it was more, even, than a conflict between strands of opinion in the

Labour Party over the direction of the government. This was a division between institutionally and ideologically distinct 'parties': the Blairites and the Brownites. The two groups had separate identities before the nominally unitary Labour Party came to power in 1997. Much of the business of government was conducted by negotiation between the two faction leaders or their representatives. Institutionally, the government operated like a coalition between a strengthened Number Ten and a fortress Treasury. A coalition agreement even existed in the form of largely verbal understandings known as the Granita deal of 1994, to which we shall come in a moment. The coalition agreement was updated several times, notably at the Admiralty House dinner brokered by John Prescott in November 2003, when Blair undertook to hand over to Brown the following year in return for cooperation on policy. This was then superseded by Blair's October 2004 declaration that he would fight the next election, but not the one after that, and his replacement of Brown by Alan Milburn as campaign manager for the 2005 election. That severing of the coalition was partially reversed in the 'ice cream' pact by which Brown was restored to the dual leadership in order to fight the 2005 election.

The Brown faction finally moved against Blair in the 'coup' of September 2006, when a junior minister (Tom Watson) and a number of ministerial aides resigned, demanding a date for Blair's departure. Fearing further waves of resignations, Blair announced that he would step down in the next year. However, when Blair left the stage nine months later and Brown took over, the new prime minister continued to operate his government as a coalition with Blair's followers. At first this was a limited accommodation, the most striking example being the retention of Adonis, by then a Blairite junior education minister in the House of Lords. Later, Brown was forced to restore a more equal balance between coalition parties, bringing Peter Mandelson, his arch-enemy, back into the Cabinet in October 2008. Later still, in June 2009, he promoted Mandelson to First Secretary of State in addition to his role as Business Secretary, and promoted Adonis to the Cabinet as Transport Secretary. By the time of the 2010 election, the manifesto was a balance of Brownite and Blairite policies.

As with the Conservative-Liberal Democrat coalition that followed, one party was dominant. In fact, for a long time Blair was in a stronger position in relation to his partner than David Cameron was in relation to Nick Clegg. Labour's huge majority of 179 seats was seen as a personal endorsement of Blair, whereas the Conservatives falling short of a majority was seen by many in Cameron's own party as a failing on his part. The balance of power in New Labour fluctuated but did not change fundamentally until Blair was weakened by the Iraq war in 2003. Until then, the Brown party was the junior partner—although Brown's Treasury was a powerful partner and Blair regarded its support as at least as important to his government's success as Cameron saw the Liberal Democrats' support to his own. Paradoxically, Blair felt he had ceded too much power to Brown in his first parliament and may have been briefly stronger against the Treasury after 2001, when he fought hard and flexed his muscles.

The Blair-Brown alliance differed from the 2010 Coalition in that relations between the two wings were characterized by mistrust, hostility, and personal ill-feeling. The other main difference was that the true nature of the relationship was concealed from the public for a surprisingly long time, while the nature of the Cameron-Clegg coalition was explicit and open from the start. These two aspects of difference were related. The pretence of unity in public, and the secrecy, subterfuge, and lack of clarity it required, ensured that the atmosphere of mistrust quickly deepened and poisoned much of the working of the Labour government. The formality and public acknowledgement of policy divergences between the Conservatives and Liberal Democrats tended to ensure that tensions were resolved with trust and mutual respect, at least in the early years of the Coalition. This politeness may have been exaggerated for presentational purposes, but it was noted by many senior civil servants that the conduct of government was more straightforward after 2010 than it had been for the preceding 13 years. This may have been partly because, in a formal coalition, the Civil Service was allowed a role in brokering agreement between the coalition parties.

Shifting poles

In hindsight it can be seen that the Labour Party was bipolar even before it was renamed 'New Labour' at its annual conference in October 1994, which assembled under the slogan 'New Labour, New Britain'.[1] At the time, the party was seen as divided between 'the modernizers' and 'traditionalists'. The 'modernizers'—shorthand for the ruthlessly electoralist tendency, a vanguard formed out of the right wing of the party and the 'soft' left—had been promoted by Peter Mandelson, appointed as the Labour Party's director of communications in 1985.

The development of this strand of thinking, and its body of supporters, can be traced through the battle against Tony Benn and the hard left, which sought to gain control of the party after the election defeat of 1979, but which was held at bay in the deputy leadership contest between Benn and Denis Healey in 1981. The momentum turned after Labour's humiliating defeat in 1983. Mandelson's appointment two years later was crucial in organizing a new leadership cadre able to take the party beyond Neil Kinnock's brave reformism and John Smith's moderate Labourism.

Brown and Blair, who were elected to the House of Commons in 1983, became the joint leaders of the modernizer faction during Kinnock's leadership, with Brown the senior partner. Philip Gould, a former advertising executive who became Britain's first US-style political consultant, offered focus group research, opinion polling, and strategic advice, not just to the Labour Party but to the modernizers as a group and then to Blair personally.

In any group and in any ideology there are tensions, but those among the modernizers' faction were mostly latent while John Smith was leader. With the hard left marginalized after Labour's fourth consecutive election defeat, the modernizers now defined themselves against the 'traditionalists' both of the left and the right in the party.

Although the gap was invisible to the naked eye, the psychological and physical distance between Brown and Blair grew between 1992 and 1994. Brown resisted Blair's encouragement to stand for the leadership against Smith in 1992, and Brown discouraged Blair from standing for the deputy leadership himself.[2] The two having had adjacent offices in a parliamentary annexe, Blair stayed put when the Treasury team moved to new offices in 1993 after Brown was appointed Shadow Chancellor.[3] As Shadow Home Secretary, Blair emerged as the bolder and more radical of the two, willing to take greater risks in advocating 'one member, one vote' against the interests of trade union leaders.[4]

When Smith died on 12 May 1994, what had been hidden became explicit, but only in the semi-privacy of discussions amid intense media interest about who would be a candidate to succeed him. From what Anji Hunter, Blair's adviser, called 'the closest male relationship that I'd ever come across', Brown's deep resentment of Blair's emergence as the favourite within hours of Smith's death turned a submerged rivalry into a bitter, permanent, and structural breach.[5] 'Until this point there had been no "Brownites" or "Blairites". It was Brown's response to the leadership trauma that invited those imprecise labels,' said Steve Richards, an author more sympathetic to Brown than most.[6]

The modernizers found that, sooner or later, they had to choose to which of the new factions they owed their loyalty. That choice was most difficult and most unsuccessful in the case of Mandelson, whose clumsy attempt to avoid being seen to take sides mortally offended Brown and planted the seed of suspicion in Blair's mind. Blair recalled his encounter with Mandelson in an empty Commons voting lobby on the day Smith died. 'Don't cross me over this. This is mine. I know it and I will take it,' Blair told him. He said Mandelson replied: 'You can't be certain of that.'[7]

The founding agreement of the Blair-Brown coalition became known as the Granita deal, after the Islington restaurant at which it was sealed on 31 May 1994. Brown agreed to withdraw from the leadership contest and to support Blair: Blair agreed that Brown would be responsible for economic policy, broadly defined. The only documentary record of the deal was—fittingly, perhaps—a briefing note for the purposes of ensuring a single 'line to take' with journalists: 'In his Wales and Luton speeches, Gordon has spelled out the fairness agenda—social justice, employment opportunities and skills—which he believes should be the centrepiece of Labour's programme.' Then the words 'Tony is in full agreement with this' were crossed out and replaced with new words in Brown's handwriting: '... and Tony has guaranteed this will be pursued'.[8] Drafts of the note were faxed between Peter Mandelson and Sue Nye, Brown's adviser. Mandelson recorded in his memoir: 'I ran it by Tony, who said no to the word "guaranteed". Gordon finally acquiesced.'[9]

During these negotiations Mandelson became the transitional hate figure for the Brown party—a feud that for a time distracted those on the outside, including most of the New Labour Cabinet in 1997, from the more serious underlying breach between Blair and Brown. The Blair-Brown coalition involved more than a breach between individuals at the top of the party, however: it reflected distinct ideologies which were also represented in party organization and even in different social groups among the electorate.

Indeed, it was a commonplace before 1997, and for some time thereafter, to refer to New Labour voters as a 'coalition', combining traditional Labour supporters with new social groups attracted to the party for the first time. But in his memoir Blair also describes the government that he and Brown formed in 1997 as a union of his supporters and Brown's: 'In my Cavalier embrace of the middle class and his Roundhead identification with the Labour tradition, there was surely a coalition of sorts that could be built and could function.'[10]

Outside the inner courts of the coalition leaders, it was not recognized at the time that the first two crises of the Labour Government owed much to the dysfunctional relations between the two parties. The first was the confusion in October 1997 over the government's policy towards the euro, which was to come into being fourteen months later, which is discussed in Chapter Four. The second was the poor handling in November 1997 of the change of policy on tobacco advertising, in response to lobbying by Bernie Ecclestone, the Formula One boss who had donated £1m to Labour.

In the first case, Brown was determined to assert his control of the policy, even to the extent, 'Blair thought, of creating differences between them when there were none', according to Campbell in his diary. Blair called in Gordon Brown 'for a very heavy session, just the two of them, telling him he needed to sort his operation out'. Then Blair brought in Peter Mandelson and Campbell and said:

> 'At the moment all the key relationships are wrong. TB/GB, GB/Peter M, Peter M/AC. Unless we get back working together, we are dead. I mean dead. I mean a lost election, and the people in this room get the blame. I cannot make myself any clearer about this.' He then turned to GB and said, 'Gordon, the key figure in this is you. If you do not face up to what I'm saying, you will ruin yourself and you'll ruin the government.' GB said fine, he was happy to work with others.

Brown promised more openness with the press and 'greater trust and co-operation amongst ourselves'. Campbell plainly did not believe him: 'TB was now convinced, for reasons I could not fathom, that GB actually wanted all this to happen.' Campbell commented: 'The big worry was what all this said about the TB/GB relationship, and the difficulty GB had with the basic idea that TB was prime minister.'[11]

The following month, Campbell thought Brown had been 'largely responsible' for what Campbell regarded as the mistaken media strategy of avoiding full disclosure about the Labour Party's relationship with Bernie Ecclestone. Ecclestone had donated £1m before the election, a fact that would have been made public under the party's self-imposed policy of openness, in September 1998. Before then, however, Ecclestone met Blair to warn that to ban tobacco sponsorship of his sport would push more races out of Europe. Blair asked Frank Dobson, the Health Secretary, to 'protect' Formula One and, with an excess of zeal, it was exempted from the ban altogether. The error of judgement was Blair's alone, but the story was more damaging because the information became public gradually over several days. Campbell wrote that he did not feel that Brown's advice could be trusted: 'TB did not believe GB was being deliberately malign. I was not so sure.'[12]

Although it was well known before 1997 that there were tensions at the heart of New Labour, most of the contemporary commentary focused on the feud between Brown and Mandelson, only dimly perceiving that for the Brown party Mandelson was a proxy for Blair. However, it was only eight months into the new government, in January 1998, that Paul Routledge's biography revealed the depth of Brown's resentment against Blair: 'The newspapers, with a few notable exceptions, did not back me—not least because I was out of fashion. I was never part of the London scene anyway. But that did not in my view mean much, once the campaign started among ordinary Labour Party members and indeed backbench MPs.'[13]

Billed as written with Brown's 'full cooperation', the book accused Blair of reneging on a deal to support Brown for the Labour leadership. Alastair Campbell retaliated by telling Andrew Rawnsley of the *Observer* that it was time Brown got a grip on his 'psychological flaws'.[14] Campbell does not explicitly acknowledge that he was Rawnsley's source, but he admits in his diaries that he 'probably went over the top'. He 'said to Rawnsley that it was all about them thinking GB was robbed of his rightful place as leader, but that anyone who seriously thought he would have beaten TB in a contest needed their head examined'.[15]

The emergence of the Blair-Brown feud into the public domain prompted *Private Eye* to run a cover headlined 'Peace Talks Resume', with Blair saying, 'I am prepared to work alongside you,' and Brown responding, 'Neither am I.'[16] Previously a matter of Kremlinology among close students of the Labour Party, Brown's brooding resentment and ambition now became part of the public story of New Labour. Even so, the extent to which he used the Treasury as an independent power base in a governing coalition, and the depth of the ideological differences between coalition partners, took longer to become known—even to some of the Blairites. In his diaries, Campbell repeatedly expresses his frustration that Blair was in denial about the extent to which the Brownites were working against him.

As with most coalitions, the two parties often resorted to informal channels of communication, especially at crisis points. In the case of the Blair–Brown coalition, this channel was provided by the personal friendship of Anji Hunter, Blair's 'special assistant', with Sue Nye, who performed a similar role for Brown. After the 'psychological flaws' episode, for instance, when Blair and Brown were barely on speaking terms, Campbell wrote: 'I got Anji to speak to Sue Nye to get their real view. Sue said as far as GB was concerned, this was a deliberate AC/Peter M operation, authorised by TB and it was therefore "war".'[17] The conversation allowed both sides to pull back from the brink. The informal channels between Blair and Brown became more formal after 2001, when Hunter was pushed out by Cherie Blair, and when Ed Balls at the Treasury and Jeremy Heywood as Blair's principal private secretary (1999–2003) became the main interlocutors.

Parties within the party

The Blair–Brown coalition bore all the marks of inter-party competition and negotiated cooperation. From an early stage, the two factions operated like parties within the party, as Brown in particular sought to secure parliamentary candidacies in safe Labour seats for his supporters. Competition between Douglas Alexander, Brown's former researcher, and Pat McFadden, Blair's political secretary, for the by-election vacancy in Paisley South in September 1997 was fierce: 'GB was pushing very hard for Douglas Alexander and it was pretty clear TB did not want to pick a fight he might lose.'[18] Alexander prevailed, while McFadden was eventually elected as MP for Wolverhampton South East in 2005.

In Parliament, each coalition party had its own whipping operation to organize its MPs. Although the formal loyalty of the Whips Office lay with the prime minister, its loyalty in practice waned and waxed. Blair hesitated over appointing Nick Brown as government chief whip in 1997. Nick Brown had been campaign manager for Gordon's putative leadership campaign in 1994, and Blair thought he had never given up that role. Having been deputy Chief Whip in opposition under Donald Dewar, he was finally given the top job in government by Blair, but outside the Cabinet and for only a year. He was then moved to the lowly Ministry of Agriculture, with the sop of a nominal promotion to full Cabinet status. Blair wrote later: 'I knew he was more or less continually working for Gordon and against me, and had actually probably been doing so all along.'[19]

The Blairites' suspicion of Nick Brown deepened in early 2001, when Jonathan Powell, Blair's chief of staff, accidentally listened in to a conversation between the Browns, Nick and Gordon:

> A turning point for me came in 2001 when 'Switch' [the Downing Street switchboard] mistakenly plugged me into a phone call between Gordon and Nick Brown, who was abroad. The call was in the context of the foot-and-mouth outbreak, and Gordon peppered it with pleas to Nick to be careful in what he said in case someone was listening. Gordon said all this presidentialism was terrible. 'We have to stop him taking foot-and-mouth away from you.' Nick Brown complained that he had to waste his time coming to Number Ten to hear Tony blather on about the disease for an hour a day. They agreed that they should not discuss the issue with Number Ten policy people but would talk again with Ed Balls later in the day. I simply could not believe the disloyal way in which Gordon talked about Tony and I saw him in a new light.[20]

Gordon Brown's unofficial whips' operation caused most difficulty for Blair during the House of Commons passage of bills to bring in foundation hospitals (2003), university tuition fees (2004), and the stillborn measure to bring in 'trust' schools (2005). It was a peculiar form of politics, though, because their role was necessarily covert, and had to tread a careful line between menace and deniability. At no point could Brown afford to be seen trying to inflict a parliamentary defeat on Blair. On occasions, he would visibly join the official government whipping effort, as before the vote on Iraq and that on tuition fees—although on the latter occasion the rebellion was led by Nick Brown, who was persuaded only at the last moment to support the government with the promise of a review of the impact of the fees.

The crowning triumph of the Brownite whips was a characteristically negative one, in securing so many nominations for the Chancellor's leadership bid after Blair pre-announced his resignation that no other candidate could secure enough nominations to stand. Thus Brown was elected unopposed to the leadership of the Labour Party three days before he took over as prime minister in June 2007. Some of Brown's own supporters thought this 'coronation' was a mistake, because it meant he was not forced to think deeply about his programme for government.

Nick Brown was restored as government chief whip by Gordon, but not until October 2008—such was the deep suspicion with which he was regarded by the Blairites; and such was Gordon's need to sue for peace with them. After Geoff Hoon, a former Blairite who had made his accommodation with the coming power, took the post, Nick Brown finally returned when the more dramatic return of Peter Mandelson provided 'Blairite' cover. (Two weeks after Ed Miliband was elected leader in 2010 he asserted his independence and sought to appeal to the Blairite wing of the party, and Nick Brown was again sacked as chief whip.)

The two parties in the coalition even had separate funding arrangements in a way that was unprecedented in British politics. In part, this arose from the wider franchise for the leadership, brought in by the Bennite revolution in 1981 and widened further by the introduction of 'one person, one vote' in the trade union section under John Smith in 1993. This gave candidates, who had previously canvassed the selectorate of Labour MPs personally, the incentive to raise money for national campaigns of mailings and tours directed at party and trade union members. Blair's friend Barry Cox raised £88,000 for his leadership campaign, and several rich donors funded his office as Leader of the Opposition.[21] Although Brown never actually ran a leadership campaign, he took the precaution of being prepared for one, and raised money to run his office in opposition. Geoffrey Robinson, the wealthy MP and Brown supporter, was sometimes unclear whether cheques he wrote were made out to the Labour Party or to Brown's office as Shadow Chancellor.[22]

Brown's competition for money was the immediate cause of his falling-out with Jonathan Powell, which happened soon after Powell joined Blair's office in 1995:

> Paul Hamlyn, the publisher and philanthropist, generously donated money to set up Tony's office as Leader of the Opposition. Gordon got to hear of it, summoned me to his office in Millbank and sat me down in front of his desk. He told me in stern terms that he had Tony's agreement that all income was to be shared half and half with his office. I knew there was no such understanding and could not stop myself bursting out laughing. It must have been very irritating, and Gordon never forgave me.[23]

Once in government, some of the separate funding of Brown's party continued. Peter Watt, the general secretary of the Labour Party 2006–7, said that a secret 'fund with no name' was maintained by the party for Brown's use, to pay for private opinion polling.[24] Also, at arm's length, the Smith Institute, a charitable think tank, was set up by Wilf Stevenson, a personal friend of the Chancellor. It provided a job for Ed Balls in the short gap between his stepping down as chairman of Brown's Council of Economic Advisers in 2004 and his election to the House of Commons in 2005. At the same time, the official funding of the party was increasingly treated as Blair's presidential property, with the 2005 general election campaign paid for by secret loans from rich donors whose support was as much personal to Blair as to the Labour Party. This money was raised by Michael Levy, a fundraiser whose loyalty was similarly as much to Blair personally as to the party, and this was to cause Levy difficulties later, when the police investigated claims that peerages had been promised in return for the loans—an allegation for which the Crown Prosecution Service concluded there was insufficient evidence.

Effect on Cabinet government

Coalition policy was shaped mainly by negotiation between Number Ten and the Treasury, with appeal not to the Cabinet as decreed by classic British constitutional theory but to the duopoly of Blair and Brown.

While contemporary comment on the machinery of government in the early Blair years developed familiar themes from the recent past, such as prime-ministerialism or even US-style 'presidentialism', bypassing of the House of Commons, and the power of 'spin', much of the real story was of Blair's tinkering with structures to try to assert his authority over his Chancellor. The plans drawn up by Sir Richard Wilson, the Cabinet Secretary, in 1998 described Number Ten, the Cabinet Office, and the Treasury as 'the centre'. They were an attempt to bind the Treasury into what was unashamedly a centralized command structure, but what was important about them is that they failed. Brown continued to assert his independence and to hoard information as power, which meant that the government continued as a coalition even in the early years when Blair was at the height of his authority. The conventional commentary at the time about the weakening of Cabinet government was only half-right, and that half was right for the wrong reason. The collegiality of Cabinet ebbs and flows in constitutional history, depending on the strength of personality of the prime minister and, crucially, the force of his or her personal electoral mandate, as we shall see in chapter 2. Thus Cabinet government was weak during the later Thatcher period and the early Blair period.

Some Cabinet ministers felt, however, that their power was diminished not by Blair's pre-eminence but by the nature of the duumvirate of Blair and Brown. The power of that axis, and the informal relationships patched together to support it, inevitably sucked power away not just from Cabinet but from much of the Cabinet committee structure. Margaret Jay, a Cabinet minister in the first term, said:

> Because there was this very strong relationship between the two principals, the Prime Minister and the Chancellor at the centre, which

meant that departmental ministers, even if they were senior Cabinet ministers with huge responsibilities for public expenditure, had to go through one or other of them in a slightly demeaning way in order to achieve what they wanted. It meant that the processes of Cabinet government were not exactly undermined, but were marginalized.[25]

The bipolar government had another side effect, by virtue of the importance of the officials—both civil servants and special advisers— who were the interface between Blair and Brown. Ed Balls thought that he and Jeremy Heywood, Blair's principal private secretary, were more powerful than they would have been in a single-party government:

> The duopoly of Blair and Brown in the Government also meant ... that Jeremy and I were probably far more influential in the shape and direction of the government than was wise or sensible or proper, but that was nothing to do with us. That was simply a reflection of the Blair-Brown approach to government, and our job was to make it work. The interesting thing when you read these memoirs, and think about it, was that my relationships with Alastair Campbell, Jeremy Heywood in particular—they were less involved in the making-it-happen side of things—were always very strong, because actually our job was to hold it together. We made it work. We made this relationship between Tony Blair and Gordon Brown, which was sometimes dysfunctional, sometimes incredibly creative, but certainly power-driven most of the time—our job was to make it work, and if we hadn't have been there, it wouldn't have worked.[26]

However, it was not until the dispute over foundation hospitals, in 2002/3, that an ideological gap opened up in public between the two wings of the coalition. Until that point, although Brown had signalled that his instincts lay to the left of Blair's, it had been hard to identify any policy issues on which they definitely disagreed. As we have seen, the confusion over the euro in October 1997, for example, was seen to be caused more by Brown's determination to control the policy than the policy itself—with Blair more concerned to keep open the option of joining before the next election. By the time of the second decision on the euro, in June 2003, everything had changed. It was by now well known that Blair was in favour of adopting the euro and that Brown was opposed. Hence the unfamiliar revival of the principle of Cabinet consultation, as Blair sought to use the rest of the Cabinet as a counterweight to Brown. The balance of power within the coalition was shifting as a result of the Iraq war, but, as we see in chapter 4, the economic and political case for adopting the euro was weak, even if the majority of the Cabinet were willing.

'I'm going to sack him'

Alastair Campbell's diaries revealed that, by the 2001 election, Blair had come round to the view that Brown was out to destroy him. The day before the election, Campbell, Tony Blair, and his wife Cherie discussed Gordon: 'Cherie had pretty much always been of the view, then I came to it, that a large part of GB was basically working against him. TB said that sadly, very sadly, he had reached that conclusion too.'[27]

Peter Mandelson testifies that Cherie was hostile towards Brown as early as the time of his first resignation from the Cabinet in December 1998, over the undeclared loan from fellow minister Geoffrey Robinson. In his memoir *The Third Man*, Mandelson described Brown as 'the engine of my destruction', and quoted from a note from Cherie Blair:

> I have no doubt you have been the victim of a vicious and selfish campaign... My only consolation is that I believe a person who causes evil to another will in the end suffer his returns. That he is prepared to risk the whole Labour government and to plot against a vital part of it means that to me he has lost any claim to the moral high ground he affects to inhabit.[28]

She was, she said, 'worried for Tony'.

Blair himself first talked to Campbell about sacking Brown a year later, on 20 December 1999, after a ridiculous episode in which the Chancellor appeared on television to announce the writing-off of debt owed to the UK by poor countries—£155m over ten years—without telling Blair. As the 2001 election approached, Brown repeatedly demanded a departure date from Blair. Blair told Campbell that, on 9 April 2001:

GB had started a conversation with him straight out with the words, 'You betrayed me. You said you would never challenge me and you took that job away from me.'... TB told him again he was happy to support him in becoming the next leader, but not if he sought to remove him. Then all bets were off. GB said to him, 'You cannot lay down conditions.' TB told him he had to accept who the leader was.[29]

On 26 April, Campbell wrote: 'I was hanging round the outer office and not for the first time we could hear raised voices, GB's the louder, and TB told us later he asked straight out, again, when was he leaving. TB said he was like a raging bull.'

As new instances of Brown's rudeness, obstruction of good government, and plotting emerged—although most of them came out only after Blair had stood down as prime minister—the puzzle of why Blair failed to sack him became insistent. Blair gave an early answer to Campbell and Cherie in that conversation on the day before the 2001 election:

> But it wasn't possible to sack him or to move him, and in the event it wouldn't be the right thing because, for all his flaws, he does have real talent, it's just that we saw the wrong side of him in this campaign. But that's us, he said. Neither the party nor the public would remotely understand if they thought I wanted to get rid of him. They would think it was just a leader trying to dispose of a rival. It would be wrong. He didn't believe GB would strike necessarily, though he might try over Europe, but he felt the party would see through it.

Brown did strike eventually, but not until after Blair had strung him along for about as long as he could be strung. And not until after Blair had thought long, hard, and often about striking first.

With the approach of the Iraq war, Brown sought to exploit Blair's distraction. Two days after the recall of Parliament for the publication of the first dossier on Iraq's weapons of mass destruction, Andrew Adonis called Alastair Campbell:

> to say GB had sent a 44-page letter to all Cabinet ministers attacking foundation hospitals [and] under-delivery by the Department of Health... Earlier, Alan Milburn had said to me that GB was positioning

himself as reforming re PFI but totally against anything that looked like private sector provision of public services... When I told TB about it, he paused for a long time and then said, 'He's brilliant and ambitious but he's also bonkers and I just can't be bothered with it.'[30]

According to Campbell's contemporaneous account, Jonathan Powell and Sally Morgan both said the next day that the letter to ministers was 'a declaration of war'. Blair spoke to Brown, who was at an IMF meeting in Washington: 'TB said I view this as very serious, to which GB said, "It is very serious," and he made clear it was deliberate too.'[31] Ed Balls admitted to us this was seen as an 'unfriendly act', but that the policy itself was resolved in Brown's favour, with Blair's support, the following month (see chapter 4).

Blair, however, told Campbell on his return from the Christmas holiday on 6 January 2003 that he had made his mind up: 'I'm going to sack him. I've come to a settled view that he has to go. There was a time when I could make the case that the tension was creative. But it has reached a point where it is destructive and it can't go on.'[32] But it was too late. The war in Iraq was approaching. Getting rid of Brown would have to wait. As for the argument that the tension was creative, this is also discussed further in chapter 4.

Even as the aftershocks of Iraq got worse, the operation was on again and off again in Campbell's diary: on 16 May 2003, 'I got a message to call TB. He asked, "Are you on a landline?" I said yes. "I think there may be a case for moving him come what may. It's just not tenable like this. He is impossible to deal with at the moment."' But it was always just as unthinkable to move against him.

In August 2003 Blair's inner circle, Peter Mandelson (at this point a backbench MP again after two stints in Cabinet that ended in 2001), Jonathan Powell, and John Birt, the former BBC director general brought in as a 'blue skies thinking' adviser, drew up a plan code-named 'Teddy Bear' to split up the Treasury:

> On the model of the United States, we suggested dividing the Treasury in two. A new Ministry of Finance would handle the macro-economics:

taxation, international markets, financial services. A separate US-style Office of the Budget and Delivery (OBD) would…deal with all government funding and spending. The idea was to leave Gordon with the Finance Ministry, but to put a different person, trusted by Tony, in charge of the departmental purse strings, so that the way was opened up for the reforms to advance.[33]

When we asked Blair about it in 2011, he said:

That never got very far actually. Because I wasn't sure it was really a good idea. The issue wasn't the power the Treasury had but how it was being used at the time. I'll be very frank here. On the tax credit stuff I would have been a lot more cautious if I had known where it was actually going. And in the end if there had been a shared sense of purpose then actually the power of the Treasury would have been a very good thing. But it's when it became obvious that we were on a different track that it became not.[34]

'It won't happen…so play along'

Thereafter, as the situation in Iraq deteriorated and Blair's confidence ebbed, the coalition entered a new phase. As 2004 approached, ten years after the Granita dinner which Brown believed had agreed a ten-year timetable for the handover, the Conservative party was convulsed. Iain Duncan Smith lost a vote of confidence among Conservative MPs, and on 6 November 2003 Michael Howard was elected unopposed to replace him as Leader of the Opposition. That day, the deal was renegotiated at a dinner at Admiralty House, the residence of John Prescott, the deputy prime minister, who was the witness, referee, and notary for the occasion.

Blair had the day before refused to reappoint Brown to Labour's National Executive, as a sign that he wanted someone else to run the next election campaign. Meanwhile, the legislation for foundation hospitals, the main reform of the National Health Service, was going through Parliament under John Reid as Secretary of State for Health—Alan Milburn had resigned in June 2003 after he clashed with Brown on the subject and Blair had humiliated him by finally taking Brown's side (a conflict covered in more detail in chapter 5). The Admiralty House dinner ended with an ambiguous two-part agreement in which both parties focused on the part that they wanted to hear. Blair agreed to stand down in the summer of 2004, provided Brown gave him his full support in pushing ahead with his reforms. The Brownite version of the conversation was relayed to Robert Peston, whose book, *Brown's Britain*, was intended by the Chancellor to set out his vision for his imminent premiership:

> 'I know things are very difficult on trust,' Blair said. 'I think in the end I will be vindicated [over Iraq]. But I'm not going to turn this around for a very long time. Therefore I am going to stand down before the election.' And turning to Brown, he said: 'I know I must leave, but I need your help to get through the next year.'[35]

Unusually, for a nominally single-party government, an agreed statement was published the next day (7 November 2003):

> The Prime Minister and the Chancellor agree that a line should be drawn under the events of this week. Regarding the NEC, the Chancellor can automatically attend whenever he wishes. Their offices will actively discourage people from speaking to the press on the events of this week and concentrate on key messages about the Prime Minister and the Chancellor continuing to work together. In particular they will concentrate on ensuring the success of the consultation exercise being launched by the party in the near future, getting across the key messages, the current and continuing strength of the British economy, constant improvement in the delivery of the public services and exposing the true nature of the Tory party under Michael Howard.[36]

The statement was both unspecific and damaging, in that it acknowledged that the two parties were in a state of dispute—and also that they had 'offices' that would try to control 'people' who might purport to speak to the press on their behalf.

John Prescott in his memoir took Brown's side:

> It was at that meeting that Tony promised to go by the next election. That's definitely how I took it and how Gordon took it—as did all the

Brownites because he must have told them afterwards. But Tony maintained later that he hadn't said it. As far as I'm concerned, he did. Tony reneged on his promise.[37]

Blair's version is nonchalant in its simplicity: 'He [Gordon] would say: I received an assurance Tony would go. I would say: I received an assurance Gordon would cooperate and carry through the agenda. You can then debate who kept his word and who didn't.'[38]

Blair gave a slightly different account of the deal to Mandelson that casts doubt on his good faith. Prescott told Mandelson about the dinner the next day and Mandelson phoned Blair in confusion, because only 'days earlier', Blair had been pondering either Operation Teddy Bear or trying to move Brown to the Foreign Office. Mandelson said that Blair explained to him:

> 'What I've told him [Gordon] and John, and I really mean it, is that if Gordon really backs me and helps me and implements my policy, I'll be happy to step down.'
>
> 'Really?' I asked.
>
> He paused a moment before replying. 'Well, I don't think he'll help me. So the situation won't arise. It won't happen. But I've got to do this—so play along.'[39]

In his memoir, Blair offers yet another account of his motives: he said that his offer to stand down had been a moment of 'the weakness of a normal person' who had been 'ground down', or 'an act of cowardice' even.[40]

The first test of the new agreement was the passage of the foundation hospitals Bill, carried later that month with 62 Labour MPs voting against. It was an ambiguous victory for Blair, and Brown's 'people' continued to agitate against the other big reform Bill, to raise student tuition fees to £3,000 a year, paid for by a loan repayable after graduation above a minimum level of earnings. This Bill was even more difficult: eventually 72 Labour MPs voted against it and it passed by just five votes, with Nick Brown declaring his support for it only on the morning of the vote. It looked as if the Brown party were trying to wound but not to kill Blair, weakening him in an attempt to

force him to abide by the Brownite interpretation of the Admiralty
House agreement. If that was the calculation, it was a poor one, because
the tuition fees revolt was one of several grievances nursed by Blair in
deciding that Brown could not be trusted to continue his reform
programme after all.

Ed Balls interpreted Brown's motives differently, suggesting that, far
from agitating against Blair, Brown was merely trying to navigate a
difficult course between the parliamentary party and a prime minister
increasingly regarded by MPs as 'not one of us'. He insisted that
Brown did not want Blair to be defeated, even on tuition fees, because
he was worried about inheriting a divided party:

> Gordon didn't sit there and think: 'How do I best wind up the
> Parliamentary Labour Party to be opposed to Tony Blair, to strengthen
> my position to be the next leader of the Labour Party?' In fact, his per-
> sonal obsession was so much, 'How do I avoid the Labour Party divid-
> ing, and therefore blighting my inheritance of leading the Labour
> Party?' If you take the big votes—tuition fees is the best example—the
> only reason why the tuition fees rebellion wasn't much larger was
> because Gordon Brown completely threw his body on the line to try
> and persuade people to support the government, and that was the reality.
> He was far more worried about—he disagreed intellectually, and he
> was worried about what Tony was doing—but he also didn't want the
> government to divide.[41]

Brown may have been positioning himself for the Hutton report into
allegations by the BBC that Blair and Campbell had interfered with
the intelligence on weapons of mass destruction before the Iraq war.
Some of Blair's critics thought that he might have to resign when the
report was published in January 2004. Instead, it exonerated the government and criticized the BBC.

However, that verdict brought no relief—it was widely derided as
a whitewash—and Blair went through his bleakest period, according
to Sally Morgan:

> What he hated was his integrity being questioned and that's what
> really got to him in the period after the war... What was clear after
> Iraq and particularly after Hutton and the aftermath if you like is that

he felt that his ability to get the other things done that he wanted to do and his strength of leadership over the Labour Party was weakened. And I think that led to some serious questioning.[42]

Sally Morgan, however, told us that she felt Blair had come closest to resigning two years earlier, and before the Iraq invasion: 'The most serious conversations I've ever had with him about whether or when he should go were in 2002 not 2004. Because in 2002 he was very seriously sitting down saying, "Is there a case for me announcing that I should go at the next election?"' José María Aznar, the prime minister of Spain until 2004, had recently done precisely that. 'Not particularly from a position of weakness but a position of feeling that maybe, maybe he couldn't get the buy-in for some of the domestic reforms. This wasn't about international [affairs] at all, but some of the domestic reforms he wanted to do.' Blair's question, according to Morgan, was: 'Would he be in a stronger position to drive that agenda through by announcing then that he would not contest the next election? There was quite a lot of—well a very small but quite heated—debate about it. And he came to the conclusion that it would leave him weakened. And for me that was a much more serious conversation than in 2004.'

Her view that Blair's 'lowest point' was 'earlier than many people think'[43] suggests that Blair might not have been sincere when, shortly after the Budget on 17 March 2004, he suggested to Brown, with just the two of them in the room, that he should, after the Easter recess, 'pre-announce' his resignation that autumn.

According to Robert Peston, Brown hesitated:

Brown did not know quite what to make of it. It would suit him to have it out in the open that Blair was going. In fact, surely this would make all his dreams come true. What he feared however was that he was being set up. He calculated that the so-called 'pre-announcement' would fire the starting gun on a bitter and divisive campaign by all the pretenders to the throne. Brown would not have a clear run. A number of senior ministers—including John Reid and Charles Clarke—would bitterly resist a seamless transfer of power to Brown. In fact Blair reinforced those concerns, by saying, 'I'm going to support you but some of these members of the Cabinet are going to be very difficult.'[44]

So Brown advised Blair: 'Don't do that, it would be crazy. You'll make yourself a lame duck. You'll send the Labour Party into turmoil.'[45] It was an extraordinary exchange, on both sides. It revealed Brown's paranoid caution and his low estimate of his support among Labour MPs—which seems misjudged compared with the outcome three years later, when no rival candidate was able to muster the forty-six nominations required to stand against him. Having revealed to Mandelson that he did not expect Brown to keep his side of the bargain, perhaps Blair really had had enough now. More plausibly, though, perhaps his motive was to flush out Brown's intentions and to confirm that the Chancellor was indeed the coward that Blair thought he was. Certainly, the information gleaned from that exchange would have helped to convince Blair that, if he decided to carry on, Brown would hold back from an attempt on the leadership.

It is not clear, however, what Blair would have done if Brown had advised him to pre-announce his resignation that year. Presumably, Blair would have changed his mind before making the announcement, on the same grounds as he later gave.

According to Peston, Brown came to regret his advice soon afterwards, when he realized that he had no guarantee Blair would stick to his intention to go. Because Alastair Campbell had left Number Ten the previous autumn, we do not have the same first-hand day-by-day account of Blair's thinking in this period, but Campbell continued to advise Blair and records in the fifth volume of his diaries, published in 2016, that he considered trying to become President of the European Commission (not the same job as the President of the EU Council, created by the Lisbon Treaty in 2009, for which he was considered but to which Herman Van Rompuy was appointed).[46] If Blair had ever genuinely intended to stand down, at some point between March and July 2004 he changed his mind.

The situation in Iraq continued to get worse, although some of those close to Blair felt that he was already regaining confidence when the photographs of Americans torturing Iraqis in Abu Ghraib prison were published on 28 April. John Prescott certainly thought the handover was going ahead when he dropped a heavy hint to Tom Baldwin, a journalist on *The Times*, on 15 May: 'When plates appear to be moving, everyone positions themselves for it.' Around the same time Prescott even confided to another person that 22 July had been set as the date for the announcement of the handover.[47]

However, media speculation about Blair stepping aside in Brown's favour prompted Blair's Cabinet allies to rally to him, urging him to stay on and warning that Brown as prime minister would be a disaster for the country. In June, John Reid, Alan Milburn, Charles Falconer, Tessa Jowell, and Peter Mandelson spoke to Blair in person, singly or in groups, and Patricia Hewitt wrote him a personal minute.[48] It may have been that Blair, minded to stay, was using the phalanx of his supporters to mobilize his part of the coalition in his defence.

As Brown and his team planned over the early summer for their takeover of government, Blair started to draw up ambitious five-year plans to accelerate his reforms. In his memoir, he dates his change of mind about the handover to the weekend of 3/4 July 2004: 'I came to one inescapable conclusion, and then another. The first was that I didn't really believe Gordon would carry on the agenda...The second conclusion was that the only reason I wanted to go was cowardice.' Blair said: 'The following week I informed him. You can guess the reaction.'[49]

The Brown version is slightly different. According to Peston, Prescott hosted another dinner at Admiralty House on 18 July, four days after the publication of the Butler report on the failure of pre-war intelligence on Iraq. Blair 'implied' that he had changed his mind about quitting: 'To go now would look like I've been defeated over Iraq...I need more time, I can't be bounced.'[50]

Either way, Blair and Brown were both now resolved against each other: Brown to push Blair out, knowing that, provided he did it carefully, he would have the support of a majority of Labour MPs; Blair to carry on. Having told Alastair Campbell a year and a half earlier that, when he came to sack Brown, 'it can only happen when the waters are calm and it's least expected, and it must be a totally ruthless operation', he now planned precisely such an operation, not to rid himself of Brown but simply to ensure his own survival.

The return of Milburn

Thus on 8 September 2004, Alan Milburn returned to Cabinet as Chancellor of the Duchy of Lancaster, responsible for policy and taking the job Brown regarded as his, of running the campaign for the election expected in May 2005. Milburn had unexpectedly left the government in June 2003, ostensibly for personal reasons, although his bruising clashes with Brown over health policy—in which he felt that Blair had failed to support his own reforms—had not disposed him to stay. Now he was back: 'The Prime Minister has decided that I should be in charge of general election planning, the overall strategy and policy presentation and crucially, the formulation and development of policies that will eventually lead, through the proper process, to a Labour manifesto in the next general election.'[51]

Looking back, Milburn explained why he took the job: 'In part it was because I was an ally of Tony's and was very much close to him and he wanted somebody in that sort of role. To be honest I didn't want to do it because I'd left government. I'd left the government in 2003, for my reasons and the last thing I wanted in all honesty was to come back.'[52] In his letter of resignation in June 2003, Milburn had said: 'It has been an enormous privilege to serve in government for six years. But I have already missed a good bit of my children growing up, and I don't want to miss any more.'[53]

We asked him why he took the job if he didn't want it. He replied:

Because I felt obliged. It's as simple as that. I mean just, believe it or not that's just sometimes how it works, that I really, really didn't want to do it and I had the sort of sense that it wasn't going to be a lot of fun and my sense was entirely right. My instincts, my antennae were sort of twitching and I knew it wouldn't be a bundle of laughs and it wasn't.

It was a very, very difficult election to fight. But it's sort of quite difficult if the prime minister, especially if he's a friend, asks you to do
something and there is no other explanation for it really.

Milburn responded to the suggestion that he was being set up as a
rival to Gordon Brown as Blair's successor:

No, because if that were ever true, I would never have walked out in
2003. The last thing you'd do would be walk away if you want to be
leader of the Labour Party. You know people might think it's [an]
incredibly clever Machiavellian game, you know, on the up escalator to
sort of say now I'm getting off. Now, I know it's unusual, politicians
usually get off the escalator going down, or they're kicked off and of
course I did neither, you know, I walked off voluntarily. Most people—
in fact the day of that reshuffle in 2003 the *Sun* were running a story
saying I was going to be the next Home Secretary, how wrong they
were. But I did it for the reasons I did it. And people find it, sometimes,
because they have a sense of what politics and politicians are like they
can't quite disentangle that from an uncomfortable reality and the
uncomfortable reality is thank you very much I don't want to be leader
of the Labour Party, I don't want to be the prime minister, end of story.
So there we were.

Milburn claimed that he had no intention at all of staying on beyond
the 2005 general election, and that he had been very, very clear to Blair:

The problem with Tony that, you know, we went through . . . a period
of sort of intensive wooing during 2004 where, he's not daft, so he
knew that he had to sort of hook me back in. So really in the beginning of 2004 I was being invited to lots of political strategy meetings
in Number Ten. So, 'Okay fine, but I'm a backbencher,' type of thing.
Then the next thing I'm chairing a meeting, so, 'Hold on a minute this
is not quite right because then there's people like Sally who are supposed to be in charge of all this.' And then you get, 'Well you've got
to come back, you've got to come back,' and I really didn't want to
come back. Anyway, so then he persuaded me to come back and I said
to him, 'That's fine I will do it but I'll only do it until the election
campaign is over and then I'm off because I don't want to do it, I really
don't want to do it.'[54]

Before Brown could regain his balance, and while he was in Washington
for a meeting of the IMF, Blair struck again, on the last day of the

Labour conference, 30 September 2004. He announced that he would be going into hospital the next day for a 'routine' heart operation to get his flutter 'fixed', and that he would put himself forward as prime minister at the next election, seeking to serve a 'full third term' but not a fourth. Simultaneously, the *Independent* reported that the Blairs had bought a £3.6m house in Connaught Square, by Marble Arch.

This last was the most significant—bricks and mortar being more substantial than affairs of the heart. The decision to buy the house had been made early in 2004. Cherie was opposed to what she saw as the surrender to Brown, but was anxious about the family's lack of a stake in the London property market. By the time contracts were exchanged, however, Blair had decided firmly to stay on.

To offset the unavoidable information about the house, and his health, both of which might suggest that he was preparing to go, Blair finally gave Brown the date for the handover for which he had been agitating—only it was May 2009, if the 'full third term' were interpreted literally (and assuming four-year parliaments, as were the norm before the Fixed-term Parliaments Act 2011). Most of Blair's friends advised him not to impose a term limit on himself, fearing that it would weaken him, at least after the election. But the surprise attack worked, in that the pressure from Labour MPs for him to stand aside in Brown's favour subsided. 'I had my operation. The house was bought. And so was some time.'[55]

Milburn had tried to persuade Blair not to do it:

> What I was worried about, as the guy who was having to deal with the campaign, was that it wouldn't make the campaign any easier and I don't think it did actually. Anyway, we know now in retrospect, words were exchanged... Well he sort of sighed and I shouted. And then he did what he wanted, because he was the bloody prime minister, you just can't control them.[56]

The hostility between the two wings of the coalition was more open than ever, represented visually when a Blair news conference on 6 January 2005 was scheduled at the same time as a Brown speech in Edinburgh, so that live television coverage employed a split screen. Brown's sense of betrayal was vividly conveyed via Robert Peston, when his book was published on 9 January 2005: 'Brown routinely says to Blair, "There is nothing that you could ever say to me now that I could ever believe."'[57] Blair's plan to fight the 2005 election on his own terms and under his own colours—'the election manifesto for this government will be unhesitatingly, unremittingly New Labour'—was heading for trouble.[58] Brown was in a deep sulk, declaring that he would fight his own election campaign, going up and down the country to listen to the people, with the implication that he was gearing up for his succession, which seemed the more certain the more it was postponed. The disunity began to look like an electoral liability for the 'Very well, alone' Blair party. Partly because the Blairites had colluded in concealing his private behaviour from the public, Brown was a towering and trusted leader, respected for having presided over eight years of steady economic growth. Opinion polls suggested that Labour would win more seats if Brown were leader.[59] Brown was preferred to Blair when Ipsos MORI asked 'Who do you think would make the best prime minister?' in January 2005 (by 39 per cent to 35 per cent) and April 2005 (by 41 per cent to 33 per cent).[60]

Panic divided Blair's advisers. Alastair Campbell, Philip Gould, and Sally Morgan urged him to sue for peace and renew the coalition with Brown. Indeed, Campbell and Gould were so persuaded by the opinion polls that they suggested to Blair that he should think of standing aside because Labour stood a better chance under Brown. Campbell recorded in his diary: 'I was trying to be honest without undermining him but failed.'[61]

Cherie, Jonathan Powell, and Peter Mandelson (now a European Commissioner, serving as 'a relief valve' in 'phone conversations we had as I continued my global travels'), on the other hand, pressed him to hold his nerve, telling him that he would never be free of his destructive antagonist if he gave in now. Blair came down on the side of caution and sought to restore the breach with Brown: 'Tony had two options: fight, or go. He ended up half-fighting and half-going,' commented Mandelson.[62] Late in the day, new coalition terms were negotiated by Campbell and Brown, after Campbell flew to Scotland to see Brown at home on 29 March 2005.[63] Brown was guaranteed his job as Chancellor. Blair unveiled a poster of Brown and Oliver Letwin, the Shadow Chancellor, which asked, 'Who do you want to run the economy?' Milburn was betrayed—again. He described his role running the 2005 election campaign as 'a very unenjoyable experience, I have to tell you'.[64]

In return, Brown endorsed Blair's conduct of the Iraq war and agreed to campaign jointly with him. A joint party election broadcast was filmed, which was awkward for the late Anthony Minghella, the film-maker, because Brown failed to conceal his discomfort at taking part in the charade. Tessa Jowell and Mandelson thought Campbell, on Blair's behalf, had conceded too much: 'Peter felt GB had outflanked me, but so far as I was concerned my main mission in recent weeks had been to build the campaign, to get TB and GB in sync, without undermining TB's authority fatally. I think I had done that. They didn't. Fine.'[65]

The leak of the Attorney General's longer advice on military action in Iraq dominated the final week of the campaign. On the day of the leak, 27 April, Brown defended military action as a 'team decision, a collective decision', and said that 'the war was right'. At a news conference the next day, he was asked about the Iraq war: 'Would you have behaved in the same way in identical circumstances?' He replied: 'Yes.'

In his memoir, Brown, as if in explanation, said that he had never criticized Blair publicly. 'Inevitably there were heated words exchanged between us privately—and, in this respect, I hated what were too many off-the-record briefings to the press about these disagreements from each of our overly loyal teams—but neither Tony nor I ever publicly disparaged the other in government.'[66] To that extent, the coalition held together.

The restoration of Brown to the dual premiership and the end of Blair's ambition to fight and win the election without him was symbolized in the pictures of Blair buying Brown an ice cream at a campaign event in Gillingham, Kent, on 2 May, the bank holiday weekend before the election.

The part of Blair's 'operation' that remained hidden—for another eighteen months, at least—was the money. It was not until March 2006 that reports emerged of several donors having secretly lent millions to the Labour Party for the election campaign, and that four of them had since been nominated by Blair for peerages. It was an unedifying, although not unlawful, spectacle and showed the lengths to which Blair would go to get over the election line. Its exposure contributed to the storm of disapproval that finally drove him from office. But, after he won the 2005 election with a majority of sixty-six, despite Iraq, and despite the accumulated hostilities of eight years at the top, he would still be prime minister for another two years, and would now enter his most creative phase, which he encapsulated in the repeated maxim: 'You are at your most popular when you are at your least effective, and at your most effective when you are your least popular.'

Running on thin air

The price Blair paid to get across the finishing line in the 2005 election was a heavy one. Alan Milburn was true to his word: 'The problem with Tony is he's sort of got selective memory recall, so then in the middle of the election campaign it was, "'Well right, so are you going to stay on?" "Well no I'm not actually, I'm going to go." "Oh really? But why?" "Because that's what we said. Remember when we had the conversation."'[67] Milburn resigned from the government again, live on air on the night of the election.

The Labour Party—in effect Blair's private faction within it— borrowed heavily and secretly from seventeen rich people to fund the campaign. He had imposed a term limit on himself to fend off demands from Labour MPs for a pre-election handover to Brown; his 'lame duck' status became a central feature of politics on the morning after polling day. And the price of the Brown party's support during the campaign had been a further strengthening of its leader's claim to the succession. At the first meeting of Labour MPs, six days after the election, with the mood almost one of defeat rather than of a third substantial victory, Brown's supporters began agitating for a timetable for the handover, and Blair used the phrase 'a stable and orderly transition' in his speech to them.

The balance of power between coalition partners had shifted decisively. Paradoxically, Brown's pre-election popularity advantage over Blair, as reflected in opinion polls, had faded. And over the next two years Blair was able to use what remained of the office of prime minister to achieve a surprising amount. The sullen state of the Parliamentary Labour Party meant that reforms that needed legislation were difficult. The schools Bill was watered down to homeopathic strength—and even then it could be passed only with the votes of the Conservatives. Yet Brown's concern not to inherit a ruin meant that he allowed Blair to take the lead on difficult decisions on nuclear power, the renewal of Trident, and pensions. Blair also used his leverage on the world stage to win the Olympic Games for London, to secure agreement on African aid and climate change, and to complete the settlement in Northern Ireland.

The next crisis for the coalition, a wave of letters and minor resignations from the government that Blairites called the 'coup' of September 2006, forced Blair to put a final, earlier limit on his time as PM. Brown characteristically held back at the last moment, agonizing when Ed Balls told him it was 'too late' to stop the rebellion.[68] In his memoir, Brown said: 'When, without my knowledge, a group of ministers resigned from their posts because of their impatience to see a change, I helped to put the rebellion down.'[69] What form this 'help' took was not clear, however, and the revolt achieved its objective: Blair said that the coming Labour Party conference would be his last. Brown finally became prime minister, after winning a Labour leadership election unopposed, and with Blair's lukewarm endorsement, on 27 June 2007.

Blair had managed to retain the leading role in the partnership long after a majority of Labour MPs had defected from his faction to Brown's. As with the revolt of the majority party in a coalition against a prime minister of the minority party in 1922, the majority finally asserted itself. Blair's skill lay in concealing the fact that he, like Lloyd George before him, was the leader of the minority party in the coalition. Even now, he was able to delay the accession of the majority party leader for another nine months.

The Brownite ascendancy

When the Brownites finally came into their inheritance, the coalition was in disarray but not broken. Brown promoted several members of the Blair party to maintain a balance between the existing coalition parties in the Cabinet. David Miliband, whom the Blairites still hoped would become prime minister, became Foreign Secretary. Jacqui Smith, Blair's last chief whip, became Home Secretary. Alan Johnson, Hazel Blears, Ruth Kelly, and John Hutton retained Cabinet rank, while James Purnell and Andy Burnham joined them. Brown even tried and failed to bring in new partners to a wider coalition by offering the post of Northern Ireland Secretary to Lord Ashdown, the former Liberal Democrat leader (this last despite his previous suspicion of Blair's dealings with Lord Ashdown and the late Roy Jenkins).

However, the Blairite party was disorganized after the departure of its leader and David Miliband felt constrained in assuming his mentor's role. The public division of the later Blair years had been damaging to the coalition and Miliband felt obliged to insist, 'I am not a plotter', and nor was he, by temperament as much as by calculation. With the balance of the coalition gone, the Brown-led government was chronically dysfunctional.

Tessa Jowell, who continued as a minister under Brown, observed:

> What happened to Gordon is like what happens in marriages, when one partner is unable to function without the other. Gordon was a bit

like the branch of a tree that had sheared off and been separated from the main body. In some respects incapable—I remember saying to Stephen Carter [Brown's chief of staff and strategy adviser for nine months in 2008]: you're going to be the one who tells him that he doesn't need to be the one who decides which of the three trains he's going to get to Birmingham. And he looked at me and said, 'You're not joking.'

He chaired the Cabinet but he didn't lead the Cabinet. That was the big difference with Tony. He would say I think we'll come back to that, so nothing was ever resolved.[70]

Despite being leaderless and disorganized, the Blairites started to agitate against Brown's leadership within months. The Blairites copied the tactics of the Brownites, with the resignations of junior ministers Siobhan McDonagh and David Cairns in September 2008. That revolt was snuffed out by the collapse of Lehman Bros, and the balance of the coalition was partly restored with Peter Mandelson's remarkable return to the Cabinet the following month. He imposed some message and policymaking discipline, while acting as an intermediary with Blairite Cabinet ministers. Also in that reshuffle, Andrew Adonis, on whose appointment as a middle-rank minister Blair had to insist against internal opposition, found himself in the Cabinet.

Even so, the Brown party was still weakening. In June 2009, Hazel Blears, Jacqui Smith, James Purnell, and Caroline Flint, a minister who attended Cabinet, resigned, but on different days and for different reasons. If they had acted together, they might have brought Brown down, but Labour MPs were reluctant to contemplate a change of leader because it would increase the pressure for an early general election, with the furore over MPs' expenses still running strong. By the time of the last attempt to bring Brown down, the 'roast goose plot' in January 2010, the agitators included, as well as Patricia Hewitt and Geoff Hoon, the two public faces of the plot, Harriet Harman, the deputy Labour leader, Jack Straw, the Justice Secretary, and Tessa Jowell, the Cabinet Office minister. The positions of Mandelson, Alan Johnson, and David Miliband were ambiguous, but the plotters were once again unable to act together.

Numerically the Blairites and Brownites were evenly balanced in the House of Commons by the end of Brown's premiership. After the election, a reduced parliamentary party preferred the Blairite David Miliband to his Brownite brother for the leadership by 53 to 47 per cent—as did party members, by 54 to 46 per cent, only to be outvoted by trade union members in the third section of the electoral college.

Ideologically, the situation had become cloudy. On becoming prime minister, Brown sought to distance himself from what he thought were the unpopular features of Blairism, but these were symbolic rather than real. He revoked the Order in Council that had permitted Jonathan Powell and Alastair Campbell, as political advisers, to instruct civil servants. He announced that any future military action would require the approval of the House of Commons, clumsily seeking to disown Iraq, which *had* been approved by the House of Commons— unlike Korea, the Falklands or the first Gulf War. The pace of public service reform slowed. The fall in NHS waiting lists levelled off in 2009 under Blairite secretaries of state, Alan Johnson and Andy Burnham. The academy schools programme was slightly diluted but continued to expand, even after Lord Adonis was promoted out of his institutionalized conflict with Ed Balls in the briefly renamed Department for Children, Schools and Families. On anti-terrorism law, Brown tried to return to the 90-day detention issue with a com- promise proposal for a 42-day maximum, but it failed to pass the House of Lords. (The Conservative-Liberal Democrat coalition reduced the maximum from 28 days to 14 in 2011.) Most significantly perhaps, Brown seemed content for his decisive and opportunistic reflationary response to the financial crisis in 2008 to be presented as a rehabilitation of the Keynesian and Fabian-statist instincts of the trad- itional Labour Party. His Blairite human shield, Lord Mandelson, fur- ther confused the ideological picture by adopting an activist industrial strategy at the new Department for Business, Innovation and Skills.

Thus the coalition parties fought their last election together, more or less, in 2010 on a Brownite manifesto that contained some Blairite language, but against an economic background that had changed out of all recognition.

'Do you give up the things you really care about?'

Blair himself compared his relationship with Brown to a coalition: 'There's a difference between managing a coalition between parties and managing a coalition within parties. I think it's easier actually to manage it within a party but the question always is at what price does the coalition come? Do you then give up the things you really care about?'[71]

However, by seeing the Blair-Brown relationship as a coalition between parties, we may be prejudging the question, which is whether Blair should have sacked Brown. It is not possible in a coalition for the leader of one party to sack the leader of another. David Cameron could never have dismissed Nick Clegg: he could only have brought the coalition to an end, which would have meant carrying on as a minority government or possibly a general election. But Blair could have asked Brown to take a different job or to go to the back benches: he had the power to decide all his ministerial appointments. Brown could ensure that there would be a cost to getting rid of him, but his base of support among MPs was never as explicit or as disciplined as that of a separate party.

So the question is not whether Blair could have sacked Brown, but whether he should have done. Blair put the case for keeping him thus:

> It suited me to have another big figure. In a funny way I was very self-confident but I liked the fact he was regarded as a big figure, as I thought it helped the government—and it did help the government. Until the end it was more of a help because if you sent Gordon off to the World Bank or IMF you were aware of the fact there was a major figure there who helped the country. When he stood up in Parliament and gave his Budget the Tories were pushed back. It would be wrong of me to not say that the fact he was of substance was of help to the government.

The problem with it was, as it so often is in politics, the disagreement. Once I got an idea fixed in my own mind, not only what the opposition concept of New Labour was but the governing concept then that was where we had the disagreement. My view of the governing concept of New Labour was all about individual empowerment, not about the state giving power to people. This was the main ideological difference between us. I wanted to break up the monoliths and give people choice and competition; slim down the centre of government. On some levels Gordon went along with that but on some levels he didn't and that's where the disagreement happened.

But I was very content in one sense to let this thing grow. Maybe, there are a lot of people who worked with me, who said this was definitely a mistake. Alastair would say it was a mistake. We allowed this kind of mythological aspect that I was the chairman and he was the chief executive.[72]

As we have seen, however, Blair himself felt at the start of 2003 that the tension had ceased to be 'creative' and had become 'destructive'. Geoff Mulgan, who was a special adviser and then as a civil servant director of the Prime Minister's Strategy Unit, 1997–2004, held the 'idiosyncratic' view that the relationship was constructive throughout:

It was undeniably a nightmare often for civil servants trying to second guess which of the work each side would want knowing who to talk to, not just the principals but their advisors, their civil servants and so on. And there was undoubtedly a lot of competition within government which sometimes caused problems. My idiosyncratic view in the bigger scheme of things is that competition and that relationship was incredibly healthy for government. It provided a check on both of them from doing things that might be self-destructive.

The most glaring example for Blair is that he might well have joined the euro had it not been for Gordon Brown, and if we had joined the euro early on like people like Peter Mandelson wanted, it would have been a one-term government. I'm almost certain of that, just because of the effects on the macro-economy. So he was incredibly lucky that there was this conflict. And it also forced a degree of rigour in the centre of government because there were these two power centres challenging each other all time. They had to raise their game in policy ideas. Whereas if you have a monopoly of power, in the way, to a degree, Mrs Thatcher did, certainly in the very last years of her time, it is much easier to make big mistakes.

One definition of power is the freedom to make really bad mistakes. And the fact that both of them constrained each other's power did reduce the number of mistakes they made. As I say, it's a very idiosyncratic view, and day to day that competition was a real pain for the civil servants involved.

Even now with a slight distance it's possible to see that it wasn't purely coincidence that they presided over this extraordinary period of both electoral and governing success. It wasn't despite that competition that the success happened, on the economy, on public services, on social policy, on elections. It was largely because of it.[73]

Mulgan's verdict judged the question by results: he argued that keeping Brown in post produced the best policy outcomes. This was not generally the view of the Blair party. Jonathan Powell, for example, said that the Chancellor's obstruction had negative consequences for the public finances:

Gordon's reluctance to agree to a Fundamental Savings Review in Tony's last years was probably the most damaging example of the stand-off... Gordon refused to allow it to happen while Tony was still prime minister. When we argued with him, he announced publicly to the *Financial Times* that it would not happen till he was leader... Tony suggested they collaborate on the plan but Gordon wouldn't. As a result there was no FSR and we missed an opportunity to put the country into a better fiscal position going into the economic crash of 2008.[74]

Blair insisted to us that he had not conceded as much as the Brown party claimed, but supported Powell on this point:

If I did make one error in domestic policy, and even economic policy, it was to allow this notion that I subcontracted out domestic policy. I kept a pretty firm grip on a lot of this stuff, except the micro stuff which in the end I came to regret. But the macro[-economic] balance, until the very end, the last couple of years when we had a disagreement about the limits of public spending. My view was that in 2005 we had reached the limit.[75]

In the end, Blair's argument always doubled back on itself. The question of whether he should have sacked Brown assumes that keeping him as Chancellor produced worse outcomes than installing a Blairite Chancellor would have done—on the deficit, tax credits, and public service reform. The problem was that sacking or trying to move Brown might have destabilized Blair's position. So if the assumption is that Blair's policies were better than Brown's, it was better to keep Blair as prime minister, and therefore Brown as Chancellor, for as long as possible.

Blair pretended in his memoir that he had been wrong to 'reach one last understanding' with Brown, at the dinner at John Prescott's flat in Admiralty House in November 2003:

> I have come in time to a different view. It was an assurance that should never have been asked or given... Whatever leadership is, that is the opposite of it...The feelings on his part of entitlement—which should never enter into a discussion of the office of prime minister because no one is 'entitled'—burgeoned still further from that moment on.[76]

However, it was not Brown in the end that did for Blair—it was the Parliamentary Labour Party. The MPs needed a candidate, of course, and Brown's evident availability was a threat to Blair, but Brown would probably have been more of a threat on the back benches, and his fearfulness meant that Blair was able to carry on long after the music had stopped. Which is the essence of Blair's explanation of why he kept Brown where he was:

> Gordon had enormous support within the party and the media. He was regarded by many as a great chancellor, and by nearly all as a strong one. When it's said that I should have sacked him, or demoted him, this takes no account of the fact that had I done so the party and the government would have been severely and immediately destabilised, and his ascent to the office of prime minister would probably have been even faster...[77]

This is probably right. Blair survived as prime minister for so long because he managed Brown—or perhaps it would be more accurate to say he coped with him—rather than confronted him. This was in part a reflection of Blair's weakness, not of character but of the forces at his disposal. His consistent lean to the centre, which is what made him such a successful election winner, meant that his base of support in the Labour Party would always be shallow and conditional. Iraq broke that base. But Blair's survival was a reflection of Brown's weakness too. One of Blair's greatest strengths as a political leader was his ability to string people along, long after they should have realized he was using them: 'You know, you've played me like a fiddle,' Peter Mandelson commented bitterly, and possibly with a trace of admiration, when he gave up British politics (as he thought) to take up a post as EU Commissioner in Brussels in July 2004.[78] Blair did it with Paddy Ashdown, Roy Jenkins, the Queen, and even Alastair Campbell. But the way he played Brown was his most important achievement in keeping himself in power by keeping the governing coalition in place long after his wing of it had lost much of its base in the parliamentary party. If Brown had not been so psychologically flawed, he could probably have taken over in 'late 2004', which is what Blair said he had in mind at the Admiralty House dinner. But Brown was, unintentionally, Blair's best ally, and Blair sometimes failed to conceal his wonder that his rival was playing his hand so badly. Campbell recorded in his diary on 29 April 2003: 'TB said surely Gordon must realise he is making it harder not easier to hand over to him. What is unfathomable is that it is such a not clever strategy.'[79]

If Brown had praised Blair, flattered his Cabinet supporters and promised convincingly enough to carry on their programme, his succession would have been so much harder for Blair to resist. As it was, Blair was able to keep their coalition going, with him at the head of it, for two months longer than a decade.

2

Sofa

Tony Blair faced a great deal of criticism that he dismissed the traditional model of 'Cabinet government' in favour of a prime-ministerial 'sofa government', a shorthand catch-all phrase that became received wisdom. In this chapter, we explore the battle of ideas over collective responsibility, examine how it played out, and explain Blair's instinctive embrace of a more modern operation. What emerges is a hinge of history, the ending of one era and the beginning of another as the generations turned, and government speeded up. Blair was not always right, but his tenure as prime minister marks him out as making a quite remarkable fist of what is often described as an impossible job.

Dead cert

Tony Blair's approach to decision-making was controversial throughout his decade in Downing Street—and beyond. Even in his 'Teflon Tony',[1] record-breaking polling, pre-George W. Bush days, Blair's cabinetry was contentious. The man who declared that his 'soul is and always will be that of a rebel'[2] was the undoubted star of a reformed and popular New Labour party that had stormed to a landslide victory in the 1997 general election and was keen to make its mark after a generation out of power. There was no inclination to be bound by the arcane, often uncodified, practices of the British constitution. That these were policed by the Whitehall 'mandarins'—senior civil servants who might be expected to be small-c conservative—meant the restless modernity of New Labour, and of Blair in particular, clashed with the time-honoured guardians of the British constitution.

Some concerns about Blair's governing style proved temporary, while others lasted throughout. But there was also an air of mischievous at best, dangerous at worst, myth-making from critics that started with the story that Blair had dispensed with the tradition of Cabinet ministers addressing each other by their formal titles with the line, 'Call me Tony'—said to suggest a damaging informality, which was, 'far from being the idea of some party apparatchik or spin doctor... actually the brainchild of Alex Allan',[3] at that time the PM's Civil Service principal private secretary. The PPS, controlling access to the inner sanctum in 10 Downing Street, forms, with the Secretary to the Cabinet and the Queen's private Secretary, the British constitution's 'Golden Triangle'.[4]

That Blair would win the 1997 general election was as near a certainty as modern British politics had ever seen, although a nervous Labour leadership understandably doubted it all the way to polling day. Blair's period as Leader of the Opposition saw the New Labour command focus obsessively on destroying an already collapsing Conservative hegemony, demonstrating an 'on-message' discipline rare to the point of unique for the Labour Party, and taking advantage of the new communications technology. Buoyed by unprecedented opinion-poll leads—Labour were 21 points ahead of the Conservatives the week before John Smith's death in May 1994 and 44 points ahead with Blair as leader in January 1995[5]—a popular and focused government-in-waiting took shape. The commentariat naturally mused as to what kind of prime minister Blair would be. The first specific sense of how this would translate to government came with the publication in 1996 of *The Blair Revolution: Can New Labour Deliver?* by Peter Mandelson, Labour's former Director of Communications and by then an MP, and Roger Liddle, who went on to work for Blair in Number Ten on European policy. The tag line of the book declared it was 'an inside account of New Labour's plans for Britain'. With both authors close to Blair, they displayed a rare technocratic interest in the machinery of government. The book later garnered infamy among some mandarins for its prescience, with its (albeit qualified) praise for Margaret Thatcher's governing style and the resounding line that Blair will have 'to get personal control of the central government machine and drive it hard, in the knowledge that if the government does not run the machine the machine will run the government'.[6] Not for nothing did Lord Wilson of Dinton in 2004, after a gruelling four years as the most senior civil servant, the Secretary to the Cabinet, solemnly refer to *The Blair Revolution* and declare: 'We were warned. It's all in there.'[7]

Another signpost to New Labour governance came in the weeks before the 1997 general election. At an off-the-record breakfast seminar for senior civil servants and business people, Jonathan Powell, Blair's chief of staff, spoke of 'a change from a feudal system of barons to a more Napoleonic system'.[8] These words leaked and Powell, as he himself wrote after a decade by Blair's side at the centre of government:

> got into trouble...The tabloids, with their vestigial hatred of 'old Boney', managed to translate what I thought was my subtle argument into the suggestion I wanted us to be more French, but I think my analogy still holds good. The British system of government is traditionally a feudal system of barons (cabinet ministers) who have armies and funds (civil servants and budgets), who pay fealty to the liege but really get on with whatever they want to. There is very little that the prime minister can do to make the government consistent or coherent. The only weapon he has in his armoury, a very blunt one, is hiring and firing people.[9]

This may be overstating the argument for effect—controlling the Cabinet's agenda and the parliamentary diary is hugely important, too—but Powell's conclusion was blunt: 'My proposition was that, if the New Labour government was going to succeed in delivering, we couldn't rely on the old ways. We needed to have greater coordination at the centre on both policy development and implementation.'[10] Sir Richard Mottram, who was permanent under secretary at the Ministry of Defence when Blair became prime minister and who served at that highest levels of the Civil Service until 2007, later observed caustically: 'Now that was a *really* good idea because Napoleon was a *fantastic* success.'[11]

Thus were the battle lines drawn, before a vote had been cast in the 1997 election. Blair's style was to be prime-ministerial, centralizing power in the person of the leader, and would clash with the traditional model of Cabinet government, in which ministers, including a prime minister as first among equals (*primus inter pares*) would discuss matters before reaching a collective decision. His critics would accuse Blair of 'presidentialism', accusing him of thinking he wielded ultimate executive power on the model of a United States president.

As the election approached, and New Labour looked on course for a mighty victory, hints about a Napoleonic revolution loomed large in the minds of the permanent tribe of government. The embodiment of the Civil Service then was Sir Robin Butler, who had been Secretary to the Cabinet since 1988 and, at that time, head of the Home Civil Service, though the two posts are not always combined. Sir Robin, later Lord Butler of Brockwell, was only the seventh person to hold the post since its creation in December 1916, the others being Maurice Hankey (1916–38), Edward Bridges (1938–46), Norman Brook (1947–62), Burke Trend (1963–73), John Hunt (1973–9), and Robert Armstrong (1979–87). The role of Cabinet Secretary is peculiarly British in that it is perhaps *the* great unelected office of state, but one which attracts relatively little attention and correspondingly scant public understanding. All information in Whitehall flows through the Cabinet Secretary's hands, with the tremendous power that that implies. Even the very well-connected Victor Rothschild—third baron of the banking family, close friends with several of the Cambridge spies, wartime MI5 officer, Fellow of the Royal Society— came out of an interview to be head of the Central Policy Review Staff in 1970 with Sir Burke Trend, then Cabinet Secretary, and Sir William Armstrong, the head of the Home Civil Service, and said: 'Not until I came to Whitehall did I learn that the country was run by two men, neither of whom I had ever heard.'[12] It was apt that the three-volume biography of the first Cabinet Secretary was subtitled *Man of Secrets*.[13]

Since the Northcote-Trevelyan Report—published in 1854 and partly implemented in 1870—the British Civil Service has prided itself on its ability to impartially serve the government of the day. Sir Robin had thus been the literal right-hand man, traditionally sitting next to the prime minister in Cabinet, first as the Thatcher years drew to an acrimonious close, then with John Major throughout his hard slog of a premiership. (When Sir Robert Armstrong became Cabinet Secretary in 1979, 'somebody said "where does Robert sit, does he sit behind the Prime Minister, behind Margaret Thatcher?" "No," they said, "he sits at the table at Margaret Thatcher's right." "God," they said, "we didn't know there was such a place." ')[14] It has been said that Stalin was shocked that the civil servants supporting Winston Churchill at the Potsdam Conference in 1945 smoothly moved across to advise Clement Attlee once the election result was announced in the middle of the conference and the new prime minister took over, the implication being that in Russia a change of government would see a change of senior civil servants, usually because the previous ones had been executed. The early New Labour years were to test the mandarins mightily. As Robert Hill, politically appointed special adviser in Number Ten in 1997, becoming the PM's political secretary in 2001, put it: 'We were in a hurry.'[15]

The novelty of Blair's arrival may have erased memories of earlier accusations of prime-ministerial abuse of the conventions of Cabinet government. Most notably, a decade before Blair entered Number Ten, Michael Heseltine strode out of it and away from Margaret Thatcher's Cabinet in 1986, accusing her of orchestrating 'the breakdown of constitutional government',[16] an attack Thatcher denied: 'We had reached our decisions on Westland in a proper and responsible way.'[17] It demonstrated a fundamental truth of the British constitution: being uncodified, and hugely complex, means much can be debated without a clear, definite answer. This is especially the case in rapidly changing times.

'Cabinet government' defined

So what exactly is understood by the concept of 'Cabinet government'? This somewhat nebulous idea is best examined by key works of authority and the analysis of those who have been a part of it. The eminent journalist Walter Bagehot in *The English Constitution,* first published in book form in 1867, gave us the classic observation:

> The efficient secret of the English Constitution may be described as the close union, the nearly complete fusion, of the executive and legislative powers... The connecting link is the Cabinet... A Cabinet is a combining committee—a hyphen which joins, a buckle which fastens, the legislative part of the State to the executive part of the State.[18]

In more recent times, Lord Armstrong explained that 'the Committee of the Privy Council which is the Cabinet, [is] the apex where politics and administration come together and where differences and conflicts have finally to be reconciled and resolved'.[19] While Lord Falconer of Thoroton, the Lord Chancellor 2003–7, explained it well when he told one of our classes:

> Historically, Cabinets had two particular purposes: one, they brought together all the factions in a political party; and, secondly, and separately, they brought together around one table all the interests of central government... two particular functions, bringing together all of the politicians at the top of a political party and secondly and separately making the machinery of government work.[20]

All this happens through a kind of hierarchical triangle encompassing officials, politically appointed special advisers, and ministers by which means decisions are taken at all levels, through committee meetings and written correspondence, with significant and/or contentious decisions rising through the chain until they reach the Cabinet or prime minister.

For Lord Wilson of Dinton, a related point of Cabinet government was 'ensuring they [prime ministers and other Cabinet members] have the best decision-making material... in front of them when they come to decide important matters of national interest'.[21] Even this seemingly positive and innocent concept becomes tricky, however, when deciding what facts are to be presented and how, as demonstrated above all by the Iraq war decision, as we shall see. Moreover, Margaret Thatcher had in an earlier generation berated her government's chief scientific adviser following a presentation 'based on the facts'. She responded in frustration: 'The facts. The *facts*. I have been elected to *change* the facts!'[22] (While in 2017, the United States Counselor to the President, Kellyanne Conway, introduced the concept of 'alternative facts'.[23])

Blair and his governing team were similarly impatient for change. Unlike Thatcher, however, who had been a Cabinet minister previously, there was no experience of—and little interest in—how the intricacies of apostolic governing traditions played out in practice. If they had seriously thought about it, which they by and large did not, they might have planned how to manage the system. But Blair had the biggest parliamentary mandate of the modern era behind him, to a large extent based upon a desire for modernization across the board. Democracy had empowered him to a huge degree.

Within months of becoming prime minister, press commentary appeared suggesting Blair was uninterested in governing through his newly appointed Cabinet and preferred a small clique of ministers and an imported network of special advisers, something expertly chronicled by Peter Riddell in *The Times*. In an article entitled 'Cracks in the Cabinet cement' in November 1997, Riddell announced: 'The long predicted demise of the Cabinet as a central organ of government has finally occurred...During a pre-retirement interview recently, [Sir Robin Butler] remarked how the Cabinet had returned to its 18th-century origins as "a weekly meeting of political friends", discussing issues informally with decisions taken elsewhere.'[24]

Butler's successor, Sir Richard Wilson, was concerned that Blair was in danger of becoming too powerful and that, influential as the prime minister inescapably is, executive power is essentially vested in the secretaries of state. He later warned prime ministers that 'formally, you're not the CEO'.[25] Sir Richard's predecessor, Sir Robert Armstrong, had previously elaborated on this:

> We have a system of cabinet government, not a system of presidential or chief executive government. Cabinet ministers are explicitly collectively responsible for the policies and actions of the governments of which they are members...virtually no powers are formally vested in the office of Prime Minister, and those formal powers the Prime Minister does have are powers of patronage not of policy. He is the chairman of a collective, which is called the Cabinet; and, once he has chosen his colleagues—and unless and until he fires them—his own strength lies essentially in being the chairman of the Cabinet.[26]

Sir Richard Mottram forcefully underlined the senior officials' concerns when he explained:

> Statute does not say the powers of the command of the armed forces are vested in the prime minister, it says they are vested in the secretaries of state. Similarly, if you looked at lots of other statutes, the powers of home secretaries and justice secretaries, they are partly in statute. But our whole constitutional edifice, the framework of law, is based on the idea that we have accountable secretaries of state, accountable to Parliament, then we have collective government and the prime minister is the head of that collective government.

> Now it's absolutely for the prime minister to decide the extent to which he or she wants to use the formal mechanism of Cabinet to give coherence to the government because nowhere in our Constitution are the powers of the prime minister or the powers of the Cabinet laid down...so what this will tell you constitutionally is that it is not acceptable for the prime minister and those around him to take decisions which are the responsibility of individual secretaries of state. Conversely, quite clearly those individual secretaries of state recognise the authority of the prime minister so it's perfectly okay for the prime minister to take decisions in consultation. This principle was only passingly recognized, if at all, in Number Ten...

> Blair wasn't that interested in full meetings in the Cabinet Room, listening to his colleagues witter on. What he was interested in was, 'I will figure out in a smallish group of people what the right answer is and then I'll tell everybody else'.... He had an exaggerated amount of confidence in the opinions he had reached...He's a man of great

confidence and conviction, and that great confidence and conviction
was absolutely instrumental in him getting the job. It may not necessarily have served him that well in some way when he had the
job...Tony wasn't sufficiently cautious about his confidence, it was
too high...

I don't want to sound too critical of him...I think it is incredibly hard,
and amazingly hard if you've no training in it—how could you possibly
succeed?[27]

Blair certainly vexed Sir Robin Butler, who retired as planned at the
end of 1997, having seen in the new government, but he looked back
with fondness:

Tony Blair arrived. And that was a very exciting time for all the Civil
Service because it was a change in government after eighteen years.
We wanted to show that we would serve a Labour Government as
committedly as we'd served the Conservative Government. We didn't
know them as well. I wanted to manage the transition to the new
Government smoothly. And so...that was a challenging but also exciting
time. I felt very fortunate really, because I had eight months of the
Labour Government. If we hadn't got on well together well, you know,
they weren't going to keep me forever. Actually I think, personally
anyway, I got on extremely well with Tony Blair. He thought the transition went well. He was grateful and kind to me personally. And so...
I left feeling I'd really left at the right time and had a very good time.[28]

For his part, Blair 'found Robin thoroughly professional, courteous
and supportive. He didn't like some of the innovations, but he did his
level best to make them work. He was impartial in the best traditions
of the British Civil Service, intelligent and deeply committed to the
country.'[29] These warm recollections came years after Blair, at the end
of his very first day as prime minister, privately nicknamed him
'Buttleshanks', perhaps conveying his impression that the experienced and respected mandarin was old-fashioned, maybe even a
dyed-in-the-wool butler.[30]

The personal warmth contrasted sharply with the senior mandarin's
concerns over Blair's cabinetry. In 2004, Butler observed, 'there is
too little of what I would describe as reasoned deliberation which

brings in all the arguments...I think I would restore open debate in government at all levels up to the Cabinet. The Cabinet now—and I don't think there is any secret about this—doesn't make decisions.'[31] While in 2012, he mused, 'Has Cabinet Government broken down?... I think it some ways it has. Of course it has changed, because the focus on the Prime Minister has become much stronger.'[32] While the traditional powers to hire and fire, and chairing the Cabinet, have not changed, the prime-ministerial focus on foreign affairs and running the Cabinet committee system have changed. Moreover, the 'twenty-four-seven media [are] very much more concentrated on the Prime Minister'.[33]

For Peter Mandelson, Cabinet minister under both Blair and Gordon Brown, the pressures of the media on prime ministers and on collective ministerial responsibility were reflected in Blair's approach to Cabinet government:

> You went into the Cabinet and the Prime Minister would come down...not that Tony was the most 'let-it-all-hang-out' and let everyone have their say, let the Cabinet go on for as long as everyone wanted, he's not that sort of guy. Nor are most prime ministers, incidentally, they want everyone in, out, with the minimum disagreement or whatever. I tell you why, because they're terrified of the press, you have to remember that the interaction of the media and politics is very important in all of this. So a prime minister will literally wince if someone so much as opened up a potential millimetre-wide variance from what he thought we should agree. He was afraid the press would say, 'Ah, terrible divisions in Cabinet'... They really fear that Cabinets are things that can lurch off in any direction and if they lurch off a centimetre too far there'll be the press before you, click.[34]

Lord Wilson explained how the burgeoning media pressure speeded up the decision-making process and pressurized the traditional model of collective government:

> You would like ministers to take their decisions on the basis of a best statement you can put together of the facts, of the options, the arguments, the costs, all the considerations and for them to have sufficient time to reflect and to discuss that you ensure that you've got proper

collective involvement in the decision and then you take the decision and announce it. That's what your heart yearns for. But, of course, in an age when the media are bellowing through breaking news and through headlines in newspapers, governments have to be much speedier than that and that changed, the pressure of media for answers and for government action and announcements is one that is now with us to stay, and has been I think with us for a decade or more, or longer than that, fifteen, twenty years.[35]

A later Cabinet Secretary, and a former press secretary to Prime Minister John Major, Gus O'Donnell, now Lord O'Donnell, was clear that 'one of the important things to learn was not to take the press side of things too seriously. It shouldn't dominate, you need to get that longer term vision'.[36] This echoed the thinking of Lord Butler:

I think the most important thing is not to take too much notice of the media because they will push you about and they will demand imme-diate responses and immediate responses are often wrong...the focus on the Prime Minister has definitely increased. However, it doesn't follow from that, in my view, that the government has got to become a presidency and I think it's a very bad thing if it does...I think that Cabinet government remains very important. It is more difficult to achieve in a very much faster moving world, but not impossible, and...my advice to a prime minister would be to make sure that collective government continues.[37]

For Andrew Turnbull, Blair's third Cabinet Secretary, 2002–5, with all the vast pressures on Cabinet government in the modern age, 'it is just how much of it is still operative which is really the notable thing rather than the opposite'.[38] Indeed, a clear-thinking member of Thatcher's Cabinet, Nigel Lawson, Chancellor 1983–9, explained:

A normal Cabinet meeting has no chance of becoming a grave forum of statesmanlike debate. Twenty-two people attending a two-and-a-half hour meeting can speak for just over six and a half minutes each on average. If there are three items of business—and there are usually far more—the ration of time just exceeds two minutes, if everyone is determined to have his say. Small wonder then that most ministers keep silent on most issues or confine themselves to brief but pointed questions or observations.[39]

Perhaps the best way any mandarin has described the overriding wish for collective Cabinet government amid all its impracticalities came from Lord Hunt of Tanworth, Cabinet Secretary throughout much of the chaotic seventies:'I do not think collective responsibility is a myth. I think it is a reality. It is cumbersome. It is difficult. It has all sorts of disadvantages ... it is going to be a bit of a shambles. But I do think it has got to be, so far as possible, a democratic and accountable shambles.'[40] On another occasion, Hunt described the limitations of the ideal collegiate deliberation:'I accept that Cabinet government must always be a cumbrous and complicated affair and that this is a price well worth paying for the advantage of shared discussion and shared decision, *provided the system can keep up with the demands put upon it* [emphasis added].'[41] From the vantage point of the twenty-first century, it looks likely that the strain placed upon an older style of Cabinet government by the onset of instant mass communications from the mid-1990s onwards changed the reality forever.

Furthermore, the prime minister is very much more involved in foreign affairs these days, explained Lord Butler:

> In the old days if you wanted to communicate with the head of another government, instructions were given to the Foreign Office, they sent a telegram to the ambassador, the ambassador would seek audience with the other government, report back to the Foreign Office, and it would come back. Now the Prime Minister picks up a telephone and an awful lot more happens from here, and because travel is so much easier there's an awful lot more personal relations and personal visits on both sides.[42]

Lord O'Donnell agreed:

> Globalization has meant that heads of state in government have to do more. There are more issues that are handled at the international level now. Take things like climate change, take things like financial regulation, and dealing with crises, these things, they go across borders very quickly and you need international solutions, and our international machinery isn't very good. The international machinery for climate change I'd say is completely broken. We have some that were left, the Bretton Woods twins—the IMF, the World Bank—after the Second

World War, but again they don't reflect the economic realities of today. You know, the weight that countries like China, Korea, have is too small. So, in the absence of that, international organisations working effectively, individual heads of government have to come together and solve those problems.[43]

If Cabinet government is anything, it should not be a court. Sir Richard Mottram certainly thought Blair operated a court system, and was scathing:

> What is very striking about all systems of courts is everybody is seeking the favour of the king or the queen and they do it in various ways, but one obvious way in which they do it is they differentiate themselves from others, so a constant theme and this was true when I worked in the Cabinet Office latterly. A constant theme of all the people in Number Ten and the hangers on around Number Ten was 'departments are useless, only because of us does anything get done'. These were people who had largely never worked in a department, so how they knew they were useless, I've no idea. 'Look PM, look what I can do for you,' not 'look how you could through me get someone to do something for you,' so in a way it became a game of who looks good and a competition over knowledge.

> Number Ten could happily spend weeks talking about things about which they knew nothing, without engaging the people who knew something, often either because that was a clever part of this game or because they didn't know who knew something so they could operate in a complete fog of stupidity while out there there were resources they could have tapped into. All because that was their model of their machine, it's us against them, they are the enemy—doesn't work.[44]

Sir Robin Butler's successor in January 1998 was Sir Richard Wilson, stepping up from permanent secretary at the Home Office. The announcement of his appointment as Cabinet Secretary came in August 1997: 'TB wanted him sold as a moderniser,' Alastair Campbell recorded, 'which Jonathan [Powell] thought was a joke. He felt he was a classic Establishment Civil Service appointment with not that great a track record on the modernising front.'[45] Powell's words presaged a power struggle between him and Sir Richard. Indeed, the turn of the century would be marked historically as one of the low-water marks for relations between the permanent and temporary sides of government—at the very top level, at least.

In Sir Richard's valedictory lecture in 2002, 'Portrait of a Profession Revisited' (the original 'Portrait of a Profession' was delivered by Sir Edward Bridges in 1950[46] and was described by Samuel Brittan as 'an inexhaustible quarry of quotations for radical critics'[47]), Wilson painted a picture:

> On the walls of my private office hang the photographs of my seven distinguished predecessors as Secretary of the Cabinet. I sometimes find myself staring at them for inspiration...A week or two ago I found myself looking at the great Lord Bridges...staring at Bridges, I could see a bubble emerging from his mouth enquiring: What precisely is happening on your watch, Sir Richard?[48]

The perennial Civil Service touchstone of 'continuity and change' was what was happening. While Sir Richard was keen to modernize, his sense of history as part of the apostolic succession (the 'classy trade union', as Hennessy put it[49]) meant change would come but only, if he could help it, at a pace acceptable to the Civil Service and its appreciation of the constitution. Posterity weighed heavily on Sir Richard's shoulders.

Wilson's view was informed by his juxtaposition of Thatcher and Blair's Cabinet style and added informality to the charge list—anathema to tidy-minded, due-process-driven mandarins. He observed:

> Mrs Thatcher was very formal. No one went into the Cabinet Room before she went into the Cabinet Room. Everyone hovered outside, no coffee or tea then. We all waited and then a buzzer would sound in the lobby downstairs and we'd all clear away from the two main entrances into the lobby and she would go into the room first. And then...there would be a slightly unholy rush to get into the room after her. Because she would sit down, put her handbag down there, put the papers in front of her and be ready to start the meeting while people were still getting through the door...Come to Cabinet with Tony Blair, we'd have coffee and tea outside the room, the Cabinet doors would be open. People would saunter backwards and forwards, they'd put their papers—you'd still have a seating plan—people would put their papers down and go do business in the corners of the room. And Tony Blair

would be having a bilateral with John Prescott in his study and would
sort of saunter in eating an apple in his shirtsleeves. I remember watching
for the first time and thinking this is a different generation. This is the
prime minister as Hamlet.[50]

Butler backed the Thatcher analysis: 'She was much more formal about
this than her reputation is. She certainly wanted to get her own way, and
she was very dominant, but she certainly took the view, as Harold
Wilson did, that important decisions should be taken by Cabinet.'[51]

Agreeing with many of the Cabinet Secretaries' criticisms, Peter
Hennessy, former journalist, full-time Whitehall watcher and,
throughout the Blair premiership, professor of Contemporary British
History at Queen Mary and Westfield, University of London, raised a
further concern. In a series of lectures he described as 'overflights',
the Cabinet government 'romantic'[52] Hennessy mixed a scholarly
knowledge of precedent with the choicest of unattributed but
impeccably sourced quotations and analysis, all packaged in a passionate, beautifully constructed and thoroughly entertaining defence of
the inescapable need for no one person to dominate British government.
'For ours is a system of government largely without maps,' Hennessy
explained:

> Our governors, elected or appointed, live by a set of constitutional
> arrangements and approaches which rest on convention and procedure
> rather than prescriptive statute. Our working constitution is a thing of
> tacit understandings, in Sidney Low's phrase, held together by notions
> of Crown power and Crown service—a world of innumerable "grey
> areas" which exist in a government machine operating within an uncod-
> ified constitution[53]

Another Hennessy lecture succinctly explained 'the importance of
being collective, both as a safeguard against overmightiness at the top
and as an aid to careful, effective and durable policy making'.[54]

The concerns of mandarins Butler, Wilson, and Mottram, and
senior journalists-cum-scholars Hennessy and Riddell, among others,
amounted to a sustained barrage of criticism. In Blair's first term,
according to Lord Wilson, he was 'the most powerful prime minister
we had had in the country for many years; [with] the most disciplined

Cabinet, the most disciplined party; with the highest ratings ever in public opinion—all the things you look to for checks and balances (including the press, Cabinet government, political parties, Parliament) were in a quiet state'.[55] A focus of attention became the newly minted *Ministerial Code*, renamed from *Questions of Procedure for Ministers*, which was first privately issued to ministers in 1945, tweaked by subsequent prime ministers, and finally published in 1992.[56] Former Cabinet Secretary Lord Trend dismissed the importance of this document in 1986 as 'not a constitution, merely some tips for beginners—a book of etiquette',[57] which has subtly changed over time but has recently ranged from the travel expenses of spouses and policy on air miles to the coordination of presentation—and, crucially, conduct of collective responsibility. Though the prime minister is not mentioned in the latter's three short paragraphs essentially concerned with presenting a united front and secrecy, this did not stop a campaign based upon the *spirit* of the publication, building upon the idea of it being the *closest* thing to a constitutional text. Blair was eventually forced to defend his governing style, declaring in the House of Commons that 'no one will be better governed through fine-tuning the Ministerial Code. Those are good issues for academics and constitutional experts, but they are not the big issues that Parliament should debate when we consider our role in the modern society.'[58]

Sir Andrew Turnbull observed that the 'style of working was not a bad habit that the Blair group slipped in to. It was a quite conscious decision. There are things they had written in advance or reported ex-post that they had been thinking, that the Civil Service process was too bureaucratic.'[59] Though the late-Blair-era Secretary to the Cabinet Lord O'Donnell came to believe that Blair himself recognized some shortcomings in his decision-making over the highly intricate and ambitious public sector reform programme: 'I think he was beginning to see, and it was beginning to emerge, that there were disadvantages...some of the most difficult issues he'd had to deal with, where I think a more formal process might have helped him.' O'Donnell also noted: 'I think [Blair was] somewhat exasperated by the, "If I don't do it myself, it doesn't happen".'[60] Blair himself did concede in retirement that 'towards the end, I would say we made much more use of cabinet committees...we did definitely transition our mode of government over time'.[61]

But Sir Jeremy Heywood, Cabinet Secretary 2012-2018, and principal private secretary 1999–2003, thought a little differently:

> I don't have a vivid memory of transition. In his first term, he was very close to Gordon Brown, closer to John Prescott in a different way but he held him close, certainly, and some senior colleagues, he kept them in touch as he needed to, discussed as he needed to. In his second term he was keener to develop a cadre of public service ministers alongside obviously the Chancellor and other senior ministers so I think he paid more attention to building up colleagues who were bought into what he was trying to achieve, had an opportunity to help him shape that thinking, and he did more meetings with ministers in his second term. So I think his style did evolve over time. Some of the Iraq discussions: the minutes have now been published, and you can see in all their detail how that operated. There were some issues that did get a lot of attention, a lot of discussion, they weren't always short meetings, but I wouldn't necessarily say there was a great trend to use Cabinet intensively or for more and more substantive purposes as the period went on.[62]

Sir Richard Mottram put Blair's initial disdain for Cabinet government down to inexperience—and, he implied, arrogance:

> There's obviously a big question mark over prime ministers who come in who've never been in charge of anything. But if you are the prime minister in those circumstances...the incoming person [should say to him or herself] 'I am now in charge of this huge machine of which I know very little, what is my best strategy? I need to put together an approach here which absolutely maximises the knowledge and skills valuable to me from this huge machine, work with all these people to produce results.' Did he do that? Did they have a mental picture, a mental map which said this is what we're trying to do?

Note the use of the word 'they' to refer to Blair and his court:

> They had a different mental map which said in structural terms, we're not into this Cabinet government lark...they held their colleagues in contempt, mainly, largely, and they had a very low opinion about a

government machine about which they knew nothing...Years later they still never learned this lesson that the most important thing you do is pick the people because they didn't think they were going to work through loads of other people, they thought they were going to do it all themselves...so if you look at the way business was conducted, throughout, from day one, it was conducted through a smallish group of people who didn't really understand the nature of running a very large organization because they'd never run one.[63]

Iraq

Iraq is the focus of greater attention later in this book. Received wisdom has it that 'sofa government' was the conclusion of the 2004 *Review of Intelligence on Weapons of Mass Destruction*, otherwise known as the Butler report after its chair, the former Cabinet Secretary. Unsurprisingly, the phrase 'sofa government' does not appear in such an official report. The use of 'sofa' owes its origin to Daniel Finkelstein, *The Times* columnist who had previously worked for John Major and William Hague and later became a Conservative peer. During the Hutton inquiry hearings, he wrote: 'A picture of Blair's Downing Street emerged in which people plonked themselves on sofas in other people's offices, shooting the breeze about the crisis, with no one in charge and no one keeping a record. Not very reassuring.'[64] The image stuck. Indeed, the final recommendation of the Butler report, on the machinery of government, said:

> We are concerned that the informality and circumscribed character of the Government's procedures which we saw in the context of policy-making towards Iraq risks reducing the scope for informed collective political judgement. Such risks are particularly significant in a field like the subject of our Review, where hard facts are inherently difficult to come by and the quality of judgement is accordingly all the more important.[65]

These are critical words, for sure, but not exactly the damning indictment Blair's critics claimed they were.

Some said the report was highly condemnatory, but required nuanced reading, written in what was sometimes described as 'mandarinese', 'officialese', or 'Whitehallese', that peculiarly British, highly skilled, euphemistic subdialect of 'legalese' made famous by the perennially popular 1980s BBC television comedies *Yes, Minister* and *Yes, Prime Minister* (still the 'unrivalled guide to British politics' according to the *Financial Times* in 2016).[66] It is now chronicled by the website, civilservant.org.uk—for example, the word 'concerned' as in, 'I was concerned to hear' is defined as 'a senior official is about to explode'; 'surprised...signifies utter horror, disgust and fury'; while 'disappointed' could be 'used by senior officials to express the view that a particular junior official is quite possibly the most incompetent person it has ever been their misfortune to come across...particularly devastating if used in conjunction with "concerned" and/or "surprised"'.[67] 'Mandarinese' undoubtedly helps to lubricate the often aggressively conflicting agendas within government—as Sir Ian Bancroft, head of the Home Civil Service 1978–81, would say, 'I think we'll have to draft around that one.'[68]

The final paragraph of the Butler report, on the machinery of government, was clear that the committee of the great and the good, politicians and officials, 'do not suggest that there is or should be an ideal or unchangeable system of collective Government, still less that procedures are in aggregate any less effective now than in earlier times.'[69] Indeed. For as Stanley Baldwin, prime minister three times between 1923 and 1937, said in 1932:

> The historian can tell you probably perfectly clearly what the constitutional practice was at any given period in the past, but it would be very difficult for a living writer to tell you at any given period in his lifetime what the Constitution of the country is in all respects, and for this reason, that almost at any given moment...there may be one practice called "constitutional" which is falling into desuetude and there may be another practice which is creeping into use but is not yet constitutional.[70]

Indeed, the Butler report was dismissed by the media at the time as a whitewash—another one, after the Hutton report into the death of Dr David Kelly, who had been the BBC's source for the allegation that Blair's office had manipulated the intelligence case for the Iraq war, and pressure for another investigation grew.[71] Sir John Chilcot's inquiry was announced by Prime Minister Gordon Brown on 15 June 2009, 'to identify lessons that could be learned from the Iraq conflict... including the way decisions were made'. Its report was published in the last days of David Cameron's premiership on 6 July 2016. Chilcot stated: 'The Report provides an impartial, fair and accurate account of events from which the Inquiry has drawn its conclusions, but which also allow the reader to draw their own'[72]—indeed, the report was cited in vindication by those highly critical of Blair, *and* by Blair himself. Everyone took from the report what they wanted. The eight-page conclusion on 'collective responsibility' started by trying to define what it is: 'Under UK constitutional conventions—in which the Prime Minister leads the Government—Cabinet is the main mechanism by which the most senior members of the Government take collective responsibility for its most important decisions.'[73] This was carefully worded: the 'main mechanism' is not the *only* way, and a convention is the way in which something is *usually* done, not a law.

The report explained: 'Most decisions on Iraq pre-conflict were taken either bilaterally between Mr Blair and the relevant Secretary of State or in meetings' between Blair, Jack Straw, Foreign Secretary, Geoff Hoon, Defence Secretary, and Number Ten defence and security officials—not the full Cabinet.'[74] It quoted Lord Turnbull, who described Blair's characteristic way of working with his Cabinet colleagues as: ' "I like to move fast. I don't want to spend a lot of time in kind of conflict resolution, and, therefore, I will get the people who will make this thing move quickly and efficiently." That was his sort of characteristic style, but it has drawbacks.' However, Lord Turnbull went on say that the group listed above was 'a professional forum... they had... with one possible exception the right people in the room. It wasn't the kind of sofa government in the sense of the Prime Minister and his special advisers and political cronies.'[75] The 'one possible exception' was Clare Short, the International Development Secretary, who was deeply sceptical about the war and who Blair and Alastair

Campbell thought likely to leak. Although she did not resign when it came to the invasion vote, she left the government shortly after.

The inquiry concluded 'that there should have been collective discussion by a Cabinet Committee or small group of Ministers...at a number of decision points which had a major impact on the development of UK policy before the invasion of Iraq'[76]—eleven occasions were detailed over a fifteen-month period—and that 'a more structured process *might* have identified some of the wider implications and risks...It *might* also have offered the opportunity to remedy some of the deficiencies in planning [emphases added]'.[77] These are the hardest criticisms in the Chilcot report over Blair's cabinetry. Again, it is critical but not damning.

None of the huge Iraq inquiries consisting of politicians, officials, and independent historians—under great public pressure to be transparent and avoid a so-called 'whitewash'—has found that Blair was unconstitutional.

Cabinet government according to Blair

Blair responded to his critics when he came to our class in 2011. He was confident that his view of Cabinet government was the more realistic in the modern age. He started by pointing out that the expectations journalists had of Cabinet meetings had changed:

> It's the place where decisions are actually formally made but it's difficult now in the world in which you live to have a 'from the beginning' discussion in Cabinet without working a lot of things out beforehand with the key players. Now, maybe that's always happened. But I remember Roy Jenkins telling me that in the old days, the 1960s, in Harold Wilson's Cabinet, they would frequently go on for two days, have a Cabinet meeting, then have a show of hands at the end of it. You just couldn't operate like that in today's media environment. If it ran on past lunchtime they'd be: a crisis! And if it ran on to the next day...! There wouldn't be much left of the government. And if you had a show of hands...!

This change had started long before he became prime minister. At a Cabinet meeting early in his government John Major noticed it had turned 1 p.m. and said: 'If we don't break up now, they'll say there's a crisis.'[78]

Blair said he doubted Cabinet had ever had open-ended discussions without preparation—the implied intellectually pure (and leisurely) debate of textbook theory:

> Personally I think there really is a lot of nonsense written about decline in Cabinet government...Leaders end up getting fired in one of two ways. They either can't make up their minds or they are dictatorial. So I chose one over the other. You work through your Cabinet but I can't imagine a situation today in which you literally just take an issue blind to the Cabinet and have a discussion and everyone makes up their minds at the end... There's a belief, I think that's understandable but I don't think very politically realistic, that Cabinet government operates in a way to constrain the Prime Minister and I'm not sure it was ever particularly like that. The most important thing about the PM in relation to the Cabinet is that he or she appoints them. So it gives you a certain amount of power in that situation. So the idea that you were ever going to have this general discussion around a table with people not being aware of the fact that obviously they are playing into a power politics of all the relationships I think is a bit unrealistic. It's also because I think the nature of the job has changed.

One important change is the speed of 'today's media environment', he said:

> I was seen by some people, and this was meant critically, as very iconoclastic towards traditional Cabinet government. But I just can't imagine running it today in the world in which we are particularly with two things that I think are very, very different. The first is the twenty-four-hour, seven-days-a-week media that completely changes the way that prime ministers have to operate. Literally, you cannot imagine how fast you have to take decisions and come to positions. Creating the space to have some huge deliberation that is then filtered out with the guy standing outside Number Ten all day is really not practical.

This was particularly important in crises:

> For prime ministers today, a lot of the job is about getting things done, it's about delivery. Particularly in relation to public services but also in relation to crises that you are expected to manage and deal with and so on. And unless you have a powerful centre, unless the prime minister has the power to do things, things just don't happen . . . with things like foot and mouth and so on, these crises that hit you, the fuel protests, if I hadn't gripped that and run it, never mind Cabinet government, run it myself with the ministers sitting round the table gripping it, salvaging it, it just would not have happened . . .

> The reality of today's world as prime minister is that you've got to grip things strongly from the centre. If you don't, you just buffer them, basically, and people end up saying you can't make up your mind, you are weak, you're indecisive . . . So I think the way government works today has changed but it has changed for reasons . . . that are far more about the nature of the job than the nature of the person because I can't imagine a prime minister running the country today and not gripping things closely . . . I think the fact you have to grip it is one aspect, how quickly you act on it is another. Gripping it is an essential part of how modern government works.

> I think the speed of decision making, I think that is a problem . . . It's partly the speed of how the world works for political leaders today they are expected to take decisions really quickly and if you don't shape events quite fast then you find that they shape you.

He summed up: 'People say that the power of Parliament has declined but what they just mean is that the government's doing things they don't like, with a majority. It's what we used to call democracy.' But he accepted that the nature of democracy had changed because society had changed:

> I think there is a big, big debate about democracy and one of the things I'd like to do is initiate and take part in that, about how you mature your democracy in the modern age which I think is a far bigger and more interesting topic than what I think some of the constitutional experts are obsessed by, which is why the world of 2011 isn't like the world of 1961. And the answer to that is, well, because it isn't.[79]

Unsurprisingly, Jonathan Powell was in tune with his former boss Blair when he spoke of 'sofa government', but made the argument more bluntly:

> What it became was a metaphor for decisions people didn't like. In other words, it was easier to attack the means [by which] you got to decisions than decisions themselves. I'm completely unrepentant about sofa government...having a formal meeting of Cabinet does not make a decision or a discussion any better than having an informal decision and discussion in a group. The key is to have the right people in the discussion and make sure their views are aired and then the right decision is reached...Criticising us just because we did it in the one office rather than the other office, doing it informally rather than formally, strikes me as not fair.'[80]

He was also crystal clear as to who he felt would own the future in an even more aggressive response to the critics in his book *The New Machiavelli*:

> The current role of the Cabinet in the British system of government...is not a policymaking body but the political manifestation of united and strong government based on collective responsibility. A dangerous myth has, however, been built up around the idea of Cabinet government in recent years, propagated by a number of retired mandarins. Their argument, somewhat simplified, is that Tony Blair murdered Cabinet government and replaced it with something called 'sofa government'. Before him, everything was well regulated, the big issues of state were discussed in Cabinet on the basis of papers provided by the civil servants in the Cabinet Office, and good decisions were reached and properly recorded. No one was kept in the dark about anything and the Cabinet Office strove to make sure that all departments had an equal say and that there was fair play. In their doctrine, it is the Cabinet that has the power, not the prime minister. He is simply a *primus inter pares* who chairs the Cabinet.
>
> This is nonsense.

Powell identified the 1970s—'not a decade we naturally associate with the success of Britain as a country'—as the 'supposed golden era of Cabinet government'.[81] 'Pendulum politics',[82] swinging between Labour and Conservative, meant weak governments leaned on a Civil Service content to organize 'the orderly management of decline'—to quote the head of the Home Civil Service, Sir William Armstrong, in 1973.[83] The Labour Party in particular was ever more riven in these years—it formally split after all in 1981 with the creation of the Social Democratic Party—and the divisions led to disagreement and great Cabinet debate; hardly, Powell suggested, 'the dignified, inclusive, evidence-based policy discussions suggested by the proponents of the golden age':

> Cabinet government of that sort, if it ever existed, died before Tony Blair went into politics, and it was finally buried under Mrs Thatcher... She did not have much time for her cabinet colleagues, she did not want lengthy discussion, and she usually knew what she wanted out of a meeting before she went to it...
>
> The division is not therefore between Cabinet government and no Cabinet government but between a weak leader and a strong one. Each time weak prime ministers succeed strong ones they invariably announce they are reintroducing Cabinet government, but all they really mean is that they do not have the power to lead their government effectively by themselves.

Powell warmed to his theme:

> There is a good reason why the mandarins' conception of Cabinet government doesn't exist in reality: it would be a singularly bad way of making decisions. Any discussion that involves twenty-five people or more, many of them uninformed about the subject under discussion unless their department is directly involved, and with many of the right people whose voices should be heard not present, will give you at best an unfocused political discussion of a subject. So Cabinet is the right place to ratify decisions, the right place for people to raise concerns if they have not done so before, the right place for briefings by the prime minister and other ministers of strategic issues, and the right place to ensure political unity; but it is categorically not the right place for an informed decision on difficult and detailed policy issues.

This is, perhaps, the most emphatic elaboration of the 'modern' model of Cabinet government. It is a persuasive argument about the most effective use of ministerial time and prime-ministerial power. And Powell sought to turn the phrase 'sofa government' against Blair's critics:

> The clue to the threadbare nature of the argument put up by the critics is their focus on furniture. It doesn't matter whether decisions are made sitting on a sofa or round a coffin-shaped table. It doesn't matter if the participants call each other President of the Board of Trade or Margaret. I was a civil servant for sixteen years and a political appointee for thirteen years, so I have seen both sides. I can tell the difference between an ad hoc committee and an Ad Hoc Committee of the Cabinet, but I don't think it matters. Those who suggest that it does are stuck in an old-fashioned mindset that cannot distinguish between form and substance. The series of set-piece attacks by retired Cabinet Secretaries and other senior civil servants on the modern system of government in reports and speeches are essentially the death rattle of the old mandarin class.

The biggest confusion of the 'old mandarin class', Powell wrote, was to think that sticking to old-fashioned procedures would have meant that the Government would have avoided making mistakes:

> I don't pretend that all the decisions that were taken in government from 1997 to 2007 were right. We made many mistakes, but they were generally made not because of process, not because we did not have the facts in front of us, not because a particular minister or Cabinet Secretaries was absent, but because we collectively made the wrong decision. That is why the propagation of this mandarins' myth is so pernicious. It is designed to mislead new governments into thinking that, if only they follow the old ways, somehow they will not make mistakes.'[84]

Powell here alludes to a theme running throughout the Blair years and especially the earlier ones—that, while the mandarins of the Civil Service were not politicized in an unsophisticated way by Blair and had not been in the Conservative years before, neither were they 'impartial' in the purest sense. They had a view as to how things should be done. Of course they did. Even the Whitehall legend Burke Trend, Cabinet Secretary to Macmillan, Home, Wilson, and Heath, and a man of legendary discretion who would not even vote in general elections lest it cloud his judgement, had clear views on governance and pronounced them often—albeit privately.[85]

A differing of opinions within the mandarinate

The common view is that the New Labour governments were in a cold war with the Civil Service throughout. This is simply incorrect. Many senior officials took the Blair-Powell view of Cabinet government. While Cabinet Secretaries Butler and Wilson, along with senior colleagues such as Sir Richard Mottram, saw real problems in Blair's approach to governing, others such as Sir John Holmes, principal private secretary to the Prime Minister 1997–9 (later ambassador to France 2001–7), disagreed. Sir John had also been the Foreign Affairs private secretary to John Major, so he had some idea of the evolution of government machinery around the historic hinge of 1997:

> I think this stuff about sofa government is highly overdone. I mean, yes, he [Blair] did have a more informal style but the idea that before that what really counted was Cabinet meetings and Cabinet Committees is bollocks. There were formal structures which continued to exist— most of the decisions in John Major's time and I'm pretty sure in Mrs Thatcher's time were taken in different ways, through kitchen cabinets and informal meetings and whatever. So the idea that...suddenly you were sitting on sofas discussing things in ways that never happened before is nonsense. It went further in that direction, no doubt, but I just don't buy this theory...it didn't feel that different. The Cabinet in John Major's day was very formalized, the only time they discussed anything serious I remember really was Europe and then it went into some kind of political format because there were so many problems over Europe and there were some very important discussions...Cabinet Committees were used for big decisions and discussions but the big decisions were not necessarily being taken there. Before as well as after.

He felt that Blair's inexperience led to a change that was more style than substance:

> What's probably true is that one of the weaknesses of Blair is that he'd never been a minister. He didn't understand how the system worked. He didn't know what it was like to be a minister, a departmental minister.

And therefore it was a weakness because he tried to operate too much through the special advisers, the bright young things telling senior Cabinet ministers what to do, and of course they didn't like that. Civil servants didn't like it either but neither did politicians. And that wasn't a way to get people to own the decisions you were trying to make. You set up resistances in the system. That was more about his style and his lack of knowledge about what it was like to be a minister than it was about politicization or anything else. There had been political advisers around before, John Major had them, the head of the Policy Unit was not a civil servant, they were people from outside...

I think people portray it too starkly a complete change. All right, it was heading more in that direction, but it was heading in that direction anyway. John Major sat around talking to us about things, to people he confided in about things, taking decisions about things, effectively, even if it was formalized later just as Blair did and just as Mrs Thatcher did.[86]

Sir Jeremy Heywood was one of the most significant Civil Service figures of the period, having been principal private secretary to Blair and having returned in an enhanced version of that role for Gordon Brown, followed by serving as Cabinet Secretary to David Cameron and Theresa May. He was in a unique position to compare and contrast the governing styles and to answer the key question: was Blair unconstitutional in his approach to Cabinet government?

I'm not sure I would use the word unconstitutional. Obviously it's the case that any prime minister has to decide how to use Cabinet best. Some prime ministers have brought lots of issues to Cabinet, including some controversial issues, and have used Cabinet to resolve them. Other prime ministers have used it to basically set out their own thoughts and haven't really invited much debate. Different prime ministers use Cabinet in different ways. Tony Blair's Cabinets were relatively short. Obviously, occasionally, we had long Cabinets but in general they were pretty short.

Would I call that unconstitutional? I think that's a very pejorative word. He used other ways of keeping in touch with people, other ways of reaching conclusions on things, but he didn't use Cabinet in the conventional way, at that stage, the conventionally understood way Cabinet would be used.

Being at the very top of government from Blair to May, Sir Jeremy explained that, though technically a prime minister can govern as they see fit, practicality over the long term demands a good degree of collegiality:

> There are certain rules and conventions, obviously, and I think in the end if the prime minister wants to maintain a coherent government in which individual Cabinet ministers are prepared to defend collectively what's been agreed in the name of the government then he has to find a way of engaging them. You can't not consult people, then expect them to go out and religiously defend everything the government is doing. So self-preservation in the end dictates that prime ministers do observe certain conventions and one of them is to allow collective discussion or at least collective written agreement to proposals.[87]

This is the state-of-the-art, clearest description of Cabinet government in the early twenty-first century. Gone are the days when a theory of traditional collective government dominated, with the Cabinet Secretary at the apex, replaced by a cool pragmatism which accepts prime ministers make decisions as they see fit—but are locked into an unavoidable collaboration if they wish to see decisions take effect. The truths to which Cabinet Secretaries of Blair's early years clung in their apostolic succession have been swept away. In a postgraduate class under the joint auspices of 10 Downing Street and King's College London in 2016, Lord Butler accepted that collectivity was only an option: 'There's nothing to say you must, you're not going to be taken to the Supreme Court if you don't.'[88] Civil Service influence has been downgraded compared to its 1970s heyday. Political power has reasserted itself.

A quiet Cabinet

There were other reasons Cabinet government was quiescent during the Blair years. The new prime minister had good cause to dismiss any potential Cabinet revolt. For Blair often referred to his leadership being the first of a 'less ideological age' following the collapse of the Soviet bloc, with a Labour Party not as riven by philosophical divisions than before and hungry for government after four election defeats—a generation out of power. Sir Nicholas Macpherson, at Gordon Brown's side throughout his chancellorship as first his principal private secretary and later as permanent secretary to the Treasury, witnessed 'an extraordinarily deep relationship based on a real mutual understanding' between his boss and Blair, a near telepathy, on issues that had been thrashed out during the long opposition years.[89] This was dominant in the early years of the New Labour government, before personality clashes and diverging ambition extended to policy differences. Blair spoke several times in Cabinet, 'stressing this was the first Labour Cabinet for a long time with no ideological divide and we had to ensure we didn't lose that'.[90] Alastair Campbell later observed that the government was:

> pretty united, [though] there were differences... would Tony Blair and Clare Short automatically agree about most things? Er, no. Were there differences closer within, sometimes Tony and Gordon, Tony and John Prescott and David Blunkett on specific areas of policy? 'Course there were, it is just inevitable no matter how many people you put together but actually they were pretty ideologically united.[91]

There was less need to use Cabinet to resolve differences, something so different from previous Labour governments.

For Lord Falconer, a pre-politics friend of the prime minister and a minister and later Cabinet minister in his government, Blair's role as New Labour's star performer in opposition with an unprecedented personal mandate led to major gains in government:

> Blair came to power in May 1997 with the majority of 179, which I think is the biggest majority that any prime minister had obtained since the Earl of Liverpool[92]... And there was a very widespread perception, whether you think it's right or whether you think it's wrong, that the result in the general election had been caused by Blair, his personality and the way that he had moved the Labour Party from one place to another. So if you have come to power with a majority of 179

and it is believed to be your own work, rather than the work of your party, then your need to hold all the factions in your political party together is quite limited. Particularly when quite significant numbers within the people who make up the Cabinet had broadly been opposed to quite a lot of that which you had stood for before. So Blair, right from the start, was very, very determined to achieve a particular agenda in relation to what happened. For example, the independence of the Bank of England...creating a Supreme Court and changing the role of the Lord Chancellor, if there had been great debates about [these] in Cabinet then the thing would have been slowed down very, very dramatically. And although there would have ultimately have been agreement to all of these things, they would never have happened in the way that they did.

So there was a huge benefit in Blair running a government which was very focused, had lots of very powerful ideas and drove very, very hard from the front...the strengths and successes, I believe, of the Blair Government, have very much to do with the fact that Tony was both a strong political leader who didn't need to make compromises with his Cabinet...he had a strong series of ideas which, because Number Ten was so strong, he was able to get the machinery of government to work on it in a hard way, in a way that wasn't dependent upon doing a deal with an individual cabinet minister or persuading a particular department to provide him with work...the country [wanted] a period of dynamic leadership, that the Cabinet should be weak and the prime minister should be strong, and that's what happened with Blair.

Falconer concluded: 'The position unequivocally was that Blair...took to himself the role of being the leader of the government, the chief executive of the organization, the person who took decisions,'[93] an analogy that was anathema to Lords Wilson and Armstrong, as we have seen.

The fear of making Labour once again unelectable was a powerful factor in Blair's alleged prime-ministerialism. From the earliest days of New Labour in 1994, it was clear that here was a master strategist, as he triangulated between the Conservatives and many in his own party, charting a course at first stratospherically popular. Blair's declaration during his victory speech at the Royal Festival Hall on the morning of 2 May 1997, 'We have been elected as New Labour and we will govern as New Labour' (words given him by Peter Mandelson[94]), meant that he was not going to be a centrist in opposition and turn left in government, but it also expressed his determination to avoid the chaotic government of the 1970s again. This point cannot be stressed enough. Blair had seen how a Labour government had been weakened by ideological division in the 1970s and how it had refused to 'compromise with the electorate' during the 1980s, which had kept it out of power. He was determined that it would not tack left again, certainly not on his watch, and not after the hard-fought reforms of the long opposition years. With Blair and Brown growing apart, the prime minister and his closest advisers became more defensive of the creed, and more suspicious of what a reversion to 'Old Labour' could bring.

As Campbell wrote of Brown and his courtiers in 2000, 'TB was worried not just that they were wrong, but it meant they misunderstood what New Labour was, and its potency as a political force' because 'we had to stay bang in the centre ground. "I know I am right. I am where the country is. [William] Hague is more right wing than the country and GB is more left wing than the country." ' Blair went further, Campbell recorded in his diary: 'He said he had underestimated the ability of the Labour Party not to be happy about winning, to want to take victory and from it sow the seeds of defeat.'[95] Resisting this pressure was why Blair was determined to keep an iron grip on Cabinet government—he believed history taught that a traditional left-wing party was unlikely to stay long in power.

Blair believed the election defeats after he stood down proved his point. He wrote of Gordon Brown's loss in 2010 that 'Labour won when it was New Labour. It lost because it stopped being New Labour.'[96] He predicted four months before the 2015 election that the result could be an election 'in which a traditional left-wing party competes with a traditional right-wing party, with the traditional result'. Asked if he meant a Tory win over Ed Miliband's Labour, Blair confirmed: 'Yes, that is what happens.'[97] David Cameron duly won a narrow victory, surprising to many but not to Blair. His analysis was ever more piquant in light of Jeremy Corbyn's victorious defeat in 2017. So far, Blair's analysis has been proved right.

In fact, the senior official Sir Richard Mottram linked this fear of 'Old Labour' ministers in post due to their political standing as opposed to bureaucratic ability or support for the prime minister to Blair's attempt to work round some Cabinet colleagues. He explained that Peter Mandelson, of the prime-ministerial court, had spoken to him about this:

> [Mandelson was] great, obviously, at it, very charming. 'You're not the problem, it's your ministers.' In other words, we haven't actually got a cohesive team of ministers in whom we have confidence and we would like to work with *you*, actually . . . we'd also like to work round the ministers through you. To which every time they tried to do it, I would explain to them that 'I'm afraid I have to work to my Secretary of State, this was the constitution of the country, and absolutely the Cabinet Secretary can tell me what to do and within reason do it, as long as my Secretary of State is happy, but you can't work to the prime minister round my Secretary of State.'

> They never, from day one . . . created a coherent government. Now this is very, very difficult and to be fair to Blair, and that's why I'm not a great critic of him, it's a very, very difficult thing to do this, but that's what he needed to set out to do, he needed to have a sense of, 'We are going to have a coherent government; I'm going to work through my ministers, not round them; and I'm going to expect the Civil Service to step up to the plate and if it doesn't step up to the plate . . . I will get the head of the Civil Service/Cabinet Secretary to take the individuals out and shoot them', metaphorically.[98]

As with many of Blair's detractors, Sir Richard appears to retreat when he might be expected to complete his argument. It turns out that he is 'not a great critic' of Blair, after all, and that Blair merely struggled with the same problems of coherence and delivery as trouble all prime ministers. Perhaps Sir Richard's strident words are born of disappointment that Blair's glittering opportunity was not fully seized.

Blair's power not untrammelled

Though 'Blair did consider Brown to be a grown-up' according to Lord Macpherson,[99] the Chancellor was always Blair's main counter-power.

In fact, Gordon Brown himself was a big reason the Blair government was less, rather than more, collegiate. The booming health of the British economy throughout the Blair years provided stability and money for the government as a whole, and put the Chancellor in a strong position. While Brown found it so difficult to accept that he was number two to Blair, he was even more determined to elevate himself above Cabinet colleagues, people he had grown up with in the party, with several of whom he had long-standing feuds—he demanded to be '*secondus inter pares*', if you will. In opposition, Brown disdained Shadow Cabinet and sought for all decisions to be taken between just him and the leader. That continued in government, and was made worse by the growing tension between the two. Peter Mandelson, wearing his thoughtful technocratic-analyst hat, observed:

> [This] had a very bad effect on Cabinet government, it effectively excluded a lot of the Cabinet. It was not a collective, working cabinet because you had the prime minister and Chancellor, which is the principal working relationship in government, operating with great difficulty and tension consuming a great deal of time and energy, which detracted from the operation of Cabinet as a whole. Second, you had Number Ten and the Treasury competing for control of the rest of the departments in Cabinet—very unfortunate for the departmental heads and members of Cabinet who had to be on one hand drawn to the prime minister because he was the prime minister and on the other towards the Chancellor because he held the purse strings. Really very difficult. But also because the prime minister and the Chancellor had to guard against exposing their disagreements, in my view that resulted in much less open and frank conversation collectively in the Cabinet amongst the Cabinet as a whole.

Mandelson described the effect this dysfunctional relationship had on meetings of the Cabinet:

> People always knew when Tony was chairman of the Cabinet, you've got Gordon sitting opposite, hardly ever looking at him, always scribbling on papers, always brought a mound of paperwork into the Cabinet which he would look through, never listened to what anyone else was saying. It wasn't a very nice atmosphere, it was constrained and it was all because of the nature of their relationship. It didn't make for

a happy Cabinet, it didn't make for an open Cabinet, it didn't really make for people feeling encouraged or able to make contributions. Some did. I remember Patricia Hewitt did sometimes, Charles Clarke sometimes did and John Reid sometimes did, but usually Tony would want the conversation closed down as quickly as possible because he would fear for the Chancellor's reaction as Gordon would usually think these things were aimed at him. And, frankly, they sometimes were. Particularly from people like Charles or John or David Blunkett or Robin Cook, all these people were very dissatisfied in their relationships with Gordon and would find some coded way to make that clear.[100]

When Geoff Hoon, Defence Secretary, raised an issue in Cabinet away from his brief, he was met with 'That's none of your concern' from the Chancellor—striking in its rebuff to the traditional idea of collective discussion.[101] With Brown the obstacle to the ideal of Cabinet government, it was sometimes Blair who defended it, once threatening for example to 'take the spending round to the Cabinet as a way of forcing Gordon's hand'.[102]

Brown was playing politics, then, when he told Alastair Campbell at the height of the foot-and-mouth crisis in March 2000: 'At some point, Cabinet government will have to be reimposed.' Campbell confided to his diary: 'The irony of his statement re Cabinet government was that his colleagues felt TB to be far more collegiate than he was.'[103] However, Campbell also noted that when Mo Mowlam and Sir Richard Wilson had urged 'more collective and collegiate government', Blair 'was pretty dismissive', responding: 'It's just a way of them saying they want to be more central, have more power.'[104]

Brown's memoir, released in 2017, was interesting for many reasons, not least for his unique reflections on the higher machinery of government—and for the belated recognition that the nature of being prime minister had changed over time but that he had failed to see it, and suffered the consequences:

Having been in government for ten years, I wanted to avoid accusations of running a 'cabal' or the kind of 'court government' which

people alleged had replaced Cabinet government...I wanted individual Cabinet ministers to play a far bigger role. I wanted the Cabinet itself to be more than a rubber stamp; more than just the sounding board it had often seemed—I wanted to see a rejuvenation of a more collective form of decision-making.[105]

The criticisms of Blair's cabinetry were clear here, and fitted well with Brown's words—if not his actions—during his chancellorship. But the really intriguing part was Brown's awakening:

> And in all candour, my attempts to move on from 'sofa' government perhaps inevitably fell short...In just about every area of central government, in fact, the media's questions landed on the doorstep of Number Ten, no matter what the issue and which department was formally responsible. So, when I now look back at the decisions we made in these first few months and how we made them, and compare this with the decision-making process of my predecessors and successors, I can see how and why the role of prime minister has kept expanding and that of the Cabinet has diminished...the transformation of the media and public perceptions has magnified the role and personality of the prime minister as the public face of the government...A restoration of what we traditionally thought of as Cabinet government was simply not possible when the engrained expectation was for the prime minister's office to answer instantaneously the media's questions on any remotely important government action...no Cabinet—not even one sitting in permanent session—could keep up with the demands for such instant responses.[106]

One might have thought that one of the, if not *the*, greatest vantage points to observe the nature of the British prime-ministership up close would have been from Number 11 Downing Street—for a decade. Many have pointed out Brown's few policy proposals once he became prime minister, but perhaps he can be equally criticized for his failure to grasp the modern demands of the top job before he entered Number Ten, in clear contrast to Blair.

The clash of the titans at the top of the Blair government meant that other Cabinet ministers were inevitably diminished. Professor Hennessy described Blair as presiding over the 'most supine cabinet' ever.[107] Roger Liddle, Mandelson's ally, remarked in 1999 to Hugo Young on the 'weak state of the Cabinet':

> There were so few strong people, he said that even Tony and Peter [Mandelson] were now worried that there was too much non-dissent... Nobody would break any new ground at all. Nowhere near like [Tony] Crosland et al. Everyone staying on the narrow track. Far too much conformity. He put this down to the price of the SDP [the Social Democratic Party, which broke away from Labour in 1981] still making itself felt...Not only did it remove a cadre of good people, but it planted the demand for total allegiance in New Labour. Nobody wanted to repeat what had happened in the Eighties: the trauma was still at large.[108]

There is evidence that Blair was concerned by the lack of forceful characters in Cabinet. In the reshuffle after the victory of the 2001 general election he appointed identifiably Blairite ministers to the main delivery departments, with the aim of their being in post for the full second term, in a riposte to Brown's manoeuvres but also as a mark of the prime minister's growing appetite for radical reform. Both David Blunkett's tenure as Home Secretary and Alan Milburn's at Health proved controversial and tough; Stephen Byers at Transport was merely controversial and Estelle Morris at Education proved anything but tough—but none lasted until the 2005 election. That the independent-minded Charles Clarke replaced first Morris at Education, then Blunkett at the Home Office, meant that, while the results of Blair's attempt to bring strength and stability to his government were disappointing, he clearly did not seek a Cabinet of stooges. His own choice of strong special advisers, accustomed and encouraged to contradict him, underlines this point, of which more later.

Blair told us:

> over time I started to get a whole new generation of Cabinet ministers that shared my kind of reforming zeal. And so...that was becoming easier, frankly, whereas at the beginning literally if I was not driving the change from the centre nothing happened or not a lot happened; towards the end...you were getting ministers that were coming into positions that shared the agenda and were really striving to implement it.[109]

Gus O'Donnell acknowledged that Blair did somewhat belatedly see that he had many big talents in the government that needed bringing on.[110]

Alastair Campbell's assertion that the New Labour government was unusually united ideologically is underlined by the absence of ministerial resignations over policy. Compared with Michael Heseltine in 1986, Nigel Lawson in 1989, and Sir Geoffrey Howe in 1990 in Thatcher's government, Blair had only Robin Cook and Clare Short in 2003. Neither was on the same scale. Cook's honourable exit before the Iraq invasion came some time after the peak of his political influence, when he had been demoted from Foreign Secretary to Leader of the Commons in 2001. Short's resignation was even less damaging, in that she had advertised her doubts about Iraq but had stayed in the government until a disagreement over the terms of the post-war occupation. Keeping Brown in post, despite all the evident difficulty, was a political choice Blair took, playing the cards he had been dealt, not living in a perfect world. Another prime minister without Blair's patience and strategic view would have put Brown on the back benches, where he would have been ready to pounce, *à la* Heseltine. However, Sir Richard Mottram caustically satirized Blair's (and Jonathan Powell's) dilemma: 'If you write a book about Machiavelli and you fancy yourselves as being Napoleonic you shouldn't have the Blair story, the story of a man who's incapable of firing his finance director.'[111]

Anyone but Major

That Blair had not experienced government office before did not mean that he had had no thoughts about the kind of prime minister he wished to be—although perhaps it might be more accurate to say he knew what kind of prime minister he did *not* want to be. For just as General Bernard Montgomery kept a portrait of Rommel pinned to his wall, so Blair focused in opposition on beating John Major. The New Labour high command contrasted Major's crumbling premiership with the determined purpose of Blair, biting at his legs. Blair became ever more disdainful of Major's supposed lack of grip, having goaded his opponent at Prime Minister's Questions in 1995 with the alpha-male jibe 'I lead my party; he follows his.'[112] The landslide of 1997 cemented his analysis.

If Major's example was how not to do it, Thatcher's was the lodestar. 'Having spent so many years in the political wilderness,' wrote Anthony Bevins, political editor of the *Independent*, in June 1997, 'many of them observing Baroness Thatcher's hardline political style, Mr Blair and Labour's most senior ministers are not in a mood for half measures.'[113] Indeed, Thatcher was the first ex-prime minister to be invited into Downing Street following Blair's election victory, so closely did he wish to be associated with her (which at the time was rumoured to have upset James Callaghan, although he only allowed it to be known that he was irked sometime later after he felt his record was unfairly denigrated).[114]

Thatcher's legend is of a dominant leader brushing obstruction aside. Unsurprisingly, this tells only part of the story. 'She was much more interesting and subtle and much more cautious and much more unsure ever of winning than people attribute to her,' according to Lord Wilson.[115] But the strength is what impressed, especially for those on the receiving end of her decade in power. Mandelson and Liddle were unstinting in their praise for her in *The Blair Revolution*, saying:

> Thatcher's success lay in her ability to focus on a set of clear goals and make everything (and everyone) conform to these priorities...her statecraft (that is, her methods of conducting government) derived a great deal from her personality—strong, decisive, uncompromising and hectoring—and it was this personality, rather than her values or ideology, which was responsible for her appeal.[116]

The history of the 1980s and the legend of Thatcher were deeply entrenched—but the strength overshadowed inevitable costs. Indeed, the paradox is that *the* most disastrous domestic policy of the modern era, the poll tax, a flagship Thatcher policy of her later years and directly instrumental in her downfall, was meticulously created through collective Cabinet government.[117]

Kenneth Clarke, having sat in Cabinet under Thatcher, Major, and Cameron, claimed in his memoir that she was a model of collegiality:

> Contrary to later popular belief, Margaret Thatcher ran a genuinely collective government in which her many strong departmental ministers insisted on taking a vocal and constructive part...but this had steadily been weakened in her last two or three years as she had quarrelled with more and more of her colleagues and become more determinedly authoritarian.[118]

Lord Lawson described a different picture, borrowing the terminology of Walter Bagehot in the nineteenth century, who distinguished between the government, the 'efficient' part of the British constitution, and the monarchy, the 'dignified' part: Lawson thought the Thatcher Cabinet had become the 'dignified' part, purely for show, with 'efficient' decisions taken elsewhere in committees.[119]

Clarke then observed a similar shift away from an initially collective government when Major took over, albeit for different reasons:

> The most noticeable change that he introduced was a reversion to a quite spectacularly co-operative and collective form of government...Now, Cabinet meetings suddenly became open-ended, wide-ranging discussions of every feature of policy...John was obviously prepared to engage at considerable length in efforts to produce truly consensus conclusions on most major issues. Some commentators picked this up and quite accurately described the new Cabinet as a 'Cabinet of chums' because we worked in such a friendly and mutually supportive way. We all genuinely found the new style of Cabinet debate enjoyable and stimulating.[120]

Chris Patten memorably described the Cabinet's mood after they had emerged from Major's very first Cabinet meeting as comparable to the prisoners in Beethoven's *Fidelio* released from dungeons into sunlight, 'blinking and singing of freedom'.[121]

But it did not, and probably could not, last and Clarke lamented that 'there was a downside to this approach, mainly the fact that John was most reluctant to make a decision that overruled the opinion of any minority within the Cabinet'. And he admitted he was instrumental in bringing an end to the early naivety:

> I was one of the ministers who rapidly decided that it was a mistake to allow any serious business affecting my department to be brought to Cabinet. I was not going to expose the details of my brief to the kind of malicious commentary that would have ensued. The then cabinet secretaries, my friend Robin Butler, unavailingly tried to find serious subjects for the Cabinet to discuss. He was usually charming and persuasive, but I fear that he was never able to convince me to raise any subject of any significance with a Cabinet from which all vestiges of sensible collective responsibility had vanished.[122]

The prime-ministerial versus collective spectrum

Sir Richard Mottram was characteristically colourful on Blair's comparison between Thatcher and Major:

> Part of the problem was the narrative which said: Mrs Thatcher, strong, no time for the Cabinet really, let's have a vote, twenty-three to one, the one has it, Mrs Thatcher in her heyday. And then you get Major: they underestimated Major, partly because they saw him through the lens of the press, and the ragged end of the Major government was hilariously bad, the Opposition just ran rings around them, it was excruciatingly bad—Cabinet government, weak. If you think about Tony, he is very binary, he's the ultimate binary, he takes binary to new heights. So Cabinet government? Weak, not going to have that. Napoleon, strong.[123]

Much of the debate around the downgrading of Cabinet government misses the point by being too polarized. While it is true that Blair's immediate choice was between the weak but consensual Major and the strong but dictatorial Thatcher, this contrast was too stark and masked the realistic, but much more nuanced reality, that every prime minister is at times collective and at others autocratic. They are all on the prime-ministerial–collective spectrum.

The furthest back our witnesses went was to David Lloyd George, prime minister 1916–22. Lord Morgan had not seen it for himself, of course, but as Lloyd George's biographer he told a Downing Street history seminar that his subject had operated 'sofa government carried to an extreme'.[124]

Here, we confine ourselves to the history of British government since the Second World War. Clement Attlee, subsequently immortalized as the gold standard of collective Cabinet governance by such luminaries as Roy Jenkins, Peter Hennessy and most recently John Bew, presided over a Cabinet of powerful personalities and not a few rivalries, and bequeathed a level of domestic delivery every bit as victorious as the war effort. But he kept the nuclear weapons programme under such secrecy that many of his Cabinet had no idea Britain was building such awesome destructive capability until Labour had left office. He originally thought that a Cabinet committee could work until the economic ministers attending, Hugh Dalton, the Chancellor, and Sir Stafford Cripps, the president of the Board of Trade, stood firm over the cost at a time of true austerity in the autumn of 1946. Attlee adjourned, and reconvened in January 1947 with a new committee, simply excluding Dalton and Cripps. And Britain became a nuclear nation.[125] Attlee later castigated his Cabinet colleagues—and cast doubt over his collegiate credentials—by defending this demonstration of stark prime-ministerial power, because 'I thought that some of them were not fit to be trusted with secrets of this kind.'[126] Lord Armstrong thought this decision absolutely right, as it was in what he considered to be the national interest.[127]

In Sir Winston Churchill's second premiership, 1951–5, the old warhorse once again sought to be the centre of decision-making. This time he tried to create a new layer of coordination with the 'ill-starred experiment'[128] of 'overlords'—in effect trusted old friends who were to keep him in post by way of being a buffer between him and Cabinet ministers—but it never really took shape and was formally abandoned in 1953. During the Second World War, he had consulted neither the service ministers nor the War Cabinet over the development of the atomic bomb, yet in July 1954 brought to full Cabinet the decision to advance to the hydrogen bomb era.[129]

Sir Anthony Eden's two-year tenure from 1955 to 1957 will be forever blighted by his handling of the Suez debacle, the invasion of Egypt before which Cabinet government was conducted, according to Lord Bancroft, 'in a hurried, reactive, almost furtive way'.[130] Eden was supremely and tragically assertive in his undoubted specialist area of foreign affairs, but was highly collegiate in domestic affairs—in effect outsourcing economic and social matters to Rab Butler and Harold Macmillan due to a chronic lack of confidence.[131]

The diaries of Barbara Castle, Richard Crossman, and Tony Benn are strewn with examples of Harold Wilson's chaotic collegiality during his 1964–70 government, with Cabinet meetings running on and on but, again, on nuclear issues he could not have been more prime-ministerial—'the smallest ever Cabinet committee on nuclear weapons policy' was convened of just him, Patrick Gordon Walker, the Foreign Secretary, and Denis Healey, Secretary of State for Defence,[132] to overturn the anti-nuclear implication of Labour's 1964 manifesto and to continue with the construction of the Polaris submarine fleet.[133]

Edward Heath's premiership started with an impressive show of collective government in which *all* ministers were expected to have an informed opinion whatever subject the Cabinet was discussing.[134] But this broke down and he became markedly prime-ministerial, and technocratically apolitical to boot, as the challenges mounted and his policies unravelled. The 'U-turn' in 1972 which jettisoned the government's economic approach (and which provided Thatcher with the material for one of her most famous speeches eight years later: 'To those waiting with bated breath for that favourite media catchphrase, the U-turn, I have only one thing to say: you turn if you want to. The lady's not for turning')[135] was not only planned away from the Treasury in the Cabinet Office by the head of the Home Civil Service, Sir William Armstrong, but the key Industry Bill was then *presented* by Heath to the Secretary of State for Trade and Industry, John Davies.[136]

James Callaghan's government is remembered for its demise after the wreckage of the winter of discontent, and thus for the prime-ministerial decision to postpone an election despite favourable opinion polling in the autumn of 1978. But his handling of the 1976 IMF crisis is perhaps one of the most significant episodes in the history of British Cabinet government. For it is still debated[137] as to whether it was 'an object lesson for all prime ministers'[138] and 'a brilliant operation',[139] as Cabinet ministers Denis Healey (then Chancellor) and Shirley Williams (Secretary of State for Prices and Consumer Protection and, from September 1976, Education and Science) respectively described it—or whether it was 'a farce and a dangerous farce at that', as Edmund Dell, President of the Board of Trade, described it.[140] The prime minister judged that the only way to navigate his government through the public spending cuts needed in order to secure the largest ever loan from the IMF, and so to avert resignations and perhaps the fall of the government, was by allowing ministers to 'talk and talk and talk' through a total of nine full Cabinet meetings, and twenty-six ministerial meetings in all, from July to December.[141]

For Dell, Callaghan should have practised 'collective tolerance' but instead showed a profligate indifference to the precarious position of the country as the government's majority evaporated and global confidence in it was collapsing.[142] Joel Barnett, then chief secretary to the Treasury, backed this view, saying that any complex financial decision always falls to the Treasury to enact—Callaghan's 'strategy was to get them [the Cabinet] bored, wanting to leave by one o'clock, and then me and the PM, Chancellor and Deputy PM could sort it all out'.[143] While it is undeniable that Callaghan used his Cabinet extensively, it is also true that he kept to himself the actual IMF letter of demands and only gave his Cabinet colleagues a verbal précis,[144] a little like Blair's failure to share the text of the Attorney General's full legal advice on Iraq.[145]

Every prime minister, then, has been both prime-ministerial and collective in their style, at different times and sometimes even at the same time. Every prime minister has kept information back from

Cabinet from time to time. Changing political standing, party divisions, and personality all combined to influence how decisions were arrived at. Moreover, there is nowhere in the British constitution a demand that the prime minister bring all issues to Cabinet. The Ministerial Code comes closest to it when it says: 'Cabinet and Ministerial Committee business consists, in the main, of... questions which significantly engage the collective responsibility of the Government, because they raise major issues of policy or because they are of critical importance to the public.'[146] This is, as usual, all things to all people and purest mandarinese. Moreover, according to a 2016 House of Commons Library briefing paper,[147] 'Collective responsibility is a fundamental convention, rather than a requirement, of the British constitution. The *Cabinet Manual* makes it clear that it applies, "save where it is explicitly set aside".'[148] The paper adds: 'When questioned about collective responsibility in 1977, Prime Minister James Callaghan famously said, "I certainly think that the doctrine should apply, except in cases where I announce that it does not."'[149]

So much depends upon whether eventual decisions are subjectively considered to be right or wrong. Thus the debate over collective Cabinet government is one that never ends. It flared to life once again after Theresa May succeeded David Cameron in July 2016, following his defeat in the Brexit referendum. In a December 2016 interview with *The Spectator*, the new prime minister was keen to stress, 'We do policy development in the cabinet sub-committees. So I have reinstated what might be described as a more traditional way of doing government.'The magazine noted:'There is now a large glass meeting table; her predecessor preferred to chat on the sofas,' a dig at Cameron, no doubt, for following in Blair's footsteps.[150] It is notable that several prime ministers, at least since Ted Heath, have started their time in office by proclaiming the restoration of Cabinet government— although it is also notable that in many cases they had little choice, inheriting deeply divided Cabinets. Indeed, just four days after May's *Spectator* interview, *The Times* claimed, 'All important decisions on Brexit have been deferred until next year amid reports that members

of a key cabinet committee are struggling to reach agreement.'[151]
May had earlier suspended collective ministerial responsibility and
allowed two Cabinet ministers, Boris Johnson and Justine Greening,
to publicly—but not in Parliament—criticize the decision to expand
Heathrow airport.[152] Less than a year later, in the days after the 2017
general election in which May lost the small Commons majority she
inherited from Cameron, her powerful joint chiefs of staff, Nick
Timothy and Fiona Hill, resigned to the accompaniment of constitu-
tionally lurid stories of how they had denied access to the prime
minister and had ensured the manifesto was written in the smallest
of groups with minimal ministerial input.[153] May's declared wish for
a traditional collective government was window dressing and hid
perhaps *the* most prime-ministerial government ever. The loss of her
majority with no personal victory reinvigorated Cabinet ministers and
ensured a more collegiate approach—albeit in a weak government.

The process by which May decided the government's negotiating
position for the Brexit talks in 2018 was a historic demonstration of
weakness. May sought to persuade sceptical ministers, including David
Davis, the Brexit Secretary, to back a hybrid scheme for customs after
Brexit. This would allow British and EU tariffs to be operated side by
side. Davis, on the other hand, argued for an independent customs
policy, saying that computers would ensure cross-border transactions
were as frictionless as possible ('maximum facilitation'). After Amber
Rudd resigned as Home Secretary over the Windrush scandal and was
replaced by Sajid Javid, May found herself in a five-to-four minority
in the EU Exit and Trade (Strategy and Negotiations) subcommittee.
She then resorted to unconventional methods to try to finesse ministerial objections. She appointed two working groups of three Cabinet
ministers to examine the rival proposals, with two members opposed
and one in favour in each case.[154] Neither group made headway,
and May decided to take the question to an all-day meeting of the
whole Cabinet, including the six ministers with the right to attend, at
Chequers on 6 July. In this larger group of 29 ministers, she had
engineered a clear majority (though no votes were taken), and so

overcame the objections of Davis and Boris Johnson, the Foreign Secretary, to arrive at a seemingly common position—a renamed version of her 'facilitated customs arrangement'. This 'Chequers deal' was immediately publicly announced, but the myth of Cabinet unity was destroyed when Davis and Johnson repudiated the decision and resigned a few days later. She had got her way, but at real cost.

The practice of suspending collective Cabinet responsibility, the so-called 'agreement to differ'—deployed over the 1975 EEC referendum and over direct elections to the European Assembly in 1977—has become a frequent resort of twenty-first-century prime ministers.[155] The coalition agreement between the Conservatives and Liberal Democrats explicitly allowed ministers to disagree on certain subjects between 2010 and 2015. Sometimes the rules had to be made up as they went along, as when Nick Clegg, deputizing for Cameron at Prime Ministers' Questions, described the Iraq invasion as 'illegal'. This was followed by hurried clarification that he was speaking in a personal capacity, 'expressing long-held views' as leader of his party and that he was 'entitled to express his own view at the dispatch box'.[156] Then, despite Cameron winning a Conservative-only majority in the 2015 election, he was forced within nine months to suspend collective responsibility again during the 2016 European referendum campaign. All of these are further examples of prime ministers doing whatever is needed to get business through. Blair simply did not need to go to such lengths.

Get the army in

It is fair to say that Tony Blair was more prime-ministerial by temperament than many of his predecessors, in an age that placed ever greater emphasis on leadership. Like many prime ministers, he flirted with the idea of a smaller, more strategic Cabinet. In times of conflict and extreme stress, the British state has often seen war cabinets of just five or so members. Peacetime prime ministers have sometimes tried to emulate this more focused executive decision-making. For example,

Harold Wilson toyed with 'inner cabinets', creating in 1968 the 'Parliamentary Committee', which he reformed as the 'Management Committee' in 1969, both essentially concerned with political and parliamentary tactical manoeuvres, but with no true strategic focus.[157] The 'Quad' of the 2010–15 Coalition, comprised of the Conservatives David Cameron and the Chancellor George Osborne, along with the Liberal Democrats Nick Clegg, the deputy prime minister, and Danny Alexander, chief secretary to the Treasury (who swiftly replaced the original member David Laws), settled the thorniest of issues between the two parties.

When James Callaghan was eventually invited in to see Blair, his advice was to find about six Cabinet colleagues upon whom he could rely and to work through them alone.[158] Blair had tried to do this in opposition, with what was known as the 'Big Guns', which carried on during 1997 and 1998 and consisted of him, Gordon Brown, Robin Cook, and John Prescott. It is indicative of changing personal and governmental dynamics that Alastair Campbell's description of this body degenerated into the 'Group of Death' during 2000. The fledgling inner cabinet had by then grown in size to incorporate Philip Gould, Peter Mandelson, David Miliband, and Douglas Alexander (who christened it thus after a particularly gruesome first round draw meant England played Germany, Portugal, and Romania in the 2000 European Football Championships), and some of the relationships had undeniably festered.[159]

While it is clear that Blair was disinclined to use Cabinet government for the sake of collegiality, he came to recognize some of its benefits as his premiership wore on and experience built. He also began to use another element of the traditional but always malleable machinery of government—the crisis-response nerve centre of British government, the Cabinet Office briefing room, or COBR (known colloquially as COBRA). Sir Ian Blair, Commissioner of the Metropolitan Police 2004–8, offered this description:

> Below ground in Westminster lies a series of government control rooms, each one deeper and further away from Whitehall than the last...The briefing room is long, low and at that time [2001] dominated by large

television screens at either end, on which CNN and Sky were playing
silently...there are officials in another room who are available to supply more information on any topic required.

COBR, according to Sally Morgan, had 'declined into non-existence'
in the years after the Cold War,[160] but it roared back to prominence
during first the fuel protests of autumn 2000, the floods of late 2000,
the foot-and-mouth crisis of 2001, and the firefighters' dispute of
2003 (what might be called the 'Four Fs'), and further included the
immediate aftermath of 9/11.

The fuel crisis started on 8 September 2000, when 100 lorries
staged a go-slow on the A1, eventually blockading a refinery in
Pembroke. In the next few days, many other refineries were picketed.
By 11 September, the government was alarmed by a combination of
growing protests, panic buying, and a rapid realization that, if it
continued, fuel would be unavailable for the emergency services, let
alone for the general public. Blair was amazed and incensed. This was
his first domestic crisis, and it was one in which the media for the first
time were largely against him over fuel prices. The centre of government looked shaky. The opinion polls turned sharply against Labour,
putting William Hague in the lead for the only time during his leadership. 'The part of a prime minister's contract with the voters on
which the electorate really expect them to deliver is crisis management,'
mused Powell. 'If they fail in that, they lose support very quickly.'[161]

According to Blair, 'Alastair was in full crisis mode [but] the rest of
the machine seemed curiously paralysed, reacting to the scene as it
was unfolding with a mixture of endless process and hand-wringing
that was not pretty to behold.'[162] Powell said: 'I pulled every lever
available and none of them seemed to be connected to anything.'[163]
The New Labour commanders were encountering what many prime
ministers in the modern era had come to realize, especially in times of
crisis, was, as Edward Heath described it, 'the need to force issues to the
fore and process them to the point of decision from the centre' or 'the
'No 10 problem'.[164] It quickly dawned on Blair, advised by Sir Richard

Wilson, the cabinet secretaries, that COBR would provide a useful focus for concentrating attention and binding in commitment, a sort of ad hoc domestic war cabinet but with a changing membership of ministers, officials, and outsiders, all to the prime minister's design.

As Blair tried to get a grip, he embraced the need for teamwork: Prescott impressed COBR attendees with his calm confidence, in contrast to the other ministers present, saying that he would take care of the unions, on which he delivered.[165] Alan Milburn was dispatched to flag up the impact on the health service, sending nurses to debate with the protesters on the picket lines and grabbing the moral high ground. Within a few days just about everything was back to the way it was, bar some minor tax changes. The opinion polls returned to a Labour lead, and the crisis was quickly forgotten by journalists and the public. But the prime minister was chastened and, according to Campbell, 'had discovered the powerlessness of government processes in such a situation and was determined that it would never happen again'.[166]

Another crisis did arrive, and soon. If the fuel crisis was the biggest political crisis of the first term, the biggest logistical one was the outbreak of foot-and-mouth disease, first confirmed on 19 February 2001. The numbers involved were huge: 2,030 cases in Great Britain and Northern Ireland; with pre-emptive culling included, the number of premises on which livestock was destroyed increased to 10,157; this amounted to the slaughter of 6,456,000 cattle, sheep, and pigs; and the total cost of the outbreak was around £8 billion. It did not subside until the summer, delaying the general election from a planned May date to June. The initial response was handled by the Ministry of Agriculture, Fisheries and Food (MAFF) with Nick Brown as Secretary of State, a strong ally of his namesake Gordon. Blair initially thought Nick Brown 'appeared to be doing well, and for once the ministry was fully apprised of the gravity of the situation'.[167] MAFF was convinced that it had the situation under control and preached reassurance but its information was flawed and out of date. The numbers of infected animals kept growing. In Number Ten, the realization swiftly took shape that MAFF and Brown were failing: 'Tony started comparing foot and mouth to the fuel crisis,' Powell remembered. 'Again we pulled on every lever and none of them was working.'[168]

The Ministry of Defence anticipated the call for military assistance, although the formal request did not come until 14 March, nearly a month after the disease was confirmed. The first deployment of troops took place two days later. Blair had finally run out of patience with Nick Brown, who was not even invited to COBR when it was convened on 22 March, meeting twice daily until 5 April.

Blair was under great pressure to show that the situation was under control, with a general election just weeks away. He was shocked at the poor performance of MAFF—and of the Civil Service in general. According to Campbell, Blair told Sir Richard Wilson on 26 March that 'the Civil Service had shown itself very good at setting up new committees but we kept announcing policy approaches which they could not implement'. Campbell himself thought: 'If people knew how hard it was to crank our machinery into gear, they would be appalled.'[169] This was in real contrast to the professionalism of the army. Blair was hugely impressed by its logistical expertise, leadership, and management skills. Military habit, communication, and structure were brought in. Real-time information was injected into a command-and-control structure and when decisions were made, they were seen as orders and were followed as such. Blair thought the army 'coped brilliantly' with the outbreak which was 'roughly several times more difficult in logistics and practicalities than the Gulf War or Kosovo'.[170] Blair was left with the impression that the armed forces were simply more effective than the Civil Service: 'The blunt truth is that it was the armed forces' intervention that was critical to delivery. Why? Because they didn't take no for an answer; they used rules as a means to an end, not an end to themselves.'[171] He may not have known it, but he was echoing his predecessor the Duke of Wellington after his first Cabinet meeting: 'An extraordinary affair. I gave them their orders and they wanted to stay and discuss them.'[172]

Blair asked Sir Kevin Tebbit, the MOD's permanent under secretary: 'Why is it we manage to achieve this with the military and the armed forces which we find almost impossible to do with civil departments?' For Blair, at exactly the time that his thoughts were increasingly turning to the challenges of public service reform, should he win a second term, graphic demonstrations of Civil Service incapacity and military delivery left a powerful imprint: 'The PM understood very clearly that there was something different about the way armed forces operated which indeed he wanted to be able to apply in the wider delivery of the Blair agenda,' concluded Tebbit.[173] 'The impact of those events,' said Sir Richard Mottram:

> provided the stimulus for a wide range of initiatives involving the centre of government after the 2001 General Election. They signalled recognition that it was no longer adequate to leave responsibility for building preparedness with individual central government departments where, even if it was done, work tended to be stove-piped; synergies and best practice were not exploited.[174]

The prime minister was to use a version of the COBR model again in the spring of 2002 to coordinate what became known as the Street Crime Initiative to counter rising levels of muggings. As Sir Ian Blair explained:

> For the first time in my life I was at a table with representatives of the Judiciary and the Law Officers who could be told, very politely, but still told—by the only person who could do so, the Prime Minister— to get the judges and magistrates to do something, to get involved, to take notice...The meetings lasted for about eighteen months and were very successful in helping the police and other agencies to bring down street robbery.[175]

If the first couple of years of the New Labour government saw Blair finding his feet, the years after 2000 witnessed his attempt to refashion central governance. The use of COBR was an example of his dissatisfaction with traditional Cabinet government, as he experimented with a development of collective working based on a group focused on a single problem with selected invitees—with few people in the room by right. However, Blair's use of COBR, rather than being contrary to the principles of Cabinet government, should be seen as complementary. It was an attempt to formalize the continuing question of getting 'the right people in the room', which is something the formal Cabinet structure, limited to ministers, is not designed to do.

It is notable that, after Blair, the COBR model was developed in Brown's National Economic Council and Cameron's National Security Council. Lord O'Donnell, Blair's last Cabinet Secretary, who implemented the model for his successors—not Cabinet committees, not a 'court', but the COBR model[176]—explained:

> You've got a mixture of officials and ministers, politics and civil servants, all working together to try and solve problems. And I think we've developed a system which has lots of meetings of civil servants, and then papers prepared that go to a meeting just of politicians, and there's obviously a case for something like Cabinet clearly being about the ultimate body for politicians. But I think along the way we could get a lot more done, and it was certainly done during the National Economic Council when Gordon Brown was prime minister, of having officials, ministers, around the table grappling with an immediate problem—the recession. And also that we bring in outsiders, outside experts, who would say what's going on out in the world, who would give you specifics about what the problem was about banks and lending to small businesses, or what specific problems individuals were facing in terms of poverty, the Citizens Advice Bureau, head of that, would come in. And so you get external experts as well.
>
> So you get all the experts round the table, and I think David Cameron as prime minister used to say what he really liked was having all the experts lay out what they knew, the evidence, the discussion, and be cross-questioned, and then the politicians have the discussion about 'OK, in the light of all of that, we've heard all this advice, what are we going to decide?' And then as well thinking about 'OK well now we've decided something, how do we present it? What are the issues? Where do we go next? What are the things we want these officials to go off and find out more about? Give us more evidence.' So I think that system works well, and could be used much more widely.[177]

This complementary addition to the collective furniture was certainly interesting—in effect, a horizontally focused, silo-busting initiative, born of deep frustration from a prime minister truly thinking experimentally. It was also, perhaps, a sign of things to come.

Conclusion

On the spectrum between prime-ministerialism and collegiate government, Tony Blair was always going to be at the 'lead from the front' end. Yet in practice he inevitably found himself constrained by politics and circumstance, as all prime ministers do. He ended up, typically, crafting an unintended third way between the two extremes, running a government organized round the twin centres of him and his Chancellor. This sucked power from the rest of the Cabinet, not to a single prime-ministerial figure but to a dual leadership, even if the balance of power in that partnership was tilted in Blair's favour for most of his time at Number Ten.

Blair's electoral success gave him a personal mandate that few British leaders have enjoyed. He was determined not to allow any return to the pursuit of unrealistic policies which had so blighted Labour in the 1970s and 1980s. But his lack of experience, coupled with a burning zeal, meant a clash was inevitable with what traditionalists believed to be a model form of collegiate and therefore cumbersome decision-making. Inexperience blended with the benefit of not knowing better—a heady concoction. His style of governance did become a bit more collegiate over time, partly due to the basic need to bring colleagues with him, but also to stand against Brown. One thing that never changed, however, was his desire to lead.

Lord Butler explained the limits of prime-ministerial power when he described the trauma of Thatcher's demise in 1990, just three years after achieving a majority of 102 seats and the third election win in a row: 'The deal is that you give people very considerable power for five years, then they can be thrown out, and, in the meantime, if things get bad enough there are ways of getting rid of them. That is the deal of our constitution.'[178]

All prime ministers want to get their business through. We have seen how Attlee, arguably the most collegiate prime minister of the modern era, when faced with defeat, simply formed a smaller, even more secret group and pushed the momentous nuclear decision through. James Callaghan allowed the Cabinet to talk itself out when the country was forced to go cap in hand to the IMF, yet, in order to get the deal through, declined to share with it the details of the critical IMF demands. Even Margaret Thatcher had her collegiate side and, although the poll tax was the product of her strong leadership, it was taken through all the sacred procedures of ministerial consultation. John Major started out as open and consultative, yet ended his premiership in a bunker.

Tony Blair wished to change his country with an ambitious pro-gramme. Perhaps he would have observed a more traditional form of Cabinet government had he had a small or non-existent majority, a more divided Cabinet, or a poorly performing economy. But he did not, and we will never know. Lord Wilson was right when he said that no prime minister has been so unencumbered by what had previously been understood as the checks and balances of the uncodified British constitution. But this was not Blair's fault. And Churchill's aphorism about democracy could in fact apply to Cabinet government too. The full passage from 1947 is as follows:

> No one pretends that democracy is perfect or all-wise. Indeed, it has been said that democracy is the worst form of Government except all those other forms that have been tried from time to time; but there is the broad feeling in our country that the people should rule, continu-ously rule, and that public opinion, expressed by all constitutional means, should shape, guide, and control the actions of Ministers who are their servants and not their masters.[179]

Power is what everyone in government desires, and Blair amassed it. Within an uncodified constitution, it was up to him how he used it.

The practice of Cabinet government is not something laid out in law; it is, as our colleague Michelle Clement described it, more of an 'ethic'.

Comparisons with US politics are generally unhelpful, but Blair acted more 'presidentially' than most prime ministers, because he could. However, nothing in his use of Cabinet government went beyond what previous prime ministers had done. He adapted the machine that he inherited and tried to make it better suited to the priorities he was elected to deliver. One of the features of British Cabinet government is its flexibility, and it continues to adapt to changing political needs. Most of the changes Blair made, although they were criticized at the time, were retained, or taken up and developed, by his successors. This was powerfully reinforced by Gordon Brown's failed attempt to return to a more collegiate model.

The notion that Blair somehow corrupted the purity of the British constitutional model is not sustainable. The idea that the core business of government was carried out through informal, unstructured chats on Downing Street sofas—beyond the first weeks of governing—was not supported by any of the people involved who came to our seminars, and Blair's critics have never sustained the allegation. Over time, some of those who stood strong against the rise of what was initially seen as Blairite prime-ministerialism have accepted that dynamic outside forces have shifted the nature of the British premiership forever. Perhaps it was simply a generational factor. But it was undoubtedly a criticism that endured.

Our findings are that Blair was neither unconstitutional nor very unusual in his approach to Cabinet government. But that is not to say that the role has not changed. It has most definitely speeded up and become much more demanding in a personal sense. The traditional model of collective Cabinet government is now, more than ever, a theory that cannot be maintained in practice.

Blair instinctively understood the dynamics of the changed role of prime minister. Decisions were sometimes right, other times wrong, popular and unpopular. But, in being a prime minister for the new age, he set the standard.

3

Spin, Spads, and Sir Humphreys

We have examined how Tony Blair approached his role as prime minister in a decade of highest-level decision-making—and how criticism of this was largely unfair by comparison with other prime ministers. We now turn to the other great complaint about his administration: the heightened role of presentation and another catch-all shorthand—'spin', personified by Alastair Campbell—and look at how this fed into the long-running theme of the loss of trust in British politics. We also examine the relatively brief spasm occasioned by the strength and reach of Blair's politically appointed special advisers ('spads'). While Blair led from the front, and spads rose in importance, we will describe how the new era saw a less powerful role for the most senior mandarins compared with their 1970s heyday (the shift in emphasis from *Yes, Minister* to *The Thick of It*, if you will). Finally, we shall look at how the furore calmed and the innovations in presentation, political advisers, and Civil Service roles became the norm post-Blair.

The media: fighting fire with fire

Upon his election as Labour leader on 21 July 1994, Tony Blair set about creating his team. Several chose themselves. Gordon Brown was the main one, and is the focus of a later chapter. Peter Mandelson was another. The self-described 'Third Man' had helped drag Labour back to reality with his appointment as director of communications in

1985, was elected to Parliament in 1992, and remained a strategic and media maestro, while Philip Gould, the pollster, had been close to Neil Kinnock and now returned to prominence as the concept of the focus group entered the mainstream. Blair's first major personnel selection decision was to be his most significant.

Alastair Campbell was from the start the main target to become press secretary. Though both Blair and Mandelson 'thought I would be best, [they] assumed I wouldn't do it. They were thinking about Andy Grice [*Sunday Times* journalist]. Peter MacMahon [*Scotsman* journalist] had offered himself. I said what about Colin Byrne [former Labour chief press officer]?'[1] But Blair knew who he wanted. He was to pursue Campbell with gusto, driving for hours across France in the summer of 1994 to persuade him when both men were with their families, supposedly on holiday (the Campbells with Neil and Glenys Kinnock).

A former alcoholic who had suffered a mental breakdown, Campbell had reformed his life but had lost none of his compulsion and intensity, and had developed into an acerbic TV pundit and senior journalist, fluent in tabloidese (that language of simplicity and sensationalism beloved of newspapers such as the *Sun,* the *News of the World,* the *Mirror,* the *Express,* and the *Mail*). Kinnock advised Campbell to turn down the job, citing his burgeoning media career, which was delivering status and salary:

> I went to see Neil again and he was more adamant than ever that I should not work for TB. He said he could not stress enough how bad he thought it would be for me and for the family. However bad you ever thought it looked from the outside, he said, multiply by ten and then ten again. It is the worst job there is.[2]

But Blair played on Campbell's political soul, offering the chance to help destroy the Conservative hegemony and install a dominant Labour government, something that proved irresistible.

Campbell had always considered the possibility of a political career, with rumours continuing to circulate during the Brown government and indeed beyond that he would stand for Parliament. He privately mused that he would not enjoy the life of an MP and admitted in 2016, 'I've thought about it, but the time has never been right.'[3] So, Campbell bought into Tony Blair, subsuming his own political ambition into Blair's, thereby creating the most successful political strategy and presentation partnership of the modern era. Blair, formidable on his own, was unstoppable with Campbell.

The Labour Party had suffered at the hands of the Conservative press in the 1980s and early 1990s. From the 'donkey jacket' worn by Michael Foot to the Cenotaph in 1981 to 'loony left' councils and endemic ideological division, the right-leaning print media tore into Labour throughout the Thatcher years and immediately after. The Rupert Murdoch press in particular became the enemy to a generation of left-wingers as it distorted, criticized, and pilloried Labour's policies and leaders, culminating in the 1992 election-day front page of the *Sun*: 'If Kinnock wins today will the last person to leave Britain please turn out the lights.'[4] Two days after Major's surprise 1992 election victory, the archetypal red top declared overconfidently, but with some truth, 'It's The Sun wot won it'—in hindsight, a high-water mark of the right-wing press's political influence.[5] Blair watched in fear and fascination as Kinnock was battered:

> I learnt a lot from him and I saw what he also had to go through and the—the viciousness of the attacks upon him and the power of the media, which probably I became too affected by, to be blunt, but . . . I watched what he went through and could see how incredibly destructive it was. Because at that point, the media was immensely powerful in its ability to shift opinion and it was so negative on him that it really didn't matter whether what he said was sensible or not sensible by the time they'd finished with it. He literally had to stand out against, I would say, I don't know, it must have been 70 per cent of the media, 80 per cent of the time . . . back then, were just determined on one thing: we weren't going to be kicked around in the way that, frankly, Neil and his team had been.[6]

One of the reasons that Blair won the leadership was because he was everything the previous leaders were not. Though technically another Celt following on from the Scottish John Smith and the Welsh Kinnock,

Edinburgh-born Blair had a classless English estuary accent and no particular patriotic affinity for Scotland itself (intriguingly, the opposite of Campbell, who was born south of the border but thought of himself as Scottish). Blair was a middle-class, London-centric Briton, who embodied the concept of aspiration in a way that Thatcher had previously done, but which the Tories were losing by the mid-1990s. Labour understood that this was a missing factor in its recent appeal, a reason why the populous south-east of England had turned towards the Conservatives. Labour under Blair was on the front foot, highlighting its new leader, not having to mask shortcomings. With Campbell on board, the fight was taken to a weary Conservative government, in power for fifteen years, in a way that would change the nature of media management forever.

The Conservative Party had always been better at using the media. From Stanley Baldwin's 'fireside chats' on the radio to Winston Churchill's wartime speeches, Sir Anthony Eden's 1955 TV election addresses, and Harold Macmillan's 1959 joint broadcasts with President Ike Eisenhower, the Conservatives embraced new technology with aplomb.[7] Margaret Thatcher continued the trend by presenting herself as the nation's housewife, combining common sense with the strength of the Iron Lady, all amplified by able practitioners of the presentational arts such as Bernard Ingham, Tim Bell, and the Saatchi brothers.[8] Labour had generally played catch-up. Though many today consider Clement Attlee's anti-presentation attractive as public relations professionalizes ever more,[9] at the time it was more likely to be considered a vote loser. Perhaps only Harold Wilson for Labour truly connected through the media, with his television-friendly, folksy, northern English image.[10]

New Labour sought to undo the Tories' historic advantage. Philip Gould joined Bill Clinton's New Democrat campaign in the US in 1992 and applied the lessons back home. New Labour built a media monitoring unit which surveyed the newly enlarged political battlefield created by the UK's first twenty-four-hour news channel, Sky News, launched in 1989, and a 'rebuttal unit' which sought to defend against Tory claims before they became accepted.

Political discipline among the Shadow Cabinet was stringently enforced, making use of early instant personal messaging, albeit one way, with the supposed tyranny of the pager (mobile phones and the Internet were becoming available but only achieved mass adoption after the 1997 election). Politicians going 'off message' were contacted by pager, which meant they had to find a landline telephone, often to receive a dressing-down or an instruction to issue a clarification.

If this was impressively defensive, it was the offensive onslaught that caught the imagination. The Conservative government under Major was dying. It was riddled with guilt over Thatcher's dethronement and divided over the looming creation of the single European currency. Britain's forced ejection from the European Exchange Rate Mechanism in 1992 had also destroyed the Tories' previously perennial advantage over Labour on economic competence. After his impressive 1992 election victory, the only real success for Major during the next five years was that he kept his party together (along with a good but thankless economic bequest), though this was pushed to the limit with a number of Eurosceptics having the whip removed and many Conservative candidates in 1997 offering their personal opposition to the single currency in addition to the official party manifesto, which kept the option open, subject to a referendum.

A further, unedifying dimension was what became known as 'sleaze'. Any party that is in power for so long sees unpleasant decisions come back to haunt them. But there was also the inevitable aspect of distasteful characters taking advantage of long-term success. This image began to take shape in the early Major period with the resignations over sexual indiscretions of ministers such as David Mellor and Tim Yeo, and snowballed with Major's 1993 'Back to Basics' policy drive, which was wilfully misinterpreted by journalists as a call for a return to Victorian values, with all the hypocrisy that predictably entailed. What followed was a deluge of stories, from perjury leading to the imprisonment of Cabinet minister Jonathan Aitken and the Scott Report over arms to Iraq to two MPs accused of taking cash from the boss of Harrods to ask questions in the House of Commons. It seemed that every week brought a new scandal. Just imagine if the news had broken before 1997 rather than in 2002, that Major himself had had an extramarital affair from 1984 to 1988 with his colleague Edwina Currie![11]

With his aggression against the Conservatives and his tabloid genius, Alastair Campbell helped to shape the idea that the Conservative Party was 'immoral' and unfit for office. It got to the point that Major's 'put up or shut up' leadership challenge to his parliamentary detractors was seen by some as Campbell's creation: 'I bumped into David Mellor... "I assume you are orchestrating this farce?" he said.'[12]

A year of huge polling leads over a disintegrating government led to a reassessment from the anti-Labour press. In July 1995 Rupert Murdoch himself, chief media hate figure for Labour, invited Blair to Hayman Island in Australia to address his News International executive team. Though Murdoch had lost faith in a lacklustre Conservative Party facing defeat, the invitation was a symbol that change was in the air. The received wisdom is that Blair's trip was part of a deal by which he yielded to Murdoch on policy in return for Murdoch's endorsement. But Blair went to recite his New Labour credo, in a way that appealed to Murdoch's anti-establishment instinct, and he *refused* to concede any pro-European ground to Murdoch's Euroscepticism. Indeed, its central message was that radical changes in the economy required investment and strengthening of society.[13] Brown endorsed the approach: 'I supported the lengths he travelled, geographically and rhetorically, to deal with the *Sun*, *The Times* and other newspapers which had so unfairly undermined Neil Kinnock.'[14] Blair, Campbell, and the rest of the New Labour command were overjoyed to receive the backing of the *Sun*, the *News of the World*, *The Times*, and the *Sunday Times* at the 1997 election.

Special advisers

Jonathan Powell was Blair's next appointment to his central team in opposition. He was plucked from the Washington Embassy in 1995 after he had followed his illustrious elder brother into foreign policy—Charles had been Margaret Thatcher's trusted Foreign Affairs Private Secretary,

1984–91, who went 'native' along with Bernard Ingham. That is to say, although they were civil servants they both became closely identified not just with Thatcher personally but her policies, leaving government soon after she did. Blair, Brown, and Mandelson had decided that they needed somebody at the centre of their operation who understood the Civil Service, but who was also committed to the New Labour vision.

As Second Secretary in Washington, the younger Powell had made his name by sensing that, against all the odds, Bill Clinton could beat George Bush Sr in the 1992 presidential election. Blair and Brown were impressed by Clinton's win and his branding as a 'new kind of Democrat'. Powell became Blair's chief of staff, a title that paid its respects to American politics, in opposition and government, leaving with Blair in 2007, the only senior member to go the distance. Powell's job was to prepare for the day when New Labour formed the government and Blair became prime minister:

> I had discussed at length with Alex Allan [principal private secretary to the prime minister, 1992–7]...Alex took me round the house and we chose where Tony would live and where all the offices would be...Politicians are simply not thinking about these sort of things before an election...if you start thinking about what you are going to do once you're in government, you're kind of tempting the gods to stop you winning, but you need people like...me to be doing that kind of planning.[15]

Blair expected to transplant his opposition team into government. This would entail a marked upturn in both numbers and quality of special advisers, unelected political appointees, technically temporary civil servants who, when the system worked well, provided specialist skills that the Civil Service *could* not and political commitment it *would* not. Though the Fulton Report on the Civil Service as far back as 1968 said of special adviserdom: 'We welcome the practice as a means of bringing new men and ideas into the service of the state,'[16] and Lord Neill's Committee on Standards in Public Life reported in 2003: 'Witnesses were in unanimous agreement that special advisers have a valuable role to play, precisely because they are free to act and advise in a way that a politically impartial civil servant cannot,'[17] the role of special advisers caused a furore in the first years of the New Labour Government. As the all-party House of Commons' Public Administration Select Committee explained in 2001, 'the issue of special advisers...exercises so much parliamentary, public and media commentary [but] it is an issue that usually generates more political heat than useful light.'[18] Blair's experience as leader of the Opposition during 1994 to 1997 had led him to build a small team of proven ability. This was not the first time in history that a dynamic leader was to rely upon a tiny team.

The worlds of officialdom and what became known as special-adviserdom were not as demarcated in the nineteenth century as they were to become, with civil servants becoming politicians or political advisers and vice versa, something which is normal in French politics. A new probity emerged before the First World War, with a drive to root out jobbery, with the natural side effect of reduced employment flexibility—but the Great War's all-consuming focus demanded quite simply the best person for the job and the new rigidity was set aside, only to be reimposed after. The hard lessons learned were passed down by the first Cabinet Secretary Sir Maurice Hankey, so that in 1939 Britain hit the ground running. Non-civil servants of all kinds, 'irregulars' in the parlance of the time, were drafted into the British bureaucracy in huge numbers. Business people, journalists, academics, all who could contribute became wartime civil servants in what Hennessy described as 'an adventure playground for all the talents'.[19] All but a handful of these energetic incomers, 'men of push and go' in David Lloyd George's pithy phrase,[20] were to leave government service in the immediate aftermath of victory in 1945, some heading out, not wanting to be peacetime bureaucrats, disliking the environment and the pay, others pushed out by the career mandarins. This haemorrhaging of talent led to what Hennessy famously described as the 'missed opportunity', whereby an unprepared and underpowered Civil Service failed to embrace the complexity of the newly enlarged welfare state, mixed-economy Cold War world.[21] As the British economy fell relatively behind competitor states such as Germany, France, Italy in the 1950s and 1960s, and Japan by the late 1960s, pressure fell upon the Civil Service to up its game. One response was to appoint special advisers.

Seen by some in 1964 as 'the thin end of the wedge',[22] special adviser numbers were low to begin with. Margaret Thatcher brought a small team of unelected true believers with her into government in 1979, as Charles Powell observed later:

> I've always thought there was something Leninist about Mrs. Thatcher which came through in the style of government—the absolute determination, the belief that there's a vanguard which is right and if you keep that small, tightly knit team together, they will drive things through...there's no doubt that in the 1980s, Number Ten could beat the bushes of Whitehall pretty violently. They could go out and really confront people, lay down the law, bully a bit.[23]

Special adviser numbers crept up over time. Thatcher's first administration began in single figures but these had doubled by the time she left office. They doubled again under John Major to 38 in 1997. Blair doubled them again from 38 to 70, and they rose to 84 in 2004/5 before falling back to 73 in 2007. Although his immediate successors were keen to distance themselves from such 'politicization', numbers remained broadly unchanged under Gordon Brown, who ended with 68, and they then increased again under David Cameron's coalition, reaching 98 in 2013.[24] Most special advisers were located centrally in Number Ten and the Cabinet Office and, since the 1970s, the guideline was that each Secretary of State was allowed two special advisers—though David Blunkett's blindness meant he needed up to four to help him get through his workload and Brown demanded more for the Treasury.

Economists dominated the first wave of modern peacetime special advisers due to a shortage in the Civil Service, especially of identifiably left-wing ones. Thus Harold Wilson reverted to wartime when he brought in the first special advisers of the modern era in 1964—Thomas Balogh to the Cabinet Office, Nicholas Kaldor and Robert Neild to the Treasury, whereas Barbara Castle, Secretary of State for Social Services 1974–6, explained to an overseas visitor the qualifications of her two special advisers: 'I appointed [Professor] Brian [Abel-Smith] for his brains, and Jack [Straw] for guile and low cunning.'[25] The description of Straw prefigured the notion that special advisers were employed to promote the political ambition of their principals—as when Clare Short railed in 1996 against New Labour discipline enforced by the 'people who live in the dark'.[26] Short's disgruntled description became a much-repeated theme, with Chris Patten, the former Conservative chairman, in the House of Lords in 2017 calling special advisers, now generally known as 'spads', 'creatures in the undergrowth'.[27]

Sir Richard Wilson, as Cabinet Secretary in 2001, explained:

> Although the distinction between political and policy advisers is clearly a useful one, in practice there are policy-skilled political advisers and politically informed policy advisers...some of them are what I would previously have described as expert advisers, and we abolished that distinction at the last election. There is a question, I think, as to whether we were right to do that because some of the special advisers have visibly no political role at all. To take the Drugs Czar, Keith Hellawell was recruited through a competition but counts as a special adviser, and he cannot possibly be presented as some kind of political spin doctor. The same applies to his assistant. There are a number of other special advisers, three economic advisers in the Treasury and a number of others, who I think have been brought in because they are experts.[28]

There was also another kind of irregular special adviser. The Public Administration Select Committee commented in its report:

> The use of special advisers is not new. The existence, since the Northcote-Trevelyan reforms of the 1850s of a Civil Service which was politically neutral and recruited and promoted on merit...has led Ministers and Prime Ministers, certainly as far back as Lloyd George, to appoint confidants. These were people who shared and understood ministerial preoccupations and had political skills and contacts that civil servants lacked.[29]

Blair was proud of his New Labour spads, as Campbell recorded in conversations with him in the first three months in government: 'He was waxing lyrical re the team he had brought in from outside, saying we were far better than most of the civil servants—"And these are supposed to be the best"';[30] 'these top Civil Service people are not as good as they think';[31] 'He was worried about the capability of the Civil Service';[32] and, 'We talked about the need for pretty big reform in the Civil Service. The place was pretty inefficient but apart from TB, none of us were overconfident we could change it much.'[33] Blair made his disappointment with the Civil Service much clearer twenty years later in a balanced assessment when he said that though he had 'seen systems all round the world now, the British system is up there with the top of the top globally, there's no doubt about that at all' and 'I love the integrity of the Civil Service', but 'when it came to trying to make change, I'm being very honest here, I found it inadequate.'[34]

Doubling the number of spads was one thing, but just as important was their quality. The New Labour influx was the strongest ever outside wartime, with one or two household names among them and several of whom would later become Cabinet ministers. Alongside Alastair Campbell and Jonathan Powell were David Miliband, the head of the Policy Unit from 1997 to 2001 and later Foreign Secretary; Andrew Adonis, who joined the Policy Unit in 1998 and succeeded Miliband as its head in 2001, later Transport Secretary; Anji Hunter, a long-time friend and confidant of Blair, who was special assistant to the prime minister in 1997; Sally Morgan, who became political secretary to the prime minister in 1997, later a minister and chair of Ofsted; and Geoff Mulgan, founder of the think tank Demos, who joined the Policy Unit in 1997 and was later head of Policy and director of the Strategy Unit—the policy wonk's wonk, and someone, interestingly, who went to the trouble of becoming a senior civil servant before he left government in 2004. Add to this Professor Michael Barber, chief adviser to David Blunkett at the Department of Education during the first term and the first head of the Prime Minister's Delivery Unit 2001–5, who was in 2017 appointed chair of the newly created Office for Students, the first regulator for the university sector.

The Treasury had its own senior spads, with Ed Balls making his considerable intellectual power felt between 1997 and 2004 as the indispensable go-between, not just between HMT officials and the

Chancellor but between the Chancellor and prime minister, before becoming an MP, Cabinet minister, leadership contender, Shadow Chancellor, and media celebrity; and his junior colleague Ed Miliband, a Treasury special adviser between 1997 and 2005 (on sabbatical at Harvard during the pivotal 2002–3 Iraq period), who rose to be a Cabinet minister and to beat not just Balls but his brother David to the Labour leadership in 2010, before taking the party to defeat in the election five years later.

Why bring in the spads?

Ed Balls explained why special advisers were necessary, as he thought back to New Labour's first term:

> Look at periods of transition in government: 1964, 1979, they were two big transitions in government. In both times, you have powerful unelected advisers who come in as part of the change of the regime, because changes of government, if they are to be effective, aren't simply about the change of personnel, or even a change of policy—it's a change of mindset, of view, of argument, of intellectual direction. You need people around you who are part of that change of intellectual direction. I spent a lot of time in the early period...if you look back...at the Treasury, we did a whole series of discussion papers which were called Lessons from the Past for Economic Policy, Fiscal Policy and Monetary Policy. They were ways in which we were, with the machine, really shaping our intellectual framework. That's something that ministers haven't got time to do, but it's not the civil servants' job to do that, and therefore you need people like me whose job it was to be part of that change of frame. As the government goes on, I think those people become less important, because you've changed the direction and your relationships with the machine are stronger.[35]

The step-change in quantity fed the suspicion that the impartial Civil Service was being politicized, as a critical mass created its own networks of power and blurred lines of responsibility. As Blair put it, 'When after a few years in government I accumulated seventy of them, it was considered by some to be a bit of a constitutional outrage.'[36] This was an argument that had been rejected at the time by Sir Richard Wilson, the Cabinet Secretary, in his evidence to the Public Administration Select Committee, arguing that '70-odd advisers could not swamp the senior Civil Service of 3,700 people'.[37]

Blair professed himself baffled by the furore when he spoke to our class in 2011:

> Spads are a vital part of the system and the prejudice against them is absurd. What they are, are people who can come in and give you a certain perspective, and a certain expertise and also they are often extremely committed. You know, why shouldn't you if you are the elected government have people who support what you are doing. I never understood that. The most we ever had in government was about 70 or 80. I think the way government works today has changed . . . it's far more to do with the nature of the job than the nature of the person.[38]

Lord O'Donnell, permanent secretary to the Treasury 2002–5 and then Cabinet Secretary 2005–11, saw good and bad in spads: 'When you get a good special adviser, they are worth their weight in gold; when you get a bad one, it's disastrous.' His view was that bad special advisers see government not through a wide, strategic lens, but through their minister, a more tactical view.[39]

Eighteen years in opposition meant New Labour were relatively detached from Whitehall culture. Read such studies as John Campbell's biography of Roy Jenkins and it is noticeable just how intermingled senior politicians and civil servants had been at university—for example Roy Jenkins, the future Chancellor, with a future Treasury second permanent secretary Leo Pliatzky.[40] New Labour prided itself on being outside 'the Establishment', a concept popularized by Henry Fairlie in *The Spectator* in 1955,[41] although it inevitably began constructing its own. (The distancing from the traditional Establishment continued into retirement: note how few of New Labour's leading lights have accepted honours—no peerages or knighthoods for Blair, Brown, Campbell, Powell, or Balls.)

The new political masters in 1997 were naive about their ignorance of government but held to the confident view that 'what counts is what works',[42] even though, as Geoff Mulgan pointed out, 'they were not people like their equivalents in France or America who had run big cities, big states'.[43] Sir Richard Wilson, Cabinet Secretary from 1998 to 2002, said: 'When the Blair government came in, they were inexperienced in government and untouched by previous models of how you do it [but] they had no doubts about their ability to run government, the key players were remarkably confident.'[44]

Order in Council

New Labour's insistence on appointing an unprecedented number of special advisers contributed to Sir Robin Butler's unease: 'Very early on,' recounted Blair, 'I could tell that [Butler] didn't really approve of the positions of Jonathan Powell as chief of staff, Alastair and, though less so, my old friend and general factotum Anji Hunter.'[45] Though Campbell's immediate impression upon entering government on 3 May was that both Butler and Alex Allan 'seemed absolutely fine about me and Jonathan, no problem at all', this was a misunderstanding.

Sir Robin Butler was perturbed by the wish to import what he considered too many senior special advisers into Whitehall, thereby sidelining officials. This most senior mandarin believed that the British constitution's traditional adherence to an impartial Civil Service had to be defended. He believed that the convention of impartiality imparted a duty on him to preserve distance between a minister's immediate wishes and the need to keep an eye on a future change of government.

While a prime minister is rarely as powerful as immediately after a general election victory, and Blair was both very powerful after his stunning success and also convinced of the need to import his election-winning team, Sir Robin Butler was determined that, though he could not stop the influx, he would to try to limit the power of the most powerful spads. An Order in Council was devised to allow only a specified three special advisers to 'direct' civil servants. Jonathan Powell said: 'When Robin put the idea to me, I thought it was completely loony; he wanted to do it, so we said okay.'[46] The Chilcot report explained:

That proposal became the Civil Service (Amendment) Order 1997 which exempted 'up to three situations in the Prime Minister's Office which are designated by him' from the principle of selection on merit based on a fair and open competition, allowing political appointees to hold central executive roles.[47]

By tradition, the British Civil Service has been governed by 'Orders in Council' emanating from the Queen's 'Privy Council' of about 500 people, including all members of the Cabinet, past and present, the Speaker, the leaders of all major political parties, and other senior public figures.

When Harold Wilson created special advisers, they were able to offer advice but not to draw up policy. 'Instead of adjusting the theory to reality, the officials wanted to protect the theory and make an exception for us,' lamented Powell, something which was to cause real difficulty.[48]

Powell and Campbell were two of the three special advisers appointed under the new provision. Anji Hunter was anointed for the third position but it never actually happened, something that she felt damaged her standing and which she was still enquiring about a year later.[49] Indeed, in March 2001, Blair indicated that he wished Hunter to receive the power, only for Butler's successor, Sir Richard Wilson, to block it.[50] This was later countered by Powell:

> I'd never thought of Anji as being the third one as I'm not sure who it was she'd have wanted to order around in the Civil Service so I'd have thought it would have been more David Miliband or someone like that...We never gave it any serious consideration to making anyone the third person.[51]

For Hunter, the situation 'was slightly laddish':

> There's no question about that. I'd been there [in government] about three or four months and I found out that Alastair Campbell and Jonathan Powell, who were my equals before the election...unbeknownst to me and certainly unbeknownst to him [Blair], had gone to Whitehall and done a deal on their salary. I went in and I was told this is your salary, and I said fine, but they had done a deal saying they were so important they had some special, what was that thing [the Order in Council] that ludicrous thing, some formal thing, that said they could boss civil servants about. It wasn't offered to me is all I can say. I think

my salary was about half as much as theirs. I kept my mouth shut for a while. Then after a few months I thought why should I put up with this? I got my salary raised to the same as theirs but it took a lot of hassle. But I had Tony's support in that. 'Of course she should have more money. How could you have done this, guys?' It was slightly laddish, because Alastair is a lad, a sort of football laddo. He is a little bit misogynist, a tiny bit. You can say this to him. He and I are really good pals. I don't really have an ego about titles and Orders in Council and these special privileges. Am I good at my job or not? Do people respect me or not? I could boss civil servants around as much as I liked and they bloody loved it. They were getting proper direction from me and they got it in a very nice way. I wouldn't think there is a single civil servant you can find who would say she was awful, difficult to work with. I hope they would say I was good.[52]

Wilson was never comfortable with the Order. Campbell recorded Blair's intention to continue the arrangement at the time of the 2001 general election, but noted: 'It was clear Richard Wilson was up to a few tricks—e.g. wanting to reverse the Order in Council that allowed Jonathan and me to instruct civil servants. Jonathan and I were now down as "advisers" on his list.'[53]

Intriguingly, Ed Balls told us he was asked before the 1997 election if he wanted to be covered by the Order too:

I actually discussed that with Jonathan [though Powell had 'no memory' of the conversation[54]] in the autumn before. I said to him that I didn't think such a power was necessary, and I didn't want it, because it always seemed to me that if the Civil Service didn't want what you said, and didn't agree with what you said, and didn't think that you reflected the view of the minister, then they wouldn't do it, even if you ordered them. Whereas if actually they thought that you knew what you were doing, you were on the same side, and you reflected the view of the minister, you never needed to give them an order and therefore it was a bit of a red herring, and that was always my view.[55]

He concluded: 'If I was seen to be close to the Chancellor, and had the respect of the Treasury, then I would be able cooperatively to drive what I wanted without having to direct anybody.'[56]

Balls's analysis was correct in that the problems created by the Order in Council were avoidable. Powell thought it 'entirely unnecessary' and this was eventually recognized: 'Later Robin graciously admitted it was a mistake.'[57] Powell explained that it was 'completely unnecessary in that heads of the Policy Unit had been telling civil servants what to do for decades, so there was no need for it at all, it was just a mistake'.[58]

In fact, the First Division Association, the trade union for the Senior Civil Service, had also called for it and later changed *its* mind:

> While they made no complaint that either post-holder had abused his authority, the experiment should reach a natural conclusion at the next general election [2001]. This was partly because it did not think it was necessary, partly because it contributed to misconceptions about the relationship between the Press Secretary and the Government Information and Communication Service and partly because it set a dangerous precedent. Mr Campbell's authority now derived from the fact that he represented the Prime Minister rather than his possession of executive powers.[59]

For Powell, 'It was ludicrous, however, to suggest that we were doing anything different from what Ed Balls was doing in the Treasury as a special adviser to Gordon Brown or other special advisers were doing elsewhere in Whitehall.'[60]

When Campbell left government in 2003, his Order in Council power was not passed on to his successor Dave Hill, nor was Powell's, when he left Downing Street with Blair in 2007. Gordon Brown made a point of formally rescinding the amended Order as an early act as prime minister, a way of sending a message that he was keen to be anyone but Blair.[61] His *Governance of Britain* Green Paper said: 'The Government believes that it is inappropriate for even a limited number of Special Advisers to have such a role and has revoked these provisions by an Order in Council.'[62]

Like Brown's belated comprehension that the nature of Cabinet government had changed before *his* premiership, he similarly came to understand that the attempt 'to revert to a more traditional Number Ten in which ministers alone made the formal decisions' was misguided and:

> the process of government came to rely even more on a close-knit team at the centre. Even if Cabinet was supposed to be the sole inner circle of decision-makers, there came to be another inner circle. Our

critics referred to them as 'courtiers', a 'cabal', a 'clique', but someone had to deal with the stream of issues that constantly arrived on the prime minister's desk every day. Formally these advisers—who were, in the main, young, up-and-coming and very bright experts in their own right—may have had no power to make decisions but in practice they became among Britain's most important decision-makers. Indeed, much of what the Cabinet now does according to textbook constitutional theory is, in practice, done by these advisers acting as a kind of unelected Cabinet. It was not, I found, a good system for governing, nor is it one that will endure without mounting criticism. The problem lies in the lack of accountability.[63]

Again, Brown tried to undo the Blair bureaucracy, misunderstood how times had changed, and then was forced to accept the inevitable—even if reluctantly.

Did the Order in Council lead to the politicization of the Civil Service? Sir David Normington, permanent secretary at the Department for Education, 2001–6, the Home Office 2010–11, and then First Civil Service Commissioner, the guarantor of Civil Service impartiality, thought not. He told us he thought the Order in Council was:

> a pragmatic step in 1997 from a head of the Civil Service who needed to win the confidence of the incoming prime minister...it never extended beyond [Campbell and Powell]; and...since these two were the greatest of class acts, they never abused their position to politicize other appointments.

Sir David was also relaxed about the growth in the number of special advisers:

> There is a long-term trend for governments to appoint more and more special advisers, particularly at Number Ten; and the Blair years saw special advisers grow in importance and numbers. I think it is likely over time that this will change the way government works with political 'cabinets' around ministers and civil servants at much more arm's length from the policymaking process. That has already happened in Australia, which until relatively recently had a system much more like ours. But that was not the position in the Blair years; and I have personally never been able to get very excited about it. There were about thirty special advisers at Number Ten...In the rest of Whitehall most Secretaries of State had two formal special advisers and some

others who occupied less formal advisory roles. One hundred or more special advisers versus 490,000 civil servants. It is hard to argue that some fundamental change was taking place.

He argued that far from undermining Civil Service impartiality, special advisers strengthen it:

> If used properly, special advisers provide the political support and advice which civil servants should not do; and, therefore, protect the Civil Service from overstepping the political line. In my experience most special advisers I encountered in the Blair years were easy to work with and wanted to be part of a team around the minister. Some didn't and behaved badly and gave special advisers and civil servants a bad name through their exploits, but they were the exceptions that proved the rule.

He pointed out another difficulty in defining politicization, which is that the Civil Service often reflects the inevitably political mood of the times:

> When there are strong leaders with a clear political philosophy who go on for a lot of years it is inevitable that the political leadership and the Civil Service get more and more aligned. That did happen in the Blair years and it was intensified by the fact that the approach of the Blair government played to the natural inclinations of many civil servants. But some of the same happened in the Thatcher years particularly in the years between 1979 and 1987. Thatcher caught a mood in the Civil Service as in the country that years of national decline needed to be reversed. It was not difficult for the Civil Service to respond to her clear leadership and the government's clear philosophy and to believe that they were involved in something important.
>
> It is the job of senior civil servants to be very aware of the dangers of this alignment, particularly as a general election approaches. In my experience they always are. But the longer one party is in power the more the Opposition will be suspicious that the Civil Service is biased and partial.[64]

Sir David is an important witness, one of the mandarin class who held central delivery jobs in education and home affairs and who enjoyed the challenge of New Labour's reforms, before going on to a post responsible for enforcing the Civil Service Code and ensuring the Service's impartiality.

Junction-box Powell

Upon the 1997 victory, Jonathan Powell continued in his position as chief of staff and took the office directly outside the prime minister's in a significant demonstration of the geography of power; he now sat atop a vast machine of information flow. The Public Administration Select Committee tried in 2001 to chart the new power in Downing Street:

> Not having been able to secure an interview with the Chief of Staff, we asked the Cabinet Secretary what his role was. In answer to the question 'Is Jonathan Powell in charge at Number Ten?' Sir Richard replied 'Yes. He is the Chief of Staff.' Subsequently he explained... 'Jonathan Powell has lines going to him from the Press Office and Alastair Campbell's side of the business. The Policy Unit, which are all the political advisers and civil servants in that area, also come under this umbrella. Then the rest of Number Ten, which is the Private Office itself, the Garden Room, the honours and appointments side and operation of the day-to-day management of Number Ten, they come under the Principal Private Secretary. What I am saying to you is that the truth is that the two of them share out the work in that way'... It is clearly an extremely significant role for a special adviser to play.[65]

When we interviewed Powell in 2014, he said:

> I see that [David] Cameron has the same thing, and I don't think it'll ever go away again to have a chief of staff that brings together all the different bits because the problem in Downing Street that I observed when my brother [Charles, senior foreign policy adviser to Thatcher] was there and actually even before that, is that there is no one who pulled all the strings together in Downing Street... that's why you now have someone like Ed Llewellyn [as chief of staff]. Of course Gordon being Gordon abolished it as soon as we left ['I also made a point of appointing a civil servant, Tom Scholar, as both my chief of

staff and principal private secretary', wrote Brown,[66] but this only lasted six months as Scholar returned to the Treasury, and the role was again split] but it's come back again and I strongly suspect it will always be there. It was an innovation whose time had come and won't go away.[67]

This was underlined when Theresa May initially appointed joint chiefs of staff in Nick Timothy and Fiona Hill, and then just one, Gavin Barwell, after the 2017 general election.

Certainly, the chief of staff role hurt the mandarins of the early Blair years. They had become accustomed to being *the* true right-hand men (relatively few women even now at the highest level and none has ever been Cabinet Secretary or principal private secretary), the repositories of knowledge and the arbiters of action—believers in their unique responsibility as civil servants to the concept of the Crown. But this could be viewed as an historical aberration: the post of PPS had been a political appointee in Asquith's time;[68] the Cabinet Office and Secretary to the Cabinet role had only been created in December 1916; and, while it is true that for both Harold Wilson and Edward Heath the Cabinet Secretary and head of the Home Civil Service were indeed the go-to advisers (the roles were divided in 1968, reforged in 1981, divided in 2012, before being amalgamated once more in 2014), others had been as close, if not closer, to prime ministers before and since. As Powell put it to us:

> When I went out to the Houston economic summit in 1990, I went on the VC-10 with Thatcher and I was a very junior official and she started off in the front cabin with Geoffrey Howe [deputy prime minister] and John Major [Chancellor], but as soon as Denis [Thatcher] got on the plane she kicked them out and replaced them with Charles Powell and Bernard Ingham and the fact is prime ministers always rely, and kings have since the beginning of time, on the people who are closest to them, rather than on figures that are further away such as Cabinet Secretaries... There's a whole myth that has been written about Cabinet government and this notion of Cabinet Secretaries... I think it's a mistake to think that Cabinet Secretaries were ever a confidant of the prime minister or the closest person to them.[69]

One month after Blair assumed power, a front-page news story in the *Independent* in June 1997 blew the lid off the simmering battle for Downing Street: 'New sleaze row knocks at door of Number Ten':

Downing Street yesterday reacted angrily to an accusation that the Prime Minister was threatening to create a new 'sleaze' culture at the heart of Whitehall. The attack follows widespread media speculation that Jonathan Powell, Tony Blair's chief of staff at Number Ten, was to be appointed to the post of Prime Minister's Principal Private Secretary. Those reports have startled Whitehall insiders, and Peter Hennessy, Professor of Contemporary History at the University of London, told *The Independent*: 'You could almost say it was sleazy. Why does he need this bauble?' But a senior Number Ten source said last night that Mr Powell had been appointed chief of staff and would remain in that job. When Alex Allan, the current Principal Private Secretary, moves to another posting later this year, he will be replaced by another civil servant...

Professor Hennessy was concerned that the Principal Private Secretary's role was that of 'junction box' for the Civil Service, involving a number of sensitive issues like security and intelligence, relations with Buckingham Palace, and honours. But *The Independent* has been told that those functions will be covered by the Prime Minister's other private secretaries, all of whom would come from within the Civil Service. Clearly disturbed by the suggestion that Mr Powell might take on that role, Professor Hennessy said Mr Blair had promised to take action against quangos and the patronage state. 'Yet what he is proposing means that working within some feet of him, at Number Ten, he will have created his own version of the patronage state.'[70]

The *Guardian* followed up a day later with what it described as 'The first serious clash between the Prime Minister and the head of the Civil Service', thereby identifying the chief opposition as coming from Sir Robin Butler, the Cabinet Secretary:

For Sir Robin, already concerned about the number of political appointments in Whitehall, it was a move too far... According to officials, Sir Robin... let it be known he was "seriously unrelaxed" about the prospect of Mr Powell taking over from Alex Allan... In what a well-placed source described yesterday as a fudge, Mr Powell will keep the title of chief of staff, while Mr Allan will be replaced by another civil servant.[71] (John Holmes started as principal private secretary in August 1997.)

These reports were a foretaste of what was to come: concern over the pace and scope of change to time-honoured practice landing up in the papers. While New Labour were rightly seen to be 'sultans of spin',[72] mandarins were not always above it.

Campbell's *Diaries* give the immediate political reaction from Number Ten: 'TB was...fed up and said he intended to send Butler a warning shot about it all [but] . . . There was no row . . . Butler came to see me and said he was sure Peter M[andelson] was behind a lot of this stuff in the press re Jonathan.' Powell later offered fascinating addenda to this story, saying that there simply was no attempt to install him as PPS and that, in any case, the conversations had taken place during the first days in power, and all had been settled by the time of the newspaper articles:

> It's the annoying thing about history, which is it's basically the sum total of press cuttings. It's completely untrue. I never wanted to be PPS. If I'd have wanted to be PPS, I'd have stayed being a civil servant and tried to be PPS that way. Robin Butler approached me actually after we got to Number Ten and said, 'Would I want to be PPS?' and I said 'No!' That's why we appointed John Holmes as PPS after Alex Allan left...He said, 'You're not very political, are you? Why don't you come and be PPS?' Because I didn't want to do that, I wanted to be political, my ambition was to be a Labour MP. I didn't want to be a civil servant, that's why I'd left the Civil Service. It's a complete myth...it's just a myth that got out there and once it's got out there you can't kill the damn thing off. I thought it would have been quite inappropriate for me to become PPS but I didn't want to. It's not the job I wanted to do.[73]

However, Lord Butler has recalled that while Blair had told him in 1996 that he had no intention of Powell becoming PPS, he reversed this a week before the 1997 General Election.[75] Sir John Holmes later reflected to us on the PPS position:

> Jonathan Powell was an obvious combination anyway of a civil servant and a special adviser and he'd been a diplomat so he'd kind of done it from that side, too. And 'chief of staff' is a kind of American term, very Clinton-influenced. I guess it made sense to call it that because it was a sort of different role in principle anyway, or in theory, from the PPS. Now, why would Jonathan have wanted to be PPS? He was chief of staff! I think they thought it would be logical for him to be the PPS but then I became the PPS because people like Robin Butler were worried that otherwise the whole thing was becoming too politicized

and the civil servants in Number Ten were reporting to someone who was a political appointee and not another civil servant, so that's why I became the PPS. It wasn't a big role, it was just to keep people like Robin Butler happy, to be absolutely honest with you, there was some kind of neutral Civil Service check on what Jonathan and Alastair and whoever else were doing...

I wasn't a PPS like Alex Allan had been a PPS, because I was simply there as the most senior civil servant in Number Ten and I didn't do very much in that role. I was too busy doing Northern Ireland, Europe, G8 Sherpa, foreign policy, defence, aid policy. So the amount of time I had to devote to being PPS was very small. Essentially I could be the reporting officer in formal terms for the other civil servants at Number Ten and I had a sort of nominal role in running the place in a sort of administrative sense, the sort of money side of it, it wasn't very complicated...Jonathan was the boss, there was no question of that.

When asked if Powell's responsibilities included security and intelligence-handling, Sir John said: 'Jonathan did that, too, but I did a lot of that anyway in my other role, with my real hat, as the overseas adviser.'

Sir John went further in describing the inescapable mix of politics and officialdom that the very top of Number Ten has always witnessed on a daily basis:

The difference between what Jonathan did and what Alex Allan did as PPS, or what Alex Allan's predecessor did, was not as much as people suggested because if you're in these positions, the distinction between what is political and what is government business is pretty fluid, obviously, so someone like Alex was very much involved with the politics as well as running the business of the government. Now, obviously he wasn't the political adviser but the distinctions are a bit hard to maintain. So the idea that there was a radical shift in the way things operated just because Jonathan came in as chief of staff and Alastair as head of the news office is not, in my view, as often portrayed. I'm not saying that Alex went over the line in doing political stuff, he was very close to John Major, it's the nature of the job, a prime minister doesn't say, 'I can't talk to him about the problems I'm having with the Foreign Secretary or the Home Secretary or whatever it is', even if they're political problems, just because he's the PPS.

The things that PPSs don't do: they don't go and meddle in party politics in a way that Jonathan *could* cross that bridge much further, but for most of the time you wouldn't have known that there was a big difference...Blair didn't make much of a distinction between special advisers and civil servants. I'd never met him before in my life but I became, for a period anyway, part of his inner circle—of course I wasn't getting involved in party politics...I was allowed into that circle, even though I was a civil servant I wasn't doing anything I shouldn't have been doing, but he wasn't making a sharp distinction between political advisers and civil servants, for him he didn't care, he wasn't interested.[76]

There is an intriguing echo here of Edward Heath, who used 'mixed' committees of ministers and officials, something Harold Wilson ended, with some civil servants thinking them 'a dangerous blurring'.[77] Holmes went further, suggesting that, while the Cabinet Secretary was clearly concerned, officials in Number Ten were more relaxed:

I and the other civil servants who were there, we didn't have a problem with this, it wasn't a big deal, honestly, we just adapted to that situation and got on with doing it. Jonathan wasn't lording it over us, I knew him quite well anyway, he was reasonably respectful of our positions within Number Ten. It wasn't a problem. It *was* a problem, I think, for Robin Butler. It was more of a problem in principle than it was in practice...I don't remember it as a conflict. Butler was concerned that there were political appointees in roles that hadn't had political appointees before so was this going to be a radical politicization, therefore there was this concern that there should be someone, and I was the fall guy as it were, who was the senior civil servant making sure that these people didn't run riot. But it was more concern about the potential than what was actually happening as far as I was concerned...He was worried about the precedents being set by this but the politicization, I don't think, became a big deal.

Blair did not try to politicize the Civil Service. He wasn't trying to say I've got to have a new lot of permanent secretaries, a new lot of ambassadors, because this lot are all closet Tories or something. He wasn't trying to do that, it was probably less than Mrs Thatcher had, who knows...The worry about the machinery of government within the system was much less than one might imagine.[78]

Yet Sir Jeremy Heywood, who replaced John Holmes as principal private secretary, saw the Powell–Holmes settlement as somewhat less than optimal:

I personally think the Order in Council thing was quite significant. I think it definitely reduced the status of the Principal Private Secretary inside Number Ten. I had a very good personal relationship with Jonathan Powell. He wasn't that interested, frankly, in running Number Ten and left me largely to my own devices on running domestic policy and therefore I was able to carve out some authority but it definitely would have been different had I not actually been reporting to him managerially and we've got rid of that arrangement now and I think it works better. You can still have very influential chiefs of staff but, in my view, they shouldn't have a managerial relationship over the senior civil servants in Number Ten. I think that was different, and different in kind.

Heywood did not, however, think that Blair's reliance on special advisers was different from what had gone before:

I think the differences can be exaggerated, for example John Major relied a great deal on Sarah Hogg, who was a very senior figure well-known across Whitehall as being powerful and Judith Chaplin as well as his political secretary was very influential, and Margaret Thatcher had similar advisers who were very influential on particular issues, so I think it's always been the case, in modern times anyway, that prime ministers have come to rely on people who are neither ministers nor civil servants and are close and often can have a variety of different roles...In general, I think the fact is there were a series of very senior people, political advisers inside Number Ten initially around Tony Blair and he did rely upon them to shape his thinking and challenge him and he used to stress-test his thoughts against them and they were powerful figures, they were prepared to speak truth unto him, so he definitely used them to shape his own thinking.[79]

For New Labour, Powell was the tame ex-official in the New Labour tribe, in effect a bridge to the Civil Service. The Civil Service in turn welcomed someone who spoke its language:

Remember I was a diplomat, not a proper civil servant, so they regarded me as pretty foreign anyway but I cannot complain at all. They treated me excellently, probably because I was in a position of power even in opposition. Nothing but politeness because I spoke their language particularly in the early stages, that Alastair and the others didn't speak. It was quite helpful acting as an interpreter between what they meant and what the other side was hearing...Once we got into government,

during the first six months, I was the only person who understood
what was going on, so, if you talk to someone like Bruce Grocott [par-
liamentary private secretary to Blair, 1994–2001], he described me as
swimming lengths in front of everyone else...then what happens,
which is very interesting, what happens to chiefs of staff or Rasputin
figures is you start attracting enmity, naturally, because you're sitting on
power and other people want to get it.[80]

But for Sir Richard Mottram, a rare senior official who straddled both
the domestic and security fields, having been permanent secretary to
the Ministry of Defence, 1995–8, Environment, Transport and the
Regions, 1998–2002, Work and Pensions, 2002–5, and the Security
and Intelligence Coordinator, 2005–7, Powell's role was a problem:

> He came to that job knowing nothing about how the British govern-
> ment worked, nothing about the British Civil Service because he had
> never worked in it...So his whole experience was actually quite dan-
> gerous because he thought he knew about it but, actually, I don't think
> he did. The weight of Number Ten was not official, the dialogue was not
> official, the decision-making was not official, they may have deluded
> themselves into thinking that, because they had Jonathan there, they
> had the official.[81]

Powell certainly had a tough bedding-in, but looking back, he
thought the difficulty was more from his New Labour colleagues.
The Campbell *Diaries* are strewn throughout the first term with
unfavourable references to Powell from the political side of Downing
Street—the real threat to Powell's position as chief of staff. Campbell
found himself 'wondering if [Powell] was tough enough, and I think he
was too'. For Blair, the key criticism was that 'sometimes his political
judgement is weak'. This translated over time into 'fretting about
Jonathan, felt he was feeling insecure and his response was to keep
Wilson out of things, but TB needed him bound in', because 'Jonathan
wasn't handling RW [Richard Wilson] well [which] would have bad
consequences for us.'[82] Campbell also records that 'Philip [Gould] was
convinced that Peter M was destabilising him [TB] by constantly

undermining the people around him. I had certainly been on the receiving end of Peter on Jonathan,' and that 'Peter M really seemed to be gunning for Jonathan at the moment.'[83]

Curiously, Mandelson's account of this is very different indeed:

Alastair, Anji and Tony's political aide, Sally Morgan, were all arguing that he [Powell] had to go. They recognised that he had a good mind, and they liked him, most of the time. But they felt he lacked the political background, and the personal skills...

I was virtually alone in insisting that Tony resist plans to redeploy Jonathan to Northern Ireland or the Middle East. It was true that he had shortcomings as a personnel manager, but that resulted mainly from his reluctance to interfere with the baronies that jostled each other in Downing Street. He had huge strengths. He worked fantastically quickly and precisely. He was good at conveying others' views to the Prime Minister and getting efficient and effective response. He could articulate and follow up on Tony's opinions and wishes—as time went on, sometimes without actually asking him. I strongly opposed moving him. In the end, Tony agreed. He never regretted it.[84]

Even so, on at least one occasion, Blair asked Wilson to find Powell a new job.[85] 'Welcome to politics,' was Powell's comment to us. 'I think I was quite lucky to survive that first year in opposition but, once in government, I was the only person who knew where the keys were in the first six months.'[86]

The doyen of Fleet Street, Hugo Young, recorded his reflections immediately after a lunch with Powell: 'Brisk, a little rough, a little simplistic, a mite unsophisticated, a trifle hesitant despite the speed of his answers: he seemed perhaps unreflective, certainly unmandarin, but very on the ball, of course, and in the end pretty open.'[87] Once Powell became accustomed to his role, the 'unmandarin' qualities that had caused difficulty became a huge source of advantage. As Campbell put it:

He never seemed to get down like TB and I did, and strangely the thing that people criticised him for—a lack of feel for politics—was sometimes what was needed, because he had a way of cutting through crap and when we said you can't do that, he would just say why not, and we would start thinking.[88]

As the second term took shape, It became axiomatic that Powell was of the highest quality, *the* indispensable aide to Blair, especially as his centrality to the Northern Irish peace process became more widely appreciated—and where his ability to act more flexibly as a political envoy rather than a civil servant allowed several undercover journeys alone into Republican Ulster.[89]

Alastair

Whereas Jonathan Powell was a power behind the throne, in a role only those at the rarefied level understood, Alastair Campbell was *the* publicly identifiable power, ever-present at Blair's side. Standing at six feet three inches, with a reputation for brawling, Campbell projected power. His past problems had been channelled into his becoming *the* most intense, talented, and focused of politico-media animals, all at the point that it went globally 24/7. He was the first special adviser of the modern incarnation to become a household name. To many Conservatives he was the feared destroyer of reputations but for them, as keen students of Machiavellian power, there was also deep admiration—just read the many entries in his *Diaries* when arch-Tories Alan Clarke and Nicholas Soames sought him out to praise him and Blair, and to ridicule their own side. For Labour, he was the leader's go-to person, the iron keeper of the clear message, Labour through and through, and with a reputation, the spin doctor mantle notwithstanding, for straightness. One is reminded of the film version of Roddy Doyle's *The Commitments*, when Jimmy Rabbitte announced to Outspan Foster that he had employed Mickah Wallace: 'You're mad, Jimmy, he's a savage!' 'I know he is...but he's *our* savage!'[90]

There is no doubt that many civil servants liked him and recognized rare quality. If he had retired before 9/11, his reputation would have been great, and mostly positive. His *Diaries* are the most wonderful primary resource for the historian. The millions of words are copious, yet concise in articulation, passionate and wide-ranging, and in effect chronicle the most extensive day-by-day downloading of a prime minister's brain ever. Studying them for patterns and hidden meanings will go on long into the future. They have been closely analysed here. There are times in the *Diaries* where one has to pinch oneself so as to understand just how far Labour had come from the days of the trashing of Neil Kinnock. For some, it was Blair's 1995 address to News International. For others, it was over the collapse of Robin Cook's marriage in 1997:

> I had got a deal from [Phil] Hall [Editor, *News of the World*] that they would let me see the copy in advance, and consult on headlines, even if I couldn't change them. It barely read like a *News of the World* exposé at all... They allowed us to make a couple of changes, for example talking of meetings rather than 'trysts'... I also persuaded them to use just two pictures and leave out the lurid detail. The only discussion now was the headline for the splash. They had 'Cabinet minister and his secret love' with 'Cook: my marriage is over' as a strap. I would have preferred the other way around, with 'Cook: my marriage is over' as the main headline. I suggested 'Cabinet minister leaves wife for secretary' which was more tabloid, but absolutely factual... It showed just how much we had changed our relations with the *NoW* and the Murdoch papers generally that they were willing to let us change the text.[91]

But perhaps a zenith was when Nick Brown, chief whip, was about to be the focus of a lurid *News of the World* story concerning an alleged relationship with a male prostitute. Conversations between the editor and Campbell saw the story spun as a voluntary 'coming out', with the result: 'We could hardly have asked for a better landing for Nick, who got good coverage pretty much everywhere.'[92]

Such was the aura around Campbell that Sir Robin Butler was recorded on two occasions by him asking for his help in rebutting media attacks on officials. The first was on Barbara Mills, Director of Public Prosecutions, in July 1997; the other was on Robert Fellowes, private secretary to the Queen, in November of the same year (Fellowes also called Campbell himself). Campbell agreed on both occasions but explained regarding the latter: 'I said all I could do was continue to talk him up, which we did.'[93] In the new government's early period, a form of presentational alchemy was ascribed to New Labour, a magic which, when times got harder, made the backlash all the greater.

One also has to remember that upon electoral victory, Campbell became the boss of civil servants who were in effect his vanquished opponents. As Blair entered Number Ten for the first time as prime minister and was spirited away for the customary security briefing:

> Jonathan Haslam [John Major's career civil servant director of com-munications] showed me around, introduced me to a few people, and it was all a bit weird. Jonathan was being very pleasant and doing what he had to do, but I felt for him. He was being kicked around out of the job, and having to guide me as to what to do next... The press office people were nervous, I could tell... They also sensed, rightly, that I had not been impressed by the JM [John Major] press operation.

Campbell's reputation and the nature of the three-year New Labour media onslaught naturally meant press officers used to a somewhat more genteel way of life 'gave off the sense of being terrified... I said it should be an exciting time for them because the PM values com-munications. But I did say I intended to change the way things were done.' A month later, and Campbell's view of them had not improved: 'They all seemed so beaten, and by what? They were full of problems, and very few ideas. The majority were well meaning, but the culture in which they had grown up was just way behind the times.'[94] One of the core concepts of New Labour was that presentation had to be built in to policy development from the very start. Previous govern-ments operated by calling in the communications staff once a policy had been agreed—something Campbell regarded as amateur and prone to mistakes.

While Sir Robin Butler was undoubtedly troubled by special advisers such as Campbell, he recognized that official media-handling through the Government Information Service had not kept pace with a fast-moving world. This was borne out by the outgoing chief communications secretary's two immediate predecessors, Gus O'Donnell and Christopher Meyer, both career officials, who advised Campbell to pursue 'root-and-branch change' and 'radical change, if not abolition' respectively. Meyer added, 'You have the political clout at the centre. Use it . . . They are so set in their ways and so out of date. They are cynical and sullen.' Moreover, new ministers who had grown accustomed to New Labour's operation in opposition complained to Campbell that their press offices were simply not up to scratch.[95] Thirteen heads of information left their posts in the first year as a partial consequence: 'Before you think this is a crime committed uniquely, it was twelve when Margaret Thatcher came in [19]79. It just happens. It happens in private practice. It's a matter of chemistry and trust,' according to Mike Granatt, who was appointed head of the Government Information Service in 1997.[96] All this concerned Butler. But he also 'agreed ministers were not happy' and so on 10 September 1997 set up a committee to reform the GIS under Cabinet Office Permanent Secretary Sir Robin Mountfield, which Campbell joined.[97]

The committee worked fast to 'consider proposals to respond to concerns about how far it was equipped in all areas to meet the demands of a fast-changing media world; to build on the skills and resources of the career GIS; and to maintain the established, and recently re-confirmed, propriety guidelines', reporting just ten weeks later. It stated from the outset that it is:

'. . . a proper and necessary function of a democratic government to inform, and to communicate its policies and achievements positively, in order to aid public understanding and so maximize the effectiveness of its policies'. The name was changed to the Government Information and Communication Service to 'imply the proactive exposition and justification of policy rather than the reactive answering of questions...'[98]

Lobby briefings were placed on the record in 2000, with Campbell named as the 'Prime Minister's Official Spokesman'. Previously, these twice-daily briefings (while the House of Commons was sitting) had acquired a mystique by virtue of being off the record, with quotations often attributed to 'Downing Street', and being limited to journalists who were members of the Parliamentary Lobby. These are holders of security-cleared passes who have access to the Palace of Westminster and specifically to the Members' Lobby outside the Commons Chamber. The passes are allocated by the Commons authorities, not the government, but the system gave rise to complaints about favouritism, manipulation, and secrecy. Sir Robin Mountfield said: 'A Lobby system which relies on non-attribution tends to give an unwarranted credibility to those unnamed sources who are always "senior" and invariably "close" to whichever Minister is the prime subject of the story.'[99] Campbell had been 'toying with the idea of going absolutely upfront on the record with briefings, both as a new challenge, but also as a freedom of information and centralisation move. It would give the centre more clout and allow us to get some message control.'[100] This last point is crucial to the dynamic that Campbell was operating within and also to understanding what he considered to be damage done by the competing sources of communication. Campbell had in mind two people in particular—Peter Mandelson and Charlie Whelan.

The early months of New Labour saw Peter Mandelson operating even more than usual in the grey areas. As Minister without Portfolio in the Cabinet Office but close to Blair, he had time on his hands and no particular focus but with a liking and ability for gossip. Campbell, however, was the official spokesman and tension was unavoidable: 'I tried to be dispassionate about Peter and work out whether my troubles were provoked by jealousy that he was a major news-making figure or whether, as I stated to him [Philip Gould] and to TB, I felt he was becoming a problem to TB and potential embarrassment to the government.'[101] The other rival was the Treasury's spokesman, Charlie Whelan. For different reasons, conflict ensued with both— Campbell often won the battles, but not before reputational damage had been done (see chapter 4).

The other change that Mountfield introduced was a Strategic Communications Unit to institutionalize the grip and power of central communication and the need for it to work side by side with policy-making. Campbell wrote: 'Clinton said his big mistake was he was so busy governing he stopped communicating and you cannot afford to do that. Trust depends on constant communication.'[102] Moreover, in June 1997, he wrote: 'The *Mail* splashed on a leaked memo from TB to the Cabinet...There was still far too much gabbing around the place.'[103] This effort to speak as one voice of centralized power enfeebled many and worried still more. The opposition days seemed long ago.

Looking back after a decade, Campbell said: 'I can't understand why there was a fuss about it to be honest, I really can't...If I am being absolutely frank, I don't think we did enough—in some ways I think we sort of pussy-footed around a bit too much.'[104] David Blunkett was one of the Cabinet ministers who wholeheartedly agreed:

> The whole thing was way back in the 1950s and therefore there was very urgent action in the months after May 1997 to try and do some-thing dramatic about that...The press generally became antagonistic to what we were doing partly because we became so much more effi-cient and effective. The idea that mumbling government is a good thing, that miscommunication or no communication is a good thing, or if you communicate badly by not knowing what your message is and not putting it out and allowing the media to make whatever they like of the policies you're trying to promote, I found that unacceptable—that's just ludicrous.[105]

One aspect of New Labour prowess was 'rebuttal', the aggressive response to an opponent's viewpoints and propaganda. In opposition, it was a touchstone of efficiency and strength, and a demonstration that what had destroyed Kinnock was not going to happen again. But once in government, the basic concept attracted unease and even constitutional objection. A commitment to comprehensive media monitoring was included in the Mountfield report, but rebuttal was another thing altogether. Campbell said that Sir Richard Wilson, Cabinet Secretary, 'clearly saw it as a totally political concept, and it was a struggle to persuade them it was a necessary part of any organisation constantly being written about, a lot of it nonsense which had to be challenged'.[106] Sir Richard agreed to try to accommodate it but it was clear he found this close to crossing what he considered to be the constitutional line, while the concept of 'prebuttal'—anticipating Conservative criticism of the Labour government—was simply beyond the pale.

Campbell's reach, aggression, and power provoked a reaction. Political and media adversaries admired and lamented his strength. The cost of his success was near warlike relations between Number Ten and the media. In December 1997, Blair observed: 'The press will kick us...because they think the Tories are useless and in a way they are becoming the Opposition, so we have to push them back in argument.'[107] This 'push' turned into conflict throughout Campbell's time in Number Ten. He fought fire with fire, unapologetically, but his very aggression started to alarm Blair, as Campbell noted in February 1999:

> The Sun front page said we were the most arrogant government in history. A lot of this was still payback for my whacks at the national press. I felt we had to keep going, ensure the public conditioned their response to media attacks with an understanding of the game being played, but TB was losing his nerve a bit. He called me at 7.20, said the front pages were ghastly. 'We are in trouble on this.' He made the same point at the office meeting, said he wasn't sure where this war with the media ends. I said it doesn't end, you have to fight the whole time, or they make sure you never get heard properly. Philip was the only one totally supportive of where I was, saying the public would be with us over time, and there was never a better time. But people were getting jumpy.[108]

A throwaway remark to Javier Solana, NATO Secretary General, during the Kosovo crisis revealed a great deal about Campbell's thinking: 'He [Solana] said he loved the way we had "tamed" the media. I said we hadn't, we'd just made them think we had.'[109] And the next year, Blair elaborated on his doubts to Campbell:

Under Thatcher, they got drunk on the power she let them wield and then they tore Major to shreds, in part with our complicity. Also, for pragmatic reasons, we entered into a whole series of basically dishonest relationships with them and now they realise that. They realised that they actually have less power than they did and they see us as all-powerful and they want their power back. So there was no point in all-out war, because at the moment we have the upper hand.[110]

Early on, Campbell started to run into another problem, which was that journalists' fascination with him began to mean that he was the story. 'John Pienaar [BBC journalist] said on the radio I was a "cult figure" to people interested in government-media relations,' Campbell recorded in November 1997.[111] 'I had...forgotten the scale of the coverage I was attracting,' he later wrote, 'not just incessant press atten-tion, but a play based on me, a website dedicated to me, books, my own impersonator on Rory Bremner's comedy show.'[112] The last was created on the familiar satirical premise that it was Blair who was deputy to the forever condescending boss Campbell, and was fed by some behind-the-scenes banter between the two captured on film as part of a documentary by the BBC's Michael Cockerell. Campbell wrote:

I did another interview with Cockerell and TB popped round, feigning surprise that he was there, and we had a not terribly natural chat about things before Cockerell drew him into a kind of interview...TB saying I was the best in the business...He was trying to downplay the media side of things and I stupidly undercut him as he left when I pointed out he had just wasted his time talking to Michael C.

The documentary caused consternation in Number Ten, with Blair concerned 'we had to watch out for the "real deputy PM" gibe because, if people believed it, it wasn't good for him or me'. When the pro-gramme was broadcast, Campbell wrote, 'The only moment I cringed was when I seemed to be taking the piss out of TB,' while 'TB's worry, that the Cockerell film stood up the Rory Bremner analysis, was slightly borne out by the [next morning's] press.'[113]

As a result of this pressure, Campbell retreated from briefing the lobby himself, but continued to wield power as a close adviser behind the scenes and, just as importantly, to be known to do so. Blair's unease was not heeded and, uncharacteristically, the prime minister had stern words with him after an outburst in front of civil servants and the wider team:

> He said you cannot talk to me like that. It's wrong and it unsettles all the others. He said this is not about vanity or *amour propre* because I am the least status-conscious politician I know, but that was bad. And the reason we have things like Rory Bremner is because that kind of thing gets out. I kind of apologised and said I felt completely stymied by the lack of follow-through from ministers and the lack of basic discipline and professionalism, and the extent to which he expected me and one or two others to pick up all the pieces. But I accepted I was too easily slipping into a mode of being critical of him. He said it was OK for me to go at him in front of Sally, Anji and Jonathan but that was it.[114]

Lord O'Donnell was one of many Civil Service witnesses who thought 'Team Tony', the political staff, were 'very nice, very able'—and very blunt to their prime minister.[115]

Looking back, Campbell mused:

> Perhaps I didn't help myself in agreeing to a documentary about our media operations. I was hoping that if people saw genuinely behind the scenes, they would realise the whole thing about 'spin' had been overblown. But BBC documentary maker Michael Cockerell later told me the film [*News from Number Ten*[116]] got more publicity than all other films he had made combined—including several on prime ministers, so perhaps that both made the point and whilst also suggesting I had defeated the object of the exercise.[117]

Campbell's intensity cut both ways. Relentless pressure, both from external forces but also from Blair himself, combined with his own ferocity, meant that he soon began to contemplate whether his position was good for him and his family. As early as March 1998, he wrote:

> The problem was the pressures on me were really growing, as TB became more and more reliant. There was no escape or release from it ... We took the kids skating, and Charlie Falconer was there and he

said it must be great to be the one that TB calls his Colossus, the one on whom it is all built, and I said no, that's what drives me crazy. I don't want power, or more pressure. Yet the more I try to devolve, the more things seem to accumulate towards me.[118]

In May 1998, just a year after entering government, Campbell first recorded the idea of leaving: 'I was thinking of quitting. It was the first time I had articulated that.'[119] It was followed by perhaps the only clear threat of resignation in anger to Blair over the 'him-or-me' sacking of Gordon Brown's press secretary Charlie Whelan in January 1999 (which will be examined in chapter 4).[120]

As soon as that crisis was resolved, in Campbell's favour, he found himself central to the British part in the Kosovo crisis. In April 1999, when the confrontation was in the balance, in no small part due to disjointed and hamfisted NATO communications, Campbell was arguably at the height of his powers:

> Jack Straw said we needed 'some good old-fashioned Millbank [the building in which the 1994–7 media campaign was largely orchestrated] discipline instilled in them'... TB called Solana to discuss presentation, thinking they would resist a UK takeover. But Solana said... I was the best in Europe... Charles [Guthrie, chief of the Defence Staff] called later, said he told all of them that I was the man to sort them out and they had better bloody well listen. It was a huge help having someone as blunt as him, and more important who got the need for the media side of things to be right... I confess to feeling a real excitement, almost exhilaration, at the thought of a new challenge, and one that both BC [Clinton] and TB had asked me to do... I was to be seen as a special envoy from the PM, on a par with a senior cabinet minister.[121]

Campbell undoubtedly contributed to NATO's success but at further cost to himself. Two months later, his wish to leave became more of a plea: 'I... told TB I'd been getting very tired and fed up and wanted to leave, and he said I couldn't.'[122] Kosovo was probably the high point for Campbell. A head of steam was building up over the concept of 'spin', every bit as catch-all and ill-defined as 'sleaze'. As Campbell mused in 2012, 'we allowed our approach to communications—which was simply a necessary shift towards a more disciplined approach—to become defined as spin'.[123] Blair drew a further conclusion: 'From the outset, deprived of a real policy attack on New Labour, this alternative attack of being a government of "spin", of "deceit", of me as a "liar", had taken root.'[124]

Understanding public opinion, Blair knew that spin was becoming a problem early on. Indeed, on the day he arrived in Belfast for the talks that led to the Good Friday Agreement, he recalled:

> [I] decided to be in practical, workmanlike, non-rhetorical mode when I addressed the press outside Hillsborough, the stately home that is the perquisite of the British Secretary of State for Northern Ireland. 'Today is not a day for sound bites,' I began eagerly, oozing impatience to get down to work and irritation with anything flowery or contrived. Then—and heaven only knows where it came from, it just popped into my head—I said, 'But I feel the hand of history upon our shoulder', which of course was about as large a bite of sound as you could contemplate. In the corner of my eye I could see Jonathan and Alastair cracking up. I decided to say no more.[125]

If Campbell had left before Iraq, or indeed before 9/11, he would have retired as the global go-to-guy for twenty-first-century government-media relations. As it turned out, he is still internationally recognized as a first-rate speaker and columnist, not to mention government media adviser, but one who is, for many, tainted.

That Campbell did not leave before the Twin Towers were felled was due to the reason he began to work for Blair in the first place: the prime minister understood Campbell in a way few did. He knew that there was mutual respect and trust but, much more, he understood Campbell's visceral hatred of the Conservative Party and his passionate wish to make the world a more progressive place. Blair played on this remorselessly and persuasively. In June 2000, Campbell said that 'TB was being exceptionally nice because he knew I was at the end of my tether.'[126] A few weeks later, Blair 'said my problem was that most cabinet ministers, certainly the important ones, trusted and respected my judgement, so I was unique. It wasn't like Ingham because in the end I was on a par with the senior cabinet guys.' But by February 2001, conversations about Campbell's departure entered a new phase:

> I asked Adam Boulton [of Sky News] up to the office to sound him out as a possible replacement in the event I went. He was clear he would want to do it as a civil servant, he would want to wait till the New Year, partly for share options, partly to be distant from the election. I was clear with him that it wasn't certain I would go but that what we were talking about was a director of communications job rather than PMOS [prime minister's official spokesman]. He was basically up for it but not straight after the election.[127]

In retrospect, it looks as if the move for Boulton was more Blair throwing Campbell a sop, because Campbell wrote in March 2001:

> [Blair] said whatever happened he would always call on me because he valued my judgement and friendship. He said part of my problem was that I like responsibility and I was good at big decisions...he still needed me for advice, politics, my feel for the party, my words and my ability to motivate...He said he felt deep down I wanted to stay and I was trying to find reasons for going so that I could please Fiona but he felt I would resent it if I went.

Campbell admitted as much a week later when he wrote: 'She [Fiona, his partner] felt I was not being honest with myself, that I was worried about losing status and power...there was a long list of reasons I wanted to leave, but a very powerful pull to stay.'[128]

Campbell's role did change after the June 2001 election, but 9/11, Afghanistan, and Iraq dragged him back to the centre of the action—and controversy. In fact, the problems that New Labour would now encounter over 'spin' in the run-up to the Iraq invasion began on the day of 9/11. Jo Moore, a special adviser in the Department of Transport, wrote an ill-judged and tasteless email to colleagues that afternoon: 'It's now a very good day to get out anything we want to bury. Councillors' expenses?' It was the most foolish own goal of the Blair government. Although, after a document written in 1983 by Bernard Ingham, Margaret Thatcher's press secretary, was declassified in 2016, perhaps we should not be too surprised. In it, he considered how to reduce coverage of Greenham Common anti-nuclear weapons protests:

> They will secure less airtime and have less impact if something more newsworthy in television terms occurs—eg (to be brutal) a North Sea blow out, an assassination attempt on the Pope, etc; some awful tragedy. All this is in the lap of the gods and all tragedies are devoutly not to be wished . . . There may be other things we can do to reduce the amount of air time available to CND [Campaign for Nuclear Disarmament] . . . I think that Good Friday is a lost cause. This is the day when the CND chain will (or will not) be formed between Aldermaston and Greenham Common. It is also a day when there is not much sport. However, what would take the trick would be press and TV pictures, for release on the evening of Good Friday and/ or Saturday newspapers, of Prince William [then 9 months old] in Australia.[129]

A day to use good news to bury bad, perhaps. In any case, further proof that there is little new under the sun.

Us and them: New Labour and the Civil Service

Looking back, one senior former official thought the Civil Service 'stale' in 1997.[130] This was understandable. Much of the Major era had been uncomfortable and demoralizing for officialdom: a fourth-term, divided government with a disappearing majority was led by a dispassionate and technocratic prime minister who helped drive the state, measured by public spending as a share of national income, to a post-1945 near low of 39.9 per cent[131] and reduced the number of civil servants, which had been over a million in 1945 and 751,000 in 1976, down to 476,000 in 1997.[132]

It was in some ways inevitable that a high-powered and confident political team of new ministers and special advisers encroaching and

usurping some traditional Civil Service roles would create friction.
We asked Jonathan Powell, did an 'us versus them' situation arise?

> Not on our side, certainly in Downing Street there was no such divide
> at all, we were very, very close in terms of Downing Street. We did
> have a problem with Cabinet Secretaries, starting with Robin [Butler],
> and with Richard [Wilson] particularly, Andrew [Turnbull] less so
> but still a problem, Gus [O'Donnell] not at all. The real problem
> I think…when we came in we had formed quite an effective guer-
> rilla operation in opposition and the trouble was what happened
> was that we carried on operating as a guerrilla operation inside
> government and just carried on doing everything by ourselves.
> I remember Tony complaining to me after a while, maybe six months,
> that the government machinery was like a Rolls-Royce parked outside
> Downing Street which he wasn't allowed to drive because he was
> still driving through our guerrilla operation…We had to, at that
> stage, start making it more inclusive and using the Civil Service. So
> it wasn't so much us and them as us still being a very tight-knit
> unit…maybe it felt to civil servants that we were a tight-knit unit
> that wasn't letting them in, that could be a fair criticism, but we'd
> adapted. Within the first six to nine months we got to a proper system
> where we were using the Civil Service.[133]

A retired Sir Richard Mottram surveyed the state of the relationship
between the political tribe and the official one in 1997:

> The really important point was that the country had been drifting,
> the government had been drifting, so come 1997, actually, there was
> an amazing amount of enthusiasm and drive in the Civil Service to
> work with the government. There were civil servants whom I thought
> were a bit on the margin of being insufficiently distant to maintain
> their political impartiality, they were sort of overjoyed that they'd
> won, but there wasn't anyone who didn't think it was a good idea
> they'd won.[134]

Jonathan Powell said that this was not necessarily good for New
Labour:

> The problem we had was that permanent Civil Service were leaning
> over backwards to convince us after eighteen years that they were to the

left of us and that's where we got into a bit of trouble with them trying to show how leftie they were…we expected them to be independent.[135]

Sir Richard thought there was a difference between New Labour's attitude to less senior civil servants and the high-ups:

> I think they had a view about the permanent secretaries which was probably based upon *Yes, Minister* and assumed they were all very homogenous and that they were all stuffed shirts, old people who constantly told people 'no'…
>
> In the old days there was a certain sort of Conservative who knew how to relate to a servant…I used to work with Lord Carrington [Foreign Secretary 1979–82] as a very junior civil servant. I was very, very fond of him. He would say to visitors, 'I never went to university so I employ these chaps because they are very, very clever'…he treated us magnificently well but he had the idea that we were servants, and most civil servants don't mind that much, the ones who do are a bit of a worry and shouldn't be civil servants really, so you like the idea that you are in that relationship. The problem for Labour, I think, is that some Labour ministers don't have the confidence to do that.

Sir Richard thought there was also a darker side to the 'us and them' divide:

> They had a view that the Civil Service was politicized [by the Conservative years] and although I never managed to get ahold of this, there was a list apparently—just a small illustration of what I mean—there was a list of people who were allegedly politicized civil servants and this was a list of people who were going to be got rid of…it may be a myth that it ever existed…but my name was allegedly on it, so I enquired gently about why my name was on it to which the answer was well, you know, they'd seen me—'they', I don't know who it was—they had seen me in the context where I was quite friendly with Conservative ministers, which led me to say, 'What? This is the basis of this list, is it?' Of course when they came in this list vanished and nothing happened…It could well be a myth, but you can imagine how such a myth could develop.[136]

Powell was adamant this was wrong: 'Certainly nothing to do with Tony. I've never heard of any such list and I would have known if there was such a list and, no, there wasn't.'[137]

That Sir Richard should believe such a 'myth' speaks volumes, but the received wisdom of a huge gulf between New Labour and the Civil Service is too simplistic. Most of the problems settled down over time, the friction centred on the earlier, older leadership. For most of the Civil Service, the New Labour team and those officials below the very top in 1997 rubbed along fine—better than fine in many cases. Sir David Normington was a case in point and told us:

> In so far as you can generalize, the Civil Service approached the 1997 election with a sense of anticipation tinged with trepidation. Although impartiality is real and deep in the psyche of the Civil Service, we are also citizens and electors; and many civil servants were caught up in the general sense that it was time for a change and that Tony Blair in particular offered something fresh and new . . .

> But there was trepidation, too. We were not sure how deeply Conservative thinking had penetrated our subconscious. There were thousands of younger civil servants who only knew Conservative government. And it was inevitable that some incoming ministers and their special advisers would be suspicious that the Civil Service was deeply Conservative with a large C. Indeed in his speech on the Civil Service in 2004 Tony Blair admitted that Labour activists in the seventies and eighties had been brought up in the belief that the Civil Service was 'Tory to its bones', quickly adding that it was a total myth.

> In the event, most civil servants working close to ministers were swept up in the excitement of a change of government. There were White Papers to write and new programmes to launch. There were task forces and working groups set up with joint membership of civil servants. There was little evidence of distrust and a seeming willingness to take civil servants at face value. There was surprise and some mild amusement at the 'Call me Tony' informality and the Cool Britannia atmosphere but most of us found these early months engaging and refreshing. I remember thinking particularly that it was a relief to work for a government who seemed to value public service and thought that the Civil Service could be part of the solution to delivering their political ambitions.

> It is inevitable in government that things get more difficult and tensions between the government and its civil servants grow. The job of government is hard. Things go wrong. Projects fail. Interest groups protest. Some civil servants are unable or unwilling to match the government's ambitions.

But in my experience, despite these difficulties, the majority of the Civil Service did not find it difficult to align themselves with the policies and approach of the Blair government; and the good relations of those early years never completely disappeared. And the reasons for this are not hard to discern. This was a government which believed in active government and thought the Civil Service was there to get things done: that created a sense of being valued which was not so apparent from the governments which preceded it. The people who did not survive or flourish were those who did not get stuck in. This was a government which wanted things to change quickly. There was no place for people who stood on the sidelines. It helped of course that this was a time of plenty, with resources being poured into public services on a large scale. This meant that there was not the same pressure to achieve savings that there was in the early eighties or after the financial crash; nor the same level of efficiency programmes.[138]

This mood was understood by Geoff Mulgan, special adviser in the Number Ten Policy Unit from the start:

The most striking thing in terms of the Civil Service mood when Labour took over was relief. Relief that actually here was a government with a majority, roughly knew what it wanted. They were pretty tired, bored, of not only Conservative rule, but even more of an administration with no majority, and therefore perpetual tactics, in-fighting and so on. And in broad terms, the five or six big goals which Blair set were ones probably ideologically shared by most of the Civil Service. I know one doesn't speak of the Civil Service as having beliefs, but I think that most of them were quite keen on the continuity of economic policy... Secondly, the revival of public services ending a very long squeeze on both spending and attention to public services which had characterized both Major and Thatcher. They were pretty keen that there should be some echelon in equality and there were lots of internal working groups in the Civil Service on inequality, social exclusion, and so on in the two or three years prior to [19]97. Most of them were fairly supportive of devolution to Scotland and Wales, and finally most of them were moderately pro-European and therefore quite keen to see a government which was trying to restore relationships with Europe.[139]

Mulgan was important to the drive to reform and re-energize the Civil Service. Central to this was an ambitious attempt to foster 'joined-up government' to mitigate the perennial problem of departmental demarcation. The Haldane report of 1918, called for by the Cabinet's Reconstruction Committee in 1917, was an early look at the organization of government:

> Upon what principle are the functions of departments to be determined and allocated? There appear to be only two alternatives, which may be briefly described as distribution according to the persons or classes to be dealt with, and distribution according to the services to be performed... Distribution according to the nature of the service to be rendered to the community as a whole is the principle which is likely to lead to minimum amount of confusion and overlapping.[140]

But organization by department meant that issues such as youth offending, teenage pregnancy, or illegal drug use fell between the vertically arranged departments. Whose responsibility were they? The Home Office's, Education's, Health's, Social Security's, Defence's, the Foreign Office's? All generally and none in particular. When many are responsible, none is accountable. These 'wicked issues', a phrase invented before the 1997 election by Sir Michael Bichard when permanent secretary of Education and Employment,[141] were to be tackled in an unprecedented way. Teams of ambitious officials (always a sign of political importance) sprang up across the Cabinet Office, such as the Social Exclusion Unit, the Performance and Innovation Unit, and the Rough Sleepers' Unit, which sought to reverse the rise in the mid-to-late 1990s of inner-city sights such as 'Cardboard City'.[142]

A further attempt to change the nature and ethos of the Civil Service came with the *Modernising Government* White Paper in March 1999, which collated policy promises and promised more strategic government in which higher-quality services would be provided with the consumer in mind, not the producer, and in which 'we will value public service, not denigrate it'.[143] The White Paper reflected Blair's frustration with the pace of reform, but some of the resistance from officialdom, that the impulse for further and faster change was unfocused, was justified.

In any event, the message of reform was muddied further on 6 July 1999, when Blair expressed his true feelings in a departure

from his prepared speech to the (of all people) British Venture
Capital Association:

> Try getting change in the public sector and the public services. I bear
> the scars on my back after two years in government and heaven knows
> what it will be like after a bit longer. People in the public sector are more
> rooted in the concept that 'if it's always been done this way, it must always
> be done this way' than any group of people I have come across.[144]

Jonathan Powell looked back on the episode:

> What we hoped Cabinet Secretaries would do was to reform the Civil
> Service because we believed the Civil Service needed really genuine
> reform, the 'scars on my back' comment was something that slipped
> out revealing that, and now we see Cameron saying the same thing
> ['enemies of enterprise'[145]] . . . What they were supposed to be was the
> person who runs the machinery of government in our system.[146]

Sir Richard Wilson was in a difficult position. Standing in the same shoes
as giants of British bureaucracy, who had evolved organically as guardians of the constitution, he knew the job he wanted to do, as did some
of his senior permanent secretary colleagues, who wanted him to stand
up for what they saw as their traditional rights of power. Yet New Labour
in general and Powell in particular had eroded the historical position of
the Cabinet Secretary being not just figuratively but actually the prime
minister's right-hand man. Dr Ian Beesley, at the launch of his book *The
Official History of the Cabinet Secretaries*, pointed out Sir Richard's dilemma:

> On occasion, in private, it can be necessary to speak up to ministers
> with some home truths. Now for those of you who have ever tried
> that, it takes a great deal of courage. Ministers are big beasts, they're
> used to getting their own way. Some of them have large egos. All of
> them sit at the top of the food chain. It's best done by someone who
> will never challenge them as ministers for political office . . . by far the
> bravest example I have seen is four documents submitted by Richard
> Wilson to Tony Blair about the Blair way of running government [in
> 1999]. The fourth of these was so sensitive that it was handed over in
> person. Its title, 'The Nature of Power'. And it contains the following,
> 'You have the levers to hand, you choose not to pull them. Do not try
> to use the Policy Unit to run the government. Do not attempt to

divorce permanent secretaries from their Cabinet ministers. Do not be tempted by a Napoleonic model, shifting resources from the Cabinet Office to 10 Downing Street. Above all, do not spend too much time on foreign affairs. It is of course fun and it's easier than domestic policy, but the Foreign Office is only one of 20 departments and it wins you the fewest votes.' Wow. One of the prominent permanent secretaries of the day said that he and his colleagues had no idea that Richard Wilson was making these submissions. That gap in knowledge must have made Richard's tasks with the permanent secretaries much more difficult, yet he could never tell them. He could never have shared that moment of truth unto power.[147]

At the same event, Lord Wilson mused that:

> There were moments when it was clear to me that the Blair team longed to import some characteristics of the American presidential way of doing things—small things—and you have to say to yourself, 'Am I being pernickety?' Quite often issues of principle are tied up in very small incidents, and you have to decide where you're going to draw the line, where you're going to fight, and where you're not going to fight. I don't want to imply it was all battle, but I do think there are moments where you have to say to yourself, 'Have I got it right? Am I being too rigid in my insistence?'[148]

Here we have—laid bare—the conflict of good people trying their best to deliver what *they* think best for government, now and in the future. Furthermore, the prime minister was to tell Wilson, 'I find your theology quite surreal,' after repeated clashes over what the Cabinet Secretary regarded as important principles of Civil Service propriety.[149] The tension between Blair and his Cabinet Secretary reached a crisis point over the question of Sir Richard Wilson's successor in 2002. Jonathan Powell explained:

> One demonstration of the ability of the Civil Service to resist change was the opposition they mounted to the idea of the recruitment of an outsider for the job of Cabinet Secretary when Richard Wilson retired. We proposed there should be an open competition so that outsiders as well as insiders could apply, but Richard was opposed. Richard proposed that he interview all the applicants and put up a shortlist of two. It was, he said, the only way to settle down the Civil Service. We had a shrewd idea of who he wanted to fill the post, while we wanted a reformer.

We counter-proposed splitting his job into two, one the traditional
Cabinet Secretary and the other a new CEO for the Civil Service. Richard
agreed but kept a close grip on the process to ensure that it didn't really
happen. I managed to sneak Michael Bichard in to see Tony as a possible
candidate. Michael was permanent secretary at the Department of
Education, but he was seen by the Civil Service as an outsider because he
had previously been a local government chief executive rather than
working his way up the Civil Service hierarchy. When Tony revealed to
Richard that he had seen Michael, Richard flew off the handle and spoke
in intemperate language he later regretted: Number Ten was a mess; we
were trying to interfere in the work of all the departments; we needed to
return to collective government. Tony gave as good as he got, and Richard
retreated through the green baize door (actually now an electronic door
controlled by a swipe card) to the Cabinet Office.

Tony thought the outburst had arisen because Richard detected political
weakness in Tony's position, but I thought he had been wound up by the
other Permanent Secretaries who always gave him a hard time. Richard
saw off our idea of an outsider as head of the Civil Service in a way
Machiavelli would have been proud of, but a prudent prime minister
would return to the idea and insist on it if they really wanted to shake
up the Civil Service.[150]

From Powell's point of view, the clash was the culmination of long
conflict over the configuration of the prime minister's office:

Because of the weakness of the Cabinet Office, we looked on a number
of occasions during Tony's decade in power at creating a separate
Department of the Prime Minister. There is an argument for the prime
minister having a larger office, with a proper staff and budget, capable
of taking on departments in argument, but when we first considered
the idea in February 1999 Richard Wilson threatened to resign. Fearing
we were trying to create one by the back door, he went even further
the next month by refusing to allow us to appoint any more staff to
Number Ten. [In fact,] although I could see the argument for more
muscle inside Downing Street, I was always opposed to the creation of a
large prime minister's department.[151]

Powell later elaborated further, putting the Blair years in the perspective
of Cameron's premiership:

We have a very small Downing Street and I think it will always
remain very small...the analogy I always thought of was that it was like

a gearstick, it needs to be very responsive to the prime minister, but it needs to connect the government machine in some way. What the Cabinet Office should be doing is connecting the government machine to make sure that all four wheels are pointing in the same direction and yet the Cabinet Secretaries we had, at least to start with, Gus was the exception, didn't really want to play that role, they wanted to play a different sort of role and that was a problem. So we had a clash between us and Number Ten, between Tony and them, because they didn't want to do what we wanted them to do, they wanted to do what we were doing.[152]

With a massive mandate from 1997, an absence of opposition, the likelihood of a second term, and an emerging budget surplus, it was unthinkable that there would be little change in the country to show for it. The pressure for public service reform built, not least in Blair's mind:

> We had proclaimed 1999 as the 'year of delivery'—a phrase that somewhat came back to haunt us. Truthfully there had been progress, but it was very incremental, not only because the money had not really started to flow, but also because, as the 'forces of conservatism'[153] speech had indicated, there was a structural problem that money alone couldn't solve. Across the piece—in schools, universities, the NHS, law and order and criminal justice—we were still only tinkering, not transforming. The speech was actually self-critical as well as system-critical. As 1999 wore on and the year 2000 turned, I began to look at how we could propel the whole question of reform further and faster.[154]

Blair realized—somewhat belatedly, but nonetheless definitively—that he needed to harness the whole potential power of not only his choice ministers and special advisers but also the Civil Service as a whole. One of the New Labour mantras in government had been 'standards not structures', which gave rise to the idea that Blair was uninterested in detail. But, within a year or two, Blair understood that structures mattered too and he threw himself into understanding the machinery of government, becoming by his third term the most powerful critic of his earlier attempts. While it is true that there was real friction between Blair, Powell, and Wilson, it is also the case that Campbell records in February 1999: 'TB felt we needed new structures and a team centrally based dedicated to pursuing departments and chasing delivery. TB also felt Richard Wilson needed to be more on the inside track with us. TB felt our overall cause would be helped if he had a better understanding of it.'[155] So began the history of the Prime Minister's Delivery Unit.

The Delivery Unit

The idea that there is a 'hole in the centre' of government had emerged many years before. Harold Wilson had called for greater back-up for the prime minister in the 1960s, while, as we have seen, Edward Heath had lamented 'the Number Ten problem'.[156] The politicians wanted greater control, while the mandarins saw a chance to buttress their own power, so what occurred was a classic fudge—the 'think tank' that the politicians wanted was transformed into the 'Central Policy Review Staff'. The CPRS lasted from 1971 to 1983, when it was abolished by Thatcher, much to the lasting lament of thoughtful Whitehall technicians.[157] It merged long-term thinking with policy analysis and progress-chasing. The Delivery Unit was in some ways a scion. Demand from Blair led special advisers David Miliband, Andrew Adonis, and Michael Barber to combine with the civil servant Jeremy Heywood, who succeeded Sir John Holmes in 1999 as principal private secretary to the prime minister. The history of this landmark Whitehall innovation is currently being written by Michelle Clement at King's College London, with the help of Sir Michael Barber's heretofore unpublished diaries. She has identified Heywood and Barber as the chief originators of the unit:

> Heywood was planning post-2001 General Election reorganisation but Barber came up with the initial design and then refined it with Heywood. I don't think there would have been an effective Delivery Unit without Barber, especially one with so much access to the Prime Minister. Barber's expertise, experience and relationships meant that he was uniquely qualified for such a role. There are other people that played a role in inspiring Barber like David Miliband and Powell who helped start the process off. Once Barber's position was confirmed, Blair and Barber refined what it would focus on and what it would not focus on.[158]

Blair used his 2001 re-election victory speech on the steps of Number Ten—always an insightful moment to know what a prime minister really cares about—to say: 'It is a mandate for reform and for investment in the future and it is also very clearly an instruction to deliver.'[159] Those words 'instruction to deliver' echoed through his second term in office, and took institutional form in the Delivery Unit.

This time, Sir Richard Wilson was supportive, as he explained to the Public Administration Select Committee in November 2001: 'The culture of the Service is going, in some respects, to need to change quite dramatically.' But he added, 'I am proud of it, I think that model is a new model, it has within it some very important new developments, including the simplification and the reduction of the number of targets.'[160] This was a reference to the hundreds of targets that had accompanied the Treasury's initial Public Service Agreement initiative in 1998—reduced to 160 in 2000[161]—by which the Treasury sought to link reform of public services to funding, but which proved complex and ineffective, and which turned out to be another source of friction with Number Ten.

The whole concept of targets became a furore, with opposition coming from those at the front line such as health staff, teachers, and police, who complained that filling in forms on performance kept them away from the delivery of their services. As the idea went, how do you measure and plot on a graph a nurse's bedside manner? But this was too simplistic, and the Public Administration Select Committee said in 2003:

> Every organisation needs to have a means for measuring its own performance internally and in comparison with others, if it is to learn, develop and motivate its staff. None of our witnesses seriously advocated that performance measurement should be swept away, and we recognise that much has been achieved by means of it. The increase in accountability and transparency which targets have brought with them has been valuable. Taxpayers and users of public services have a right to know how well their services are being delivered and who is accountable for them.

It went on to point out that greater empathy and sophistication needed to accompany the evolution of what it called 'the measurement culture'.[162]

Another criticism of the Delivery Unit came from those looking at its constitutional dimension. Technically, secretaries of state are legally responsible to Parliament for what goes on in their fiefdoms. But a prime minister's power means this is blurred in practice. The Delivery Unit took individual highly specific aims and sought to deliver them. But what of the ministers—and senior civil servants—whose departments were being monitored and 'supported'? Michael Barber saw no problem with this. In fact, he explained:

> I said to the permanent secretaries when we were set up in 2001 that I hoped we would be so successful that in three or four years we would be able to abolish the Delivery Unit because they would be good at delivery. When I went back to see them in 2004 to ask them, I said, 'Shall we abolish the Delivery Unit now?' And they said, 'No, we find it very helpful because we like the consistency of the priorities, we like the fact that you have a small number of very helpful people and that you keep us straight and honest and focused on our priorities, even though there are many crises going on affecting all the departments.'

What is more, 'The Delivery Unit enabled the government to keep focused on those priorities even when there were crises pulling the prime minister and other ministers off that core agenda.'[163]

Sir David Normington spoke for many when he praised the Delivery Unit:

> After the honeymoon was over the emphasis was relentlessly and continuously on delivery. There is some cynicism about this now but at the time the focus on the delivery of targets and outcomes was very real and came from the top. And in many areas it produced results.
>
> Most departments had targets and outcomes in their public service agreements for the delivery of which civil servants were accountable and which were constantly monitored. But the four so-called delivery departments—Education, Health, Transport, and Home Office—received extra attention.
>
> In the Department for Education, the Secretary of State and the Permanent Secretary and some other key civil servants were called to Number Ten every six to eight weeks for a stocktake with the prime

minister. We were quizzed on how we were raising standards in schools. The latest data was pored over and analysed. The message about the need to raise standards, to improve discipline and attendance, to be intolerant of failing schools, to drive forward the first programme of setting up sixty academies was consistent and unchanging. We were expected to follow through from the centre to the front line and to know what was actually happening in the school.

Sir David said that 'the prime minister never let up', and that his personal commitment to the Unit was crucial to driving change:

I vividly remember an education stocktake after 9/11, on the morning that the prime minister was departing for Washington to show his solidarity with the American government and people. I have a similar vivid memory of the last stocktake I attended in 2007 when I was in the Home Office, two weeks before the prime minister stood down: when we examined forensically why it was so difficult to return failed asylum seekers to their country of origin. The prime minister was invariably on top of the detail and knew the answers better than the officials in front of him...

These occasions were nerve-racking and demanding, particularly for civil servants who did not know their stuff. But ultimately they were energizing and empowering. In the Department for Education we really were encouraged to believe that that we could change the education system for good and for a time the evidence suggested it was happening. More important we, as civil servants, were being invited to be partners in a great endeavour to modernize public services.

I would argue that this focus on delivery and outcomes was more significant in changing the way the service thought and acted than any individual reform measure. Of course it had its problems. It was too centralist and too top-down. Some targets had a distorting effect. There were problems for civil servants in particular when the prime minister was driving in a direction that the Secretary of State disagreed with. It could be frustrating for politicians and civil servants when a programme which seemed settled received a blast of attention and criticism from Number Ten, which threw everything up in the air.

Nevertheless, for many of the Blair years the leadership from Number Ten was the single most important reason why public services improved. And for me and for very many civil servants who experienced it, it is what made the Blair premiership unique.[164]

Blair became hugely proud of his Delivery Unit. In his memoir he described it as 'an innovation that was much resisted, but utterly invaluable and proved its worth time and time again'.[165] Speaking to the Strand Group at King's College London in 2015, he lauded it as 'quite revolutionary, more so than we realized at the time'.[166]

The revolution occasioned unusual unity between the Blairite and Brownite wings of the coalition. Ed Balls wrote in his memoir:

> In particular, having a Delivery Unit outside the Treasury close to the Prime Minister, coupled with the weekly meetings Tony and Gordon would have with different Cabinet ministers to discuss how they were delivering better public services, worked incredibly well. It was a process which could never have been managed solely from within the Treasury. Of all the reforms dismantled by David Cameron and George Osborne, I think one of the most retrograde steps was their scrapping of the Delivery Unit and the output targets for public spending that we introduced. It was, at best, short-sighted of the Tories to scrap them, and, at worst, a cynical attempt to avoid comparisons with our record under the guise of cutting bureaucracy, but the quality and effectiveness of public services has suffered as a result.[167]

Sir Michael Barber is, however, one of a kind. When he left in 2005, the Delivery Unit never had quite the elan again. It was allowed to wither on the vine after 2007—when it was absorbed into the Treasury—and Prime Minister Brown was heard one day to shout in great frustration, 'Where is my delivery unit? Where is my Michael Barber?'[168] (Brown did try to rehire Sir Michael, as a minister in the House of Lords on the Adonis model, but to no avail.[169]) And, although Cameron did abolish the Delivery Unit in 2010, he in effect recreated it in 2012, renamed away from Blairite connotations as the 'Implementation Unit'.

The evolving Cabinet secretaryship

The unhappiness that had accompanied Sir Richard Wilson's tenure as Cabinet Secretary came to an end with his retirement in 2002. His successor, Sir Andrew Turnbull, had been in the running for the job when Sir Richard was 'interviewed' for the job he took up in 1998:

In [19]97 there were several candidates but the Prime Minister Tony Blair hadn't worked out what the process should be. And it consisted of: bring us in here [Number Ten] to talk to him on something... And then the only idea... that Tony Blair had got was to send us off to talk to Derry Irvine [the Lord Chancellor]... I went around to see Derry Irvine. He was in his dinner jacket at the Lord Chancellor's rather splendid apartments. And he said to me: 'You're a Christ's [College, Cambridge University] man, are you?'... And we talked about Christ's for about ten or fifteen minutes... And then I thought, I've got to get this off this subject because I would need to lay out what I can do with this job. And then I was just about to get to it and he said: 'I've got to go off to my dinner now.' So I completely blew that...

In 2002 it was different in the sense that it was much more systematic. There was a pre-assessment by Civil Service Commissioners... And we were all asked to put in a note on what we would do, that I've always called 'The Prospectus'... it was largely about what I thought he... wanted the Cabinet Secretary to do which was about the reform of the Civil Service, what I thought the changes that needed to be made. And also some structural changes in the role.[170]

Sir Andrew did oversee the splitting of the role, with Sir David Omand (a rival for the Cabinet secretaryship) assuming the position of Security and Intelligence Coordinator, as those issues mushroomed in importance and scope after 9/11, while Sir Hayden Phillips of the Lord Chancellor's Department took over responsibility for the honours system. Sir Andrew retired himself in 2005, by which time the friction of the Wilson years had calmed, as Sir Andrew recognized a changed role for officials away from policy advice. He accepted that Blair wanted not a chief *consigliere*, but a project manager for the Civil Service. Sir Andrew's tenure did not energize the service in the way that Blair desired. His three years, after Wilson's four (both men retiring at 60), compared with an average tenure of eleven and a half years over the preceding 81 years, since the appointment of the first Cabinet Secretary in 1916. Blair got through them at an unprecedented rate.

Gus O'Donnell succeeded Turnbull in 2005 and became Blair's last Cabinet Secretary. His classless accent was a product of a state Roman Catholic school in South London and, while his Master's was from Oxford, he took his first degree at Warwick and and a PhD from

Glasgow, an unusually unprivileged path for the time. 'I always felt an outsider', he told us.[171] A man of 'wondrous interpersonal gifts',[172] in appearance and manner he was the Civil Service mirror image of Blair—to Jonathan Powell, he was 'the first modern Cabinet Secretary in my view, with more sinuous political skills'.[173] Upon his appointment, he announced a 'Capability Review', explaining that this would 'do for departmental capability what [had been] done for delivery'[174] and later explained to MPs: 'What I want the Prime Minister's Delivery Unit to do is to enhance its role by looking at the capability of departments to deliver.'[175]

Sir David Normington explained that, until O'Donnell's arrival, reform of the Civil Service had stalled:

> Tony Blair made two major speeches about Civil Service reform in 1999 and 2004 and in them you can find the same restlessness for reform which he brought to everything. But in truth there was never the same drive for Civil Service reform per se. Indeed it is one of the paradoxes that for all the pressure on the Civil Service to change and deliver, the actual changes to the way the Civil Service was organized and run in this period were modest.

Like Thatcher before him, Blair brought in experts from outside to try to force the pace of change:

> The government went through a phase of bringing in gurus from the private or other parts of the public sector usually to tell civil servants how to improve efficiency. This reflected a frustration that the drive for change was not coming sufficiently from the Civil Service itself. On one memorable occasion in 2003 the Secretaries of State and permanent secretaries of the four delivery departments were called to Number Ten to be told by the PM, with John Birt, the former Director-General of the BBC beside him, that we had to cut our head offices by 30 per cent and to produce by Christmas a plan for doing so.

The Civil Service, however, remained largely unreformed. One reason, said Sir David, was that Blair was 'much more interested in wider public service reform—teachers, health service workers, local government—than in Civil Service reform. You can see that from his speech in 1999, which was much more about modernizing the wider public service.' Another reason was that:

> Tony Blair rightly believed that reform of the Civil Service was the job of the Civil Service leadership; and it was only towards the end of his time, when Gus O'Donnell became Head of the Civil Service, that he had a leader who, he was satisfied, brought a sense of direction and purpose to that task. But by then he was in the ninth year of his premiership.[176]

Conclusion: more spinned against than spinning

As Tony Blair entered his third term, he faced the paradox that, politically, he was running on empty, whereas, as a director of the government machine, he was just getting into his stride:

> I was now completely on top of the policy agenda. I had ministers in key positions who understood what I was trying to do and why...I really did feel absolutely at the height of my ability and at the top of my game. I appreciated the bitter irony that this had happened when my popularity was at its lowest, but I also knew that in May 2005 I had won, not lost, and that there was a residual respect for and attachment to strong and decisive leadership...In my last two years, they would constantly say that we were running out of steam, when on any objective basis we were full steam ahead, at least on domestic reform.[177]

Blair finally understood how government worked—the amalgamation of strong, evidence-backed policy, clearly articulated and driven through the system, properly financed and progress-chased, arguably a great demonstration of what government could do in the modern era. It certainly laid to rest the early view of Blair that he either simply could not 'do' detail or that his barrister training meant he could master a brief but that, once he had won or lost his case, his attention turned elsewhere like a lighthouse.

In retrospect, what did the Civil Service make of Tony Blair? Sir David Normington, who was at the time guardian of the service's ethos as First Civil Service Commissioner, was full of praise when he came to our class in 2016:

> For me personally, and for many civil servants at the heart of the government's policy agenda, the Blair years were some of the best of our careers. We were set an ambitious agenda to change people's lives for the better and to improve public services and we were trusted to be part of the solution and valued for what we contributed. We believed we were doing something important and sometimes it succeeded beyond our expectations.
>
> And yet paradoxically the Civil Service itself did not change much in these years in its structures and its organization. Some of the reforms which I have described were important and lasting but they did not change the Civil Service fundamentally. Maybe this doesn't matter. Most programmes of 'reform' of the Civil Service are dull and uninspiring. What the Blair years show is that what makes the difference is leadership; and in the Blair years we had that in abundance.[178]

Sir Jeremy Heywood, who had been such a central official under Blair and who went on to serve his three successors—and indeed was still in post when interviewed in 2016—would not be expected to be critical, but nevertheless offered a thoughtful assessment that the Civil Service adapted well after the initial shock:

> I don't think there's one view in the Civil Service and I don't think there would have been one view that was fixed throughout all that time. I don't think Tony Blair and his senior ministers used the Cabinet Secretary role to its maximum effect, I think they probably inherited a series of permanent secretaries who were in many cases older than them and they didn't really trust them or they didn't really feel comfortable with them, I don't know whether it was the permanent secretaries' fault. But for whatever reason, the top tier of officials, including the Cabinet Secretary, they didn't have as much impact and influence over the incoming ministers and above all the incoming prime minister and Chancellor as would have been expected. So that set a tone over the New Labour government that it was against the Civil Service, but that is a very big misunderstanding.
>
> There may have been issues with some of the most senior people as there had in fact been when Margaret Thatcher came in, if you recall, so to some extent that's natural, in some cases some of the permanent

secretaries had always intended to retire after the election and stayed on only to see the new government in, so I don't want to exaggerate this. But it was definitely the case that all of these ministers, certainly Tony Blair and certainly Gordon Brown, quickly found civil servants who they thought they could trust, they thought were good, they thought were swinging into action immediately. This wasn't a matter of those civil servants being politically aligned, but they were just civil servants who were keen to impress the new ministers, but also civil servants who liked working for government ministers who had a big agenda of reform...most top-quality civil servants are keen and interested to be asked to advise on major changes in laws and so on, that's what they came to the Civil Service for, to help change things.

So lots of people responded really very positively to the demands of a new government coming in with fresh ideas wanting to change things, wanting to harness the power of government, wanting legislation, and with money, and I would say overall the Civil Service had a very good relationship with that Labour government as it does with all governments. I mean, the caricature of ministers versus officials is just that, a ludicrous caricature, and we go through cycles of the media reporting this, picking up on one observation and extrapolating that. But there's a reason why the Civil Service model endures, which is that fundamentally ministers like having clever people who are loyal to them for their period of office and get in the trenches to help them deliver things, and that was no different under New Labour [than] it has been under the coalition government or the Conservative government we've had since.[179]

The criticism that spin and special advisers undermined the Civil Service is simplistic and misleading in the extreme. 'Spin' was a product of changing technology and increasingly professional media management: something that each prime minister since has embraced. No doubt it was overdone in the initial move from opposition to government, a phase that lasted too long. That it was delivered by Alastair Campbell, one of the most compelling personalities in the New Labour cast, gave it piquancy. He once complained that he was 'more spinned against than spinning',[180] and it was true that after about 2000 the reputation for spin acquired by him, Blair, and New Labour generally allowed journalists to attack any attempt to present the government's case. His status as a special adviser added to the furore about unelected power at the centre, but this was hardly new or something that will be reversed. What is more, the idea that the Civil Service and New Labour were at loggerheads is simply wrong. It is true that some senior mandarins found the New Labour years unpleasant, uncomfortable, and even unconstitutional, and this has informed the debate since, but they were in a minority, largely from the first years.

Governing is never easy. To govern is to choose. To choose is to disappoint. Mistakes are made. But, after a bumpy start, Blair turned out to be one of the most effective prime ministers in operating the government machine.

And, on at least one occasion after he stood down, permanent secretary after permanent secretary at their Wednesday morning meeting lined up to bemoan just how good things had been under Blair.[181]

4

The Treasury: The Brown–Balls Partnership

The history of the Treasury during the Blair years is the stuff of legend. We have seen in the first chapter how the personal rivalry played out between the prime minister and Gordon Brown, the Chancellor for the whole of the momentous decade. In this chapter that rivalry is still apparent, but the focus is on the machinery of government and the major policy decisions, such as granting operational independence over the setting of interest rates to the Bank of England and the decision to not join the single currency. We also look at the troubled legacy of the Treasury and the Labour Party during the twentieth century and assess how this influenced Brown and his unprecedentedly powerful adviser Ed Balls, without whom Brown could not have achieved so much. The picture that emerges is one of ten years of unbroken growth, leading to unprecedented spending on public services and a changed role for the Treasury (one that largely snapped back once Brown was gone), but one that does not support the accusation that the financial crisis that engulfed Britain in 2008 was New Labour's fault.

The rise of Ed Balls

Perhaps the only other time in modern British history that an economic record smouldered so long after the flames had disappeared was the

Thatcherite era, its economic policies still generating debate about their short-term necessity, long-term effectiveness, and the fact that some communities still raged at what they felt was deep unfairness a generation later. For the 2010 general election was dominated on the Conservative side by a determination to blame the deficit on Labour's profligacy in government—rather than on the American-born global financial crisis. David Cameron and George Osborne argued that a structural deficit was apparent before the collapse of Northern Rock, Lehman Brothers, and the Royal Bank of Scotland. While the 2015 election saw a rerun of the same argument, with Ed Miliband as Labour leader and Ed Balls Shadow Chancellor, blasts from the New Labour past, each having been young but influential special advisers to Gordon Brown for much of his long chancellorship—a continuum of nearly two decades.

Balls, especially, was powerful from the very beginning. Described by many during the Blair years as the 'deputy Chancellor', in opposition he had been an informal economic adviser to Brown from 1992, formally appointed in 1994, Treasury special adviser once in government in 1997, and then crowned Chief Economic Adviser to the Treasury in 1999. Here was *the* expert economist fuelling Brown the politician by translating and explaining his complicated boss. How did Balls come to be by Brown's side?

> I was the leader writer at the *Financial Times*, we'd just come out of the Exchange Rate Mechanism (September 1992). Geoff Mulgan had this big event to launch [the think tank] Demos at some restaurant in Islington and I get invited to go. Mo Mowlam [Labour MP and member of the Shadow Cabinet] pulls me aside and has this long conversation with me and the next day rings me up to say you've got to come in and meet Tony Blair. So I come down and have this meeting with Tony Blair in a tiny office with Anji Hunter [Blair's adviser] about employment policy and then he never really followed up, and then Gordon jumped in very quickly afterwards. But when I started with Gordon in autumn of 1992, I had no idea that I was choosing. Tony became leader in 1994 and, in the September, the US raised interest rates for the first time and Gordon was on holiday and I get summoned over to Tony Blair's office

in Parliament to discuss this interest rate thing. I said why it was a problem for Britain, Tony says, 'Can you write me an article?', so I wrote Tony's first article on the economy, which went in his name in the *FT* the next morning and Gordon said, 'Why have you written an article for Tony Blair?' Well, because I thought he is the leader and we all work for him and I think at the time I didn't realize how naive that was.[1]

Balls had risen to public prominence very quickly, unusual for an opposition adviser. In 1994 he had written a speech for Brown which included a reference to 'post-neoclassical endogenous growth theory', which the Shadow Chancellor said was not the stuff of soundbites. (Balls much later explained that it means 'the rules of the game that the government sets on taxes, spending and regulation are not irrelevant to growth but can have a profound impact'.)[2] This attracted the attention of Michael Heseltine, President of the Board of Trade and virtuoso of anti-Labour performances, who gave Balls top billing in his conference speech that year. He told Conservative representatives: 'The speech hadn't been written by Gordon Brown at all but by a 27-year-old choral-singing researcher named Ed Ball [*sic*]. So there you have it. The final proof. Labour's brand new, shining, modernist economic dream. But it wasn't Brown's, it was Ball's [*sic*].'[3]

That Balls and Miliband were on the front line of British politics from 2010 to 2015 meant that their history was very much of the moment, intensely probed and fought over. There had not been a clear-out, a fresh start for Labour. It also meant that no real tell-all narrative memoir emerged until Balls' *Speaking Out* in 2016, followed a year later by Brown's *My Life, Our Times*.[4] Big gaps in the understanding of the period were filled by conjecture and factional briefing and counter-briefing. Furthermore, Brown's intensely difficult three years as prime minister, culminating in electoral defeat, directly after his decade as Chancellor, naturally caused a reassessment of his stewardship of the Treasury. What had seemingly been a great decade of uninterrupted growth for the economy seemed less impressive in hindsight. The leftward shift of the Labour Party after 2010, and especially after Jeremy Corbyn became leader in 2015, saw the New Labour record criticized, often from within Labour itself. Even what had originally seemed a solid success story, the early reform of the Bank of England, became debatable.

The long road to Bank independence

The first important decision of the New Labour Government—and one of the most significant of its entire period in power—was the granting of operational independence to a new Monetary Policy Committee of the Bank of England to set interest rates, a function heretofore exercised by the Chancellor in conjunction with the prime minister. The doyen of economic commentators, William Keegan of the *Observer*, charted how the British aversion to ideology has in reality been a litany of lodestars by which to navigate monetary policy. Dogmatism masked by pragmatism.[5] For example, the Conservative government which embraced the monetarist experiment under Sir Geoffrey Howe, Chancellor in 1979, abandoned the policy by the mid-1980s. Whereas Howe's successor after the 1983 general election, Nigel Lawson, had written in 1978: 'Rules rule: OK?'[6] Seeking new rules to guide policy after measurements of the money supply failed to behave as expected, he tried to persuade Thatcher to join the European Exchange Rate Mechanism but had to settle for a policy, initially covert, of shadowing the Deutschmark, which eventually contributed to his resignation and that of Thatcher's economic adviser, Sir Alan Walters, in 1989. The self-imposed discipline of the ERM was finally embraced just before Thatcher resigned in October 1990. British recession and German inflation following reunification led to mis-matched interest rates which culminated in the conflagration of Black Wednesday in 1992—and the destruction for a generation of the default Tory reputation for economic competence.

It is hard to convey, a quarter of a century later, quite how profoundly insidious Britain's ERM meltdown was, and Prime Minister John Major and Chancellor Norman Lamont's subsequent blood-letting through their memoirs did little to help restore their reputations. Paradoxically, leaving the ERM was christened 'White Wednesday' by Anatole Kaletsky of *The Times*, who held the view that the ERM was shackling Britain to an increasingly sclerotic European economy.[7] It was a factor in an unprecedented sixteen years of unbroken growth between 1992 and 2008—while between the first quarter of 1991 and the third quarter of 2009, the UK's gross domestic product rose by 48 per cent. Put into context, that was against 35 per cent in France, 22 per cent in Germany, 19 per cent in Italy, and 16 per cent in Japan.[8] But the benefits of this economic run did not benefit the Tories. The main effect of the collapse of Major's ERM policy at the time was his political humiliation.

The ERM policy vacuum was filled by a tentative new framework between the Treasury, the Bank of England, Prime Minister John Major, and Chancellors Norman Lamont (1990–3) and Kenneth Clarke (1993–7): an inflation target of 2.5 per cent (along with a quarterly inflation report) coupled with a published account after a six-week delay of Chancellor Clarke and Governor of the Bank of England Eddie George's monthly meeting—'Once I'd labelled it accidentally "the Ken and Eddie show", suddenly it became a major thing,' Clarke remembered. 'It made Eddie George the first governor that 90 per cent of the general public had ever heard of.'[9] Though Gordon Brown had backed the ERM policy to buttress his and Labour's pro-European and economically responsible modernism, and had taken a personal hit when the policy came crashing down, a strategic opportunity presented itself.

Brown and Balls knew their Labour Party history. Brown had completed his doctoral thesis, published in 1986, on the life of James Maxton, leader of the Independent Labour Party in the 1920s and 1930s.[10] Balls had been a teaching fellow at Harvard in the Department of Economics and a journalist for the *Financial Times*, the *Guardian* and the *New Statesman*, and was a keen student of Labour's economic crises past. The dates to make Labour politicians shudder were 1931, 1947, 1949, and virtually the whole of the 1964–70 and 1974–9 governments, years littered by devaluations, rampant inflation, public spending crises, party splits—and, subsequently, a rapid return to opposition. Brown and Balls were obsessed with avoiding the disasters of Labour's past and with taking advantage of the Tories' economic disarray. The precocious Balls in particular had long hankered to reforge British economic policymaking, and audaciously told Labour MP and Treasury adviser Geoffrey Robinson in 1997: 'I've always wanted to sort the Bank out.'[11]

The post–ERM framework led many to believe that the logical conclusion was an independent Bank of England, emulating the examples provided by the German Bundesbank and New Zealand. In private, Nigel Lawson had come to the same conclusion four years before the ERM disaster, submitting a memorandum in November 1988 to Margaret Thatcher setting out a proposal for an independent Bank, first revealed in his resignation speech to the House of Commons eleven months later:

> An independent Bank was to some extent an alternative way of entrenching the commitment to stable prices...An independent Bank would not, of course, have had the merit of ERM membership of replacing discretion by rules. But it would at least, in the words of my paper, 'be seen to be locking a permanent anti-inflationary force into the system, as a counterweight to the strong inflationary pressures which are always lurking'. In particular, it would do something to 'depoliticise interest rate changes'...She did not ostensibly reject it out of hand, but argued that...[it] would look as if the Government were admitting that, after all, it was unable to bring inflation down itself, which would be highly damaging politically.[12]

John Major, who succeeded Lawson as Chancellor in 1989, and Thatcher to become prime minister in 1990, believed that such decisions were an important weapon in a government's armoury, and should be left under democratic control[13]—much the same thinking as Thatcher's. Norman Lamont, Major's first Chancellor, did not start his term in favour but, by the autumn of 1991, privately raised the concept with the prime minister; he sought to include the policy in the 1992 Conservative manifesto, and was much strengthened over independence after the ERM crisis. He even spoke to Blair and Brown on the subject before the 1997 election, saying that it was going to be a winner and in the national interest, so much so that when Brown called him to announce the decision, he said, 'We have decided to take your advice.' (Moreover, Lamont wrote that permanent secretary Burns was 'not at all in favour' and that 'independence had surprisingly little support in the Treasury'.)[14]

Kenneth Clarke, who succeeded Lamont in 1993, and was favourite to win the Conservative leadership contest which followed the 1997 election defeat, apparently told Brown 'he would publicly and strongly oppose the move'.[15] Yet in 2017 he explained:

> I was never against it . . . I've often been accused of being against independence and nobody's found any quotations to support that . . . The reason for me sitting on the fence [in 1997 was that] . . . had I supported independence for the Bank of England [publicly, the Eurosceptics] would have been convinced it was all part of a Euro-conspiracy.[16]

How Labour's Bank policy emerged

The origin of the independence decision in Labour's policymaking is disputed. Until the publication of Tony Blair's memoir in 2010, it was seen as a Brown–Balls co-production. But Blair belatedly laid claim to be the driving force:

> I had no doubt it was right. I had been convinced long ago that for politicians to set interest rates was to confuse economics and politics, the long term with the short term, the expedient with the sensible. I had watched the game played out as governments carefully calibrated the interest rate movements with the electoral cycle . . . The result was the country effectively paid a political premium on the interest rate . . . I had talked about it often with Roy Jenkins . . . Gordon had come to the same conclusion, and so when I suggested it, he readily agreed.[17]

When asked about Blair's words in 2011, Ed Balls 'thought that was a bit odd [but] he was the prime minister so in that sense everything that happened in his government he is entitled to take credit for . . . At all stages, Tony Blair was supportive and he may have been in favour before we realised.'[18] Derek Scott, Blair's economic adviser in opposition and up to 2003 in government, wrote that during the run-up to the Mais Lecture delivered by Blair in 1995:

> I was drafting the speech and discussing its contents with Tony. I suggested that it include a commitment to make the Bank of England independent, something I had been urging on him from the very start. However, Tony was not persuaded about this, largely I think on the sensible judgement that there was little to be gained politically and the costs attached to an early announcement were perhaps too great, but also because Gordon had not made his own mind up.[19]

Balls himself had publicly advocated Bank independence as far back as December 1992 in a Fabian Society pamphlet, *Euro-Monetarism: Why Britain Was Ensnared and How It Should Escape*. Geoffrey Robinson, moreover, claimed that Balls told the future Paymaster General that 'it was his idea, which he had put to Gordon in mid-1995. Gordon discussed it with Tony, who was very pro-independence and it was agreed Ed should take a week off from the day-to-day political battle to write it up.'[20] This happened on 3 March 1995, at a New Forest meeting of the New Labour heads (which much annoyed the uninvited deputy leader John Prescott).[21] The paper that Balls presented to Blair and Brown was entitled 'The Macroeconomic Framework' and described the benefits of an independent Bank along with its knock-on effects vis-à-vis the euro, 'given that the Maastricht Treaty requires moves towards independence'.[22] Balls also said that:

> this reform was vital to Labour winning not just a first, but a second term in office. I must have seemed a bit obsessive about my plan, and —at a time when people were so focused on what we needed to do to get into government—it was genuinely difficult to persuade them to concentrate on how we would avoid stuffing things up when we got there, in the way that previous Labour governments had done on inflation and interest rates.[23]

Balls's planning for the Bank continued throughout the run-up to May 1997. But the Chancellor-in-waiting had yet to take the decision to hand over democratic control—an essentially irrevocable move, almost impossible to unwind barring a crisis. Brown was again demonstrating what initially looked like 'prudence' but came later to be seen as a lack of political courage. Robinson, in 2000, thought this was a virtue: 'It was a pattern of decision taking I was to see often repeated. He was not hasty; he would listen to a lot of people; he would think it over; then he would decide, mostly on his own, and announce his decision. Gordon has great self-reliance and inner self-confidence.'[24] Another admirer of Brown, Bill Keegan, thought that the Bank decision revealed him as 'a great agoniser and this was certainly an issue of such major importance that it called for a lot of agonising'.[25]

Brown's indecisiveness contrasted with his predecessor Kenneth Clarke. Sir Nicholas Macpherson, the official in charge of continuity during the handover of power as principal private secretary to the Chancellor, said: 'The case against Ken was that he took decisions too quickly.'[26]

Clarke explained his approach:

I ran [the Treasury] as a kind of debating society. I liked to have the meetings...liked to encourage a lot of discussion, because that clarifies one's own mind. I rather impulsively came to decisions...the Treasury was the best department I ever worked in because the intellectual quality of the people was undoubtedly higher, almost universally across all the officials, than any other I was in. I could run it like a debating society, because the then permanent secretary encouraged it, Terry Burns, who hadn't started as a civil servant either. But what I liked about it was you could get a group of officials around the table and they would all join in and the most junior guy at the table, just out of school I used to say, no doubt just come out of university with a reasonably good degree, he or she would argue with the permanent secretary, or me, with the same vigour as anybody else. And we would all clarify where we would go. And it was a very stimulating atmosphere, which I used to compare with something like a high table at an Oxbridge College. The mood, I picked up from it, was similar. I used to say they were just like an Oxbridge College—frightfully bright and not one of them capable of running anything. Not actually running anything, but they had policies and ideas—they were brilliant...

I was a complete contrast in every way with Gordon Brown who followed me...I had had this rather impulsive way of making my mind up...Terry Burns [permanent secretary to the Treasury, 1991–8] used to say that he used to come running round the corridor when we had a crisis, so that he got to my room before I had started to decide what we were going to do, so he could talk to me about it . . . Gordon Brown, of course, took ages to take a decision.[27]

Brown confirmed his work-pattern changes:

The way the Treasury then worked was, in my view, unmanageable—gatherings of countless officials assembled around this massive oval table. It was also a waste of valuable time for senior officials, since only one or two of them were ever expected to speak. Almost immediately, I put decision-making on a more focused and professional basis—small meetings, with only relevant officials and advisers present—and I made a point of inviting the person doing the actual work on a project, rather than their superior two or three rungs up, who in the past would attend on grounds of seniority.[28]

Another difference emerged when Brown asked his Private Office what they used to do for lunch with Clarke. An incredulous Chancellor learned that lunch often took place at the Pimlico Tandoori. Sandwiches in the office duly became the new norm.[29]

The tipping point for Bank independence appears to have arrived on 20 February 1997 at a meeting between Brown and Alan Greenspan, the chairman of the US Federal Reserve, who explained that he thought it 'unfair' that politicians were made to take unpopular interest rate decisions.[30] On the last weekend before the May 1997 election Brown demanded Balls dust off the independence blueprint. In Robinson's words, Brown 'felt that the external pressures would inevitably push us into Bank independence and concluded quite sensibly that if that were the case, it was surely better to take the initiative and get the political kudos associated with the move'.[31]

Many discreet conversations took place between the Opposition advisers and senior civil servants before the May 1997 election. Such meetings were first accepted by the prime minister in 1964 to facilitate an efficient handover of power, and the 'Douglas-Home Rules', named after Sir Alec,[32] allowed Brown's lieutenants Balls and Robinson to meet Treasury and Bank officials over almost a year to discuss the fateful Bank decision amongst other policies,[33] as Terry Burns explained:

I had a great number of meetings with Ed Balls, two or three with Gordon—Gordon's mind was on winning the election, Ed was very much planning the programme for after the election—the first almost a year before the election, but particularly from December 1996 onwards. They were very informal, where I would have lunch or breakfast with him and he would go through the agenda of what was on their mind. In headline terms these were things that were known because Gordon was giving lectures and making known what he would do, in terms of monetary policy and comprehensive spending reviews, over EMU [European Economic and Monetary Union], over wanting a welfare-to-work programme, and of course the windfall profits tax on the utilities. These were all major issues and we spent a lot of time trying to firm them up and deciding on the work the Treasury would need to do…they'd had a lot of work done themselves on these topics, they were themselves extremely well prepared…I think that side went pretty well.[34]

Balls corroborated this:'We had been in some quite intense discussions for over a year…I probably spent three hours with Terry twice a week for nine months. Much, much warmer than you might have thought.'[35]

Brown finally takes the plunge

As Margaret Thatcher once said,'Advisers advise and ministers decide.'[36] Brown decided to go for Bank independence just days before the 1997 general election on 28 April: 'The Monday before the election, I had said to Ed Balls that if I became chancellor on Friday I wanted to go ahead immediately with Bank of England independence. Prior to that conversation, we had been working on the assumption that we would deliver independence sometime in a first term.'[37] Balls replied:

'You're right about this, and I don't want to delay. We'll tell them on Friday and we'll move quickly.' I remember at the time taking it in my stride, thinking:'Let's see if he sticks with this.' But I could also sense he was serious. Regardless of the timing, just the fact that Gordon seemed to have made his mind up was significant. For the past three or four years, we'd been discussing whether it was strengthening or weakening for the Chancellor to give up control of setting the interest rates. Gordon never took steps he thought were weakening, so I'd always expected him to be more equivocal on the risks, but this was him at his decisive best.[38]

The Labour manifesto said: 'We will reform the Bank of England to ensure that decision-making on monetary policy is more effective, open, accountable and free from short-term political manipulation.'[39] Peter Mandelson's diary entry for polling day, Thursday, 1 May 1997, intriguingly suggested that Brown had still not definitively decided on immediate operational independence. Mandelson reported that Blair 'wanted my views [on] whether we should press ahead quickly on independence of the Bank of England which he was keen on and pressing Gordon to do'.[40] Balls remembered that 'On polling day, Gordon talked Tony Blair through the plan over the phone... as often happened between them, Gordon most likely hung up thinking everything was squared off, while Tony most likely hung up not entirely sure what Gordon was on about.'[41]

On election day, Burns deduced from a conversation with Balls that 'something is going on on the Bank of England and European front'.[42] The Treasury had spent weeks on the groundwork for bringing Britain into line with European rules on an independent central bank, a legal prerequisite for joining the euro,[43] in case New Labour wanted to pursue it. Balls explained why he and eventually Brown thought the immediate Bank move was the right idea:

> At that time, there was a deeply personalized relationship between the Chancellor and the Governor, Ken Clarke and Eddie George had this continual spat almost weekly in the newspapers and I think what Gordon saw was that the moment he became Chancellor and he got locked in to that kind of relationship where the Governor and he met head-to-head every month. The Governor made his recommendation, the Chancellor then decided, and remembering that pretty much every previous Labour government had a tense relationship with the Governor of the Bank of England, whether it was Montagu Norman in the 1920s or Lord Cromer in the 1960s, the moment you got into that relationship, the danger was that whatever you did was from a

position of weakness. So let's say the Governor says, 'We should raise interest rates by one per cent' at the first meeting, and the Chancellor says 'I'm not sure we can cope with one per cent, why don't we do half a per cent' and the Governor says, 'Well, that's your decision, but my advice is one per cent.' If you then make a move on central bank independence, the danger is it looks like the Chancellor has said, 'This is all too difficult' and therefore it's from a position of weakness and so Gordon therefore decided that the only way to avoid that kind of relationship, if you were going to make the Bank independent, was to do it on the very first day so that you never ever had that kind of tension. We'd done a lot of preparation, all the building blocks, but until that Monday morning, I had no idea that he wanted to go that quickly, and I don't think until the Thursday Tony did either.[44]

In fact, Balls recalled that Blair was surprised: 'I think he fell off his chair when we told him we were going to do it. Bloody hell! He was very pleased.'[45]

Intense conversations ensued once Brown had been confirmed as Chancellor. An invaluable contemporary record of many of these conversations was captured by a Scottish Television documentary team which was filming Brown and his inner circle in those first days. The programme was broadcast as *We Are the Treasury* on 7 October 1997, although copyright confusion between HM Treasury and STV prevented repeats. Burns lamented: 'It didn't help that there was a team from Scottish Television with cameras to make a movie.'[46] Balls told us: 'To be fair to the Treasury—actually to be unfair to the Treasury— nobody was strong enough to say no.'[47] The documentary did not enhance the reputation of Brown's inner circle. Brown said that he had not mentioned Bank independence in the election campaign because no one had asked him. Charlie Whelan was shown saying he was sometimes 'economical with the truth'. Nevertheless, the programme is a valuable contemporaneous record. Balls was filmed explaining the policy: 'In order to do what a Labour government should do, you've got to earn credibility first.'[48]

The meeting that confirmed the decision to give the Bank operational independence with the new prime minister took place at 3.30 p.m. on Friday, 2 May. On the Saturday morning there was a meeting at Tony Blair's house in Islington with Brown, Balls, and Moira Wallace, a Treasury private secretary in Number Ten. Brown later explained:

> At this point, Tony was still working out of his London home and so, over cups of coffee and seated in comfortable chairs, we discussed the change. What would become known as 'sofa government' was quite literally starting in the informal atmosphere of his living room in Islington...Moira, who was as intelligent as she was forceful, had a very different view from mine—and I think Tony's—on how the issue should be handled. She advised us that we ought to wait until we had run the gamut of a whole series of formalities. To be fair, she had been advised by the Cabinet Secretary, Robin Butler, that this was proper procedure, and it was—in normal circumstances.[49]

According to Balls, Wallace said: 'Don't you think, Prime Minister, that we should commission papers and look at this carefully over a period of time and not rush to any hasty decisions?' To which, Tony Blair replied: 'No, it sounds fine to me, these guys know what they're doing, we'll just get on with it.'[50]

The Bank was given a target for inflation of 2.5 per cent, although it was subtly different from the previous target, allowing a 1 percentage-point margin up or down instead of requiring inflation to be 2.5 per cent or *lower*. The governor would be obliged to write an open letter to the Chancellor to explain the situation if this was not met. Balls recalled: 'There were people in the Bank of England who thought we would arrive and try to impose some form of growth target on the Bank as well as the inflation target, so that they had to balance the two, which would have been economically ridiculous.'[51] Treasury officials admired the 'careful plans'[52] for Bank independence that Brown's team produced on arrival, not expecting such 'precise ideas' or 'detailed homework'.[53]

Sir Robin Butler, Secretary to the Cabinet, told Paddy Ashdown, leader of the Liberal Democrats, that New Labour were better prepared than any other government he had worked with, referring specifically to the draft letters prepared for the governor Eddie George,[54] but he was perturbed that Blair and Brown had taken such a momentous decision without recourse to Cabinet. Butler suggested to Blair that the Cabinet should be informed. Blair replied: 'I'm sure they'll agree.' Butler pressed but was told: 'They'll all agree.' Butler's final attempt was to ask: 'How do you know that the Cabinet will agree with the decision when it's still a secret?' To which Blair simply said: 'They will.'[55] And they did. It should be noted, however, that Blair was careful enough to suggest to Brown that he inform former Chancellors[56] along with John Prescott, the deputy prime minister, and Jack Straw, the Foreign Secretary, while Blair himself called David Blunkett, the Education Secretary.[57]

Brown was actually filmed in *We Are the Treasury* calling George Robertson, the new Defence Secretary, with the news:

> I'm taking the chance to honour the manifesto in practice on the question of the Bank of England. I'm announcing that we are going to bring in legislation to make the Bank operationally responsible for interest rates. I just wanted every member of the Cabinet to know and why I couldn't tell people earlier or have a meeting of the economic committee to discuss it or anything was the sensitivity of all this.

Blair and Brown were informing selected members of the Cabinet, not discussing it with them. The first major decision of the new government had been made away from Cabinet. Brown later wrote:

> That weekend we broke with all the conventions—detailed Civil Service papers, long subcommittee meetings of officials then ministers, a Cabinet discussion and decision. While Robin Butler, Terry Burns and Moira Wallace were justified in their reservations, I was absolutely convinced that Britain needed this new start, and the best time to make it was at the very beginning of our first days in power. I was also learning about leadership. Without a clear vision and determination to see it through, you could easily be knocked off course.[58]

Though the main reason for the decision was to take the politics out of interest rate policy, there was another angle to the decision. Lord O'Donnell, later permanent secretary to the Treasury, explained that operational independence was also about 'taking power away from the governor', as it was now one (Eddie George) versus the nine others on the Monetary Policy Committee.[59]

Although Bank independence was announced with speed, it would take a few weeks to set up the machinery. So there followed the only discussions between Blair and Brown, followed by a meeting between Brown and Eddie George, to decide the interest rate. Brown and Balls favoured a 0.5 percentage-point rise to counter any inflationary pressure built up by Kenneth Clarke refusal on three occasions to raise rates in the run-up to the election. George thought it too bold a move, one which might spook the markets, and advised a 0.25 percentage-point rise. Blair agreed, supported by his economic special adviser Derek Scott, and Brown demurred, satisfied that on this issue at least he would not be in the same position a second time.[60] 'Despite a lot of hassle,' wrote Robinson, 'the bank rate was increased by just 0.25 per cent. It was our first run-in with Number Ten. We could do without that. And in future we would be free of it.'[61] But only over interest rates.

We Are the Treasury broadcast scenes of Treasury officials lining the corridors and noisily welcoming the New Labour team. Nicholas Macpherson, who was then principal private secretary to the Chancellor, a position usually subject to public exposure, explained on camera: 'The Treasury's not given to outbursts of emotional enthusiasm and it's in fact a fairly staid, cynical institution, and I was astonished to see all these people standing on the steps cheering genuinely spontaneously and reflecting a wider sense one had on the Friday of a new beginning.'[62] But all was not well. Friction and bad blood between senior Labour figures—in particular with Brown and those around him—and some of the mandarinate was evident from their first days in government in 1997 to the very last in 2010. Brown's wife Sarah in 2011 wrote in her autobiography of Sir Gus O'Donnell as Cabinet Secretary:

> You need to be really confident that the whole of the civil services is there to serve the government of the day...You need to be very confident that what you're getting is that support...and it's a bond of trust. And I just felt at the end that I wasn't confident of that with Sir Gus.[63]

However, as we will see, most of the early difficulties came to be seen as teething troubles and were later smoothed over—remarkably like the picture in Number Ten.

Reaction was overwhelmingly favourable from the press and the markets. Peter Riddell in *The Times* wrote of Brown's 'flying start'.[64] Hugo Young in the *Guardian* lauded the 'economic sense' of the move and its long-term perspective as a 'bulwark against inflation'.[65] A handful of critics did exist. Anatole Kaletsky, for example, denounced the government's 'naïve commitment to transparency'.[66] William Keegan was characteristically frustrated by what he thought was too narrow a focus on low inflation, not enough on growth, and was moreover dismayed by the transfer of policy to unelected officials, something he called an 'insult to democracy'.[67] Nevertheless, the markets welcomed the news.[68]

In 2015, Balls looked back over his handiwork:

When the economy started to slow down, the Bank of England was much more aggressive about cutting interest rates in the autumn of [19]98 into [19]99 than people expected. The way I always thought about it was that if a Labour Chancellor had cut interest rates three months in succession it would have been a crisis. The Bank did it basically nine months in a row and people thought 'Thank God, we've got them now on the case'... Over those two or three years, the way the debate went, the way the Bank operated, and Eddie's contribution, meant that Bank independence went from being something people feared might be unaccountable and undemocratic to something people felt really worked, was more responsive...

One of the things we underestimated was that it actually strengthened the Treasury's hand within Whitehall rather than weakened it. You might have thought that this was the Chancellor giving up power but the reality was it wasn't clear to us that we would end up making very different decisions from the Bank of England; once you'd got the structure right, the decisions they made and the decisions we would have made would have been the same ones, but any time you wanted to get your way with the prime minister, on any economic policy matter, you'd just say—we had a big debate at one point about the minimum wage, where DTI and Downing Street want[ed] to go for a higher minimum wage than the Low Pay Commission looked like they were going to recommend.

Our argument was, we understand the arguments, but, um, how will the Bank of England react? They're independent now. If they end up raising interest rates because they're worried the minimum wage might be inflationary, what do we do? Tony Blair said: 'That settles it then!'...

It also freed us from what was a hugely debilitating monthly cycle. If you look back over the previous twenty years, the Civil Service's senior figures in the Treasury and the Chancellor would probably have spent in good times a quarter of their week, and in bad times most of the time, worrying about monthly interest rate decision making.[69]

Some see giving operational independence for setting interest rates to the Bank of England as 'an incremental change dressed up as a dramatic reform'.[70] It certainly was swimming with a strong historical tide. But this was a brilliant move, one that Labour will long be able to look back upon as a bona fide achievement. If it was incrementally inevitable, then perhaps it was akin to scoring an easy goal in a World Cup final—you had to earn your right to be there, and it becomes legendary. Sir Nick Macpherson went further: 'We should be in no doubt that this was an absolutely critical moment in post-war economic history and took macroeconomic policy off the table for ten years, which is probably the longest period macroeconomic policy had been taken off the table.'[71]

Tension between the Treasury and the Bank

The pre-election Treasury analysis that Bank independence went hand in hand with a snap decision to join the euro in the first wave of 1999 proved false. There was no appetite for that at all, as we shall see. But there was another side to reform for the Bank, and that was a hiving-off of banking supervision with the creation of the Financial Services Authority. This was another point included in Balls's prescient 1992 pamphlet.[72] Though Eddie George saw regulation as intrinsic to the Bank's mission, New Labour had come to the decision, backed by Treasury second permanent secretary Steve Robson, that existing regulation was neither comprehensive nor robustly pursued.[73] While the announcement to grant operational independence was accepted, even welcomed, by just about all, the FSA announcement was botched, drove a wedge between Brown and Burns, and very nearly caused the resignation of the governor of the Bank. Had this happened, it would have been a catastrophic start to a New Labour government desperate to demonstrate competence, comfort with the modern financial world, and a clear break with past Labour debacles.

Burns had been recruited by the Thatcher government in 1980 as a monetarist economist, but had matured into an effective and impartial mandarin, becoming permanent secretary in 1991. He spent a fretful few days after the election writing letters and generally lobbying Brown to de couple independence and regulation. Balls explained to camera their approach: 'The governor had to be presented with a package, make his mind up, then agree to the package. The Bank was getting what it needed to be successful. We needed to ask to get what we needed to make that possible. There couldn't be a negotiation.'[74] The Permanent Secretary and most of his senior colleagues were concerned that a 'big bang' approach to Bank reform was too much, too soon. Only Steve Robson was fully behind the drive to reform regulation and he observed: 'You don't give the good news now and the bad news later.'[75] For Balls, 'It was a big mistake to separate the two letters. I think we knew that at the time.'[76]

The New Labour team initially resisted, fearing leaks and a Civil Service rearguard action but, as one senior official recounted, 'You're Chancellor of the Exchequer, you've only been in the job 24 hours, and your Permanent Secretary has three times tried to advise you to do what you think will be the wrong thing... So Gordon really could not say no to him again.'[77] (Although, as we have seen, Blair withstood Sir Robin Butler's advice to summon a Cabinet meeting on the actual Bank independence decision.) The plan was eventually divided. When Brown met Eddie George, the governor was overjoyed to hear the news regarding operational independence, essentially his heart's desire. The power and prestige of an institution he had been heard to say he 'loved' would be immeasurably enhanced.[78] 'It was,' he thought, 'absolutely the right thing to do.'[79] But Brown and George left the meeting with differing understandings of what had been agreed. Robinson explained the problem:

> The original proposals embodied in a single package of reforms were divided into two separate letters from the Chancellor to the Governor. The first set out the proposals for the Bank's operational independence... The second letter dealt with the removal from the Bank of... its regulatory role... [It] was to be treated as 'confidential' [and] its contents were not released with the press statement handling the independence issue. Predictably, the Governor felt that since the second letter enjoyed this exempt status it was an open matter, up for consultation. This was not the Chancellor's intention.[80]

A fortnight later, the picture turned so sour that all New Labour's good work on the economy was threatened. Derry Irvine, the Lord Chancellor, in charge of the government's legislative timetable, told the Chancellor that there would be time enough for only one Treasury bill that year. Regulatory reform could not be delayed indefinitely and so it was tacked on to the bill establishing the Monetary Policy Committee, 'hardly an elegant solution... the Chancellor had no option but to press on despite what we knew would be a huge row'.[81] *We Are the Treasury* shows Brown explaining it was:

> Very important that the Bank does not start to get a view across that this has been a bad exercise. I'm not saying that there had been great consultation with the Bank, I'm not intending to say that... And I will not make any secret of the fact that the Bank have not really been supportive of this.[82]

Burns explained: 'I was a bit nervous that coming so hard on the heels of the other move that this was quite quick.' He told Brown—*on camera and in no uncertain terms*—'there are two things you should not say, you should not say that this is being done because of Barings and BCCI [banks that had collapsed in 1995 and 1991, respectively], nor should you say that Barings and BCCI could not have happened had this been done earlier', to which Brown replied, somewhat offhandedly, 'Terry, please! I am not proposing to make an issue of the Bank's failures in the past.'[83] One can only repeat that for this kind of exchange—something that has happened as long as there have been ministers and officials but *always* behind closed doors—to be captured on film was, frankly, astonishing. Balls was then filmed talking to the *Financial Times* journalist Robert Peston:

> The Bank wanted to have its cake and eat it. But it was made clear to it many years ago that if we were to move to independence this would happen to regulation. They made no secret that they didn't want it to happen, and they probably would rather it wasn't, but that wasn't really their choice.[84]

Burns had called George after the first meeting to reassure him that the regulatory issue was not imminent and that consultation would of course take place in any event.[85] The governor then explicitly assured the Bank's senior officials that there would be consultation before any decisions were made—now he had to return to them humiliated, the worst experience of his long career.[86] The second meeting of Brown and George on 19 May was, consequently, very uncomfortable (the House of Commons was informed of the reforms on 20 May). The governor was incandescent, thinking that he had been lied to by the Chancellor, and even went public at a press conference on 21 May when asked if he had considered resignation, answering: 'All sorts of things go through your mind.'[87] Burns, who was close to George, later said: 'I was able to calm him down, slow him down, as he was very close to resignation.'[88] (This related to the decision to set up the FSA and remove banking supervision—not the independence decision.) However, Brown was to dismiss this: 'Eddie was later reported as saying that on hearing of my plans he had thought of resigning. But there was no substance to this; he was undoubtedly angry, but I found Eddie more intent on using the initial misunderstanding to claw back some of the powers we were to give to the FSA.'[89]

The New Labour team were unhappy with the governor, hoping he would not seek reappointment for a second term.[90] Robert Peston went further and quoted an anonymous member of the government saying that George had 'played into our hands'.[91] Geoffrey Robinson later wrote: 'Perhaps, so far from Gordon being high-handed, the Governor had overplayed his hand. This seemed uncharacteristic for so skilled a bridge player. Perhaps he had been encouraged to do so. That is how it seemed to me,'[92] a thinly veiled criticism of Burns.

Sir Nick Macpherson was critical of the process but sympathetic to the intent:

> Communication in the early days was hopeless. The Eddie George thing was just symptomatic of a wider set of issues, it wasn't that Gordon Brown was particularly trying to ... he had no interest in upsetting him, it was the last thing on his mind, there was just a hell of a lot going on, they wanted to hit the ground running and inevitably people handling became quite difficult in those circumstances.[93]

What was in no doubt was that Brown was unimpressed by Burns and swiftly returned to a more tightly knit operation in which only Balls was truly trusted. This inevitably brought its own problems, as Macpherson noted: 'One of the difficult things for Terry and myself was that the political team would all go off [to] the top of the Grosvenor Hotel every night and everything would be determined there and then you never quite knew where things were.'[94] This was a reference to Geoffrey Robinson's permanent suite, used as a base for the Treasury team in opposition, a practice which continued as an office-away-from-office for some time into government.

Perhaps the last straw for Burns and the New Labour team came when the *FT* published the latest in what was becoming a series of leaks from inside government, several aimed at Burns. Blair asked the Cabinet Secretary to investigate. Sir Robin Butler naturally contacted his friend Burns, who said circumstantial evidence pointed to Balls and Charlie Whelan. Butler told Blair, who confronted Brown, who called Burns into his office and said if conclusive proof could be presented, he would sack Balls and Whelan. It could not, and Brown decided he would not include Burns in the gathering cold war with Number Ten.[95] This was a graphically poor example of the mistrust that existed in the first year between Numbers 10 and 11, politicians, special advisers, and career officials. It couldn't carry on.

Brown and Balls—the Blair and Campbell of the Treasury

Burns lasted a year until he left the Civil Service:

> If you find yourself as Permanent Secretary in the role where the major impact you are having on people's lives is to be seen to be awkward and to be stopping them doing things they want to do, it isn't comfortable …It was more sensible all round, for everybody, that I should go.[96]

Burns came to be seen as another embodiment of early misunderstanding between New Labour and the Civil Service. The exalted position of Balls was the main cause. He had in effect been promoted above Burns in the Treasury's decision-making processes, in a way that Jonathan Powell and Blair had sought in Number Ten, but which had been frustrated by Sir Robin Butler.

Balls was trusted by Brown in an unprecedented way, a tough, yet incredibly supportive special adviser to a Chancellor like no other: 'My role was always to be quite robust. It was necessary. But I actually generally had good relationships with him all the time he was at the Treasury.'[97]

Not only did Balls become the conduit from Chancellor to machine and vice versa, but he did it at a time when the Treasury was changing away from what ex-Treasury official Peter Jay once described as a 'suffocating layer cake of successive administrative generations filtering every initiative to purest innocuity'.[98] Balls said he and Brown tried to cut through the layers:

> [We] helped to drive what was an evolving process of culture change in the whole Treasury, most importantly in terms of changing the policy-making process from an entrenched hierarchy into a true meritocracy… We always insisted on having in the room the individuals who had actually done the work on an issue under discussion, not the people who had signed it off. And when Gordon wanted to discuss any particular point, we'd tell him who we regarded as the best person to speak to.[99]

Balls thought the effect was to increase the self-confidence of Treasury civil servants, which in some cases was already high. Sir Nick

Macpherson said: 'Much as I think the Civil Service important, I'm afraid I've always seen myself as a Treasury official first and a civil servant second.'[100] The officials debated at all levels, but then came to a collective decision, at the apex of a solid triangle—more institutionally powerful than that of the Number Ten–Cabinet Office near merger which Blair was presiding over, with its disparate units devoted to everything from Civil Service reform and social exclusion to intelligence assessment, and in different physical locations.

Moreover, Balls demonstrated his foresight had been right to reject an Order in Council giving him explicit authority to direct Treasury officials (see chapter 3), which paradoxically let him assume an informal power of pivotal significance. His links with and understanding of the Treasury went back several years. While Brown's Treasury experience, pre-government was non-existent—'I had been a Member of Parliament since 1983, I had never once, in those fourteen years, crossed the road from the House of Commons into the Treasury. I had never been inside it or sat down with any of its senior officials'[101]— Balls had worked in the Treasury in the summer of 1989. Furthermore, he had gained a place on the Civil Service fast-stream scheme after graduation, but deferred the full-time post in favour of a Kennedy Scholarship at Harvard University. He appraised the department fast:

> For all the arcane practices, this was the Treasury, the beating heart of economic policy, the most powerful department in government, the place where economic and political history was made. And what struck me most about the Treasury back in 1989 was the sheer excellence of the people who worked there, the volume of data they had access to, and the quality of their research and analysis. My boss was a first-rate economist and a wonderful teacher. It was without question a Rolls-Royce operation, even if it was a rather vintage model.[102]

As a result, Balls told us:

> I think I understood quite a lot about the culture . . . I always had a really close relationship with the Treasury principal private secretary and I never ever wrote, there's no piece of advice in email or note to the Chancellor from me saying here is my view and why it's different from

the Treasury because we never did it that way, and the only reason you were ever in need of an Order in Council is that somehow you were asserting your right to have an alternative view or the most important view or the decisive view, but I didn't think it was necessary.[103]

The new regime's approach did attract criticism, with Balls accused of being over mighty:

What I did the whole time, myself plus two or three key policy-forming civil servants, most important of which would have been in the Treasury Gus O'Donnell, in the government, me and Jeremy Heywood when he was working for Tony Blair, we would basically hold meetings in the Treasury [and in the now closed Churchill Cafe on Whitehall across from Downing Street—'canteen government', according to Sir Jeremy[104]—especially when tensions between Blair and Brown were high] where we would talk through what we're doing, what the outcome was we were trying to achieve, what the policy should be, where we were trying to get to, reach a view in the meeting and that view would be the advice that would go to the Chancellor and the advice was always written by the civil servants, it was never cleared by me, it was never vetoed by me, it was never second-guessed by me, but it was also the case that they never really put up advice I didn't agree with because we'd gone through that process...

The Civil Service never wants to put up advice to the ministers which the ministers think is the wrong advice. Challenging advice is important, but not if you don't understand what you're doing: 'Where did this come from, it's out of left field!' Especially in the early period of government you need to have a person who together you can work out what we're trying to achieve and where we're going. If the independence, objectivity or critical faculties of the Civil Service are suspended during that process then that's very bad but I think most people whom I worked with in the Treasury would have thought the opposite. I would spend more time challenging them than they would challenging me, but the result was we worked it out.

Terry Burns used to complain that there was a paper flow problem, that I would hold things up. The truth was the opposite of that, it wasn't that I ever said to the Treasury that you can't put that piece of advice up to the Chancellor, it was that the Treasury didn't want to put up advice to the Chancellor until they had had their meeting with me because they knew that was the best way to work out what we were trying to achieve, and you could see how if you were the person who used to be the clearing house that would be a bit frustrating. But it wasn't being imposed by me, it was the other way round.[105]

Sir Nicholas Macpherson corroborated the view that Balls became a conduit between the Chancellor and the Treasury: 'In part, yes, driven as much by Gordon Brown's style of working',[106] a man who was 'remarkably uninterested in the trappings of power', who found 'multitasking really quite difficult' and had an 'element of the tortured genius about him'[107]:

> Gordon Brown was far more interested in big-picture objectives than the rather boring sort of detail of how you got from here to there, he was interested more in ideas than the specifics. Having a very lateral mind, I think he just was not someone who was particularly turned on by churning through the rather sequential, linear bits of Treasury advice. He preferred to develop his thinking by writing speeches, writing things himself which allowed him to grapple with the arguments. So he desperately needed someone who would complement him by delivering on the detail and that is really where Balls came in. He was like some sort of *consigliere*-type figure, a man of affairs, whose job it was basically to deliver. Now Brown had huge trust in him based on their time in opposition because this was the guy who could get through an extraordinary amount of work, had a very impressive intellect, and he probably had a lot of influence in influencing economic strategy in opposition, because again Brown just was not very interested in the deep detail of economic strategy and so it worked quite well.

This kind of relationship was not, however, what Treasury civil servants had been expecting, according to Macpherson:

> The issue of 1998 was that the senior officials couldn't quite come to terms with the fact that if you wanted to influence and develop policy you probably wanted to engage more with Ed Balls than with Brown, because with Brown you probably wouldn't get an answer, you just get some lateral question. I think the skill which you had to develop over time was, not to forget about Brown, because Brown was still Chancellor and ultimately took the decisions, but there were whole areas of policy which actually Balls was the special adviser lead—but you kind of had to realize that you had to work with and through Ed Balls as much as with Brown because often it would only

be Ed who could intermediate with the Chancellor and get him to sign up to a policy.

Macpherson explained how Brown worked through Balls and Ed Miliband, his special advisers:

Brown had many positive qualities but one thing that made him very difficult to work with was, if you asked him a straight question, would you get a straight answer which would allow you to move a policy on to the next stage? It wasn't as if he was being sort of clever or obstructive or annoying, it was just not how his mind worked, so the challenge was to get him signed up to the broader strategy which he'd be very keen on. For example, I worked on tax credits, you know he was very keen to promote this agenda. He saw it very much as a way of how you could legitimize giving more money to the less well off in society. In that instance, I would work with, say, Ed Miliband, to develop the policy detail, it would be Ed Miliband's and my role to test the assumptions, whether we could make it work, we'd have meetings with the Inland Revenue and so on, and having satisfied ourselves with that, Brown would sign off the policy and he would want to be able to articulate what it meant in a Budget speech. But it wasn't really his thing to spend lots of time worrying about disregards or tapers and the other really tedious aspects of what constitutes a tax or benefit policy.

Actually, there's a real risk for any minister that if you get too involved in the detail you start to miss the big picture and, certainly as Chancellor Brown had a very good grip of the big picture and the overarching story of what he was about and probably did that better than any Chancellor I've come across, with the possible exception of Nigel Lawson.

My view of Balls and Miliband—I worked extensively with both of them—was on the one hand these were relatively young people suddenly immersed in a job that gave them a lot of power and influence and I'm quite sure that back in 1997, occasionally, that might have gone to their heads, but actually what was a pleasure was working with people who were real experts. They had a deep understanding of what they were trying to do and they were incredibly enthusiastic and driven, and I personally enjoyed working with them a lot.[108]

Balls said he and Ed Miliband, far from lording it over civil servants, saw it as their job to restrain Gordon Brown:

I was always seen as a cautionary influence around Gordon when we were at the Treasury, as was Ed Miliband. The then Permanent Secretary,

Sir Andrew Turnbull, gave an interview to Larry Elliott [of the *Guardian*] early on in our time in the Treasury in which he said there were two types of advisers: amplifiers and absorbers. And the reason why the Treasury worked well in those years was that both Ed and I were absorbers who would not wind Gordon up but hold him back, make certain he was sure, get the evidence, test every issue.[109]

For Sir Terry Burns, an illustrious career had come to an abrupt end due to the new Treasury culture:

There was a feeling, inevitably, that somehow or other the organization had become itself associated with the policies of the outgoing government. The new ministers arrived with their supporters and they adopted a style of working they had established when they were in opposition. They had won the election so they thought that they'd been doing it pretty well... They wanted to carry on working the way they had done; they wanted to have private telephone calls which were not recorded; they wanted to negotiate with people without notes being taken; they wanted to have a lot of things done in a sense 'off piste'... I think the formalization of process... in [19]97 happened quite slowly...

The actual working style was difficult, partly because of the Chancellor's own particular working style. Then there was the cost-benefit balance of Ed Balls, who is extraordinarily clever and was right on top of all the policy, but it meant that he became the Chancellor's real filter and so our official teams had to spend a lot of time dealing with Ed rather than the Chancellor. The Chancellor really wanted to spend his time with relatively few people. He wanted things sorted out and then put to him, where he could reflect and think about it and weigh the messages he wanted to get out, leaving others to do the detailed work and this was a huge change.

I wouldn't say they were rude or anything. But it was a way in which the Chancellor wanted to work and it's done him pretty well in his life. I think that people who lead organizations have a right, frankly, to have quite a lot of scope over how they wish to organize their own lives and how they want to make their decisions; whether they want to make them around a table with twenty people the way that we had basically done business, or whether they wanted to have this filtering.[110]

Brown provided an intriguing thought in his memoir when he compared and contrasted his productive Treasury days with those less successful ones in Number Ten:

At the Treasury I brought together a team of civil servants and advisers who grew in government and learned together. As prime minister, I found that after the great collective efforts to surmount the initial crises of my first months in Number Ten—from the terrorist attack to foot and mouth and Northern Rock—engendering the same kind of team spirit we had in the Treasury was more difficult. In part, it was because after ten years in power Labour was running out of steam. In part, it was the modern nature of prime-ministerial politics, having to handle a multiplicity of crises in a twenty-four-hour cycle. In part, it was the difficulties in creating the right balance between ministers, officials and advisers, which meant I found myself with too little time to focus on longer-term strategic issues where I think I had most to offer and where my input might have made more of a difference.[111]

One might also suggest, in part because Balls was not central to Brown's operation by 2007 (of this, more later).

Sir Nick Macpherson acknowledged the pain and the wonder of a peaceful democratic transfer of political power when he observed:

There was a brief period where you thought this is a transition and then things will settle down, and they did settle down, but they didn't settle down to the old model, it was a new equilibrium...Through [19]97, [19]98, [19]99 there was a slow evolution...By about [19]99 it had adjusted and moved on...The problem with 1979, the earlier sea change, had not been about personalities and the way the Civil Service worked because the Tories had been in power as recently as [19]74, it was that the Civil Service simply didn't understand and couldn't absorb what the Thatcherites were on about...In [19]97 there had been huge preparation...We were all over the policy, there were about 400 pages of briefing, nearly none of which ever gets read...Policy-wise we were incredibly well prepared. I think the Treasury high command were not prepared for the sea change in political style.[112]

Ed Balls agreed that Treasury civil servants had 'spent a huge amount of time preparing for the implementation of our new policies, but did very little to prepare for Gordon's personality, and that made things very tough when we arrived'. He wrote in his memoir:

We faced a constant battle in the early weeks and months, with the officials saying, 'This is how it works,' and us saying, 'Yes, but this is how Gordon works.'...For all of his passion and brilliance on the big picture, Gordon was never very good at making the Civil Service machine work for him.[113]

Macpherson also saw New Labour's arrival as the changing of the generational guard:

Time has elapsed and it's amazing how time does give you perspective. My view of what happened in 1997 about the Civil Service and New Labour is that this is as much a generational thing as anything else...

There were very few civil servants in the Treasury born, say, between 1955 and 1963, because there were recruitment freezes when this lot all graduated in the early [1980s] and so increasingly you had almost a bifurcation. You had a whole lot of senior civil servants who were probably past fifty; you had a lot of younger civil servants who around 1997 were between thirty and thirty-five; I was slightly older because I came in by accident, born in 1959 so I was thirty-eight in 1997. If I define myself as the top end of that younger age group, we'd all greatly enjoyed working for Ken Clarke, we were very motivated but we had only worked under Tory governments, and wanted to experience a Labour government. We knew the world was changing. Blair and Brown represented a significantly younger generation. They were born in the 1950s. Clarke was born in 1940. Major the forties [specifically, 1943]. There was a generational shift here. I think people recognized there could be a different way of working, but they found it difficult to adjust. There was huge energy and enthusiasm created by this new government coming in...

My view of [19]97 was, yes, there was a degree of confusion. If you were at the top of the Treasury, the role of special advisers was very novel but, if you were a younger person, you thought fine, this is just a new government with a new way of working. And so my view was that it's a bit like Bob Dylan's 'The Times They Are A-Changin'.[114]

And back to the TB-GBs

After just a fortnight in power, the New Labour Chancellor and his Treasury team had scored a mighty victory with Bank independence, one which was to shape the future for economic policy and set the pattern for relations within the Treasury. Operational independence over interest rate decisions was not just a success, one that was hardly questioned for two decades, but underpinned a decade or so of unbroken growth to add to the five years already banked, in total sixteen, unprecedented in the history of the UK, and unmatched by any near competitors. It immediately cemented Brown as a huge figure, above his Cabinet colleagues and strengthened his wing of the New Labour coalition.

In hindsight, Blair rued the power he had ceded:

> I allowed Gordon to make the statement [on Bank independence] and indeed gave him every paean of praise and status in becoming the major economic figure of the government. I did so firstly because I thought he deserved it, secondly because it was good for the whole thing not to look like a one-man show, and thirdly not doing so would have created considerable tension. But it had an unfortunate and long-lasting consequence. I have many faults, but one virtue I have is that I don't mind big people around me . . . So when I consciously and deliberately allowed Gordon to be out there as a big beast, as the acknowledged second most powerful figure in the government, I did so without any fear of being eclipsed or outmanoeuvred . . . The office were less sanguine. Alastair [Campbell] in particular worried that a picture was being drawn that I was 'the chairman' or 'president', and that Gordon was the 'chief executive' or 'prime minister', which, as he pointed out with vigour, easily translated into the person who simply does the glad-handing, and the hard-working guy who runs the country.[115]

According to Terry Burns: 'He was a prime minister not in control of his economic policy and people in Number Ten hated this, *hated* it.'[116]

While the endemic tension between a prime minister and a Chancellor over interest rates had indeed been removed, the difficulty between the two biggest beasts was only in its early stages. Sir Nicholas Macpherson explained that Brown's determination to be not just number two in the government but to push constantly to be number one, brought about a renaissance in Treasury confidence:

> You had a Chancellor who could get things done, which was absolutely critical. I go back to the Bank of England independence: 'Don't you have to get that agreed by the Cabinet?', 'No, I'm seeing Tony

tonight, I'll sort it out, we'll do it.' And if you're in the Treasury, you want to be involved in things happening. By 1997, there's a general view that it was time for a change, you could do things differently. It was not just about the Bank of England; it was also about looking at tax and spend, public services, looking at how you got people into work, looking at poverty, these were all really exciting agendas. Now, with the benefit of hindsight, making progress on these things is a hell of a lot more difficult than it appeared in 1997, but in 1997 the starting point was always that these things had been starved of money so if we can just get some money and then intervene in a sensible way then you can actually make a difference. The Treasury as an institution likes powerful Chancellors, it likes Chancellors who can get things done. If you work in the Treasury, it's not your problem how the Chancellor engages with Number Ten. You want a Chancellor who can go to Number Ten and come back with agreement to do what he wants and what the Treasury will have advised him to do. That was extremely liberating because, even working in the Chancellor's office, historically you were slightly patronized by the Number Ten private secretaries: you knew you weren't allowed in meetings because Number Ten jealously guarded access to Number Ten. But that changed in [19]97.[117]

The 1994 Granita deal (see chapter 1) in effect divided Whitehall between those departments Blair would take the lead on and those in which Brown's word held sway. But what of those 'wicked issues' which crossed departments? And to what extent would Blair and Brown's understanding of Granita remain constant or be a cause for dramatic instability? Balls described the approach and ambition in *We Are the Treasury*:

> We had all been frustrated for ages about not having responsibility, not having machinery to do things and we've got on despite that and suddenly there's this whole place designed to make this happen and to do things. It's great . . . The only point of doing the things we're doing in terms of stability is in order that we can do what we want to do in terms of education, of unemployment, fairness, if you don't do those things then this is all a joke. This is not some kind of ego trip for the Chancellor. He doesn't want to be a traditional Tory Chancellor, he wants to be a Labour Chancellor. But Labour Chancellors have got

blown away in the past by not doing tough things first. But if we don't meet our Labour objectives then it was a waste of time.

New Labour had done its homework, won big, imposed political control, and made early historic moves. Internal challenge had been dismissed. Though narrowly avoiding a very early and messy resignation of the Governor of the Bank of England, and forcing the somewhat unedifying retirement of the Treasury permanent secretary, Brown, Balls, and the rest had forged a powerful start to the new government. The decision over Bank of England independence was hugely successful, and testament to the quality of the New Labour team.

The great euro decision

The old order at the Treasury had been swept away. The hierarchy that would sustain it for the foreseeable future had been set—at least until Ed Balls left in 2004, won a seat in Parliament at the 2005 election, and returned in 2006 as a junior minister, Economic Secretary to the Treasury. Those not in tune with the new times had gone. The internal battles were over. The competition in future would be an outward-facing one across the rest of government and beyond. The first of these came with the perennial challenge of European policy. One of the monumental decisions facing the new government was whether it should join what was to become the single European currency.

As Balls reflected on his time in government after losing his seat in 2015, he was keen to counter the idea that New Labour's entire history had to be seen through the prism of the battle for supremacy between Tony Blair and Gordon Brown:

> It is well known that one of the great political battles of recent history was fought between Blair and Brown. But ironically, if any two people demonstrated the ability to maintain their essential kinship whatever their own rivalry and the day-to-day difficulties, arguments and conflicts going on beneath them, it was Tony and Gordon.[118]

While Blair and Brown's relationship did not break down to the point of resignation, the tension between them coloured much of the period. The decision on the euro was one of the first big clashes.

Charlie Whelan, the Chancellor's press secretary and a special adviser, caused especial difficulty for Blair and his press secretary, Alastair Campbell, with his aggressive and unbridled support for Brown. A former foreign exchange dealer and member of the Communist Party, Whelan became a researcher in the Amalgamated Engineering and Electrical Union, a forerunner of the Unite trade union. He was recommended to Brown by Peter Mandelson,[119] somewhat 'ironically, given the intense fights they would have later', wrote Brown in his memoir.[120] Whelan promoted Brown irrespective of, and often in conflict with, the wider view of the government and certainly its leader. In opposition, all focus for Labour was on the winning the election. But, once won, Blair sought to stamp his authority on Brown's political team. Just after the exit poll was published on 1 May 1997 suggesting the landslide, the soon-to-be Prime Minister demanded that the soon-to-be Chancellor's special advisers, Charlie Whelan and Sue Nye, be excluded from the move into government. Brown refused, a first test of his own independence. Balls said that Brown could not have agreed to Whelan's exclusion, 'not least because I regarded Charlie as so essential to our operation I would have resigned in protest'.[121] Lord Burns recalled the tension:

> The relations with Number 10 were terrible. Most of my problems weren't necessarily because of the relationship between the Chancellor and the prime minister but between the team supporting the Chancellor and the team supporting the prime minister. On the first day, I had a message indirectly from Number 10 telling me that the prime minister didn't want Charlie Whelan to come to the Treasury as special adviser and would I like to stop it? I said that's very interesting, but it's the prime minister who approves all appointments of special advisers and if the prime minister doesn't want Charlie Whelan to be in the Treasury it is a matter for him... 'Oh no, we can't do that!'[122]

Blair and Campbell's fears were confirmed, however, in Whelan's first few months as a special adviser. Anonymous quotations later attributed to him included: 'Blair's lightweight'; 'He's not real Labour, Gordon's doing all the real work'; 'Blair doesn't understand anything about economics'; and 'Gordon has all the power because Tony's so useless.'[123] An infuriated Number Ten had no doubt at the time that they were Whelan's work.

The euro debacle in the autumn of 1997 provided another early case study of Blair-Brown dysfunctionality, not to mention laying bare the mechanics of New Labour spin, and all around one of the most profound issues facing modern Britain—an 'extraordinary mishap...a mess', according to Burns.[124] The question of the single European currency had dogged British politics for a decade, providing the final denouement for Thatcher and the destabilizing backdrop to the entire Major premiership. New Labour positioned itself from the start as pro-European, partly to distance itself from the wilder excesses of 1981–3, when Labour's policy had been one of withdrawal from the European Community, but also to seek to embarrass the increasingly Eurosceptic Conservative party.

Sir Stephen Wall, the UK's Permanent Representative to the EU in Brussels from 1995 to 2000, noted that the difference between the two parties was more apparent than real:

> In practice, both parties had promised a referendum on entry into the single currency and neither was ready to recommend membership. However, as the 1997 general election approached, hostility to the single currency, and indeed the EU as a whole, grew in the Conservative Party while Labour's approach became more positive.
>
> Nonetheless, what is interesting is the similarity, rather than the differences, between the manifestos of both parties...The Conservative manifesto kept open the option of joining the single currency while stressing the importance of the opt-out and of a referendum. The Labour manifesto...talked of the 'formidable obstacles' in the way of Britain joining in the first phase should [the single currency] go ahead in 1999. It emphasised the triple safeguard of the need for a favourable decision by Cabinet, a vote in favour in Parliament, and then a referendum...
>
> This caution on the part of the Labour Party reflected the lack of popular support for EMU [Economic and Monetary Union], the need to avoid alienating the Murdoch press...and an unsurprising reluctance

on the part of New Labour to believe that their lead in the opinion
polls would translate into victory on the day.[125]

Opinion polling throughout the 1990s consistently showed a clear
majority of the electorate against joining a single European currency.
John Major sought valiantly to keep open the option of joining should
the euro prove a success, trying to balance his increasingly Eurosceptic
party with strong pro-Europeans in the form of heavyweights Chancellor
Kenneth Clarke and Deputy Prime Minister Michael Heseltine. The
Conservatives' civil war concealed Labour's similar ambivalence. Blair
had written a pre-election article for the *Sun*, 'My Love for Pound', an
extravagant attempt to align with popular Euroscepticism without
ruling anything out: 'I know exactly what the British people feel when
they see the Queen's head on a £10 note. I feel it too.'[126] Andrew Adonis
thought, 'Tony didn't dare move on the Euro before the 1997 election
because he was simply not prepared to have a full-frontal argument with
the Tories and the Murdoch press. He thought it might imperil the
election; but in truth, Tony never liked arguments to his right, only to his
left, and the problem with the Euro is that it united the entire Right, plus
Murdoch and [*Daily Mail* editor, Paul] Dacre.'[127]

The electoral landslide of 1997 provided a temptation to spend the
massive political capital. Certainly, this was the advice to Blair from
Roy Jenkins when the great political historian, ex-Labour Chancellor,
and former President of the European Commission urged him to
become 'the weather-maker', a phrase he borrowed from Churchill's
description of Joseph Chamberlain.[128] Jenkins artfully dangled in front
of the young prime minister the prospect of a lasting legacy, finally
putting Britain truly at the heart of Europe.

Blair came to be seen as more pro-euro than Brown. But this was
not the case in the run-up to government in 1997. 'Oddly—you may
think now—' Balls told us in 2016, 'Gordon was always mistrustful of
what Tony's intentions were towards Europe, Gordon was more pro-
European.'[129] But neither Blair's nor Brown's position became clear
until press speculation—such as by that Robert Peston in the *Financial*

Times, 'Cabinet shifts towards EMU'—began to move the markets in late September 1997.[130] The government had to respond.

Robert Peston recounted most of the ensuing mess in his book *Brown's Britain* in 2005. The book itself was part of the Blair–Brown conflict, then reaching its penultimate stage at Blair's third election, and so Peston's account, though accurate, was mostly based on off-the-record sources. When Ed Balls came to our class, he placed the story on the record, with the added benefit of hindsight:

> The day before, on the Thursday [16 October 1997] Gordon Brown and Tony Blair met. As so often happened, they had a conversation that wasn't really overheard by anybody else. Alastair Campbell was there but I'm not sure if he was concentrating. I was ill, actually, at home. Gordon was really worried that instability over whether we joined the single currency in the first wave was going to destabilize us. He had a conversation with Tony Blair. We had already spoken to Alastair about doing an interview to say we weren't going to join the single currency in the first wave. Gordon has a conversation with Tony where Gordon says he told Tony and Tony agreed. They come out of the meeting and Gordon says to Alastair, 'It's all agreed.' Alastair says, 'Fine.'
>
> On the Friday, Gordon is doing the 'interview' with Phil Webster. [Brown later added: 'Ed Balls called Philip Webster, the Westminster political editor of *The Times*, and it was agreed to give him an exclusive interview on the euro. At the time, Philip was out playing golf with his opposite number from the *Sun*, Trevor Kavanagh.'[131]] The interview didn't actually happen until four in the afternoon. I was speaking from home, ill, to Phil, where I said, 'I'm not sure I can get Gordon to speak to you until four but I can tell you what he is going to say,' and Phil Webster said, 'Don't worry, I've already spoken to Alastair, I know what the story is.' Alastair, not wanting to be behind the curve, and thinking that Gordon and Tony have decided to rule out joining the single currency, has already rung Phil Webster from Number Ten on Friday morning to say we're all on course for ruling out the euro. Alastair Campbell did that. I'm listening to this and thinking I'm not quite sure what is going on.
>
> I then speak to Phil, in a sort of clearest hint yet. Gordon, from Scotland, has a short conversation with Phil where he basically pretty much says the words that have to be said but, you know... Phil on the basis of

the conversation he's had with Gordon which was a bit unclear, the conversation he's had with me which is considerably clearer, and the conversation he's had with Alastair Campbell which is very clear, then writes the story with the headline, 'Britain rules out joining the single currency'. Phil writes the story because he's been told it by Gordon Brown, me pretty much, and Alastair Campbell definitely. The paper comes out. Tony Blair says how have we ended up so definitively ruling out the single currency and starts trying to ring people. He can't get hold of Gordon, [who] doesn't answer his phone. Can't get hold of Alastair Campbell.[132]

As news of Webster's front-page report spread, Charlie Whelan's phone became white-hot. That he was in the Red Lion pub across the road from Downing Street was not unusual, nor was the fact that he conducted his business pint in hand. Unfortunately for him, he was overheard by a Liberal Democrat staffer, and the euro story became fuelled by the idea that the Chancellor's press secretary, a controversial special adviser to boot, was making policy on perhaps *the* issue of British government for decades from a bar, after alcohol.

The media smelt a crisis, perhaps even a scandal. But Balls was adamant that this was a series of misunderstandings, rather than a conspiracy by the Treasury against the prime minister:

> Tony Blair through the Downing Street switchboard rings Charlie Whelan in the Red Lion. The [Liberal Democrat] special adviser overhears Charlie Whelan taking a call from the *Prime Minister*. The prime minister says, 'Is it true we're ruling out joining the single currency?' and Charlie says, 'We've already done it! It's on the front page of the *Sun*!' Tony comes away thinking, 'Oh my God, how has this happened?' then rings Alastair who says, 'But I thought you agreed it with Gordon on Thursday in the meeting.' So the idea that this was a Treasury manoeuvre over Tony was not true.[133]

Much later, however, Brown was to write: 'According to one account, Charlie suggested to the *Sun*'s editor Stuart Higgins that the headline in his next day's edition should be 'BROWN SAVES POUND'.[134]

A journalist called up the Treasury and a spokesperson, unaware of the activities of some of New Labour's finest, stated unequivocally

that there had been no change in the government's official position.[135]
But when it emerged that neither the Deputy Prime Minister, John
Prescott, nor the Foreign Secretary, Robin Cook, had been consulted,
the lack of collegiality at the top of New Labour, just months into
power, was laid bare. Over that fraught weekend, even Peter Mandelson,
at that time Minister without Portfolio and the leading pro-European
and specifically pro-euro member of the government—not to mention
one of Blair's closest confidants—had cause to remonstrate with a rattled
prime minister that he had not been party to this policy shift. Worse,
an openness to adopting the euro was one of the reasons big business had
in recent years leant towards New Labour rather than to the Europhobe
Tories. The Conservative Party saw a rare chink in New Labour's armour
and demanded an emergency Commons statement.

When the markets opened on Monday, 20 October, one of the
central questions of the government's economic policy was still unclear.
Brown issued a holding statement that the government would do
what was right in Britain's interests. While the media bayed for blood,
no real market crisis arrived, providing the government a little time.
Throughout the rest of the week and over the weekend, with Blair at
a Commonwealth summit in Edinburgh, Brown and Mandelson,
along with the senior teams of Number Ten and the Treasury, were
joined by Derry Irvine, the Lord Chancellor and the prime minister's
troubleshooter, in agreeing a statement to be delivered by Brown in
the Commons on 27 October. Number Ten wanted the Chancellor to
apologize for the debacle. Number Eleven resisted and turned defence
into attack by latching onto opposition leader William Hague's shift
towards ruling out the single currency for a decade, which gave
Labour a chance to claw back some ground with the pro-European
lobby. The statement and subsequent debate on what Brown described
as 'the most important question the country is likely to face in our
generation' went smoothly and Brown managed to put a firm stamp
on what had been a shambles of a week. In fact, his statement set the
tone for the next six years: 'We believe that, in principle, British membership of a successful single currency would be beneficial to Britain

and to Europe; the key factor is whether the economic benefits of joining for business and industry are clear and unambiguous.'[136]

For Brown:

> There was not a conflict, in truth, between the Treasury and Number Ten: it was between those who accepted the hard realities and those who wished they were different. It was obvious that if we did not join the first wave of the euro in 1999 we would not be in a position to join in the run-up to the 2001 election.[137]

This was corroborated by Balls, whose assessment was that there was in fact no difference in policy between Blair and Brown at the time, although it may have suited Blair to pretend that there was in order to appease the euro supporters around him led by Peter Mandelson:

> What happened was that Alastair, who thought we should rule it out, like I did, thought that's what they'd agreed, wanted to be in the mix. I think the truth is that...Alastair hardened it up more than I was intending. I was thinking that it would be the clearest hint yet but there was no clearest hint, it was kaboom, emphatic. So the question is, did Tony Blair on the Thursday know that's what we were doing? Tony undoubtedly said to Peter Mandelson he didn't. But as is always the case with politics, that's where the wrinkles of ambiguity may conceal dust and fluff...

> My interpretation is Tony knew exactly what was going on, it was exactly the right thing to do, actually. Gordon, Tony, Alastair Campbell, and me were totally united, but there were people slightly on the outside of it who didn't like it very much. And when they rang up Tony, he said, 'How do these things happen?'... The thing about most senior politicians is that they often want to have their cake and eat it. It was the classic example. They simultaneously wanted to be able to say we haven't actually done it—but make it pretty much clear they had.

> We can debate and discuss moments when there was a fundamental divergence of view but actually that day is not it. It's actually probably the day where there was the most unity between Number Ten and Number Eleven throughout the whole period. It was the crossover point because three months before, people often say why did we come up with the five economic tests before the election, was it to stop Tony Blair joining the euro? The reason we came up with the five economic tests was to stop Tony Blair *ruling out* joining the euro on political

grounds. Gordon wanted to say we're going to make this decision in a careful way on the five economic tests, to stop what he described as 'the Rupert Murdoch thing' before the election becoming 'Blair says no' on political grounds. And then you get to that point where they agree. And then it moves in the other direction, where it ends up Gordon being the one who's against it and Tony seemed to be more in favour. But the closest convergence is probably that Friday.[138]

This may be the most plausible demystification of the episode. Certainly, Sir Dave Ramsden, the Treasury official who would soon be put in charge of the assessment of the case for the euro, said: 'The October 1997 EMU policy was unchanged right into 2001. This unusual policy stability reflected political discipline underpinned by the Treasury taking on economic ministry, delivery, and coordination functions.'[139] Sir Stephen Wall, who was later Blair's main Europe adviser, rationalized it all when he wrote:

While the manner of the announcement was unfortunate, and a harbinger of things to come, the decision itself was not surprising given Tony Blair's earlier public caution. In retrospect, there was probably never a better time to hold a referendum on entry into the euro. But it remains questionable, even so, whether the moment was good enough.[140]

Brown underpinned this when he explained:

In July 1997, Tony was persuaded by Philip Gould that he should break with tradition and campaign as prime minister in a by-election in Uxbridge. In the event, the Conservatives not only held the seat but secured a swing of 5 per cent from Labour to their candidate. It was only a few weeks since the general election but it was already clear that if we opted to join the first wave of the euro, we could not assume a clear run in any referendum.[141]

Wall also rejected the idea that, by allowing the Chancellor to set the five tests for adopting the euro, Blair lost control of the decision: 'In political terms, the five tests were no more than a confirmation of the obvious point that the Prime Minister and his Chancellor had to be in complete agreement for there to be any hope of a successful EMU referendum campaign.'[142]

The five tests

Folklore had it that the five tests were invented in the back of a New York taxi, an early example of a 'window dressing' charge—that the UK was not going to join the currency but needed to go through the rigmarole of pretending that we wanted to in order to keep pro-Europeans onside. The idea of the 'back of a taxi' may have been an echo of George Brown being offered the job to split the Treasury and create the Department of Economic Affairs in 1964 in a cab on the way to the House of Commons—'true, but not by any means the whole truth', he later wrote.[143] Balls explained the modern take: 'It's been said many times that the five tests were invented in the back of a New York taxi. That wasn't correct, but it was in the back of that taxi, via the front page of the *FT* [after a call to Robert Peston], that the world came to hear about them.'[144]

Gordon Brown had set out Labour's pre-election position on a trip to the US in February 1997, which was the first mention of the five 'British Economic Tests'.[145] The five tests were based on the economic literature on optimal currency areas, which had been applied to the UK's situation in Balls' 1992 Fabian Society pamphlet, *Euro-Monetarism*. Balls explained their development:

> We've announced the five economic tests, pre-election... We then arrive in the Treasury; three days later we have a meeting; Nigel Wicks [number two in the Treasury Civil Service hierarchy] asked for a meeting, the senior official is Melanie Dawes, we sit round the table and Nigel says, 'Melanie can you introduce it?', and Melanie says, 'Ed, we've thought about this hard and we actually think there's only four tests. We don't actually think the fifth one works, the impact on greater employment.' And I said this is kind of difficult really because we said there's five, the manifesto says it's five, and the growth of employment is quite a big deal, but intellectually, Dave Ramsden's looked at this, you know, Mundell–Fleming comes in [an academic model looking at small open economies], there's only really four, the final one doesn't really mean anything, but this is quite a problem really as I think we're going to have to stick with five... the compromise was there was only four

tests, we'll call the fifth one the conclusion, that can be the summary... By the time we got to the five economic tests in 2003, I would say we ended up putting more intellectual effort into the fifth test than into the first four but in that early period people didn't think it existed. One of those things where it did exist and yet it really didn't.[146]

The five tests were:

1. Are business cycles and economic structures compatible so that we and others could live comfortably with euro interest rates on a permanent basis?

2. If problems emerge is there sufficient flexibility to deal with them?

3. Would joining EMU create better conditions for firms making long-term decisions to invest in Britain?

4. What impact would entry into EMU have on the competitive position of the UK's financial services industry, particularly the City's wholesale markets?

5. In summary, will joining EMU promote higher growth, stability, and a lasting increase in jobs?

While the Treasury was conducting the biggest economic analysis in recent times to try to clarify the euro question, over the years 1998–2001 Blair's mind was changing. He had won an historic landslide, presided over a buoyant economy for a parliament, led the world over Kosovo, and was headed for another huge electoral mandate. He was beginning to think seriously about his legacy and the spending of his bank of political capital. His thoughts dwelt on the euro. Having started from a more Eurosceptic stance than Brown, by the time of the 2001 election, Blair's position had shifted, as Stephen Wall made clear:

I believe EMU was probably always going to be an issue for the second term, in the absence of a shift in public opinion that was never probable... There is equally no doubt that the Prime Minister hoped to take Britain into the euro in the second term... Tony Blair made no secret, in discussion with other EU leaders, British business leaders, and trusted journalists that he was in favour of Britain's entry.[147]

Balls agreed, and from the Treasury side traced the hardening of Brown's opposition:

> Tony and Gordon were always pro-European. Tony and Gordon saw this as central to modernization for Labour and the country and it's right to say that as the first parliament went on, the nature of being a finance minister, you have to become tougher, and the nature of being a prime minister, to succeed, is you have to become more consensual in your pro-Europeanism within the [European] Council, because that's how it works.

> Definitely over that period Gordon's rhetoric became tougher and Tony's became more consensual within a pro-European context. Tony used to meet Ken Clarke and Michael Heseltine in the first parliament and bring Gordon in to try to persuade them we weren't against it in principle. There was an attempt to keep them on board. But the point where it changed was the days after the 2001 election where suddenly this big briefing went out because Tony Blair had now actually decided the euro was the way he was going to express his pro-Europeanism. Until then we had thought that the euro was more form rather than content.[148]

So begins one of the last really curious, largely unanswered episodes of the Blair years—why Blair suddenly became pro-euro in the face of unchanging public disaffection? The received wisdom is that Blair had decided that, alongside his focus on reform of public services, he would push to join the euro, but that events—the al-Qaeda attacks—were to intervene. As Adonis explained in 2017,

> Just before the 2001 election Tony, for about the twentieth time recorded in my diaries, told Roy Jenkins that he was going to go for the euro. Roy told me: 'Tony says this time he's really going to do it: he is going to call a referendum very soon after the election, whatever Murdoch does'... [However t]here were three months between the 2001 election and 9/11... and there was intense internal debate on what to do about the euro in these two months. By 9/11 this debate had been resolved—in favour of doing nothing.[149]

Blair saw the political rationale for joining through a heretofore unacknowledged historical analysis:

If we can we should do the euro in this Parliament. I am absolutely clear how I see this. There are two sides to the British character: the cautious and the adventurous side. The cautious side has dominated us for the last 40 years and done untold damage. John Major and David Owen epitomize it perfectly. It is the cautious side which wants us to wait another 4 to 6 years, to wait and see how it all goes, but I tell you if we do that—and I can already see all the forces of caution uniting, on our side also—we will repeat the mistakes of the past. . . . We should do it in this term. There is no point being prime minister unless you take risks to do the right thing. If we don't go in, we will be a supplicant in 5 or 6 years' time.[150]

He was about to address the annual Trades Union Congress to ramp up the pro-euro rhetoric, with a speech containing the lines 'A successful euro is in our interest', and 'So provided the economic conditions are met, it is right that Britain joins.'[151] But before he could deliver it, the 9/11 attacks happened in the USA. The speech was abandoned and his political capital was instead spent on supporting President Bush over Afghanistan and Iraq.

While Blair continued to plug away at his pro-euro policy, with less focus than he previously intended, the Treasury took the idea of the five tests seriously. The analysis was painstaking as Sir Dave Ramsden, the official who coordinated the process, explained:

All the material was submitted to Ed Balls . . . This reflected Balls' centrality to the work in his role as chief economic adviser. He had been thinking about the issues for ten years, and he linked the team to the Chancellor, with whom we had little need for direct contact . . . From the start of 2003 our key 'stakeholders' became the prime minister and his close officials and advisers, particularly Jeremy Heywood [the prime minister's principal private secretary], Stephen Wall [Europe adviser] and Jonathan Powell [chief of staff] . . . With the invasion of Iraq becoming ever more likely the seminars didn't always take place on schedule, but they did happen . . .

Our conclusion was that the five tests had not been met and a clear and unambiguous case for joining EMU had not been made . . . First the studies and then the assessment were shared with members of the Cabinet bilaterally in the second half of May. There was a meeting of the full Cabinet to agree the policy in the week before the 9 June announcement... only one of the five tests—the City test—was passed unconditionally. The two key ones, Convergence and Flexibility, were failed, and the Investment and Jobs tests were passed, conditional on passing Convergence and Flexibility.

Ramsden rejected the suggestion that the conclusion was fixed in advance:

> Most agreed it was a weighty contribution... We delivered a major logistical exercise to time. It is one of the myths of Whitehall that the Treasury can't do delivery... [Robert] Peston says it was clear from his contacts with the Treasury in the summer of 2002 that the five tests were going to be failed. For me the issues only started to crystallize in February 2003... as our analysis of the challenges of life in a single currency came to the fore.[152]

Robert Peston's claim about the timing may be questioned, but his reading in *Brown's Britain* of the outcome was that it was correct:

> The man in the white coat [as Blair called Ramsden] and the Treasury team were right: this was the wrong moment to participate in monetary union. So it is possible to view the process as a vindication and rehabilitation of the Whitehall machine and the mandarin class: for the only time since 1997, a momentous decision was taken in the old-fashioned way, of civil servants doing a serious piece of work which was subsequently adopted by ministers.[153]

According to Balls, Blair 'absolutely had the Foreign Office breathing down his neck, including some people from the Foreign Office within Downing Street saying, get the Treasury out, you should decide this, you're the prime minister... and it was not what he wanted to do'.[154] The fateful head-to-head showdown on the euro between Blair and Brown 'had not gone well', said Balls, who recalled the after-effects two days later:

> 'Are you still the Chancellor?' I asked Gordon as he burst into the ground-floor study in 11 Downing Street. 'I genuinely don't know,' he replied, slumping into one of the luxurious armchairs. 'I don't know whether Tony's sacked me, or whether I've resigned, or whether we just

carry on.' Fifty yards down the corridor in the prime minister's office,
I was sure Tony Blair was in exactly the same state of uncertainty.

For Balls, 'This was a decision we had to control, and a battle we had
to win, and if Gordon had needed to resign to make that happen, I'm
sure he would have done and so would I.'[155] He pointed out that Blair
could have pushed it to the point of Brown's resignation and chose
not to: 'In my view, Tony Blair did not actually want to join the euro.
For the reasons... that he did not think a campaign could be won... and
that he actually understood the economics and was really worried
what the economic implications could be.'[156]

Even so, Balls was happy to take the credit, on behalf of Brown, for
having prevented Britain adopting the euro. Usually, he said in his
memoir, 'you think of your biggest achievements as being the things
you create,' but this was different: 'Sometimes in politics a decision not
to do something can be just as significant—and there is no doubt that,
for Britain, the decision not to join the single currency has been the
most successful economic decision of the last thirty years.'[157]

With the publication in 2017 of Brown's memoir, which contained
no new information regarding the euro, the definitive story of the
euro was possible. As in so many cases, Balls gave a credible analysis:

> I don't think Tony Blair actually ever wanted to join the euro through
> a referendum and I think he would have been horrified if it had ever
> got to that point. This puts me in a different position to lots of other
> people, maybe even Gordon Brown... I think there was an element of
> him needing to show his European colleagues that he was more pro
> than Gordon because if he wanted to be the president of Europe, he
> couldn't do that from a position of being a sceptic on the single cur-
> rency... And, in the tussle with Gordon Brown, it's clear that Tony goes
> to John Prescott, Clare Short, and Alastair to say, 'Go to Gordon and
> say if you let me join the single currency, I will then stand aside for you
> in this Parliament.' He does the same thing through Sue Nye.
>
> Did he do that to say, 'Okay, I'll do the deal to join the single currency
> then stand down?' Of course he did not. That's not why he did it, he
> did it so that Gordon would say no and Tony could then say the trouble
> with Gordon is he's so unreasonable, I can't work with him, he won't

give me what I want. He kept choosing people who were close to Gordon to be the conduit so that when they couldn't deliver, because Gordon said no, Tony could say to Alastair and John Prescott and Clare Short, 'I tried, but he's so unreasonable.' If Gordon had turned around and said 'Okay', Tony would have thought, 'So you actually want me to take on the Murdoch press, fight a referendum that we might well lose? Oh my God. No way.' Luckily for Tony, Gordon always said no.[158]

It now looks likely that Blair recognized that Britain had nowhere near a majority interested in joining the euro, or 'scrapping the pound' in media-speak. This answers one of the lingering questions of the Blair years over why the master politician would seemingly be so intent on an unwinnable enterprise. To cap it all, Blair explained in his own memoir: 'My disagreement with Gordon was that he was express-ing himself negatively on the euro. I was always saying, even if we don't join and maybe especially if we don't, for reasons of diplomacy always sound positive.'[159]

All the same, Blair demanded that the five tests were kept open beyond 2003 through a small analytical team. This only came to an end at the 2010 election, as Ramsden explained: 'The [coalition] gov-ernment ruled out joining EMU for the duration of the Parliament to 2015. The role of the five tests was over. The Chancellor announced in his June 2010 Budget speech that the last Treasury staff member working on UK Euro preparations was being redeployed.'[160]

Brown's spin doctors: Charlie Whelan and Damian McBride

The long analysis of the five tests took the heat out of whether or not to join the euro. But other issues arose to fuel the animosity between Number Ten and the Treasury, something Balls thought was due to lack of an effective Conservative opposition: 'Labour was the only show in town when it came to political news, and the biggest story was the rivalry and argument—whether real or imagined—between Tony and Gordon.'[161] This rivalry was stoked by Gordon Brown's press secretaries, first Charlie Whelan and then Damian McBride. Between them, they did as much as the controversy over Alastair Campbell's part in making the case for the Iraq war to tarnish New Labour's reputation as the party of spin, spin doctors, and politicized civil servants. Whelan was a special adviser, while McBride started out as a Civil Service press officer, but one who crossed the line into political activity.

Whelan's promotion of the Chancellor to the detriment of other Cabinet ministers, not to mention the prime minister, came to a head at the end of 1998. Peter Mandelson had been 'the Third Man' (as he entitled his 2010 memoir) to Blair and Brown since the mid-1980s, a position he found most difficult in the days after John Smith's death in 1994. While Blair was the frontrunner in the subsequent leadership contest, Brown's deep frustration at being usurped focused on Mandelson, who had tried, unsuccessfully, to be neutral between the two. Brown saw the hand of Mandelson in just about anything that caused problems for him, not knowing *who* Mandelson was talking to in the media, or about *what*, but sensing that he *was*.

In opposition, Mandelson had borrowed money from Geoffrey Robinson to buy a house in London. After Robinson had been made a Treasury minister, his company Transtec was investigated by the Department of Trade and Industry. A clear conflict of interest arose when Mandelson was appointed to the Cabinet as Trade and Industry Secretary in July 1998. To make matters worse, Mandelson had not told his permanent secretary of the private arrangement. So when news leaked to the *Guardian* of the loan, it created a furore, ultimately leading to both Mandelson's and Robinson's resignations. Suspicion naturally fell on Whelan, who knew about the loan, had the means and the motive to damage Mandelson, and through him to damage Blair.

Campbell finally lost his patience. In a long-distance phone call to the Seychelles on 3 January 1999 between Campbell and Blair, who was in a boat, with his protection officer, catching a fish (Campbell's *Diaries* are nothing if not graphic!), Campbell's frustration boiled over and he threatened resignation for the first time: 'I said my perspective is too often having to deal with rubbish created by Whelan and I'm not prepared to do it a day longer, and you had better get that message. It was clearly OTT and he was taken aback, but I had decided he had to get the message.'[162]

Campbell then spoke to Brown:

> I said I was not prepared to work with him [Whelan] any longer, that whether he was responsible for the loan story or not, there was enough of a track record for me to have reached that judgement, and I felt it was impossible to have him around. It was not just one thing—it was a modus operandi over years that made him an impediment to effective and professional politics or communications. Whelan had to go...He added nothing on the economy, nothing on Europe, he was there to arm himself with information and then go out and act as an unofficial source thought to be in the loop.[163]

Whelan went. He reappeared publicly in 2007 as political director of the Unite union, was copied into the infamous 2009 emails that brought down Damian McBride, who by then was press secretary to Prime Minister Brown,[164] and in 2010 was active in campaigning for Ed Miliband and against the Blairite favourite, his brother David. One commentator even declared, implausibly, that Whelan had 'single-handedly turned Labour's leadership election' in Ed's favour.[165] Whelan announced in the aftermath that he had resigned from Unite, and would retire to fish the River Spey in the Scottish Highlands.[166]

McBride inherited Whelan's mantle in 2003, after an interlude when the Treasury's Head of Communications was a career civil servant, Michael Ellam. McBride too was a career official (in HM Customs and Excise), but quickly became noted for his aggression and devotion to Brown. He was nicknamed 'Mad Dog' or just 'Dog' by lobby journalists, and he too soon became a thorn in the side of Number Ten and Blairite ministers (but not of Campbell, who had left government in 2003, although he still advised Blair and returned for general elections). Just a year later, McBride's position was under pressure after he leaked the critical opinions of departmental heads of communication regarding Number Ten. At the time, the high-level leak inquiry conducted by retired Special Branch officers decided that McBride was probably the culprit, but could not be conclusive. Brown warned

McBride: 'They're out for you now. Blair keeps going on about you. They're into your phone records, so watch who you're talking to.' We know McBride leaked the information because he admitted it in his confessional memoir *Power Trip*, as amazing for what it contains as for the fact that it was written at all. In it, he admits smearing the prime minister's wife Cherie Blair and the leaking of top secret honours, in sections with such lurid titles as 'Slow Ascent into Hell', 'Going to the Dark Side', and 'Mad Dog on the Loose'.[167]

Brown's warning only led McBride to intensify his activities to the point where it became impossible for him to remain a civil servant. McBride admitted that, as the 2005 election approached, he was committed to the Labour Party and to Brown 'in a way that many other officials in the Treasury were beginning to find frankly unpalatable'. The final straw was the release, in the weeks before the election, of Treasury documents about the 1992 ERM crisis. The papers had been requested under the Freedom of Information Act by the *Financial Times*, and McBride was able to read them while Treasury officials discussed how and when to publish them. McBride explained in his memoir:

> Given they were papers relating to a previous administration, Gordon was not supposed to have any knowledge about their contents, or any influence over the handling of their publication, but—while I was careful not to speak to him directly about it—I got word to him…that I knew the significance of the papers and would handle them appropriately.

McBride's definition of the word 'appropriately' was a flexible one. He was worried that publication might be delayed until after the election, and so encouraged *Times* and *Financial Times* journalists to report that there were 'fears' that Sir John Major and Norman Lamont, prime minister and Chancellor at the time of Black Wednesday, were trying to stall publication. 'I thought that would guarantee the civil servants wouldn't be able to hold things up any longer,' McBride admitted. He went on:

> That's how it proved, but all hell broke loose in the meantime as a result of the stories. Sir John went bananas, issuing formal denials and calling for official apologies. When one Sunday paper suggested to me

there were suspicions Alastair Campbell was orchestrating the whole thing, I gave them enough rope to run the story as a splash, and Sir John took the bait, going on broadcast news again to accuse Labour and Campbell of pre-election dirty tricks and ensuring the row ran for another couple of days.

When the documents were duly published, McBride, having already been through the hundreds of pages in advance, 'was able to point the journalists to all the best bits—by which I mean the most damaging bits for the Tories'. McBride thought his work 'might have gone undetected', but Gus O'Donnell, who had been Sir John's press secretary at the time of Black Wednesday, and who was now Permanent Secretary at the Treasury, was not fooled:

> It was only years later that I discovered Gus had spoken to Gordon after that episode, told him I'd become too political and needed to be moved. It was put to me rather differently at the time by Ed Balls when he took me for a coffee in Le Club Express on Petty France: 'If you want to carry on working for Gordon long term and see him through to No 10, you can't carry on as a civil servant...' I asked Ed what he thought I should do. 'All I know', he said smiling, 'is you seem to enjoy the work, and you seem to like the politics.' Then, not for the last time, he said quietly: 'And Gordon needs you. Without you, he'd be so exposed. So exposed.'...
>
> I should have taken longer to make up my mind, but I felt like I was part of Gordon's Praetorian guard by then, and going over to the political side would cement that.[168]

Brown clearly attracted strong characters who became devoted to him. But McBride was protective to the point of unscrupulous. He reflected the darker side of Brown's own personality somewhat—the most serious commitment to progressive humanism indivisible from the hardest of political brutalism. McBride followed Brown to Number Ten in 2007. He lasted two years before emails from him were published which contained invented rumours about senior Conservative politicians and their families, and he was forced to resign. Like Whelan, he too returned to the political fray after a while, reappearing in 2015 as an adviser to Emily Thornberry, Shadow Defence Secretary, later Shadow Foreign Secretary and in effect Jeremy Corbyn's deputy.

Welfare to work and public services

Gordon Brown's wish to bestride the government's domestic policy led to a rapid expansion of the Treasury's empire. The welfare-to-work agenda and the tax credits policy in particular were complicated and costly. Blair, 'not being a fan of tax credits' in retrospect, hinted in his memoir at his doubts about 'putting so much' public money into them.[169] The policy was ambitious, and transformed lives, but attracted years of opprobrium for the Treasury over its implementation. It was part of the Treasury transforming itself into a spending department, and widening away from the core Treasury business of economics and finance. Moreover, a question emerged at this time—if the Treasury scrutinizes departmental spending, who will challenge the Treasury?

Another way in which the Treasury extended its control of 'delivery' departments was the Private Finance Initiative. First announced by Conservative Chancellor Norman Lamont in the 1992 autumn statement regarding 'ways to increase the scope for private financing of capital projects',[170] the PFI sought to address the problem of large public sector infrastructure projects ending up over-time and over-budget; it was partly inspired by the experience of London's Jubilee Line tube extension, and was a form of public-private partnership (or PPP). Balls explained that part of its attraction to the Conservatives was that it was 'off-balance-sheet' funding, allowing them to borrow money without it appearing in the national accounts. Brown was often accused of taking up PFI for that reason, but Balls said its usefulness to New Labour was slightly different:

Tony Blair and Gordon Brown in [19]92, 93, 94, the biggest things in their minds were, 'How can we avoid being the Labour Party of 1978, 1979?...How do we avoid being irresponsible in our approach to public finance, irresponsible in our view of public spending, swayed by vested interests in our decision making, and locked into a public vs private view of the world? How do we break out of that?' In 1994...John Smith was in a real state because...John Prescott has done an interview where he says, 'We should use public–private partnerships for capital investment.' For John Prescott, there was an element of 'How can I lever more money without having to borrow directly?'...But I think from our point of view, it was at least as much about saying, let's break out of an ideological public versus private view of what the state does. Therefore, if you can use partnership between the public and private sector, in the building of hospitals, or in the building of roads, that would show that we've moved beyond the more divided state view of the late 1970s.[171]

In his memoir, Brown recognized the controversy behind the PFIs (or PPPs—Public Private Partnerships—as he described them) but was completely in accordance with Balls's analysis:

> For some, PPPs were simply a halfway house to privatisation. The public sector, they said, handed over control of projects to private contractors who, in return for paying upfront capital costs, charged exorbitant interest rates over the next thirty years. For me, PPPs looked different: they were a way of mobilising private funds for public purposes and offered a better route to building our infrastructure than the old ways of financing. After all, we had always hired private builders to construct our schools, hospitals, roads and public buildings. But we had enjoyed little control—leading to run-on costs, delays and often poor quality. With PPPs we were not only mobilising private sector skills for public purposes, ending the sterile and self-defeating battle for territory between public and private sectors, but building in tougher contractual requirements that secured far better value for money for the taxpayer. There were to be teething problems—some projects were poorly structured—and in an environment of low interest rates, legitimate issues about the rates of interest being charged. But, at their best, PPPs married the long-term thinking and ethos of the public sector with the managerial skills of the private; and, in truth, we could not have commissioned more than a hundred hospitals and built, rebuilt or refurbished 4,000 schools by 2010 if we had not.[172]

Indeed, Balls pointed out to us that PFI funding was quickly brought onto the national accounts, so the reason for its expansion could not have been to conceal public borrowing:

What then happened was, as the Government went on, increasingly the Office of National Statistics said all of this should go on public balance sheets. By the time we got to the Tube PPP, the whole of the Tube went on the public balance sheet, even though it was going to be done by public-private partnership...PFI, by the time we got to 2002–03, was pretty much all on the balance sheet.

The reason we'd been doing it was not because we wanted to sort of go off budget, it was because it was actually a better relationship between the public and private, and actually delivered better value for money. At every stage, you could only agree to a PFI if it was better value for money than a public comparator, and the truth was that we had had a country under the Labour and Conservative governments where we'd built loads and loads of really shoddy hospitals, over budget, late...My first memory is of 1977, and the Queen opening the Queen's Medical Centre in Nottingham, which my Dad went to work in, which was a new, direct build, private built, public procured hospital where the lifts didn't work from the first day.

Now—we didn't get everything right. The Tube was too complicated, some of the early PFI hospitals were over-engineered, but the truth was that public sector was often a very bad client, which was always why the private sector ripped us off.

Overall, however, Balls thought:

It was exactly the right thing to do...it was exactly right that it shouldn't be off budget, it should be on budget; it was exactly right for us to do it as a political signal; it delivered us much better value for money...Personally, I'm not going to defend every PFI contract, but in general I think it was completely right, and I'm totally robust on it.[173]

In opposition, Balls observed, George Osborne made 'a big song and dance of abolishing PFI' but, as Chancellor, 'a few years later—with rather less fanfare—it was reintroduced, as he belatedly learned it was the only way to do things'.[173] In fact, in 2012, the coalition government announced Private Finance 2 (PF2).[174] Not for the first time, the contrast between Conservative criticism of New Labour and the reinvention of New Labour policies by the Conservatives in office recalled the sardonic anecdote after the massive 1968 Fulton Report concerning reform of the Civil Service—'Oh, there have been lots of changes. We have renamed everything.'[175] (However, perhaps this story was indeed coming to an end in 2018, when the Chancellor Philip Hammond announced the abolition of PFI and PF2 for future projects. But it still remained the case that something would have to replace it.)

The 'limitations of markets' speech

'It was sometimes said that Number Ten believed in something called "creative tension" and that the friction between the departments would produce the desired pearls,' James Callaghan wrote of his time as Chancellor, 1964–7, when part of the Treasury was split off to form the Department of Economic Affairs, adding: 'This was not my experience.'[176] Fast-forward three decades and it became accepted wisdom that the competition between Blair and Brown, and between Number Ten and the Treasury, was debilitating, thwarting great promise, and leading to the common belief that Blair's greatest mistake was his failure to rein in his overmighty Chancellor (Peter Riddell's book, *The Unfulfilled Prime Minister*, captured the mood perfectly).[177] While it is undoubtedly right that too much energy was spent on internal feuding, it is equally true that the conflict often produced rigorous policy and state-of-the-art thinking. This was at its zenith in the 1999–2003 period which began the second phase of New Labour. As the cap on public spending was lifted, the question of how to spend this once-in-a-lifetime largesse became a central concern for a prime minister at the height of his powers and finally beginning to understand how government worked, and an experienced Chancellor focused upon the top job, which he believed would become his before the next election. Government was fizzing with new ideas as the creators of New Labour flexed their muscles and tried to own the future. In 2002, it was a tale of two speeches.

Blair set out his stall in his Labour conference speech: 'I believe we're at our best when at our boldest. So far, we've made a good start but we've not been bold enough.' He framed contemporary history and juxtaposed it against his vision:

The purpose of the twentieth-century welfare state was to treat citizens as equals. The purpose of our twenty-first-century reforms must be to treat them as individuals as well. It means putting power in the hands of the patient or parent... Why shouldn't an NHS patient be able to book an appointment for an operation at their convenience, just like they could if they paid for it?[178]

This was a bold reference to Margaret Thatcher's unapologetic explanation of why she went private for her treatment at the 1987 election: 'At the time I want, and with a doctor I want.'[179] Under Blair, this would be achieved 'for the many not the few' by market mechanisms— albeit funded by taxation and always free at the point of delivery.

The Treasury's first retort came the next month, when Balls gave an interview to the *Guardian* in which he said there were limits to markets in the provision of public services: 'If you go down the road of thinking you can apply market principles to a good like health, the evidence is that you end up with inefficiency and escalating costs, two-tierism, and you can do grave damage to that ethic of public service.'[180] According to Balls, the interview caused a reaction: 'The PLP [Parliamentary Labour Party], and especially the Blairites, went totally bonkers.'[181]

The next response was a heavy, measured one. To the Social Market Foundation in February 2003, Gordon Brown spoke on the subject of 'A Modern Agenda for Prosperity and Social Reform', an address otherwise known as 'the limitations of markets'. Balls explained that he and Brown 'spent ages on that speech'.[182] It was to become a milestone in centre-left economic thinking.[183] In it, Brown staked his own claim to understanding the past: 'Every modern generation since Adam Smith counterposed the invisible hand of the market to the helping hand of government has had to resolve this question for its time: what are the respective spheres for individuals, markets, and communities, including the state, in achieving opportunity and security for their citizens?'[184] The model that the Brown Treasury espoused was one of redistributive market liberalism, with a role for government in remedying market failure, such as, crucially, in healthcare. 'Politically,' explained Balls, 'it was seen as Gordon staking a position against the...sort of Blairite view of reform but, on the substance, I don't think there was ever a big argument because actually Tony never disagreed with what we were doing.'[185]

That was not how Blair saw it in his memoir:

Ed had worked out a strategy for Gordon that sort of went like this: there is a trade-off between equity and markets; Blair is pushing us too far towards 'marketisation' and thus away from equity. So all of this language around choice, competition, diversity, flexibility; all of it is in the end an attempt to move us to a system that is intrinsically inequitable; and what's more poorly motivated, since it's all part of an obsession with the middle class—historically a small part of Labour's support—at the expense of our 'core' voters.[186]

Balls refused to accept that Brown was merely engaged in positioning for factional advantage, and defended the Brown view on its substance:

Was Gordon the drag on public sector reform because he wasn't willing to embrace the market and the private sector? Our view was we were totally in favour of the private and market sector where it worked well. We didn't want to renationalize any of these big industries like telecoms or gas or anything. In the public sector, we were all for tough really disciplined productivity and reform and purchaser-provider rights and responsibilities, but what we weren't going to do was introduce the political rhetoric of the market into public services where we thought it would actually end up being more expensive.

So Gordon's 'market' speech...that was our way of explaining why you could have a tough approach to public sector reform as we saw it, which wasn't about the privatization and pricing and markets stuff.

Indeed, he turned the argument round, accusing unnamed Blairite ministers of manufacturing difference to position themselves, and claiming to be more New Labour than Blair himself:

My real view is that the Cabinet ministers who got included in that dispute were trying to have a factional fight with Gordon about public sector reform and maybe people at the time were happy to have that argument at the political level to go on but actually in terms of policy and substance, Gordon and Tony were in the same place, we never really disagreed...

I don't think there's anybody more New Labour than me. I was the only one in the 2010 leadership election to say I was New Labour, I'm still proud to be New Labour. Tony Blair wasn't more New Labour than me—I wanted radical public service reform as did he, as did Gordon.[187]

Lord Macpherson offered a more equivocal backing for the Treasury's New Labour credentials: 'Brown may have positioned himself to the left of Blair, but he really believed in markets.'[188]

Foundation hospitals

Tony Blair warned on the eve of the 1997 election that voters had '24 hours to save the NHS'.[189] Health reform was put on hold in the first term, as Balls recounted:

On the NHS, it was an explicit policy from Tony to be not reforming about the health service. If anything there was a frustration in the Treasury that we weren't doing enough reform. The decision to have Frank Dobson as the Health Secretary was a decision not to destabilize a complex thing like the health service.[190]

Blair tried to stop the musical chairs of some of his 'delivery' ministers and, from 2001, thought that in David Blunkett at the Home Office, Stephen Byers at Transport, Estelle Morris at Education, and Alan Milburn at Health, he had a settled team to make big changes. While all had gone by the end of 2004, Milburn's departure was the only one that had a policy battle at its roots, one that saw Blair at first back the Health Secretary against Brown—and then abandon his support at the decisive moment.

The conventional view at the time was that Blair had appointed Milburn to drive through market-based reforms of the NHS, which were opposed by Brown at the Treasury as a way of enhancing his reputation with traditional Labour-minded backbenchers and party members who would decide the leadership succession. In his memoir, Blair suggested that the otherwise New Labour Brown had been led astray by Balls: 'He believed, and I think persuaded Gordon, that you could be a traditional Labour leader and still win.'[191]

Ed Balls, on the other hand, blamed Milburn for the division, implying that if it had not been for *him*, Blair and Brown would indeed have agreed. Balls said the idea of 'a class of hospitals who had more freedoms and flexibilities in scope because they were high performing' was something he and Jeremy Heywood had agreed in discussions between the Treasury and Number Ten before the Budget of 2002. 'In the immediate period after the Budget, Alan Milburn is incredibly upset about getting all this money and not being consulted and not being part of the reform process…it was essentially done between the Treasury and Number Ten,' Balls told us, with absolute clarity about the duopoly that controlled much of the Blair government's domestic policymaking. In his account, it was Milburn who came up with a 'new idea', that the flexibility allowed to the best hospitals, known as foundation hospitals, had to be that they had to be allowed to borrow money:

> Therefore that would mean them being classified in the private sector not in the public sector. Either this meant they were public institutions, who somehow were borrowing unlike local government and every other government institution, [and were] outside Treasury control, or they had to be allowed to go private because they would have a sep-arate sort of charging arm.

The suggestion that Milburn was proposing charging for healthcare may be a little propagandist, but there was a genuine difficulty over the status of foundation hospitals' debt and whether they could be allowed to go bust. Presented in this light, Treasury opposition was reasonable and inevitable:

> We were very sceptical about this and we thought this was going to be a big waste of money, a big getting-around [of] proper budgetary con-trol. We didn't think introducing charging for the health service was going to help anybody. We just fought really hard to raise taxes for a free at the point of help health service and inventing charges to pre-tend they were off-budget so that they could borrow off balance sheet was not really where we were at. In advance of a big Cabinet awayday in early September, I think it was, we did a really long paper which we circulated the night before to every cabinet minister basically saying that we were in favour of freedom and flexibility for high-performing hospitals but we weren't going to get into this quasi-private, off-budget,

public sector delivery because this would be inefficient, unfair and wasteful and we weren't going to do it.[192]

Balls admitted that 'this was seen as quite an unfriendly act from the Treasury and an unfriendly act particularly towards...Alan Milburn, but also towards Number Ten', but he insisted that 'when we came to the actual meetings which finally sorted this out in October', Blair shared the Treasury's concerns about Milburn's foundation hospitals:

> The idea that they should be just allowed to borrow money without Treasury control, he thought, 'Why would I agree to that?' And this was one of those moments where, when it came to the crunch, he actually agreed with Gordon...
>
> And then Milburn was very bitter because he thought his foundation hospitals had been destroyed, but they weren't destroyed by Gordon, they were destroyed because Tony agreed with Gordon. There was never an argument between me and Gordon, between me and Jeremy, Gordon and Tony, we all sort of agreed.

More clarity here, that the important domestic policymaking in this period was decided in an early 'quad' (prefiguring the Quad of the coalition government: see chapter 2): the prime minister; the Chancellor; the prime minister's Civil Service principal private secretary, Jeremy Heywood; and the Chancellor's special adviser, Chief Economic Adviser Ed Balls.

Milburn seemed to have felt let down by Blair, but expressed himself in terms of being let down by the government's structure:

> A prime example was NHS Foundation Hospitals. So there's Tony here, Gordon here, and then there's someone called me in the middle, caught. [Claps hands.] Like that. [Claps again.] Happy-slappy, getting it from both sides. It was great! And so if you've got a disagreement on a policy issue, then having twin centres of domestic policy doesn't work. Where you've got agreement, say, on child poverty, which people think was a Brown thing but was actually a Blair thing. It was Tony who said, look, we want this target whatever, however difficult it is to achieve, of abolishing child poverty by 2020, and [if] Gordon's in agreement with it, then you can have a unified effort. If you've got policy disagreement, as happens, it's quite difficult. So structurally there's something not quite right in my view. I think, you know, sort of within the next

ten years that is, you know, one government or another will sort that out because they'll have to.[193]

Alan Milburn resigned as Health Secretary in June 2003, before returning for a short stint in the lead-up to the 2005 election. It was left to John Reid, Milburn's successor as Health Secretary, to take the watered-down legislation for foundation hospitals through the House of Commons, against a rebellion by sixty-two Labour MPs, in November 2003.

Education, education, education

Two months later, in January 2004, came the second great Commons clash over public service reform, with Gordon Brown again seen as covertly supporting Labour opposition, this time to higher university tuition fees, to be paid by student loans repayable after graduation. In the early New Labour years, education policy had been a difference of tone rather than of policy between Blair and Brown. At the 1996 Labour Party Conference, Blair had said: 'Ask me my three main priorities for government and I tell you: education, education, and education.'[194] In the first term, the main focus was on primary school standards, which had broad cross-party support, including in the Labour Party. But as the second term arrived, differences emerged between Numbers 10 and 11 over reform to the secondary school system and—most acutely—over how to fund university expansion.

In the end, the important secondary school policy of the second term was the academy schools programme. It was pioneered by Andrew Adonis, the special adviser brought into the Policy Unit in 1998, who rose to become its head in 2001, and was ennobled in 2005, becoming Minister of State for Education. Adonis enjoyed Blair's total support—but not Brown's, not least because he had been a member of the Social Democratic Party and, quite recently, of the Liberal Democrats, as Balls explained:

> I think Gordon would have been very suspicious of Andrew Adonis in that period; he didn't have any relationship with him at all, and I think

Gordon was always very suspicious of the Tony, Roy Jenkins, Paddy Ashdown link...

The academies programme in the early period—there was a divide. I don't think Gordon was very involved in education policy at all, he just thought there was this really, really expensive attempt to divert money away from mainstream education...I think the Treasury's view was that it was really very bad value for money and it was a pet project, and, if I'm honest with you, the Treasury and Gordon thought that Tony's kids had gone to the Oratory [the London Oratory School was a high-performing Catholic boys' school, not technically a selective private school, but repeated questions over its admissions policy caused Blair difficulty in a party vehemently opposed to anything but state schooling] and what he was doing was trying to spend a whole bunch of money to build a bunch of Oratories around London for people like him to send their kids to.[195]

In the dying days of Blair's reign, Adonis was unsurprisingly convinced that he would be unwanted by the new regime, and that he did not want to stay in any case. But he received a call from Brown in early May 2007: 'It was to be my first conversation of any length with Gordon for nine years, since I went to work for Tony in 1998. Before then, we had had a regular and friendly dialogue, but it stopped overnight.'[196] For Balls, this, too, was unremarkable: 'Tony didn't talk to anyone in the Treasury and Gordon didn't talk to anyone in the Policy Unit.'[197] Brown disarmed Adonis by saying he had been doing 'excellent work' at the Department of Education and he wanted it to continue. Adonis wrote:

After two hours discussing everything from academies and apprenticeships to universities and umpteen other things, including the latest books we had both been reading, we agreed to visit an academy together and I said I was looking forward to working for him. I left in a bit of a daze, and walked around St James's Park admiring the pelicans and contemplating the peculiarity of politics.[198]

Balls now became Adonis's boss, appointed to Brown's Cabinet as Secretary of State for the renamed Department of Children, Schools and Families in 2007, and Adonis stayed in post as Minister of State for Education. The academies programme continued and indeed flourished, with some changes: 'Another example', said Balls, 'that when it came to the substance, we were on the same side.'[199]

While academy schools occasioned Treasury suspicion, but not outright opposition, and eventual acceptance once Brown and his lieutenants took power in 2007, the conflict over tuition fees for universities was altogether more heated, and more politically dangerous for the government's survival. Balls explained to us that he had originally wanted to keep the option open and he was opposed to David Blunkett's decision to rule out higher tuition fees in the 2001 manifesto:

> I sat in David Miliband's office in Number Ten in the election campaign of 2001...There was a thing in the newspapers over how David Blunkett was wanting to rule out tuition fees...why would you want to do this? Surely you want to keep your options open because it makes sense for there to be some kind of contribution from graduates? David comes back in after seeing Tony and said, 'I'm really sorry but Tony said he's got to agree with David on this.'

Balls presented Blair as coming round to his view:

> Tony himself was clearly frustrated because once we got through the election he then made it absolutely clear that he wanted to ignore the manifesto and what he had agreed with David...We said we think we could find a way to make this work. It was very complicated...While we were thinking it through, I agreed to see Charles Clarke [the new Education Secretary, succeeding Estelle Morris] who, to begin with, didn't want these fees and it is true that a part of [the] Education [department] will have been saying to him you can't be confident the Treasury will find a solution.

Clarke was soon persuaded that a fee-paying system was the right way, strongly backed by Blair. Balls suggested the policy was then caught up in the Blair–Brown rivalry, with Blair playing politics:

> Gordon did a paper to the Cabinet, saying we should first of all investigate whether the principle of graduates paying can be done through a graduate contribution or graduate tax rather than fees, but we hadn't worked it out yet...it was short-circuited by Charles essentially saying, pushed by Number Ten, no, we're going to do it through a fee instead. It was a political decision. I think what happened was—thinking it through the way we discussed the NHS, the same thing manifested

itself—they [Number Ten] alighted on the principle, of having a top-up fee as a sign of reform, and our view was we were really in favour of the reform of universities and making graduates pay but there were better ways to do it.

In the end, Gordon decided that he couldn't fight that one as well . . . and I think he suspected that this was being turned into a Blair–Brown fight, therefore whatever he put down was going to become the alternative and there would be a fight and he chose not to have the fight . . . It was nothing to do with policy, it was all to do with politics. The politics was Tony wanted domestic definition and the assumption in this period was that he wasn't going to fight the next election. And people who were wanting to succeed him instead of the 'less ambitious and dead-weight Gordon Brown' thought [the question was] 'Are you a modernist, yes or no?'

Balls saw the debate in straightforward factional terms, talking about Brownites and Blairites as 'us' and 'them':

Our approach was always, we've put forward more public service reform than any of you so far, we actually know what we're doing, tell us what your reform is and we'll tell you whether it [is] a good reform or a bad reform. 'Are you for public sector reform?', our answer was always yes, but there's good ones and bad ones, but people on the other side never wanted good or bad but are you New Labour or Old Labour, are you a reformer or are you a drag?

We were the ones who set up Wanless [the inquiry into future funding for the health service] because we wanted to match resources and reform, we were the ones who got through the tax rise, we were the ones who . . . were working on how you make the purchaser–provider split [in the NHS] work.

He stressed that he and Brown were not opposed in principle to graduates making a greater contribution to the costs of expanding universities:

I've always thought a graduate tax could work. I still think it could . . . I actually wrote a pamphlet for Gordon for the Fabians in 1994 called 'Fair is Efficient' which advocated graduates making a contribution towards their higher education because of the earnings they got. It was in Gordon's name . . .

If we'd sat down and talked about what we were trying to achieve, like on foundation hospitals, I don't think in the end Gordon and Tony would have particularly disagreed, because they were quite similar in their views but on that one, people wanted a fight. And they got their fight. With most of the Parliamentary Labour Party. And the decision to divide the PLP on 'Are you a modernizer or not?' ended up being a bigger deal than the actual outcome of the policy because lots of people who voted against tuition fees actually supported graduates making a contribution through a tax. But it had become a political thing. During this there was a desire to divide on domestic policy, the policy issues were secondary.[200]

Blair in his memoir credits Balls, who 'was and is immensely capable intellectually', with being the driving force behind Brown's opposition to his policies:

Over time and the innumerable meetings with Ed and Gordon, I gradually got Ed to lose his reserve—after all, I was Prime Minister—and provoked him into his true opinions. His basic sense was that this whole assault on traditional party thinking was to prove I was 'exceptional'. 'Exceptionalism', he called it. What he meant was that I believed only I could win, and that all these rows—over tuition fees, schools reform, health reform, ID cards, asylum, law and order, welfare—were almost manufactured, in order to create the sense of a leader above the party.

Blair took the opposite view: 'I didn't choose to have rows with the party; I chose to reform. But if the reform was resisted, then you couldn't avoid the row.'

With the question of universities funding 'stuck' throughout 2002, in early 2003 Blair said:

I insisted that the Treasury come forward with a specific alternative, rather than continually raising objections to the tuition-fee proposal we had outlined...Eventually, we flushed out of the Treasury a kind of alternative, which was to all intents and purposes a graduate tax, pure and simple...it amounted not to a personal repayment of a personal debt, but a general graduate repayment of the collective student debt. I didn't like this at all...

Eventually in mid-2003 I just said: we will meet again in a month's time; the final decision will be taken; at that point you put up or we proceed. We proceeded, but we had wasted valuable time.[201]

Finally, in January 2004, the Bill for tuition fees, raised to £3,000 a year and charged to soft loans repayable by students after graduation, was carried by just five votes in the Commons—the closest Blair had yet come to defeat, at a time when he enjoyed a notional majority of 167. This was the day before the publication of the Hutton report into the death of David Kelly, which exonerated Blair and the government, but which many had expected would be the end of his premiership. Blair would now continue in power for more than another three years.

Historic Number Ten–Treasury dysfunctionality

Alan Milburn reflected on his ministerial experience and on how such conflicts could be remedied when he came to our 'Blair Government' class in 2009:

> If you've got really big strong personalities in any organization, in gov-
> ernment, it would be naïve to assume everybody is going to agree all
> the time because they don't. Secondly…although we don't have a
> written constitution, there is a constitutional necessity in my view that
> the Chancellor of the Exchequer, responsible for public finances, fiscal
> policy and so on, can say to the prime minister, 'Hold on a minute.'
> Because prime ministers will always want to do everything because, if
> you're the boss guy, that's what you want to do. So you've got to have
> a foil. So that is a necessity.
>
> Was the relationship always easy? Well, obviously not. Did it mean that
> sometimes we didn't achieve 100 per cent of what we could have in
> terms of our potential? I think that is probably right. I think if every-
> body had been on entirely the same agenda all of the time then Labour
> would have done more than it's done. And I actually think Labour has
> done quite a lot, but it could have done more than it's done.
>
> Some of this is just inevitable I'm afraid. It's a product of politics and
> it's the product of a structural relationship between the finance minis-
> ter and the prime minister.

He recalled discussions before the 2005 election about whether the lessons of the tension between Blair and Brown were that the prime minister needed a stronger office, variously described as 'the centre' or a prime minister's department:

> There were definitely discussions going on about how, post the elec-
> tion—this wasn't really a sort of personality point, it was a sort of centre

of government point—given that we'd been in [power] quite a long time, in the end we'd learnt quite a lot about what worked and what didn't in process terms. And one of the things that I and others—and I think maybe even Tony—were thinking is have we got the centre of government entirely right? And so for example we have a very big department in the centre of government, the Cabinet Office, which nobody, even people in the Cabinet Office, are quite sure what it does. That seems quite odd because they employ several thousand civil servants. And then we had a sort of strategy unit doing blue-sky thinking out here, you had a Number 10 Policy Unit responsible for the day-to-day, and the Delivery Unit... making sure things we said were going to happen in hospitals and schools, etc., were actually delivered.

What had happened over a period of eight years is that rather than reforming the heart of the government machine, the centre of the government machine, what we'd done was bolted on bits to the central government machine... And so there was a taking-stock period, particularly in the autumn of 2004 when we were considering what actually is it that the centre of government needs? And I always thought that the centre of government needed [reform, but] there would have been a huge sort of controversy and all that jazz. Look if you've got a prime minister and you've got all these little units and which really are a prime minister's department in all but name, why don't you have a prime minister's department? Then the prime minister can drive his or her agenda through the whole of Whitehall instead of having to go through a little unit here and a little unit here, having to sort out all the arrangements with the Treasury and so on and so forth.[202]

This was a reference to Number Ten planning that had happened in 2005—and also in 2001—that envisaged a major reconfiguration of Number Ten, the Treasury, and the Cabinet Office. With both, Blair led his troops halfway up the hill then down again in the wake of electoral victory, as Brown privately made it clear that his Treasury would not be touched, nor would a move to the Foreign Office be acceptable—an honourable option in a less aggressive atmosphere, especially for a would-be future prime minister with only domestic political experience. The counter-threat was that either would result in Brown and his allies heading to the back benches and conducting a guerrilla war.

This was only the latest episode in a long-running saga at the heart of British economic policymaking. Throughout history, the two roles of the Treasury, of balancing the books and of trying to foster growth, had seemed antithetical. To address this, there was an internal reorganization within the Treasury, explicitly recognizing the two functions in 1962. This became a formal split in 1964, with the economic side becoming the Department of Economic Affairs. It did not last, being abolished in 1969, and its various functions returned to the Treasury or handed to the Ministry of Technology and the Department of Employment and Productivity. The Heath years saw the Treasury at its lowest ebb, with the rise of the Department of Trade and Industry, when Sir William Armstrong, head of the Home Civil Service—an unelected official—coordinated much economic policy quietly from the Cabinet Office, attracting the sobriquet 'deputy prime minister'. Heath considered splitting the Treasury too,[203] while Callaghan said if he had won in 1979, he would have divided the Treasury into a Ministry of Finance and an Office of Management and Budget.[204] This is what Blair allowed Milburn and others to reconsider in 2005:

> I think that would have made some sense. I think actually the prime minister being able to say, 'This is what I want for the totality of the government machine, this is what I want for how we drive public expenditure,' would have made sense. And I think actually it will come back . . . Because, and this is beyond a Tony Blair versus Gordon Brown type of thing, people think that the machinery isn't quite right. It isn't.
>
> Because what happened de facto during the Blair years is that, although this was never written down as part of the organic plan for how Whitehall would work, in effect you had two centres of government. You had a Prime Minister's centre, the Cabinet Office, Strategy Unit, Delivery Unit, etc. Then you had a Treasury with quite a broad remit over areas of both of public expenditure, fiscal policy and domestic policy. Well, that's fine when they are all agreeing. But, occasionally, they don't.[205]

Quiet planning got under way in the run-up to Brown moving to Number Ten, as Nick Macpherson, permanent secretary to the Treasury from 2005, described:

> There was a period, I guess from early 2006 onwards, where there were some people in the organization who were basically helping Brown develop his programme for government and I can remember John Kingman [senior Treasury official] doing a lot of work on the machinery

of government which, with the benefit of hindsight, was probably a red herring. But Brown was very focused on whether there was a better way of arranging the deck chairs in Whitehall. There was a lot of interest in how you would organize Number Ten and the Cabinet Office which Gus [O'Donnell, then Cabinet Secretary] and I got involved with Ed Balls.[206]

With Brown about to become prime minister, and after the election-that-never-was, he immediately proposed doing precisely what he had blocked just two years before:

In May 2007, and later again in November, I asked Ed Balls to be minister in charge of No. 10 and the Cabinet Office, but understandably he preferred to be a departmental minister in his own right and I felt it wrong to deny him that chance. He was probably right to refuse: whoever I brought into that job would, I knew, be constantly accused of being an unelected second prime minister.[207]

Under the Brown plan, Balls would become Chief Secretary to the Treasury, the second-ranking minister below the Chancellor, Alistair Darling, but with a joint role as lead minister for the Cabinet Office. Balls said in his memoir:

I thought this was a doubly bad idea. Firstly, because people would inevitably conclude I was being placed in the Treasury to keep the new Chancellor in check. Secondly, we'd always both believed that the Treasury played an important constitutional role in balancing against Number Ten, especially in a government with a majority. That's why we'd fended off Tony Blair's attempt in 2005 to create some hybrid of the Treasury and the Cabinet Office. Having held that position for the previous decade, it would be illogical and unprincipled to try to fudge the divide just because Gordon was now the PM.[208]

In Brown's autobiography, which arrived a year after Balls's, the former prime minister reflected on the future demands and needs of the very centre of British government when he wrote: 'As the complexity and scale of government grows ever greater, the legitimate demands for accountability mean we will have to find new ways [including] a reorganisation of Number Ten, reform of the Cabinet Office, a better system for appointing ministers and stronger parliamentary scrutiny.'[209] The financial crisis drove Brown's thinking—and he discerned the Treasury reverting to type, pre-2007, and a renewed focus on balancing the books and sound money:

> As the recession started to bite, I could sense from my new vantage point in Number Ten that there was a change in the air at the Treasury. By moving to the forefront of its role promoting industry, productivity, science, healthcare and poverty alleviation, the Treasury was praised and criticised in equal measure as it bestrode Whitehall between 1997 and 2007...But as I surveyed the response to the recession, I was alarmed. Was I now witnessing this once powerful institution retreating into a shell? Was it shifting away from being the activist department that said 'yes' to innovation and reform and reverting to its traditional role as the finance department that specialised in saying 'no'? When the recession started to engulf us, I could see the need for far more effective coordination across government.[210]

Intriguingly and, should it have happened in the way Brown sketched in his memoir, quite hypocritically, he considered an approach not dissimilar to Edward Heath's increasingly apolitical and technocratic one, both of them at a time of intense economic and political pressure:

> I thought of changes that would have put Gus O'Donnell, who had experience in both the Treasury and the Cabinet Office, in charge of a joint operation, with Nick [Macpherson, permanent secretary to the Treasury] becoming Secretary to the Cabinet. When I told Gus very confidentially what I was considering, and simply asked him for his personal and private view, he broke my confidence by telling Nick, who clearly—and wrongly—regarded it as a demotion. Between them they scuppered the plan.[211]

This would have been government, not by unelected adviser, but certainly by unelected civil servant, a bold move for a prime minister who wrote in the same book of his fear of the unelected usurping democracy.

History tells us that there is no easy way to share out the functions of Number Ten, the Treasury, and the Cabinet Office. There may be a more efficient way, but this would increase the power of the prime minister, certainly over the Chancellor, and probably over other Cabinet ministers as well. It is, however, an issue that simply does not go away. Should Theresa May have won a convincing victory at the 2017 general election, her joint chief of staff Nick Timothy was said to be planning a Treasury break-up due to 'a longstanding belief that the Treasury had too much control'.[212]

Treasury core business

After the pitched battles between Blair and Brown over the public service reform bills of his second term, a fresh dynamic emerged in Blair's final term, 2005–7. New analysis from senior Treasury officials looks back at the Brown chancellorship after the seemingly never-ending crises of his short premiership and the subsequent austerity of the Coalition with a sense of unavoidable regret in hindsight. Sir Dave Ramsden, who ran the euro assessment in 2003 and who left the Treasury in 2017 to be a deputy governor of the Bank of England, told us that 'these huge public service reforms' after 2003 'don't feel like core Treasury business'.[213]

He wondered if the focus on the euro question, at least until 2003, and the assumptions of continuous economic growth, meant that the Treasury and British government at the centre took their eyes off the ball at precisely the wrong time:

> The Treasury has always had the things it cares about. These change a bit over time, different of us would put different emphasis [on] whether the focus should be sound finances or a growing economy. But the Treasury also likes and is at its best when it has strong political leadership and people who really have ideas for the Treasury to implement, including in that good leadership from the special advisers. I think we still had the capacity to do things, but we and the Bank of England, and we were told this by the IMF, just began to believe that we were in this Great Moderation and that things were going to go on as they were, the trend was going to continue…We were into the sixty-third or sixty-fourth successive quarter of growth; it just stops you challenging yourself; it wasn't even that we were in 'group think', you just stop asking yourself questions over what could go wrong and I do think that things like the euro were so all consuming that they displaced a lot of activity.

The 'Great Moderation' is the term economists use to describe the period in the Western economies starting sometime around 1990 and ending with the financial crisis.[214] Economists differ about the causes:

better monetary policy, often coupled with central bank independence, a shift from manufacturing to service-based employment bringing greater flexibility in the labour market, the increased use of information technology, and simple good luck have all been mooted.[215] The period lasted so long that policymakers had stopped thinking about how it might end, according to Sir Dave:

> Somehow the culture and the capability of not just the Treasury but the wider environment meant we weren't asking ourselves the right questions. We had loads of opportunities to ask them if we had wanted to, we just got lulled into this false sense of security as a country. And we're still trying to make sense now … about what we've got, we're still trying to work out what the new normal is, we got so used to the Great Moderation.[216]

Ed Balls agreed:

> Because every major crisis in the last fifty years had been driven by inflation and inflationary pressures in the housing and labour markets, the fact that inflation was low and stable in Britain, and the labour and housing markets were operating relatively normally, gave us a confidence that we shouldn't have had. We weren't worried enough about whether banks on our high streets were sound and whether our financial system was stable. We weren't even asking those questions. We were scanning the horizon for global risks, rather than focusing on the risks at the end of our nose.[217]

What is more, Sir Dave thought the Treasury was going through a period 'where it lost some of its capacity to think for itself', as it 'went through a phase of getting outsiders to do big reviews':[218] Derek Wanless on health funding,[219] Peter Gershon on public sector efficiency,[220] Adair Turner on pensions,[221] Kate Barker on housing,[222] David Miles on mortgage finance,[223] and Rod Eddington on transport.[224]

What shape was the Treasury in 2007 and was there a structural deficit before the crash?

In retrospect, the main argument against Brown's chancellorship was that he bequeathed a structural deficit which left the country in a poor state when the Great Recession began in 2008, and which damaged him so much as prime minister. David Cameron and George Osborne exploited his difficulty ruthlessly: 'This government has maxed out our nation's credit card' (Cameron);[225] and 'He didn't fix the roof when the sun was shining. His eleven Budgets have left us with the worst public finances in Europe' (Osborne).[226] These were open goals against a backdrop of harder times. The preceding years had been described as 'nice'—non-inflationary consistently expansionary—by the governor of the Bank of England, Mervyn King, in 2003, a period in which growth was above trend, unemployment fell steadily, and inflation remained low and stable, which he predicted in 2004 was to be followed by another decade 'not of the same order but also desirable, or *not so bad* [our italics]'.[227] Four years later, this prediction fell apart.

Did Brown preside over a structural deficit? Balls pointed out that in 1997, 'When we came into the Treasury, the deficit was still above 3 per cent,' but the commitment to match the Conservative's planned spending plans, something Clarke later said he would probably not have followed,[228] squeezed government spending and by 1999 had created a budget surplus. Balls observed to us, sardonically, yet with some truth:

> None of us expected those surpluses, it was a complete disaster, it was not the plan...we wanted to get to the point where you had a small deficit for capital and an overall surplus...The 3G mobile phone auction was a complete catastrophe! We were auctioning the 3G mobile spectrum, estimates are that we were going to raise between £5m and £7m, they do this market auction which raises £22bn, massive shock to us, even more of a shock to the shareholders of the companies paying £22bn.[229]

Macpherson took this point and linked it to what came later:

> The revenues took a long time to revive but by the late [19]90s the revenues were for the only time in modern history persistently outstripping expectations. That hasn't happened since and it didn't happen much before that time. I remember at various points being almost embarrassed by how much we had coming in...We were literally

awash... it was becoming a problem because once you have a surplus, everyone wants to spend it.[230]

Once the commitment to match Tory spending plans came to an end in 1999, New Labour changed tack. Pressure built for spending to rise markedly. Labour supporters and MPs alike began to ask: 'What is a Labour government for if not to spend on what we believe in?' Planning was under way for an unprecedented increase in public service spending. This caused the famous outburst from Brown, after Blair announced on Sunday morning TV that the government would bring health spending up to the European Union average over five years, that the prime minister had 'stolen my fucking Budget'.[231] There was even the 1p rise in the rate of National Insurance contributions (basically a form of income tax) for the NHS in the 2002 Budget.

Kenneth Clarke insisted in 2005: 'I passed on to Brown the strongest economy and the soundest public finances for a generation... It remains an iron law of politics that the job of Conservative governments is to clear up the mess left by Labour governments.'[232]

Macpherson took a philosophical view:

This was a period where it was legitimate to conclude in a sense that we had mastered macroeconomic policy. As a policymaker, it's always the most dangerous point, where you think that you've solved the problem, you're almost certainly presiding over the next... The extraordinary force of revenue in that [earlier] period, in my view, with the benefit of hindsight, encouraged the view that we could afford to spend a bit more than I think we should have done and that then sowed the seeds of the deficit. But even as the deficit got bigger, it wasn't that big... It was quite interesting if you heard the political debate, about what the Institute for Fiscal Studies was saying through the late period, it was that there was a black hole in the government's public finances and then you'd ask what is the size of this black hole and it was £10bn max, and when the financial crisis happened it turns out the structural black hole was over £100bn.[233]

Gordon Brown used the Treasury as a shadow Number Ten and turned it into a spending department in the process. Never before had the

Treasury been quite so powerful and feared. But it would be again. As John Kingman, who ended his term in the Treasury as acting permanent secretary, noted in a valedictory lecture:

> People sometimes forget that Osborne in opposition was a fierce critic of the way Brown had extended the role of the Treasury beyond its traditional remit; in government, Osborne proclaimed, 'The micro-management and empire building would stop...the era of the expanding Treasury empire is over.' In practice, of course, it didn't work out quite like that.[234]

Yet the true question was not whether the 'imperial Treasury' approach was right—a politician and a leader of a huge organization has rightfully much scope to organize the way they see fit (and can get away with)—but whether or not changing the core functions of the Treasury meant that it missed dark clouds gathering. For Treasury civil servants, their very 'competence was in question; they needed to show they could still do the day job', according to Jonathan Portes, now at King's College London but a Treasury official and economist at the Cabinet Office before 2009.[235]

Nick Macpherson thought that the received wisdom that Gordon Brown and the Treasury were in the ascendant during this period was simplistic, that Blair's lament over his stillborn Fundamental Savings Review in his last term not getting off the ground was damaging to Brown too, and that in retrospect the dynamic of Brown moving two years into a Parliament from the Treasury to Number Ten caused him later difficulties:

> The interesting thing about 2005 to 2007 is that, again with the benefit of hindsight it may have weakened Brown's position when he finally became prime minister, was that not a huge amount happened. We'd had a spending review in 2002 and 2004, in a normal world you'd have had a spending review in 2006 and we actually started a spending review in 2005 which was subsequently postponed. It ties in with the point about the Fundamental Savings Review: Brown was very keen that this would be his spending review, he didn't want to reach the climax of negotiations with Blair in charge because then Blair would have imposed his stamp on it, so I think that was relevant.[236]

The purpose of the Fundamental Savings Review was to 'move beyond the catch-up in investment in public services', Blair said in his memoir, and to deal with fears that Labour was the party of the 'big state' and of 'tax and spend... arguments that I was sure, in time, would pull apart our coalition in the country, and therefore our ability to win'. He admitted he could not overcome Brown's obstruction:

> Unfortunately, the FSR was fought every inch of the way and was the one element I was unable to put in place prior to departure, it being the one that really did depend on Gordon's cooperation... We should also accept that from 2005 onwards Labour was insufficiently vigorous in limiting or eliminating the potential structural deficit. The failure to embrace the Fundamental Savings Review of 2005–06 was, in retrospect, a much bigger error than I ever thought at the time.[237]

Balls dismissed the idea that Blair had reversed the presumption that a prime minister wants to spend public money and a Chancellor wants to save it: 'Tony Blair was quite keen on spending money on public services, never in favour of big cuts in it.'[238]

Macpherson told us that Blair in fact won at least one big battle with the Treasury in his third term, 2005–7, that resulted in higher spending:

> He was more determined than ever to make progress on the things he really cared about, so you have the Adair Turner pensions review which in the end was in my view a defeat for the Treasury, signing up to reintroducing the earnings link on the pension, added a significant cost pressure on the public finances.[239]

Later, Macpherson was blunter, describing the decision as, 'a monumental mistake—we're still paying the price for it, which is why the old age pension will take up ever increasing amounts of public spending'.[240] There was also, Macpherson noted, 'an EU finance deal where Blair disregarded the Treasury's position'. These defeats for the Treasury continued a string from the second term:

> There was the debate before 2005 on foundation trusts; university finance was another area which I can remember the Treasury lost on, Brown submitted a paper on a graduate tax and it was totally disregarded, so it may seem that this was a period when the Treasury was

in charge, but if you were in the Treasury you felt we were losing too many of the arguments.

Macpherson also admitted that there might have been some truth in the suggestion that in his last Budget, Brown could have demonstrated more control over spending because he was hoping to become prime minister and did not want to make any unpopular decisions:

> Normally, what you do in a post-election Budget is...tighten policy and, to be fair to Brown, the Budget in 2006 did that to a degree, I mean it probably had a number at the bottom which was positive rather than negative, i.e. it tightened policy, but he probably, understandably, didn't want to take on interest groups at that time and it meant that the normal cycle of doing quite a lot of nasty things at the beginning of a parliament to set you up to do nice things later was missed out on. But, in the event, the scale of the financial crisis from late 2007 made that slightly academic.[241]

Blair was nearing the end, but as Brown assumed the ascendancy, to borrow Peter Mandelson's dichotomy, the incumbent became the insurgent.[242]

Balls's final analysis

Ed Balls was central to the New Labour project. He was the 'hyphen which joined, the buckle which fastened' Brown to the Treasury mandarins, the special adviser who seamlessly connected the political to the official. While we have demonstrated that the New Labour division between Blair and Brown did not ever totally break down, it is undeniable that the problems lasted throughout the thirteen years of Blair's leadership. Did Balls, as the thinker, instigator, and coordinator behind much of the Treasury's power during the Blair years have any regrets?

> The reality is that you always look back and regret that you didn't do more, and things which went wrong and the arguments which happened which didn't need to happen, and also we did some really great things and we did them often in a very cooperative and purposeful way, and so I'm very proud of what we did, and so I can have regrets and not regret what we achieved and those things are consistent.

This was a really unprecedented time in British politics where you had a government for ten years which had a huge working majority, it had relatively strong public finances, it had no financial crisis knocking us off course, and it had a very intellectually powerful leadership between Number Ten and the Treasury which meant that we could do what we wanted to do and we weren't fighting events, we weren't on the defensive and we had big choices to make which we could deliver.

Now that's really unusual to be in government when we were deciding spending allocations and devising budgets, it wasn't, we're hugely under pressure with our backs against the wall, what thing do we have to manoeuvre to get us out of this hole we're in? It was, we can make big decisions about how to reshape things and what are we going to do. And, of course, within that there are arguments and disagreements and different priorities and Tony would say can't we just abolish inheritance tax, and Gordon would say the most important thing is to have a new Scottish parliamentary settlement and are we going to join the euro or not, but in the end we were able to do big things and we did loads and loads of big things.

In that situation you are bound to have different groups develop around the key figures and that's not so different from the past, but because you had such a big majority and such strength at the centre and so much room for manoeuvre you are bound to have a jostling for power and control and I think on both sides that's always a danger of being destructive, because people around Tony were probably more frustrated with Tony than with Gordon because Tony wouldn't do what they wanted, and people got frustrated with Gordon because he didn't do what they wanted vis-à-vis Tony, and Gordon couldn't always give appointments to people he wanted to support. Tony would have given in too many times on appointments, and so you would have a natural but potentially quite destructive polarization into two groups.[243]

Balls went further in his memoir, saying that Blair and Brown's failure was that 'they did not reveal more openly the reality of their comradeship . . . If anything, several of us old-timers sometimes thought that the friendship between them got in the way of good decision-making.'[244]

To 'The Blair Years' class, he elaborated:

The 1997–2001 Parliament, on policy it was a markedly common agenda, in my experience, they actually got on pretty well, but the political tensions which had started in [19]94 continued to grow.

They grew because there was a large majority and people gather around the poles, and the poles here were not Labour or Conservative, they weren't even left or right, they were two personalities with actually really rather a common agenda both of which were New Labour, but people started to become a Tony Blair person or a Gordon Brown person... Into the second Parliament, all of these trends in my view continued, fundamentally there was a common agenda on policy, the relationship in my view continued to be stable actually for most of the time but the politics became much, much more messy.[245]

He expanded in an interview with us on where he thought the differences between Blair and Brown had occurred. He said Blair needed to be the bigger man:

There were differences on policy. There's no doubt that after 2001 Tony wanted to go harder on antisocial behaviour. Tony was right and Gordon was wrong about that... From a Treasury point of view we were always sceptical that ID cards would work... By 2005 it was hugely frustrating to some of the people in the factions on either side who thought they would gain more from a breaking-up than a coming-together... But even up to 2007, I don't see any big parting of the ways on New Labour policy...

Alan Milburn and Stephen Byers were both Gordon Brown's chief secretaries but they always at every stage acted like they weren't. And I think those kind of guys encouraged that polarization and they did so and others did so for their own purposes, and that's particularly true of people who are elected. I think my big regret and annoyance is that in the end I think Tony Blair and Gordon Brown pandered to that too much and didn't do enough together to have a sense of common purpose, collective purpose which could transcend all of that. Because in the end they either tolerate or slap down that growing-up of views and the truth is they both politically tolerated it even though it wasn't substantively based, so when I look at the arguments there were political arguments that weren't actually based on a substantive difference of view...

I think that they had a huge opportunity and they made loads of ground, the polarization is inevitable and they were both not big enough to see that together they would have achieved much more if they had knocked down the polarization rather than built it up, and they both built it up.

I think that in the end they both should regret that. Normally, events come along and knock you off course way before but because it didn't, I think that Tony ought to have got key people round more and said, cards on the table, we're in this together, here's what we've got to do, let's have more of a collective sense. He never did that, he was useless at that collective sense of purpose and he didn't even do it well amongst his own group. If he had tried, Gordon would have been sceptical and obstinate and wouldn't have engaged, wouldn't have liked it, and that was bad as well because Gordon was not the leader Tony was.

Maybe Tony concluded that because Gordon wouldn't have engaged, he himself didn't try but actually he should have tried much harder because most of us wanted to work for Tony Blair and Gordon Brown and the fact that they allowed the division to happen... they didn't need to.[246]

For the 'The Blair Years' class, Balls had the final word:

To the extent that there were mistakes made by New Labour in that period I think they were mistakes that were genuinely common to Tony Blair and Gordon Brown. I think both of them were not tough enough on financial regulation in this period but it wasn't one or the other. If anything, Tony was urging a softer position. We shouldn't have used the rhetoric of boom and bust, Tony used to do that just as much as Gordon Brown. [In actual fact, ' "No return to boom and bust" was a phrase I coined when I was chancellor,' wrote Kenneth Clarke in 2005.[247]]

On policy I would say it was a 90 per cent common agenda. In terms of the friendship, on the day Tony Blair finally announced that he would be standing down the following summer after the events of that weekend, the divisive events of that weekend, I can remember Gordon Brown on the phone with Tony having a very long conversation about exactly what words Tony should use and the best way to say it. You wouldn't have sat and listened to that phone conversation and said that these guys had an irrevocable breakdown in the friendship of their relationship. There were tensions and pressures, but they were still considerably closer than anybody realized from the outside. But in that final period, things had really pulled apart, because the people around Tony didn't want him to go, and the people around Gordon, I'm talking about in Parliament here, thought Tony should have gone in 2004, and in the end it was undoubtedly pulling apart.

Normally, what happens is you have a government which is beset by external pressures and challenges, a financial crisis or a huge big financial event which throws government off course. The reality was that between 1997 and 2007 we had a strikingly stable period in our economic history, so we didn't have a government thrown off course by the economy. Secondly, throughout that entire period we had a huge working majority with a really quite disciplined Labour Party in Parliament. And, thirdly, the Conservative Party which, until David Cameron became the leader, was not at the races and in those circumstances the issue is not dealing with the outside world or dealing with the Opposition, the issue is whether or not you can hold together the collective in any political system, especially in our system where the Executive is so strong, there are always forces which pull apart rather than unite.

In the end, the frustration I would have with Tony Blair and Gordon Brown was that given throughout that period they were on the same agenda far more than anybody would like to admit, the two of them didn't do enough to hold it together. Individual tensions are transcended by the collective purpose. Now, I'm not sure after 1994 how receptive Gordon would have been to that and I also don't think that Tony Blair ever tried anywhere near hard enough to do that. My reading of it, and you may think this self-serving, but I think Gordon was more difficult in his dealings with Tony than Tony was with Gordon, but the people around Tony Blair were far more difficult with Gordon than the people around Gordon were with Tony Blair. But I think both of them in the end didn't do enough to transcend division and say there is a common agenda here and a common purpose. I think that in the end both of them historically pay a price for that.[248]

Conclusion

For the first time since 2007, both the political and official sides of the Treasury have gone on the record looking back over the Blair-Brown years. What we have is the story of a very complicated Chancellor who saw a bigger picture than most, but who required the skills of Ed Balls to distil and translate to the wider Treasury machine.

The Brown-Balls relationship was every bit as trusting, important and effective in its own way as the Blair-Alastair Campbell axis in Number Ten. Both axes will go down in history as outstanding examples of governmental partnerships. In fact, it is an emerging truth that Balls was *the* most impressive special adviser of the Blair years, eclipsing even Campbell after the Iraq imbroglio. (Perhaps one of Blair's biggest mistakes was not to choose Balls for his own team.) That Balls barely left the Treasury after he became an MP in 2005, formally returning to the Treasury as a junior minister in 2006, was beneficial to Chancellor Brown. That Balls wanted to become a Cabinet minister in his own right—and not accept Brown's strange request to wield centralized power in a new part-Cabinet Office-part-Treasury hybrid—weakened Prime Minister Brown.

Moreover, once the early difficulties with an older order of mandarin had been navigated (like, as we have seen, those in Number Ten), the Treasury settled and evolved into perhaps its most powerful incarnation in modern times, certainly for a century. Against the background of strong and unbroken economic growth, the Treasury engaged—sometimes too much and too self-confidently but undoubtedly effectively—in the Blair government's reform of public services, taking on the hugely complex modernization of health and education. Though the policy differences appeared fierce—on foundation hospitals, tuition fees, and the euro in particular—in retrospect, the lack of resignations and eventual agreement between Number Ten and the Treasury lead to the conclusion that the real issues were personality-driven. In each case, as Ed Balls repeatedly pointed out, it is unclear how much Blair and Brown genuinely differed. Blair sided with Brown against Milburn on foundation hospitals; Brown failed to produce a workable graduate tax on student finance; and Blair's political antennae must have told him that he was unlikely ever to win a referendum on abolishing the pound.

Will we ever again see a prime minister and a Chancellor both in post for ten years, side by side? We saw six and six with Cameron and Osborne, and while there clearly was a strong element of 'creative tension' in the Blair years, the Conservative duo were throughout their tenures at huge pains to avoid the 'TB-GBs', a lesson learnt in how not to do it. This went to the extent of Osborne suppressing—for the sake of public unity—his private misgivings about his friend's decision to promise a referendum on Europe.[249] Cameron and Osborne certainly took their chance to paint Brown's chancellorship as a reason for the 'Great Recession' and the deficit it left, but this is difficult to sustain in light of the evidence, while the Bank of England machinery built in the very first days of the New Labour government remains in place two decades later.

A decade on from the Blair years, the story of Brown's Treasury goes down as one of solid achievement, the unnecessary factionalism failing to prevent broadly sound policymaking, which was in the end overshadowed from a quite different and unexpected direction, by the financial crisis of 2008. Brown's New Labour Treasury was a colossus. We are unlikely to see something similar for quite a while.

5

The Iraq War

The Iraq war poses a challenge to historians similar to that posed by the First World War. For people at the time there was no such thing as the First World War; it was just the War or the Great War. Similarly, to most people, 'the Iraq war' means something different now from what it meant then, even though the name is the same. Afterwards, most British people who expressed an opinion agreed that Tony Blair 'lied' to take the country into an 'illegal' war.[1] At the time, opinion was more equivocal, with more people opposed to military action than supporting it, until the invasion began, when it was strongly supported.[2] The general view was that Saddam Hussein was a threat, and the debate was mostly about whether the threat could be contained without military action. After the invasion, Saddam's weapons of mass destruction were not found, and the idea that Blair had made the case for military action in bad faith became widely accepted. Equally, the descent of Iraq into sectarian violence ensured that the policy was seen not just as a failure but the defining one of Blair's time as prime minister, a verdict confirmed by the report of the Chilcot inquiry in 2016.

Chilcot criticized Blair's decision to support the United States invasion on four grounds: (i) planning for the aftermath was inadequate; (ii) decision-making was poorly structured, making it hard to challenge assumptions; (iii) the way legal advice was sought was 'unsatisfactory'; and (iv) the use of force was not a 'last resort'.

In seeking to rebalance the assessment of Blair, we accept that George Bush and Blair failed to recognize the significant risk that the invasion could have disastrous consequences. However, the criticisms of procedure, to the extent that they are not a restatement of the first criticism, seem misplaced. Different processes would not have produced different outcomes. And the 'last resort' is a difficult standard to apply in practice: it is always possible to argue that more time is needed. Our argument is that Blair's decision was made for good reasons in what he thought was the national interest. In this chapter, we look at the background to the Iraq war, from the start of Blair's time as prime minister. Drawing on the accounts of special guests at our 'Blair' history classes, we offer a view of the findings of the Chilcot report informed by the politics of the decision, which the inquiry could not fully take into account.

We make two additional arguments. One is that Blair's decision should be seen as subsidiary to Bush's. Much of the debate about Iraq in Britain is remarkably Anglocentric, premised on the assertion that Blair was personally responsible for much of what followed. For example, Kenneth Clarke, the leading Conservative opponent of the war, said in the House of Commons debate on the Chilcot report: 'The decision to invade Iraq was the most disastrous foreign policy decision taken by this country in my lifetime. It did not cause, but it greatly contributed to, the extraordinary problems that have persisted in the Middle East and the wider world ever since.'[3] In fact, the US government had already decided to invade Iraq and the decision for the British government was whether United Kingdom forces would join them. If it had decided that they should not, the invasion would have gone ahead anyway—'A coalition would be nice, but not essential,' said Vice President Dick Cheney as early as March 2002; 'There are work-arounds,' said Donald Rumsfeld, Secretary of Defense, as late as on the eve of war in March 2003, when it looked as if there might be a last-minute problem with the legal advice. Nothing the British government decided would have made much difference to what happened in Iraq, or to the bloodshed that followed the invasion, or to subsequent events such as the rise of the Islamic State across the Iraqi–Syria border.

Our second argument is that historians need to try to recapture the world as it seemed before the Iraq war, when Islamist terrorism was poorly understood. Although Blair should have given more weight to warnings of disorder in post-invasion Iraq, we argue that he should not be faulted for giving too much weight to the fear that Islamist terrorists and rogue regimes such as Saddam's might at some point work together against the West.

When we asked him in 2011 to reflect on how he reacted to 9/11 ten years earlier, he admitted that it was 'shocking' how little he knew at the time:

> If I knew then what I know now then I would take a far deeper approach to deal with the international terrorism situation. We thought if you knock out al-Qaeda and [Saddam] Hussein, things would sort them-selves out. Which they should have done but I think now I would have had a far clearer understanding of the fact that you were dealing with deep cultural, religious, tribal issues that do not go away just because Saddam wasn't there. That's not to say you should leave Saddam there but it's to say you were in deeper and longer than you imagined. The most interesting thing is that it's quite shocking to me how much more I understand it now than when I was prime minister. I know far more about it now. That doesn't make me any less worried by the way. It's very positive on one level and very challenging on another. The superficiality of knowledge after 9/11 is a real problem.[4]

'It really is pretty scary'

Iraq was one of Blair's first foreign policy problems before he became prime minister. As leader of the Opposition, in September 1996, he offered the Labour Party's support for US air strikes against Baghdad in retaliation for Saddam's attacks on the Kurds. As a condition of the ceasefire that ended the Gulf War in 1991, the UN had required Saddam Hussein to give up his biological, chemical, and nuclear weapons programmes and to submit to inspections to confirm his compliance. Saddam had tried to acquire nuclear technology but had been thwarted when the Israelis bombed the Osirak reactor in 1981. He had used chemical weapons against Iran in the war of 1980–8, and against Kurdish Iraqis at Halabja in 1988.

Blair had been prime minister for only six months when in November 1997 Saddam expelled the UN inspectors in a dispute over access. As it was the latest instalment of a familiar story, media interest was low, but Blair became animated about it. Paddy Ashdown, leader of the Liberal Democrats, recorded his private conversations with Blair in his diary. The two of them were engaged in secret discussions about a possible coalition, including Cabinet appointments for a few Lib Dems, which came to nothing, and Blair was keen to take Ashdown into his confidence about some of his foreign policy concerns:

> I have now seen some of the stuff on this. It really is pretty scary. He [Saddam] is very close to some appalling weapons of mass destruction. I don't understand why the French and others don't get this. We cannot let him get away with it. The world thinks this is just gamesmanship. But it's deadly serious.[5]

Intelligence briefings may have had more impact on Blair because he had had no experience of such things as a minister, but there were good reasons to find them 'pretty scary'. Since the fall of the Berlin Wall in 1989, the Secret Intelligence Service (SIS, popularly known as MI6) had regarded the proliferation of biological, chemical, and nuclear weapons as the greatest threat to the security of the UK. The intelligence services in the US took a similar view. Libya, Iran, Iraq, and North Korea were causes of concern, as were non-state networks such as those of A. Q. Khan, the scientist responsible for Pakistan's nuclear bomb who had gone rogue in the 1980s.[6] Small groups animated by quasi-religious ideology, such as the Japanese cult Aum Shinrikyo (now known as Aleph), complicated the picture. 'Ever since March 1995, American officials had had in the back of their minds Aum Shinrikyo's release of sarin nerve gas in the Tokyo subway,' which had killed thirteen people in five coordinated attacks.[7]

Islamist terrorists based in Pakistan, Afghanistan, and Sudan and able to travel to the US and Europe were not well known, but after the truck bomb attack on the World Trade Center in 1993, which killed six people, the American agencies were beginning to see how they might feature in their worst-case scenarios. That attack, intended to bring down a symbol of American confidence, was the work of Ramzi Yousef, a Kuwaiti-born al-Qaeda sympathizer whose uncle, Khalid Sheikh Mohammed, was later held by the US to have been an organizer of the 9/11 attacks; Osama bin Laden's involvement in the 1993 attack was 'cloudy', according to the *9/11 Commission Report*.[8]

Separately, American and British analysts had become more worried about Saddam Hussein when his son-in-law Hussein Kamil defected to Jordan on 8 August 1995:

> He had been responsible for the development and manufacture of Iraq's proscribed weapons programmes... [He] said that, after inspections had started, Iraq had destroyed its biological weapons and he himself had ordered the destruction of Iraq's chemical weapons. In addition, all Iraq's SCUD missiles and their components had been destroyed, although two launchers had been dismantled and hidden. Lt Gen Kamil also referred to a nuclear project that inspectors were not aware of, at the Sodash site, where equipment had been buried.[9]

Instead of reassuring agencies that Iraq had disarmed, however, the new information of previous concealment convinced them that Saddam must now be concealing more.[10] Tim Dowse, chief of the assessments staff in the Cabinet Office, told the Chilcot inquiry: 'He [Kamil] also exposed an organised Iraqi campaign of deception directed from the top—so I think in many ways what he revealed to us very much coloured our approach thereafter.'[11]

Blair was not inclined, in any case, to take risks with national security. In part, this was a matter of electoral strategy. The Labour Party had stood on a manifesto promising one-sided nuclear disarmament only ten years before, and his own past membership of the Campaign for Nuclear Disarmament was an embarrassment. Just as Bill Clinton had to live down his draft-dodging past, Blair was determined that a Labour government would not be seen as soft on defence. So when Saddam expelled the UN weapons inspectors in November 1997, Blair's tone was uncompromising: 'It is absolutely essential that he backs down on this, that he be made to back down,' he told the House of Commons. 'If he does not, we will simply face this problem, perhaps in a different and far worse form, in a few years' time.'[12]

By then, Blair had invited Margaret Thatcher to Number Ten twice, and discussed the Balkans and Iraq with her. She was strongly of the view that the only way to deal with tyrants was by the credible threat of military force.[13] Blair may have had his ideas about the nature of 'leadership' confirmed. In any case, her advice was now put to the test, as if under laboratory conditions. The November 1997 crisis was temporarily resolved, but Saddam continued to try the bars of his cage, backing off each time his intransigence succeeded in reuniting the main players at the United Nations. There was another confrontation in February 1998, when Blair, possibly through inexperience rather than democratic principle, asked for a vote in the House of Commons on the use of force against Iraq. This was the first time any prime minister had sought such authority and Blair regretted it, because it gave twenty-three Labour MPs—including Jeremy Corbyn—the chance to vote against the government.[14] But the threat of bombing, by the US and UK, had the required effect on Saddam, who allowed the inspectors to resume their work.

This lasted eight months, and in that time President Bill Clinton was distracted by the investigation by Kenneth Starr, the special prosecutor, into his affair with Monica Lewinsky, a White House intern. On 7 August 1998, simultaneous truck-bomb suicide attacks on US embassies in Kenya and Tanzania killed 200 Kenyans, 13 Americans, and 12 Tanzanians. Both the suicide attacks and the response to them look very different when viewed from the other end of the kaleidoscope, after 11 September 2001, because of Osama bin Laden's likely involvement.[15] The significance of the date of the attacks was that it was the anniversary of US military deployment in Saudi Arabia in 1990, which had been in preparation for action against Saddam, who had just invaded Kuwait.

In response, the US launched cruise missile attacks on the Al-Shifa drugs factory in Khartoum, Sudan, and on alleged terrorist training

camps in Afghanistan, on 20 August 1998. The Al-Shifa attack was a
premonition of the 2003 Iraq war in miniature. Blair issued an immediate statement of strong support. The attack was seen as a crude attempt
to distract public opinion from Clinton's domestic problems, not least
because it echoed the plot of the 1997 film *Wag the Dog*, featuring a
president who faked a war to distract attention from a domestic scandal;
and Blair's support was seen, especially by Old Labourites, as slavish
poodle-ism. Michael Foot condemned it: 'Clinton's bombing of
Khartoum and the terrorists in Afghanistan was a scandalous misuse
of power and it was improper of the British government to give its
support.'[16] Even the Foreign Secretary had his doubts. 'Robin Cook
refused to go on the *Today* programme to defend it, saying there might
be collateral damage and it could be difficult.'[17] The intelligence case
for destroying what purported to be an aspirin factory in a country in
need of cheap medicine was weak and contested. US intelligence had
reported that the factory was used for making precursor ingredients
for nerve gas, with Bin Laden's financial support. 'Analysts in the [CIA's
bin Laden] unit felt that they were viewed as alarmists even within the
CIA.'[18] In Britain, George Robertson, the Defence Secretary, was
prepared publicly to defend the strikes and claimed Britain had 'independent evidence' that bin Laden was 'seeking to acquire chemical
and biological weapons'.[19] This was not evidence that Al-Shifa was a
legitimate target, but it did suggest that the British intelligence
agencies were concerned about bin Laden and his jihadist network,
al-Qaeda, previously based in Sudan and now based in Afghanistan.
Al-Qaeda became better known when it carried out a suicide attack
on the *USS Cole* in the Yemeni port of Aden on 12 October 2000;
seventeen sailors were killed. Alastair Campbell recorded in his diary:
'The bombing, probably Bin Laden's lot, of a US ship. Grim.'

Meanwhile in Iraq, Saddam withdrew cooperation with the UN
inspectors again in October 1998. The US and UK military were
already alarmed by Saddam's probing of the no-fly zones that they
sought to enforce over the north and south of Iraq. These had been
imposed since 1991 to protect the Kurds in the north and the Shia in

the south, but Saddam was trying to shoot down coalition planes. Sir Kevin Tebbit, permanent under secretary at the Ministry of Defence, said the risk of attack was becoming serious: 'The British and the Americans were left with three options. Stop flying and patrolling the no-fly zones; or continue and have your plane shot down; or you did it a third way and attack the infrastructure.'[20] Clinton hesitated long and hard, with Blair pressing him to strike, before he ordered the bombing of suspect sites. Saddam backed down at the last moment and US aircraft were recalled while in the air on the way to Iraq on 14 November. Blair drew his own conclusions in the House of Commons:

> When he [Saddam] finally saw, correctly, that we were ready to use force on a substantial scale, he crumbled. I hope that other countries more dubious of the use of force may now see that Saddam is moved by the credible threat of force. He has exposed the fact that his fear is greater than his courage. Let us learn the lesson of that.[21]

Saddam, however, learned a different lesson, which was that his brinkmanship sustained his authority in Iraq. Richard Butler, the UN weapons inspector, reported the following month that the Iraqi regime was again failing to cooperate, and this time a bombing campaign, known as Desert Fox, went ahead for four days from 16 to 19 December 1998. Although this attack was supported by the Conservative Party and most of the British press, its timing was again regarded with scepticism, as it coincided with the start of impeachment proceedings against Clinton. Hardly remarked on at all, however, was the legal basis of British participation, which rested—in the absence of specific new authority from the UN Security Council, which would have been vetoed by Russia and China—on the enforcement of the disarmament provisions of Resolution 687, which ended the Gulf War in 1991, and on which the 2003 invasion would also rest.

Kosovo and Sierra Leone

Our purpose here is to show that Iraq was a preoccupation of Tony Blair's long before the US planned a land invasion in the wake of 9/11, in the Labour Government's second term. At this point we should also touch briefly on the other foreign policy questions of Blair's first term. The British military interventions in Sierra Leone and, as part of NATO, in Kosovo, were less controversial than in Iraq, and have been studied in detail elsewhere.[22] We rehearse them briefly here, not least because they were important in shaping Blair's, and his Government's, thinking about the arguments for joining the US military action in Iraq.

Kosovo was the last of the conflicts to emerge from the break-up of Yugoslavia in 1991–2, after the collapse of communism. A province of Serbia, it had a mainly Muslim and ethnic Albanian population which was subjected to a campaign of 'ethnic cleansing' by Slobodan Milosevic, the Serbian nationalist leader. In opposition, Blair had criticized John Major's government for its failure to stand up to Bosnian Serb aggression in the multi-ethnic state of Bosnia and Herzegovina. In that case Bill Clinton had finally led NATO in a limited bombing campaign that produced a negotiated settlement. Now Blair rallied NATO again, and a reluctant President Clinton, to bomb Serbian targets and to threaten the use of ground forces, which eventually prompted a Serb withdrawal. Within months, Milosevic was toppled and brought to justice at The Hague, although he died before the trial ended. It is hard to recall now the extent to which Blair staked his credibility on his ability to persuade the US president, and the extent to which NATO's success in Kosovo, which had seemed so unlikely, was attributable to Blair's personal leadership.

Sierra Leone was a different kind of conflict, although it too featured war crimes and British military intervention in defence of a predominantly Muslim population. Ahmad Tejan Kabbah, the elected president of Sierra Leone, a former British colony in West Africa, was overthrown by army officers three weeks after Blair's election as prime minister in May 1997. Blair took up Kabbah's cause and supported his restoration to power in a counter-coup led by Nigerian forces in 1998. This government collapsed two years later, and Foday Sankoh, leader of the Revolutionary United Front, took several hundred UN peacekeepers hostage. Blair, emboldened by his success in Kosovo, ordered British special forces to join a UN operation which secured the release of the hostages. British paratroopers were then deployed to defend the main airport in Sierra Leone, initially to allow the evacuation of foreign nationals, but in practice to help defeat Sankoh's gangster army. Sankoh himself was arrested and tried for crimes against humanity—although he too died before the trial concluded.

Both interventions were generally regarded as successful, most importantly by the peoples of the two states, among whom Blair is widely hailed as a hero. Blair himself was so impressed by his own role as Clinton's backbone in the Kosovo conflict that, even before that conflict was resolved, he elevated his instinct for leadership on the world stage to his own doctrine, the 'Doctrine of the International Community', set out in his Chicago speech of April 1999. In it he set out the tests for outside intervention in the affairs of sovereign nations:

> First, are we sure of our case? War is an imperfect instrument for righting humanitarian distress, but armed force is sometimes the only means of dealing with dictators. Second, have we exhausted all diplomatic options? We should always give peace every chance, as we have in the case of Kosovo. Third, on the basis of a practical assessment of the situation, are there military operations we can sensibly and prudently undertake? Fourth, are we prepared for the long term? In the past we talked too much of exit strategies. But having made a commitment we cannot simply walk away once the fight is over; better to stay with moderate numbers of troops than return for repeat performances with large numbers. And finally, do we have national interests involved?[23]

It could be argued that these tests were met in Afghanistan after 9/11, but it is harder to apply them to the case of Iraq. There were, in any case, other warning signs in Kosovo for Blair's future. The main one was NATO's dependence on US military power. For Blair, that held two lessons: that the European Union should increase its collective defence capability (for which he found an ally, briefly, in Jacques Chirac); and that British influence in world affairs required absolute loyalty to the US. Four years later, he told the House of Commons:

> I believed this before I became Prime Minister, but I believe it even more strongly—in fact, very strongly; it is an article of faith with me—the

American relationship and our ability to partner America in these
difficult issues is of fundamental importance, not just to this country
but to the wider world.'[24]

By the end of 1998, there was little prospect of further action against
Saddam. The Iraqi dictator was known to be trying to bypass the
sanctions regime imposed on his country. The debate about how to
contain him became more fraught, without looking as if it would ever
become critical. There were American foreign policy thinkers who
advocated the deployment of ground troops to overthrow Saddam,
but they were few. The Project for a New American Century, a think
tank, published an open letter to President Clinton entitled 'Remove
Saddam from Power', on 26 January 1998. In October 1998, before
Desert Fox, Clinton had signed the Iraq Liberation Act, which declared:
'It should be the policy of the United States to support efforts to
remove the regime headed by Saddam Hussein from power in Iraq
and to promote the emergence of a democratic government to replace
that regime.' This was later cited by George W. Bush as evidence that
he was merely continuing his predecessor's policy of regime change,
but the Act clearly did not envisage that the US should bring it about.
Before 9/11, the idea that the US would use its troops on the ground
to achieve such an aim was outlandish.

11 September 2001

'It was, in a very real sense, a declaration of war. It was calculated to
draw us into conflict,' commented Tony Blair in his memoir, published nine years later.[25] If so, the al-Qaeda attacks on the World Trade
Center and the Pentagon were wholly successful.[26] After 9/11, military
action in Afghanistan became nearly certain and the invasion of Iraq
became likely. The attacks changed two things: the US administration's perception of risk; and the willingness of the American people
to support foreign wars. Speaking outside Number Ten on 11 September
2001, Blair said that the British stood 'shoulder to shoulder with our
American friends'. When Bush and Blair met in the next few days,

they agreed that Afghanistan would come first and that Iraq was 'for another day'.[27] After a five-week aerial bombing and special forces campaign the Afghan Northern Alliance toppled the Taliban government in Kabul on 13 November 2001—'another day' had come.

As Blair already held the firm view that military action was justified against Saddam Hussein, and as he had been more hawkish than President Bush's predecessor on both Iraq and Kosovo, his attitude towards the prospect of a US-led land invasion was never in doubt. Partly for that reason, however, he may not have fully appreciated the danger to the venture, and to him, of the way that the Bush administration came to its decision. While America's perception of risk may have changed, it was not obvious that the risk posed by Saddam to America or anywhere else had increased. Some intelligence analysts were worried because they thought that Saddam was weakening the sanctions against his regime. The Iraq specialist at MI6, known as SIS 4, told the Chilcot inquiry eight years later:

> The lack of our response to the re-emergence of Iraq as a serious regional power was like having tea with some very proper people in the drawing room and noticing that there was a python getting out of a box in one corner. I was very alarmed at the way that Iraq was eroding the sanctions regime and evading it.[28]

The conventional view, however, was that the threat was if anything diminishing, because the Iraqi economy was wrecked.

Nor was Saddam responsible for 9/11, except inadvertently: by invading Kuwait in 1990 he had caused US forces to be deployed to Saudi Arabia, which was one of the supposed affronts to Islam that most animated Osama bin Laden and his followers. The common description of Iraq as a 'pre-emptive' war was accurate but did not capture its peculiarity, which was that the threat it sought to pre-empt had not changed much. What had changed was the perception of it. President Bush's argument was that 9/11 demonstrated that America should have been more assertive in tackling threats to its security at source.

Sally Morgan, one of Blair's close advisers at the time, said his motives for supporting Bush as he developed his policy were simple:

Lots of people say it was it was all about politics, all about sucking up to Bush, all about the poodle stuff. I'm completely clear that that was not the case. There were three main reasons really as far as he was concerned for action in Iraq. The first, and the strongest for him, although not the legal base, was moral. Whether that comes from the fact he has got a strong sense of religious faith or whether it was wider than that, I'm very clear that he had a very strong moral drive. He had a general view that it was right to deal with this man and what he was doing to his people. Secondly was indeed the political, the pragmatic one if you like, about Britain's place in the world and Britain's relationships with America. And the third was his commitment to liberal interventionism in a wider sense.[29]

Bush's decision to confront Saddam was probably taken early in 2002. It is hard to date precisely. Bush said in the State of the Union address on 29 January 2002, that Iraq was part of an 'axis of evil'. He had already asked for military planning as to how Saddam might be brought down. Early plans were for special forces to infiltrate Iraq, but this was quickly dismissed as unrealistic. At the same time, he asked for intelligence briefings on Saddam's non-compliance with UN resolutions, which meant assessing the regime's biological, chemical, and nuclear weapons capability. The Chilcot report found:

From early 2002, there were increasing indications that key figures in the US Administration were considering military action to achieve regime change in Iraq and there was an emphasis on the potential nexus for the fusion of WMD proliferation and terrorism.

Mr Blair stated that regime change would be desirable. If Saddam Hussein wanted to avoid war, he would need to agree to the return of inspectors.

Mr Blair told President Bush on 6 February that he agreed on the importance of sending a strong signal to the countries identified as an 'axis of evil' that their behaviour needed to change.[30]

Blair wrote in his memoir that, as late as July 2002, the president had not firmly decided on military action:

It's impossible . . . to read the accounts of the meetings during that time without an assumption of a decision already taken.

But here is the difference between everyone else and the final decision taker. Everyone can debate and assume; only one person decides. I knew at that moment that George had not decided. He had . . . a conceptual framework in which the pivotal concept was that Saddam had to come fully into compliance and disarm but he had taken no final decision on the way to make him.[31]

By the time that Vice President Dick Cheney visited London on 6 March 2002, however, he appeared to be canvassing support for military action. Privately, Cheney said to Blair that 'a coalition would be nice, but not essential'.[32] The first long discussion of Iraq in the British Cabinet took place the next day, when ministers considered a Foreign Office 'options paper' for 'the best part of an hour'.[33] At this meeting, several ministers expressed their doubts, and Blair assured his colleagues that 'the management has not lost its marbles'.[34]

The implications of the decision to confront Saddam became clear to Blair the following month: 'The first time we got to grips with it properly was on my visit to Crawford, George's ranch in Texas, in April 2002.'[35] By then, the direction of US policy was clear. 'I made up my mind that Saddam needs to go,' Bush said in an interview in Texas for British television.[36] There was nothing secret about Bush's intentions—although he did not say that he had already asked General Tommy Franks, Commander of US Central Command, to be ready to invade by October.[37] Nor was there anything secret about Blair's support for the principle of 'confronting' Saddam. What was controversial at the time was the question of whether he supported Bush's language of 'regime change', given that British legal opinion was clear that this would be contrary to international law. At the press conference on 6 April, Blair dodged that question and said only that 'doing nothing' was not an option: the threat of WMD was real and had to be dealt with.[38]

The case for war

The important question for Blair—assuming Saddam refused to surrender—was not whether there would be a land invasion of Iraq but whether he could persuade the British people, Parliament, and Cabinet that British forces should be part of it. Blair now knew that his leadership was on the line. At a meeting with his advisers on 23 July 2002, Blair 'was pretty clear that we had to be with the Americans', according to Alastair Campbell. He said, 'It's worse than you think, I actually believe in doing this.'[39]

An official record of this meeting, which became known as the 'Downing Street Memo', was leaked to the *Sunday Times* on 1 May 2005, four days after the leak of the long version of the Attorney General's legal advice from 7 March 2003. Both leaks were intended to destabilize Blair in the days before the general election on 5 May 2005, and both became central to the post-war argument that the case for military action had been manufactured.

The memo recorded the report by Sir Richard Dearlove, head of MI6, 'on his recent talks in Washington. There was a perceptible shift in attitude. Military action was now seen as inevitable. Bush wanted to remove Saddam, through military action, justified by the conjunction of terrorism and WMD. But the intelligence and facts were being fixed around the policy.'[40]

The word 'fixed', having been made public after the Hutton inquiry found that the British government had not 'sexed up' the intelligence, has become a staple of the anti-war case. It is worth quoting the Chilcot report at length on the point:

> In his memoir published in 2007, Mr Tenet wrote that Sir Richard Dearlove had told him that he had been misquoted. Sir Richard had objected in particular to the word 'fixed' and offered a correction. Mr Tenet wrote that he had been told Sir Richard had '...expressed the view...that the war in Iraq was going to happen. He believed the momentum driving it was not really about WMD but rather about bigger issues such as changing the politics of the Middle East.'
>
> Mr Tenet added that Sir Richard
>
> *...recalled that he had a polite, but significant, disagreement with Scooter Libby [Chief of Staff to Vice President Cheney], who was trying to convince him that there was a relationship between Iraq and al-Qaeda. Dearlove's strongly held view based on his own Service's reporting, which had been shared with the*

CIA, was that any contacts that had taken place had come to nothing and that there was no formal relationship . . . He believed that the crowd around the Vice President was playing fast and loose with the evidence. In his view, it was never about 'fixing' the intelligence itself but rather about the undisciplined manner in which the intelligence was being used.

Sir Richard Dearlove told the Inquiry that, during his visit to Washington in July 2002, he had had 'quite contentious and difficult conversations' with Mr Libby as well as discussions with Mr Tenet, Dr Rice and Mr Stephen Hadley, US Deputy National Security Advisor. He had returned from Washington 'deeply concerned that there was momentum in parts of the [US] Administration', and he had warned Mr Blair about that momentum.

In relation to his 'alleged comment' about the intelligence being fixed around the policy, Sir Richard told the Inquiry that this was really a reference to the attempts 'to join up terrorism and Iraq' with which he 'radically disagreed'.

Asked if Mr Blair had taken the conjunction between terrorism and WMD seriously, Sir Richard replied:

. . . I don't think the Prime Minister ever accepted the link between Iraq and terrorism. I think it would be fair to say that the Prime Minister was very worried about the possible conjunction of terrorism and WMD, but not specifically in relation to Iraq . . . [I] think, one could say this is one of his primary national security concerns given the nature of al-Qaeda.

Sir Richard added that he sought an amendment to Mr Rycroft's record of the meeting on 23 July to clarify the meaning of his remarks.

The Inquiry has seen that document.

In response to subsequent questioning, referring to a manuscript note made by Lord Goldsmith during the meeting, Sir Richard accepted that he might well have used the word 'fitted'.

Mr Rycroft confirmed that Sir Richard had challenged his record of the meeting but, after checking his notes and discussing it with others present, he had taken no further action. Mr Rycroft told the Inquiry that he had understood Sir Richard to be making the point that intelligence was going to become part of the public justification for the known US policy of regime change . . .

Lord Wilson [Sir Richard Wilson, who was Cabinet Secretary at the time] told the Inquiry that he didn't think the meeting on 23 July had 'decided on much'.

It had been a 'taking stock' meeting, but what had struck him 'was that some of the language used implied that we were closer to military action than I had imagined that we were'.

Lord Wilson told the Inquiry that two elements of the meeting stood out in his memory: First, there was 'an underlying tension...between the Prime Minister and his Foreign Secretary'. Mr Straw was 'very much in the business of saying: "The crucial thing is to get all this to the United Nations. That's the way we are going to play it. We are nowhere near military action at the minute. All the military things the military are saying need to be seen in the political context."' Mr Straw had been 'pleading quite strongly for the political nuances'; and that he was 'working very hard to keep the Prime Minister...focused on the United Nations and away from getting too...gung ho about military action'.

Second, Lord Wilson remembered 'quite vividly' that Lord Goldsmith

...gave his legal advice...which was you would need the authorisation of a United Nations Security Council resolution if you were going to specifically undertake military action and if you didn't do that, his strong advice was that it was illegal to take military action. The Prime Minister simply said 'Well...' and that's it. I remember thinking 'There is an unresolved issue there.'[41]

Even with Sir Richard's 'correction', it was plain that parts of the Bush administration wanted the intelligence to show that Saddam was linked with al-Qaeda. However, they were unable either to 'fix' or 'fit' the intelligence around that link, and when it came to military action, the cause was Saddam's failure to comply with UN disarmament obligations. The intelligence case on which this rested turned out to have been mistaken, but this was not the result of political manipulation. It was the result of what the US Senate Intelligence Committee called a 'global intelligence failure' caused by 'collective groupthink'.[42]

In the British case, Chilcot concluded:

The ingrained belief that Saddam Hussein's regime retained chemical and biological warfare capabilities, was determined to preserve and if possible enhance its capabilities, including at some point in the future a nuclear capability, and was pursuing an active policy of deception and concealment, had underpinned UK policy towards Iraq since the Gulf Conflict ended in 1991.

While the detail of individual JIC [Joint Intelligence Committee] Assessments on Iraq varied, this core construct remained in place.[43]

The origin of this 'construct' was succinctly summarized by Gordon Corera, the BBC's security correspondent: 'As with Soviet military and economic power, it was safer to err on the side of caution because normally the costs of being wrong that way were lower.' With no UN weapons inspectors in Iraq from December 1998 to November 2002, 'intelligence analysts were left with history. Worst-case assumptions had become just assumptions, which were left unchallenged.'[44]

The Chilcot report was the third independent inquiry to come to the same conclusion about the British intelligence case. Indeed, it reversed the common criticism of Blair, that he manipulated the intelligence to 'sex up' the threat from Saddam, and said that he should have done more to 'challenge' what the Joint Intelligence Committee (JIC) was saying. It acknowledged Blair's conviction, which had been built up over the years, that the Iraqi dictator was a threat. The effect of Saddam's own behaviour and of warnings by intelligence services meant that conviction was shared by most of those in government who took an interest in Iraq. So powerful was the collective belief in the danger posed by Saddam that any sign of his weakness was seen only as further evidence of his duplicity.

As Chilcot said: 'The extent to which the JIC's judgements depended on inference and interpretation of Iraq's previous attitudes and behaviour was not recognised. At no stage was the hypothesis that Iraq might not have chemical, biological or nuclear weapons or programmes identified and examined by either the JIC or the policy community.'[45]

Blair's problem, after the 23 July 2002 meeting, was that the British people were not as certain as he was that Saddam was a threat to them. He decided that the best way to persuade them would be to compile the intelligence reports so that everyone could see what had convinced him. However, partly because his conviction was based on history and worst-case assumptions rather than hard evidence, the dossier published and presented to a recalled session of Parliament on 24 September 2002 was not as persuasive as he had hoped.

The Chilcot report said surprisingly little about the drawing up of the dossier. Its Executive Summary did not even mention the claim, which became contentious after the invasion, that Saddam's chemical and biological weapons could be made ready for use within forty-five minutes. It did not refer to the BBC's allegation, made in May 2003, that 'the Government probably knew that the forty-five minute figure was wrong, even before it decided to put it in'. Chilcot merely said: 'The statements prepared for, and used by, the UK Government in public from late 2001 onwards conveyed more certainty than the JIC Assessments about Iraq's proscribed activities and the potential threat they posed.'[46]

But it concluded: 'The JIC accepted ownership of the dossier and agreed its content. There is no evidence that intelligence was improperly included in the dossier or that No 10 improperly influenced the text.'[47]

This was a notably downbeat conclusion to a controversy that prompted the resignation of the chairman and the director-general of the BBC—after the publication in January 2004 of Lord Hutton's report on the death of Dr David Kelly, the weapons inspector who was the BBC's source. Lord Hutton, whose report was received badly by journalists who had expected a different verdict, reflected on the response two years later:

> If I had delivered a report highly critical of the government in terms which conformed to the hopes of some commentators I have no doubt that it would have received much praise. However, in reality, if I had written such a report I would have been failing in one of the cardinal duties of a judge conducting an inquiry into a highly controversial matter which gives rise to intense public interest and debate. That duty is to decide fairly the relevant issues arising under the terms of reference having regard to all the evidence and not to be swayed by pressure from newspapers and commentators or from any other quarter.[48]

Lord Hutton's findings were confirmed by a second inquiry, led by Lord Butler, the former Cabinet Secretary, in July 2004 into the reasons for the intelligence failure. The main explanation was: 'Weaknesses in the effective application by SIS of its validation procedures'.[49] However, Sir John Chilcot said, a year after his report was published, that Blair was 'entitled to rely' on the minute from Sir John Scarlett, the chair of the JIC, on the eve of the invasion: 'The JIC view is clear. Iraq possesses chemical and biological weapons, the means to deliver them and the capacity to produce them.'[50]

Chilcot's third exoneration of Blair and Campbell on the charge of interfering with the intelligence had little effect on the common belief that Blair had lied to take the country to war. The *Sun*'s front-page headline the day after Chilcot's publication, for example, was: 'Weapon of Mass Deception.'[51]

In the end, the most persuasive refutation of the idea that Bush and Blair fabricated the intelligence on Saddam's weapons of mass destruction was made by President Bush himself in his own memoir: 'If I wanted to mislead the country into war, why would I pick an allegation that was certain to be disproven publicly shortly after we invaded the country?'[52] To put it more bluntly, if Bush and Blair were dishonest enough to invent the weapons of mass destruction, would they not be dishonest enough to plant some in the deserts of Anbar?

With you, whatever

A note from Tony Blair to George Bush on 28 July 2002, began: 'I will be with you, whatever. But this is the moment to assess bluntly the difficulties. The planning on this and the strategy are the toughest yet.'[53] Although the whole document was not published until the Chilcot report in 2016, the gist of its opening sentence had been reported as a theme of conversations between Blair and Bush for some time.[54]

David Manning, Blair's foreign policy adviser, and Jonathan Powell, his chief of staff, tried to persuade Blair to take it out:

I went to Jonathan and said, 'The Prime Minister should not say this', and we went up to the flat. We talked [it] through with him [Mr Blair], and I said that the first sentence should come out and Jonathan agreed, but the Prime Minister decided to leave it.

I have always assumed, incidentally, because he saw it as a rhetorical flourish, not because at that stage he was thinking anything in terms of what the scale of commitments might be. But it was a sort of emotional statement, I think. But it seemed to me that it went further than we should have gone.[55]

Blair told the Inquiry he did not mean it:

I was going to take the view, and I did right throughout that period, there might come a point at which I had to say to the President of the United States, to all the other allies, 'I can't be with you.' I might have said that on legal grounds if Peter's [Peter Goldsmith, the attorney general] advice had not, having seen what the Americans told him about the negotiating process, come down on the other side. I might have had to do that politically. I was in a very, very difficult situation politically. It was by no means certain that we would get this thing through the House of Commons...

I was going to continue giving absolute and firm commitment until the point at which definitively I couldn't... I wasn't going to be in a position where I stepped back until I knew I had to, because I believed that if I started to articulate this, in a sense saying 'Look, I can't be sure', the effect of that both on the Americans, on the coalition and most importantly on Saddam, would have been dramatic.[56]

The publication of the whole note ought to have helped Blair's case, because what was important about the phrase, 'with you, whatever', was that it was followed by 'But...' The rest of the note was also a thoughtful rehearsal of the dangers of the policy. One line in particular was significant, as Blair, in listing the potential problems of an invasion, said, 'Suppose Saddam felt sufficiently politically strong, if militarily weak in conventional terms, to let off WMD,' confirming that his fear of them was genuine. However, it was the first sentence that dominated the reporting of the publication of the Chilcot report. It appeared to confirm one of the main criticisms of Blair that arose after the Iraq war, namely that he had pledged the UK in secret to join the US in military action many months before he did so in public.

In principle, the criticism was unfounded, because Blair was unable on his own to commit UK forces, having to win the approval of the Cabinet and having already conceded the principle of a vote in the House of Commons. However, Manning and Powell seem to have thought that Blair's personal commitment limited his freedom to distance himself from Bush later. And Chilcot agreed:

> Mr Blair's Note, which had not been discussed or agreed with his colleagues, set the UK on a path leading to diplomatic activity in the UN and the possibility of participation in military action in a way that would make it very difficult for the UK subsequently to withdraw its support for the US.[57]

This is a contestable conclusion, given Blair's very public support for Bush, and his open advocacy of the use of force if Saddam did not comply. It would have been politically difficult for Blair to back out regardless of his private assurance of personal support. Although it was certainly true that 'I will be with you' was more than a personal opinion: in a conversation with Bush on 31 July, for example, Blair said there was 'no doubt that the UK would be with the US on Iraq', which was not something that he could guarantee.[58] Perhaps Manning and Powell thought Blair would lose leverage by having committed himself too early and too wholeheartedly. Yet, as Manning acknowledges, the first line of the note seems to have been designed to gain Bush's attention for the argument for building a wider global coalition. It was consistent with Blair's belief that it was in Britain's interest to hug the US President close, in order to maximize British influence on American policy. And Blair did succeed in persuading Bush to take his case to the United Nations, even if he was less successful in persuading him to advance the Israel-Palestine peace process at the same time, which was Blair's other hope.

As a matter of diplomatic tactics, Manning pointed out to the Inquiry that he could advise, but 'he [Blair] was elected and it was [for] him to decide'.[59]

In any case, there is plenty of evidence that President Bush understood the British political situation. One of the reasons for his admiration of and gratitude to Blair was that he realized what a risk his ally was taking. Indeed, the Americans may have been less certain than a nervous Blair that he would win the Commons vote when it came.

The fundamental problem, however, was not one of tactics, but that the very idea of a US-led invasion to depose Saddam was flawed. No British influence to promote coalition-building at the UN, to advance the Israel–Palestine peace process, or UN leadership of a post-invasion civil administration in Iraq (all suggested in Blair's note or in subsequent communications) could put that right.

No plan

The most important question about the Iraq war, and therefore about the British decision to join the American invasion, is whether the disorder and violence that followed could and should have been foreseen. As early as June 2002, the Ministry of Defence's Strategic Planning Group described Iraq as 'potentially fundamentally unstable'.[60] By December 2002, a Ministry of Defence paper called 'UK Military Strategic Thinking on Iraq' described the post-conflict phase of operations as 'strategically decisive'.[61] On 15 January 2003, Blair told the chiefs of staff 'the "Issue" was aftermath—the Coalition must prevent anarchy and internecine fighting breaking out'.[62] Blair himself was most blunt with Bush, in a note on 24 January 2003: 'Internecine fighting in Iraq when a military strike destabilised the regime would be the "biggest risk": "They are perfectly capable, on previous form, of killing each other in large numbers."'[63]

However, said Chilcot,

> when the invasion began, the UK Government was not in a position to conclude that satisfactory plans had been drawn up and preparations made to meet known post-conflict challenges and risks in Iraq and to mitigate the risk of strategic failure...
>
> UK planning and preparation for the post-conflict phase of operations, which rested on the assumption that the UK would be able quickly to

reduce its military presence in Iraq and deploy only a minimal number of civilians, were wholly inadequate.

The information available to the Government before the invasion provided a clear indication of the potential scale of the post-conflict task and the significant risks associated with the UK's proposed approach.

Foreseeable risks included post-conflict political disintegration and extremist violence in Iraq, the inadequacy of US plans, the UK's inability to exert significant influence on US planning and, in the absence of UN authorisation for the administration and reconstruction of post-conflict Iraq, the reluctance of potential international partners to contribute to the post-conflict effort.[64]

This was primarily an American failure, and the failure of the British was to hope that they could persuade the US government, because President Bush and the State Department seemed to agree with them, when the war was really being run from the Department of Defense.

By the time of the invasion, such hopes were unsustainable, Chilcot concluded: 'Despite being aware of the shortcomings of the US plan ... at no stage did the UK Government formally consider other policy options, including the possibility of making participation in military action conditional on a satisfactory plan for the post-conflict period.'[65]

Blair accepted in his memoir that the planning for the aftermath was 'inadequate'.[66] In his response to the Chilcot report he offered a fuller defence:

The Inquiry makes several criticisms of the planning process for the aftermath of the invasion. I accept that, especially in hindsight, we should have approached the situation differently.

These criticisms are significant and include failures to seek assurances of better planning from the American side which I accept should have been sought. The failures in American planning are well documented and accepted.

I note nonetheless that the Inquiry fairly and honestly admit that they have not even after this passage of time been able to identify alternative approaches which would have guaranteed greater success.[67]

This is where his defence is weakest. The reason the inquiry was unable to identify better approaches to planning for the aftermath of an invasion could be that their consequences were likely to be bad, and foreseeably so. Blair's second line of defence, therefore, is that Iraq would have been plunged into internal conflict anyway in the Arab spring of 2011, eight years later:

> Had he [Saddam] been left in power in 2003, then I believe...he would once again have threatened world peace, and when the Arab revolutions of 2011 began, he would have clung to power with the same deadly consequences as we see in the carnage of Syria; whereas at least in Iraq, for all its challenges, we have today a government, recognised as legitimate, fighting terrorism with the international community in support of it.[68]

This is plausible but not provable, and, if the likelihood of sectarian bloodshed was foreseeable in 2002–3, the possibility of popular risings across the Arab world nearly a decade later certainly was not. Blair engaged in a similar exercise in counterfactual history in his memoir:

> The picture that emerges [from the Iraq Survey Group Report] is of a regime whose only constraint was one externally imposed...I don't claim that the thesis is an indisputable one, that had we failed to act in 2003 Saddam would have re-emerged stronger, a competitor to Iran both in respect of WMD and in support of terrorism in the region...but it is surely at least as probable as the alternative thesis, namely that he would have sunk into comfortable, unmenacing obscurity and old age; and his sons, groomed to succeed him, would have reformed.[69]

The calculus of Blair's decision at the time—we can only speculate about this—is that he knew the Americans did not have a good plan for occupying and administering Iraq after the invasion, but that he assumed that a nation so rich and powerful would be able to manage it.

It could be argued that the danger of disorder and sectarian violence was not the main argument against military action at the time. Indeed, it was hardly part of the public debate. Robin Cook, the only Cabinet minister to resign from the government before the invasion, opposed military action for other reasons. He thought that Saddam probably had some 'biological toxins and battlefield chemical munitions', but he had had them for some time and it was better to contain him.

He was worried about the damage to international alliances and in particular by the weakness of support from the British public.[70] One important question is why Foreign Office officials failed to warn of the possible dangers. As we shall see, Jack Straw, the Foreign Secretary, supported military action when it came to it, although he was acutely aware of the political dangers with UK public opinion. But senior officials supported it too—or at least saw no problems with the enterprise sufficient to warrant formal dissension or, still less, resignation. The most significant warning given to Blair that the consequences of invading Iraq 'will be much, much more difficult than you may have been led to believe' was delivered by a group of academics who visited him, with Straw and senior officials also present, in November 2002.[71] This meeting was organized by Sir Lawrence Freedman, professor of War Studies at King's College London (later a member of the Chilcot inquiry), rather than by the Foreign Office. The Chilcot criticism of failing to think through the likelihood of disorder and sectarianism applies as much to officials as to ministers. The only official to resign over the war, Elizabeth Wilmshurst, the Foreign Office's deputy legal adviser, did so on quite different grounds, namely the legal case for military action, which we shall consider in a moment.

However, not even Cabinet ministers could have been expected to know enough about Iraq to be able to judge the likely effects of the invasion. And if they could not, other MPs and members of the public certainly could not have been expected to do so. On the intelligence, Blair is entitled to say that the pre-war debate had been open and public. He had sought to present what he knew, even if it later turned out to be wrong. But on planning for the aftermath, he failed to consider how badly it could turn out and, although some academic specialists publicly expressed their forebodings, most MPs and citizens were not in a position to assess the likely consequences. If a fraction of the intelligence effort devoted to weapons of mass destruction had been devoted to war-gaming the results of toppling Saddam, a better decision might have been reached.[72]

The origin of the myth of sofa government

In assessing how this decision was made, it is impossible to separate politics and procedures. As we discussed in chapter 2, the phrase 'sofa government' arose out of commentary on the Hutton inquiry into how the Iraq decision was taken. Hutton himself made no findings on this point, although the Butler report on the intelligence failure spoke of the 'informality and circumscribed character' of decision-making, and the Chilcot report repeated those criticisms. If more people who understood Iraq had been in meetings to work through the likely consequences of overthrowing Saddam, it suggested, Blair and other members of the government might have had their assumptions challenged.

However, it was partly because of those assumptions, which were widely shared, that procedures were as they were. And it is hard to imagine that different procedures would have produced a different decision. Robin Cook, the former Foreign Secretary who had been demoted the year before, said of the 7 March 2002 Cabinet meeting:

> This was the last Cabinet meeting at which a large number of ministers spoke up against the war. I have little sympathy with the criticism of Tony that he sidelined the Cabinet over Iraq. On the contrary, over the next six months we were to discuss Iraq more than any other topic, but only Clare Short and I ever expressed frank doubts about the trajectory in which we were being driven.[73]

Cook's claim about the following six months is not supported by the Cabinet records published by the Chilcot inquiry. The Chilcot report says that there was no 'substantive' discussion of Iraq after this until 23 September 2002, before Parliament was recalled to debate the dossier on Iraq's weapons of mass destruction. However, this may have been, as Cook suggested, mainly because most ministers agreed with the policy. Aspects of Iraq policy were often reported to Cabinet, even if they were not discussed at length. However, the formal Cabinet minutes do not necessarily give the full picture. Jonathan Powell told us in

2009, before the Chilcot inquiry was set up: 'When they are released they are going to be fundamentally boring because all Cabinet minutes are deliberately written to be fundamentally boring; they don't actually tell you anything.'[74]

One of the surprises in the Chilcot report is that Alastair Campbell's diaries are often a better record of the working of government than the official minutes. On several occasions, Chilcot gives a brief account of the official record of Cabinet meetings, followed by a fuller account of who said what taken from Campbell's diary.[75]

After the March options paper, few documents went to Cabinet. Jack Straw told the inquiry that this was because the paper was leaked: 'Any prime minister, faced with leaks like that, is bound to take appropriate alternative action.'[76] Geoff Hoon, the Defence Secretary, told the inquiry: 'Tony Blair was well known to be extremely concerned about leaks from cabinet discussions...It was my perception that, largely as a consequence of this, he did not normally expect key decisions to be made in the course of Cabinet meetings.'[77] As we note in chapter 2, Cabinet had often ceased to be a forum for 'substantive' discussion and decision-making long before Blair became prime minister. In any case, the Chilcot report criticized the way Blair managed Cabinet on only two limited points: for failing to debate the 'principles and implications' of military options; and for failing to provide the Cabinet with the full version of the Attorney General's legal advice.[78]

The report quoted Jonathan Powell on how Cabinet government worked under Blair:

> Most of the important decisions of the Blair Government were taken either in informal meetings of Ministers and officials or by Cabinet Committees...Unlike the full Cabinet, a Cabinet Committee has the right people present, including, for example, the military Chiefs of Staff or scientific advisers, its members are well briefed, it can take as long as it likes over its discussion on the basis of well-prepared papers, and it is independently chaired by a senior Minister with no departmental vested interest.[79]

However, Chilcot suggested that this model was not followed on Iraq:

The Inquiry concurs with this description of the function of a Cabinet Committee when it is working well. In particular, it recognises the important function which a Minister without departmental responsibilities for the issues under consideration can play. This can provide some external challenge from experienced members of the government and mitigate any tendency towards groupthink. In the case of Iraq, for example, the inclusion of the Chancellor of the Exchequer or Deputy Prime Minister, as senior members of the Cabinet, or of Mr Cook, as a former Foreign Secretary known to have concerns about the policy, could have provided an element of challenge.[80]

This is all very well, but Gordon Brown and John Prescott both supported the policy on Iraq, albeit with less enthusiasm than Blair. Even Clare Short supported the policy in the end, although she resigned a few weeks after the invasion. She and Robin Cook might have asked more difficult questions about the planning for the aftermath, but it would have been hard to include them in more discussions because of Blair's fear of leaks designed to disrupt the policy. The concern about leaks meant that there was less written material going to Cabinet than might have been expected. Blair said in his response to Chilcot: 'I accept that I could and should have presented a formal options paper [to Cabinet].'[81] But Chilcot made clear that information had not been withheld from the Cabinet in order to influence ministers: 'As Mr Cook's resignation statement on 17 March made clear, it was possible for a Minister to draw different conclusions from the same information.'[82]

Nor is it obvious that including other points of view would have produced a different outcome. Blair's response to this criticism in evidence to the inquiry was blunt: 'Nobody in the Cabinet was unaware of . . . what the whole issue was about. It was the thing running throughout the whole of the political mainstream at the time. There were members of the Cabinet who would challenge and disagree, but most of them agreed.'[83]

Politically, this is the important point. If more Cabinet ministers had had stronger reservations about the policy, it might not have been possible to go ahead. In particular, if Brown or Jack Straw, the Foreign

Secretary, had opposed it, Blair would have had to think again. Given that the tension in the relationship between Blair and Brown was particularly acute in the run-up to war (see chapter 1), the case for war could have been an issue between them but was not. Ed Balls, then Brown's chief adviser, recalled:

> The important thing about Iraq to remember is that how people feel now about Iraq is very different from how people were feeling at the time. Was there a bit of unease around the table of people feeling, 'I've seen the information, I'm not really sure it stacks up, what are you doing'? There wasn't. You could say that was a big mistake, and actually there should have been more demands from the machine, and from Cabinet ministers to know more about the facts. The truth was, Tony Blair was saying, 'This is what I've seen, and what I've been doing,' and most people said, 'OK.'[84]

As the prospect of the invasion of Iraq approached, however, Brown held back. He was aware that there was substantial opposition to it among Labour MPs and among the public, and he avoided being identified with it. Just as Blair realized that this decision could be the end of his leadership, Brown was acutely aware that it could the start of his. He could not afford to be seen to be playing games with such an important question, and his instincts were similar to Blair's in wanting to maintain the US alliance, but he wanted to position himself, as ever, as just to Blair's left. Brown 'wanted to be part of it and to keep his distance, in the way he does', said one of his advisers.[85] Thus Tam Dalyell, an anti-war Labour backbencher, claimed after Blair's meeting with George Bush at his ranch in Crawford, Texas, in April 2002 that Brown had told him of his 'grave misgivings' that the prime minister was 'too gung-ho' about Iraq.[86] Nick Brown, Gordon's close friend and later his chief whip, spoke to Chris Mullin, another anti-war and generally anti-American MP, on 6 September 2002: 'He says Gordon is against an attack on Iraq and that he—Nick—would have to consider his position if we became involved in a war.'[87] Gordon Brown was asked on 30 September 2002 in a rare interview on BBC2's *Newsnight* to endorse Blair's policy on Iraq and avoided the question.

According to Ed Balls, however, Brown privately agreed strongly with the Iraq decision:

> The truth on Iraq was: Gordon was, rightly or wrongly—some people would retrospectively say wrongly—Gordon was as gung-ho as Tony Blair. Gordon would have liked nothing more than for Tony Blair to ring him up more and say, could he go and do some more interviews supporting it. I think he was, for a range of reasons, some of which were very principled, he thought it was the right thing to do. But if Gordon Brown had done such interviews, when the Iraq thing was succeeding, certain columnists would have written, 'Why is Gordon Brown trying to upstage Tony Blair? Is it political over reach of ambition?' Then because he didn't, because he was never asked to, he didn't push his way in, then when it was more difficult, the same columnists would then write, 'Why wasn't Gordon Brown there supporting Tony Blair at a difficult time? Surely that shows that he never supported it for his own ambitions?' The truth is, you can never win.[88]

In the end, however, Brown publicly supported military action on 12 March 2003, six days before the Commons vote. He endorsed not just military action but Blair's leadership, saying, 'He should be given 100 per cent support in his efforts, not only over the next few days but over the next few years.'[89] Brown then engaged enthusiastically in tactical discussions, in particular advising Blair to blame the French for the failure to secure more explicit authorization from the UN. For once, he did not have the support of his principal adviser Ed Balls, who said he asked, 'a bit incredulously: "Are we really sure we want to end decades of foreign policy cooperation with France just to get a better headline?"' According to his account, 'the others' had replied: 'Of course we do; that's the whole point!'[90] At the Cabinet meeting on 13 March, 'Gordon launched a long and passionate statement of support for Tony's strategy,' according to Robin Cook, who added: 'The contribution was rather marred by an outspoken attack on France: "The message that must go out from this Cabinet is that we pin the blame on France for its isolated refusal to agree in the Security Council."'[91]

Straw was more closely involved in the policy throughout, and he too tended to be more cautious than Blair. On the day which

Brown ended by publicly supporting military action, six days before the Commons vote, Straw asked Blair if he was sure he wanted to go ahead with it. Chilcot reported:

> The Inquiry was told by a witness it agreed not to identify that, in a meeting on 12 March, with officials from No 10 present, Mr Straw had advised Mr Blair that he had 'the final opportunity to decide on a different track'. Mr Straw had suggested to Mr Blair that he had a 'way out and why don't you take it'. The witness had been 'struck' by 'the speed' and the 'absolute insistence' of Mr Blair's response: 'he had got his arguments all marshalled and all laid out'. The witness did not think there was a risk of Mr Straw resigning.
>
> Mr Straw confirmed that the anonymous witness had given 'a fair summary' of both his and Mr Blair's positions.[92]

Straw told the inquiry that he supported the war, but that he was 'anxious that we should explore all possible alternatives' and 'owed' Blair the 'best and most robust advice I could give him'.[93]

The legal advice

With Blair's Chancellor and Foreign Secretary committed to military action, the only person who could have prevented the UK taking part in the invasion would have been Peter Goldsmith, the Attorney General. If he had refused to advise unequivocally that military action was lawful, the government could not have put the question to a vote in the House of Commons. The 'way out' to which Straw referred in his meeting with Blair on 12 March 2003 was the uncertainty—even at that late stage—that such clear advice would be forthcoming. It was on that day that Blair and Straw 'reached the view that there was no chance of securing a majority in the [UN] Security Council' for the further resolution explicitly authorizing, or reauthorizing, military action.[94] This meant that the legal case for war rested on the authority of UN Security Council Resolution 678 in repelling the invasion of

Kuwait in 1990. This authority, Lord Goldsmith argued, had been suspended by the ceasefire of 1991, when the UN imposed disarmament obligations on Saddam Hussein's regime, which included its renouncing chemical, biological, and nuclear weapons. The authority was revived by UN Security Council Resolution 1441, passed unanimously in November 2002. This found Iraq to be 'in material breach' of the 1991 ceasefire terms and afforded Saddam a 'final opportunity' to comply or to face 'serious consequences'.

Lord Goldsmith had changed his earlier view that military action would be unlawful, and had set out in his formal advice of 7 March that there was a 'reasonable case' in law for it, even without a further UN resolution, but that he did not rule out legal challenges being brought against the British government. This was not what Blair wanted, or what the military chiefs and Sir Andrew Turnbull, the Cabinet Secretary, on behalf of the Civil Service said they needed.

On 11 March, Donald Rumsfeld, US Defense Secretary, said at a Pentagon news conference that Britain might not be able to take part in military action, but that 'there are work-arounds'. He had just spoken to Geoff Hoon, his British opposite number, who had spelt out the possible legal difficulties. Later that day, Blair discussed with Goldsmith the form his advice should take for the Cabinet, the Civil Service, and the military. Blair 'knew', as Campbell recorded, 'that if there was any nuance at all', Robin Cook and Clare Short 'would be straight out saying the advice was that it was not legal, the AG was casting doubt on the legal basis for war'. Lord Goldsmith told Blair 'that he wished he could be much clearer in his advice, but in reality it was nuanced'.[95]

On 13 March, Lord Goldsmith came to what he called a 'better view'. He met Straw and said that 'having decided to come down on one side (1441 is sufficient), he had also decided that in public he needed to explain his case as strongly and unambiguously as possible'.[96]

However, Lord Goldsmith still wanted to explain the 'nuances' to the Cabinet: 'He thought he might need to tell Cabinet when it met on 17 March that the legal issues were finely balanced.' Straw persuaded him that this would not be a good idea, saying he 'needed to be aware of the problem of leaks from . . . Cabinet'.[97]

Later on 13 March, Lord Goldsmith also met Sally Morgan, Blair's political secretary, and Charles Falconer, a junior Home Office minister who was a friend of Blair's and, like him and Goldsmith, a lawyer. This was one of a series of meetings, which Morgan described thus:

> They were really about—Peter wouldn't describe it like this but— slightly holding Peter's hand through what he had to go through in terms of the presentation of the legal advice. I'm not a lawyer, and he is a very serious lawyer; he took his own soundings on the legal advice and took some very serious pieces of advice himself. And so the legal advice wasn't what I was there to discuss. What I was there to discuss was how grim in some ways this was going to be for him, because he would be in the spotlight and sooner or later it would become very unpleasant for him . . . It was really about saying to Peter—it was really about giving him a timetable about when he would be asked to give the legal advice. His concern was that he was involved properly with Cabinet discussions as well around that point and he was in fact, from what I remember, he attended all the kind of war Cabinets. And from that period on he largely did attend Cabinet meetings. He was anxious not to just come in, out of context almost, give his legal advice and then be outside the door. It was not about what the detail of the legal advice was; it was such a huge thing he had taken his own counsel on that from lawyers, not from people like me.[98]

Thus Goldsmith finally produced, on 17 March, only three days before the invasion, a statement of just 337 words, which concluded that 'the authority to use force under resolution 678', which was passed by the UN Security Council in 1990 in response to Saddam's invasion of Kuwait, 'has revived and so continues today'.

This was the one sheet of A4 that was presented to the Cabinet that morning:

> Lord Goldsmith told Cabinet that it was 'plain' that Iraq had failed to comply with its obligations and continued to be in 'material breach' of the relevant Security Council resolutions. The authority to use force under resolution 678 was, 'as a result', revived. Lord Goldsmith said that there was no need for a further resolution . . .

There was little appetite to question Lord Goldsmith about his advice, and no substantive discussion of the legal issues was recorded.[99]

Lord Goldsmith was asked by Sir John Chilcot at the Iraq Inquiry: 'Did you at any point find in your own mind that it might get too difficult to give advice that would be acceptable, in which case you might have had to say, "I'm sorry, I can't go on"?' He replied:

It cannot be the job of a lawyer to decide that you can't decide to give advice, and it was not a question, as far as I was concerned, of giving advice that was acceptable. It was a question of giving advice which was correct, and if the question is: did I ever think this is all—the pressure—that I should resign? No, I didn't...

If the Government—if I had given advice—for example, if I had given advice that a course of action was not lawful and notwithstanding that, the Government goes against it, then that creates a very important moment of constitutional crisis and the Attorney General, at least if it is an important matter, would, in those circumstances, resign, and that would then force, I would think, a constitutional crisis on the Government, and that is ultimately where the authority of the Attorney General comes from.[100]

The Chilcot panel was, however, unimpressed by the way the legal advice was decided. In particular, its report said it was wrong that Blair alone should have confirmed to the Attorney General that Iraq was still in breach of its obligations to the UN:

It was Mr Blair who decided that, so far as the UK was concerned, Iraq was and remained in breach of resolution 1441 ... the precise grounds on which [that decision] was made remain unclear...

Senior Ministers should have considered the question ... either in the Defence and Overseas Policy Committee or a 'War Cabinet', on the basis of formal advice. Such a Committee should then have reported its conclusions to Cabinet before its members were asked to endorse the Government's policy.[101]

However, Lord Goldsmith had pointed out to the inquiry that 'at the discussion [at the UN] no member of the Security Council took the view that they [breaches] had not occurred', and Blair's response to the Chilcot report added: 'As the A–G has explained, my view was not legally necessary, since [UN Security Council resolution] 1441 had determined what constituted a breach. But nonetheless the A–G sought my confirmation of what I thought. Saddam was accepted by everyone including the Inspectors not to be fully complying.'

Blair said he 'understood' why Chilcot had concluded that 'the circumstances in which it was ultimately decided that there was a legal basis for UK participation were far from satisfactory'.[102] But he did not accept its main criticism of the process. The Chilcot report concluded: 'Lord Goldsmith should have been asked to provide written advice which fully reflected the position on 17 March, explained the legal basis on which the UK could take military action and set out the risks of legal challenge.'[103]

It is impossible to know what the Cabinet would have made of the Attorney General's long advice of 7 March, had all its members seen it (only Blair, Straw, Hoon, and John Reid, Minister without Portfolio and Labour Party chair, did).[104] No doubt Cook and Short would have been, as Campbell said, 'straight out' saying there were doubts about the legal basis for war. It would have made the Commons vote significantly harder to win.

One thing that is clear in hindsight, however, is that, on the binary question of whether military action was lawful or not, the Attorney General's short advice was correct. The longer advice of 7 March was too cautious. Despite opponents of the war often describing it as 'illegal', no case against any of the governments of the coalition has even been started successfully in the years since. Nor was Lord Goldsmith's opinion capricious. The Australian government, operating in a similar legal culture to the British, received similar advice.[105]

Blair, in his response to the Chilcot report, said:

The report does not dispute the legal judgement of the then Attorney General.

This is for very good reasons. The whole negotiating history of resolution 1441 in the UN made it clear that the USA and UK had refused language that obliged a second resolution. The defining of the obligations of Iraq and the agreement that failure fully and immediately to comply was a material breach was a reasonable basis for the action.

The advice of the A–G was in line with that of other law officers in other nations and distinguished legal experts though I fully acknowledge others took a different view.

Where the politics is hotly contested, the law will be also.

I understand why the Inquiry finds that the process of coming to the legal opinion was far from satisfactory. But it does not alter the legal conclusion.[106]

He is justified in pointing out that the legal objections to the Iraq war were and are essentially substitutes for political arguments about the war. For example, the Chilcot report concluded its criticism of the legal basis for military action by arguing:

> The Charter of the United Nations vests responsibility for the main-tenance of peace and security in the Security Council. The UK Government was claiming to act on behalf of the international com-munity 'to uphold the authority of the Security Council', knowing that it did not have a majority in the Security Council in support of its actions. In those circumstances, the UK's actions undermined the authority of the Security Council.[107]

Blair responded:

> The reality is that we—Britain—had continually tried to act with the authority of the UN. I successfully convinced the Americans to go back to the UN in November 2002 to secure resolution 1441.
>
> After the initial conflict it was again Britain which put UN authority back in place for the aftermath so that from June 2003 British troops were in Iraq with full UN authority.
>
> However as at 18 March 2003, there was gridlock at the UN. In resolution 1441, it had been agreed to give Saddam one final opportunity to comply. It was accepted that he had not done so...
>
> The undermining of the UN was in fact the refusal to follow through on 1441. And with the subsequent statement from President Putin and the President of France that they would veto any new resolution authorising action in the event of non-compliance, it was clearly not possible to get a majority of the UN to agree a new resolution.[108]

Neither point of view can be definitive. The reader may share the Chilcot panel's opinion or Blair's opinion. There is no court to which either side can appeal. Such is the nature of international law on such questions. There is no court that could try a decision such as that to invade Iraq. The British government needed to be satisfied only that its decision to take military action would not be successfully challenged in any court.

Some might wish that the UK government would never take part in military action without current and explicit authorization by the UN Security Council, but they would have to accept that this would give Russia, China, and France a veto over the use of British force, and they should abstain from using legal language to express that opinion. The actions in Sierra Leone and Kosovo did not have such UN authority. Nor, strictly, did NATO action in Afghanistan, which the US undertook under the UN Charter right of self-defence, for which it did not seek Security Council approval. Nor did, for example, Tanzania's rescue of Uganda from Idi Amin, or Vietnam's removal of Pol Pot from Cambodia in 1979. Such actions might now be justified by the UN's 2005 doctrine of the 'Responsibility to Protect', but that is a norm rather than a law.

When Kofi Annan, UN Secretary General, described the Iraq invasion as 'not in conformity with the UN Charter', it could just as well have been argued that it was *not* 'not in conformity with the UN Charter'. When he went on, 'from our point of view, from the Charter point of view, it was illegal', he was expressing an opinion, not passing a verdict.[109]

Advocates of rules-based international relations ought at least to welcome progress, in that the UK government now pays attention to legal advice. In 1956, Anthony Eden was advised by Reginald Manningham-Buller, the Attorney General, that 'it is not true to say that under international law we are entitled' to intervene in the conflict between Israel and Egypt and to take control of the Suez canal—and he went ahead anyway.[110]

Last resort?

The final criticism made by the Chilcot report is that military action was not a last resort. 'In the Inquiry's view, the diplomatic options had not at that stage been exhausted. Military action was therefore not a last resort.'[111] Blair made the point, which he was usually reluctant to do, that his decision was subordinate to President Bush's:

> Given the impasse at the UN and the insistence of the USA—for reasons I completely understood and with hundreds of thousands of troops in theatre which could not be kept in situ indefinitely—it was the last moment of decision for us, as the report accepts. By then, the US was going to move with us or without us.[112]

In effect, Chilcot's criticism was that the Americans were wrong to invade because it was not a last resort, and that the Blair government was wrong to go along with it.

This resumes the endless argument over whether the weapons inspectors should have had 'more time'. Seth Center, US State Department historian, commented on Chilcot's findings:

> Exhaustion seems an elusive strategic criterion in light of the interminable Security Council deliberations and differences over inspections laid out earlier in the Inquiry. An advocate for prolonging diplomacy would have had to have believed that extra time would yield a successful second resolution authorizing war or confirmation by inspectors that Iraq was fully disarmed, or would demonstrate that obstruction in the Security Council prevented a resolution, thereby proving diplomacy was indeed 'exhausted'. Scholars can debate these counterfactuals, but the evidence could explain that policymakers made a reasonable judgment in March that prolonging diplomacy would not clarify the situation.[113]

It is worth noting that UN Security Council Resolution 1441 gave Saddam a 'final opportunity' to comply. Many of the countries that voted for it argued that this did not mean that the use of force would follow, in which case it is hard to know whether the words meant anything at all.

In any case, the 'last resort' debate seems secondary to the main criticism, which was that the risks of invasion—at any time—could be disastrous.

Conclusion

The British decision to join the American invasion was a political one, which was finally and formally taken, on the day before military action began, by the House of Commons. The vote was decisive, a majority of 412 to 149, but it had not looked that way for the whole year beforehand when military action had been in prospect.

To try to recover a sense of how uncertain things seemed at the time, Sally Morgan recalled how she approached the vote: 'If we hadn't got a parliamentary majority obviously we couldn't have done it because we said that was the decision. If we hadn't got a majority of Labour MPs, I think Tony would have been out by summer, and I think he would have felt he couldn't carry on actually.' When asked if he would have gone on with the military action, she said: 'Yes.' We asked if he would have done so without a majority of Labour MPs, then later resigned, and she said, 'Yes,' again. We commented that this would have been very strange and she replied:

> Yes, but I think that's what he would have done. I mean that's me thinking. He never said, 'This is what I'm going to do, Sally,' but my take on it is that he would have gone ahead with the parliamentary majority because it was the right thing to do, as the troops were down there, would see it through as prime minister but not as Labour prime minister in a way. And see that through for as long as that took to see it through while signifying to the Labour Party that once that was over that would be it. And I think that is what would have happened.[114]

When it came to it, on 18 March 2003, Blair did win a majority of Labour MPs: 254 of 413 supported the government, although about half of his backbenchers, 139, voted that 'the case for war against Iraq has not yet been established', and a further 20 did not vote. Although he continued as prime minister, even as 'Labour prime minister' in Morgan's terms, for another four years, those votes broke New Labour and were the beginning of the end for Blair.

His main misjudgement, as the Chilcot report found, was to assume that removing a dangerous dictator would make things better for Iraq, the region, and the world. He knew that there was a risk that 'internecine fighting' might break out in the occupied country, but he gambled that 'his departure would free up the region', as he said in his 'with you, whatever' note to President Bush.

If the lesson of the Chilcot inquiry is that leaders contemplating military action should imagine the worst-case scenario, then Blair's error was that he imagined the wrong one. For him, the worst case was that biological, chemical, and even nuclear weapons produced by rogue states such as Iraq, Libya, and North Korea would fall into the hands of al-Qaeda-inspired terrorists, who had killed 3,000 on 9/11 but who would have killed 30,000 or 300,000 if they could—and that he had a chance to help stop them.

The other criticisms made by Chilcot—that more people should have been consulted, that the Attorney General's legal uncertainties should have been advertised, and that the Americans should have given Saddam more time—seem beside this larger point. In particular, the criticism made by Sir John Chilcot himself, a year after his report, that Blair had not been 'straight with the nation' was not sustained by the report itself.[115]

To see the British decision to join the Iraq operation in historical perspective, it is also worth repeating that the situation in Iraq would have been similar whether or not UK troops had been part of the invasion. Indeed British troops would probably have been sent to Iraq as part of the UN-endorsed occupation afterwards, and the situation there would be roughly the same as it is today. Much of the British debate about Iraq since the war has been argued as if the UK were the only actor in what was, in fact, overwhelmingly a US operation. This Anglocentrism has been encouraged by Blair's acceptance of personal responsibility for the British decision, when he could have pointed out that, formally, it was a collective government decision, taken by Cabinet and supported by the House of Commons.

Finally, we should note the effect of the failure of the Iraq intervention on future possible interventions. Not only did Blair's decision to join it obscure his achievements in securing good outcomes in Kosovo and Sierra Leone, but it would make similar operations harder in future. As the Chilcot report noted: 'The widespread perception that the September 2002 dossier overstated the firmness of the evidence has produced a damaging legacy which may make it more difficult to secure support for Government policy, including military action, where the evidence depends on inferential judgements drawn from intelligence.'[116] This was confirmed when David Cameron published the intelligence on Assad's use of chemical weapons against his own people in Syria in August 2013, to widespread scepticism, when the House of Commons refused to support UK participation in planned US strikes to deter Assad from doing so again.

John Sawers, British ambassador to Egypt, who, as the Iraq Inquiry noted, 'had been closely associated with the development of the UK's policy on Iraq as Mr Blair's Private Secretary for Foreign Affairs', wrote on 21 February 2002 to Sir Michael Jay, the top civil servant at the Foreign Office. In his view the UK needed to say:

> clearly and consistently that our goal is Regime Change—for the sake of stability in the Middle East, for the Iraqi people, and for the goal of controlling the spread of WMD.
>
> Whether or not we actually express it is purely a matter of tactics. So the lawyers and peaceniks should not prevent us from saying what we really want in Iraq. And by associating ourselves with Bush's heartfelt objective of seeing Saddam removed, we will be given more house-room in Washington to ask the awkward questions about how.
>
> And there are many such questions. What is the plan? How long would it take for a direct confrontation to succeed? How do we retain the support of our regional friends ... If we were to build up the Kurds and Shia as proxies, what assurances would we have to give them that we would not let them down yet again? How would we keep the Iranians from meddling? How do we preserve Iraq's territorial integrity ... How would we provide for stability after Saddam and his cronies were killed?

All these are much more important questions than legality, the Arab street and other hardy Foreign Office perennials. On a tactical point, I recall Colin Powell [the US Secretary of State, who had been chairman of the Joint Chiefs of Staff from 1988 to 1993]...in 1993 saying that one of the blessings of retirement was that he would never have to listen to another British legal opinion. Presenting Washington with one now will both irritate and weaken him. We can look for the legal basis once we have decided what to do, as we did in Kosovo.[117]

This candid observation prompted David Manning to add a handwritten note to Jonathan Powell, not disagreeing with his views but horrified by his indiscretion: 'Not helpful to have this winging its way around the world as a restricted teleletter. If John/other HMAs [Her Majesty's ambassadors] want to offer views they should be in personal letters to Michael Jay.' Powell replied: 'I was gobsmacked. John deserves a slapping down.'[118]

What is important about Sawers's teleletter, though, is that it probably closely reflected Blair's thinking at that early stage—and that, by its own tests, Blair's policy, as it developed, was a failure. Those 'awkward questions' were never satisfactorily answered, and by Sawers's own tactlessly pro-war argument, Blair should have declined to offer British support when it came to the point of decision.

Contrary to conventional wisdom, political leaders often come to grief because of their principles rather than the lack of them. Blair supported US military action because he believed that Saddam was a latent threat to the British people; that getting rid of him would be good for the Iraqi people and Iraq's neighbours; and that Britain should support the US, which stands however imperfectly for liberal democracy, and try to influence US policy. He should have realized these objectives were outweighed by the risk that it would go badly: if he had been more of a 'politician', he would have seized on the Attorney General's equivocal advice as a pretext to stand aside.

Just as David Cameron, had he not believed in Britain's membership of the EU, could have used the ambiguous conclusion of his renegotiation of its terms to argue for a 'Leave' vote in the referendum, which he would have won comfortably. He might still be prime minister now. That this is even more unthinkable than Blair backing out of a joint US–UK military operation only reveals how committed Cameron, who had once called himself a 'Eurosceptic', really was. Similarly, John Major was too attached to the European Exchange Rate Mechanism as the guarantee of the credibility of his counter-inflation policy. He could have suspended the pound's membership of the ERM before it was forced out in 1992. It would have been an embarrassment rather than a humiliation, and might have saved something of his and his party's reputation. And Margaret Thatcher's determination to protect home-owning ratepayers from the arbitrary demands of Labour councils was also too strong. She could have been prime minister for even longer if she had abandoned the poll tax.

In every case, as a result of their deep conviction, each prime minister became boxed into a course of action from which it became inconceivable to them that they could escape. Politicians usually understand, as they are rising up the ladder, the importance of keeping their options open, but it becomes progressively harder to stick to that rule after years in the highest office.

Conclusion

It is often said of an unpopular politician that history will be kinder to them. For some time we assumed that this would be true of Tony Blair, but it is now apparent that such a verdict will not be clear-cut. Will posterity see him as brilliant? Probably. Will it see him as tricky? Also likely. But will the overall verdict be positive or negative? We are not sure. As prime minister, he was popular enough to stay in office for ten years and to leave pretty much on a date of his own choosing. In his final months, his rating in opinion polls was strongly negative, although no more so than most recent prime ministers.[1]

Since then, however, his reputation has failed to recover, as the Iraq war, the financial crisis, and immigration became the dominant themes of his record. Although Blair won the 2005 election two years after the invasion of Iraq, the belief that he deceived Parliament and the nation in making the case for the invasion has become firmly established. The financial crash of 2008 has cast a shadow over the golden economic record of the previous decade. And, as the free movement of workers became the focus of the campaign to leave the European Union, Blair's decision to allow the citizens of new member states to come to the UK from 2004 without the delay imposed by Germany and France has often been cited as a reason for the vote to leave the EU in the 2016 referendum.

In recent polls Blair continues to be viewed negatively, with only 22 per cent saying he did a good job and 49 per cent a bad job as prime minister. Gordon Brown's rating is worse, while Margaret

Thatcher's reputation is now positive. John Major and David Cameron, meanwhile, seem to be subsiding into indifference, still rated unfavourably but with large numbers of don't knows.[2]

Much of the difference between Blair and Thatcher is explained by how they are regarded by supporters of their own party. Where Blair is reviled by many Labour voters, Thatcher is revered by Conservatives. In both cases their successors in the same party tried to distance themselves from them, and in both cases their legacy was a divisive one in their party. But Thatcher was always seen as representing core Conservative values, whereas Blair had built his electoral success on appearing to repudiate much of the Labour tradition.

And while Conservative MPs deposed Thatcher reluctantly because she had become an electoral liability, most of the pressure from Labour MPs for Blair to hand over to Brown was ideological, in that they wanted a swing back to 'Labour' values. Opposition to the Iraq war was the most important symbol of this, and it was notable that it was another foreign policy crisis, when Blair refused to condemn the Israeli retaliation against Hezbollah in Lebanon, that prompted the September 2006 'coup' that finally forced him to put an end-date on his time at Number Ten.

When Brown became prime minister the following year, he tried to distance himself from 'Blair's war'. He expressed an interest in formalizing the convention that the House of Commons should vote to approve the use of military force (a convention instituted by Blair, ironically) and later, in 2009, when the last British combat troops were withdrawn, he commissioned the Chilcot inquiry into his predecessor's Iraq policy. He also found himself facing, within two months of Blair's departure, the first signs of the financial crisis which led to the run on the Northern Rock building society in August 2007, and its nationalization six months later. The credit crunch, which turned into the 'Great Recession' after the collapse of the American bank Lehman Brothers in September 2008, damaged Labour's reputation for economic competence. This had been jealously guarded by Brown since the Conservatives conceded it in the European exchange rate mechanism crisis of 1992. Not only did the reputation for competence go, but the drop in living standards may have affected attitudes towards immigration, which had previously been tolerated as long as the long economic boom continued.

We had thought, all the same, that a more balanced assessment of the Blair period would assert itself in time. Instead, far from 'history' being kinder to him, there are signs that it is becoming harsher. When Robert Tombs's bestselling *The English and their History* was published in 2014, it repeated all the negative readings of the country's most recent period. New Labour, Tombs said, was 'authoritarian'; it was too attentive to the rich in general and to Rupert Murdoch in particular; it was responsible for 'bypassing Parliament', 'subverting normal administrative methods (such as taking minutes of meetings), and tending to politicise or bypass civil servants'; it used the press as an 'instrument of politics' and was guilty of 'spin'; and it achieved a settlement in Northern Ireland only at 'a cost'.[3]

The election of Jeremy Corbyn as Labour leader in 2015 completed a process of reaction against Blair's politics within the Labour Party that took elements of all these criticisms and added to them the charge that he had continued Thatcher's policy of venerating the market and of 'privatizing' public services.

The EU referendum in June 2016 suggested that Blair's Europe policy had been a failure. Whatever the complex reasons for first holding the referendum and then for the result, the outcome was a repudiation of Blair's ambition nineteen years earlier to 'put Britain at the heart of Europe'. To the extent that the vote was read as a rejection of the free movement of people, it was also seen as confirming the error of Blair's policy on immigration. The publication of the Chilcot report two weeks later, and particularly the reporting of it as confirming that Blair had lied, even though it specifically but unobtrusively absolved him of that charge, further suggested that our expectation was premature.

Finally, although it is not the subject of this book, Blair stands accused of enriching himself in his post-prime-ministerial career.

That he gave large sums of money to charity, including the £4m advance for his memoir, *A Journey*, and made no personal profit from the most controversial contract he agreed, with the government of Kazakhstan, only seemed to make matters worse.

The case for the defence

Let us try to summarize our conclusions about these criticisms in turn.

Our view is that the decision to join the American invasion of Iraq was a complicated one, where no decision would have been in effect a decision in itself. The decision to take part was made for good reasons on the evidence available at the time, but where Blair erred was not so much in failing to probe the intelligence provided to him about weapons of mass destruction, but in failing to give enough weight to the risk of sectarian bloodshed as a consequence of toppling Saddam Hussein. It seemed reasonable to suppose that disarming Saddam, which probably meant in practice removing him, was a worthwhile object in itself; but the possible consequences should have outweighed that judgement. They were foreseeable and should have been foreseen, as the Chilcot inquiry found. It would have been hard for a pro-US government such as Blair's to have stood aside, but that was the test.

Nor should Iraq be allowed to eclipse all of Blair's foreign policy. The creation of the Department for International Development and the progress towards the target of 0.7 per cent of national income on aid spending (it rose from 0.26 per cent in 1997 to 0.57 per cent in 2010 before finally reaching 0.7 per cent under David Cameron in 2013)[4] were substantial achievements. The rescue of the Muslims of Kosovo from the attempted 'ethnic cleansing' of Slobodan Milosevic, and of the (mostly Muslim) people of Sierra Leone from the murderous hand-choppers of the Revolutionary United Front were unarguable credits in the ledger of history. The intervention in Afghanistan, while widely accepted as justified initially[5]—except by Jeremy Corbyn, who founded the Stop the War coalition to oppose it—produced mixed results. Life expectancy and the proportion of girls in education rose, but the task of suppressing the Taliban was misconceived, and Blair agreed to a US request, supported by John Reid, Defence Secretary, and the army, for UK troops to take over the deadliest province, Helmand, in 2006. It was not until 2014 that UK combat troops were finally withdrawn from Afghanistan.

On the economy, our view is that the New Labour record was good overall. Despite the foolish rhetoric of 'no more boom and bust', a phrase used by both Brown and Blair, the economic cycle had not been abolished, and when the recession came it came in a form that had not been widely expected: a credit crunch in the banks. (This was despite the Treasury under Ed Balls, as City minister, having war-gamed a scenario involving a run on a northern building society that uncannily prefigured the run on Northern Rock in 2007.) Even then, after sixteen years of unbroken growth, eleven of them under New Labour, there were two things in New Labour's favour, and both of them were thanks to Gordon Brown. Brown's reforms of the labour market, and in particular the tax credits that Blair disliked, meant that the 2008 recession, deep though it was, caused a surprisingly small rise in unemployment—and employment recovered quickly thereafter. Secondly, Brown himself was a good person to have in charge in that crisis, in that he understood both the economics and the geopolitics behind the economics. He realized the importance of coordinated government action to sustain demand, rallying the larger group of G20 countries (rather than the G7) to keep the world economy afloat. He had the good judgement and the authority to ignore David Cameron and George Osborne, who were against nationalizing banks (however much he too had initially tried to avoid it) and opposed to the large increase in public borrowing—two policies that helped stave off a serious depression.

Even after the crash, real national income per head was 17 per cent higher in 2010 than it had been in 1997—a modest gain but a better record than in the US, Germany, France, Japan, and Italy.[6] As for the distribution of income and wealth, Peter Mandelson's much-quoted claim to be 'intensely relaxed about people becoming filthy rich' is often quoted without the second half of the sentence, 'provided they pay their taxes'. New Labour managed an economy that was rich enough to afford renovations of the public services, particularly health and education, and to prevent the gap between rich and poor widening. The national minimum wage, tax credits, and rising employment were all important. The failure to narrow that gap disappointed rigorous egalitarians—that is, most of the Labour Party—but it is hard to see how much more could have been done in an open economy, while maintaining a viable electoral coalition.

That open economy meant immigration, on which the verdict of history will probably depend on the jury's prior assumptions. The European single market, legislated for by Thatcher, and its opening-up, driven forward under Blair, was good for the British economy, and a factor in turning the UK from the 'sick man of Europe' into one of its more dynamic and successful economies. Expanding the EU to the east had long been a strategic objective of British foreign policy, to dilute the German-French domination of the EU and to lock in the democratization of the former Soviet bloc. Even the decision not to impose a seven-year delay on the free movement of workers from the new members was uncontroversial at the time. For those who agree with it, it was a brave, principled, and liberal decision, but in fact, as Ed Balls told us: 'We didn't see the extent to which low-wage people would move—fundamentally, we didn't think they would.'[7] What was surprising about it was that Blair, so sensitive to popular opinion on matters of immigration and asylum, and so able to respond to concerns in the short term, failed to see the longer-term problems that were being stored up. Indeed, he turned the immigration issue against Michael Howard in the 2005 election, using it to portray the Conservatives as mean-spirited and backward-looking. So successful was he that David Cameron backed off the subject completely, and it then became a force behind the rise of Nigel Farage's UK Independence Party and the campaign for a referendum on EU membership.

Immigration undoubtedly contributed to the dynamism of the British economy and in particular to the success of London as a world city, but the scale of it alarmed people. Net immigration rose above 100,000 a year in 1998, and then above 200,000 a year in 2004,[8] contributing to a feeling among most of the population that they had not been consulted about the country changing in ways that they did not like.

The dynamism of the economy in turn produced the tax revenue that paid for better public services. The criticism from the Corbyn wing of the Labour Party that New Labour was bent on 'privatization' seems to rest on a confusion. As long as services were free at the point of need, New Labour did not care who provided them: 'What matters is what works.'[9] In practice, few NHS services were contracted out: in many cases, the mere possibility of rival providers offering NHS services was enough to change the behaviour of the NHS. In the NHS, the main change, however, was more public money, with spending doubling in real terms over the New Labour period.[10] Schools were improved, with better pay for teachers, more staff, rigorous national standards for primary school teaching and later the academies and similar reforms to secondary schools. The results were mixed and hard to measure, but one study of the 1997–2010 record found that 'there is a broad trend toward small reductions in attainment gaps' between pupils from low- and high-income families.[11] The proportion of young people attending university rose from 39 per cent in 1999 to 46 per cent in 2010, including a greater proportion from lower-income families, under the system of student loans repayable after graduation.[12]

Northern Ireland

Finally, it is worth paying some attention to one of Blair's least-contested achievements in government, the settlement in Northern Ireland. The breakthrough in principle occurred in the Belfast Agreement of 1998, and it was secured in practice in the St Andrews

Agreement of 2007, under which the Democratic Unionist Party, by then the largest party on the Unionist side, and Sinn Fein, the largest party on the nationalist side, formed a joint devolved administration.

Jonathan Powell, Blair's chief of staff, played a central role as a fixer endowed with the prime minister's personal authority. When he came to talk to our class in 2009, he warned against the tendency to go from thinking the problem was 'insoluble before it got solved' to it being 'inevitable that it was going to get solved' once it had been:

> It's quite important that people don't think either that Northern Ireland was insoluble or that it was inevitable because it has an impact on people trying to solve other crises around the world. They do need to understand their problem—how much they put into the detail of it, it's not insoluble, nor is it inevitable that someone's going to come along and solve it for them, they're going to have to work and actually do it.[13]

Powell responded to the critics of the settlement, with their variations on Robert Tombs's theme about it having been bought 'at a cost'— principally that of empowering the extremists (Sinn Fein led by Gerry Adams and Martin McGuinness on the nationalist side, and the Democratic Unionist Party led by Ian Paisley on the Unionist side) at the expense of the moderates (the Social and Democratic Labour Party led by John Hume, and the Ulster Unionist Party led by David Trimble):

> Their criticism really is that we sacrificed that moderate centre in Northern Ireland; we gave into the terrorists when we should have beaten them through counter-terrorism; that it was better to have the moral clarity and certainty of the Troubles than the seedy compromise that we came up with; and that we left the extremists in power in Northern Ireland. I'll take those elements in turn. Firstly, we tried to build a centre in Northern Ireland, and we tried to build up from the SDLP and the Ulster Unionist Party to construct the peace, but we couldn't do it because the SDLP were not in a position to move ahead without Sinn Fein moving with them. We tried repeatedly to get them to do so, they weren't prepared to, they weren't in a position to do so after John Hume had started his negotiations with Adams, which was

a brave and great thing that he did and he sacrificed his party on that. So we couldn't build from the centre in that way. We tried stick to David Trimble for as long as we possibly could—Tony Blair was still supporting David Trimble even after he lost the elections in 2003 in Northern Ireland because he thought he was the only person who could make peace; he didn't think Paisley would make peace. So he stuck with Trimble long after his own people had given up on him, let alone the Irish government and the Northern Ireland Office. But Trimble was simply not in a position to deliver peace in the end. So I think to say that we didn't build from the centre is just wrong. We certainly didn't give in to terrorists: they didn't get a united Ireland; they didn't get what they wanted in terms of the terrorist campaign. So that criticism is also misplaced.

Powell sought to assign credit for the settlement between 'big economic and social changes' and 'the role of individuals'. The settlement would not have been possible, he said:

if you hadn't had Ireland turning into a Celtic tiger, if it had remained or gone backward you wouldn't have been able to shift the unionists— and Ireland itself wouldn't have had the confidence to take the bold steps it later took; and if the British Army hadn't shifted in about the mid-Eighties to realizing that they couldn't win militarily; this wasn't Malaysia, they couldn't actually suppress a terrorist movement totally; they could keep violence on an acceptable level but never knock it out entirely; it had to be won by hearts and minds. The IRA itself reached a similar sort of position, a little bit later, probably the late Eighties. Adams and McGuinness understood that they could keep on fighting forever but they were never going to achieve their aims by military means and they would have to find a political solution. Those big forces by themselves wouldn't have been enough. If you hadn't had Adams and McGuinness, politicians of stature easily big enough to play on the British stage who led their movement—a movement that never knew where it was being led to—crab-like, to a peaceful settlement without a united Ireland. If you hadn't had people like that, it wouldn't have happened. If you hadn't had the political change in Britain; if you hadn't had Mo [Mowlam] replacing Patrick Mayhew [as Northern Ireland Secretary], it would be very hard to get to an agreement. Mo was a necessary addition to reaching peace, her very personality. If you hadn't had David Trimble and Ian Paisley, who were also playing this in their own way. And Tony, who is much blamed for his messianic zeal in other issues, if he hadn't had that in this case, we wouldn't have had an agreement. If we hadn't believed absolutely that he could do it, hadn't believed absolutely that it could be done, it wouldn't have been done. He was constantly ordering us to make water to flow back up hills and to go back into negotiations at two o'clock in the morning and keep going.[14]

After nearly ten years of devolved administration, the Northern Irish government collapsed in 2017, and the situation was complicated by Theresa May's need for DUP votes at Westminster after the 2017 UK election, and by the Brexit negotiations. However, at the risk of sunny optimism, it seems that a resumption of pre-1998 levels of violence is unlikely.

The conduct of government

As was inevitable with any government impatient to make changes, Blair's was criticized for the way it made decisions. He was accused of excessive prime-ministerial power, riding roughshod over collective Cabinet decision-making and excessive informality—a welter of complaints summed up in the phrase 'sofa government'. Once these criticisms are broken down into their constituent parts, however, we believe most of them to be unfounded. It was certainly true, as most of our witnesses testified, that power in the Blair government was concentrated in the Blair–Brown axis. All important decisions were taken by those two, at first in an informal if fraught partnership, later in an increasingly hostile negotiation. That duopoly drew power away from the rest of the Cabinet. But to suggest that this was a break from a long tradition of broad-based collective decision-making is unconvincing. Our view is that the waxing and waning of collective decision-making is the product of politics, rather than the determinant of it. Margaret Thatcher had been criticized as an overmighty prime minister and praised as a strong one. John Major was praised for his more consensual style and criticized for his weakness. In the previous Labour government, James Callaghan used long Cabinet meetings to try to wear his colleagues down to a common position, a necessity forced on him as he lost his parliamentary majority.

One of the most striking vindications of Blair's governing style, paradoxically, came from Gordon Brown, who admitted in his memoir that he tried to 'move on' from 'sofa government' and to restore a traditional form of Cabinet government, but that he had to accept that times and the media environment in particular had changed.[15]

There may be three models of Cabinet government: primeministerial, core-group, and collective. Blair's was mostly the second; and there were good reasons why, under the Conservative-Lib Dem coalition that followed, the Blair-Brown duopoly was replaced by the Quad of David Cameron, George Osborne, Nick Clegg, and Danny Alexander.[16] These four, prime minister, Chancellor, deputy prime minister, and chief secretary to the Treasury, two from each coalition party, made most of the important decisions, while the rest of the Cabinet remained secondary. Theresa May, on the other hand, seemed to go straight from the first model to the third. In her first eleven months as prime minister, she drew all power to herself and her political advisers; after the disastrous election of 2017 she changed tack and consulted Cabinet and Cabinet colleagues more widely.

As for the charge echoed by Tombs that New Labour subverted 'normal administrative methods...such as taking minutes of meetings', this may reflect two things. In the first few days after the 1997 election there was some confusion about unminuted meetings—between Blair and Brown, naturally—as they carried the working style of opposition into government. This was quickly formalized. Procedures were changing fast with the use of email and texts, although they did not seem to become a problem for the bureaucracy until the arrival of Brown as prime minister, with his more disorganized methods. The other source of the idea that New Labour was cavalier about recordkeeping was the Butler inquiry's comment about the 'the informality and circumscribed character of the Government's procedures' before the invasion of Iraq, which we discussed in chapter 2. However, the idea that decisions might have been different if more 'traditional' procedures had been followed is unconvincing. Neither the Butler report nor the Chilcot report contains any evidence to suggest that different procedures would have led to a decision to stand aside from the US-led military action, as we discussed in chapter 5.

Much the same can be said of the complaint that New Labour 'politicized' the Civil Service. Again and again, this was rebutted by the officials who came to talk to our seminars. They all welcomed political advisers, now universally known as special advisers, as providing additional political capacity at the top of government and, paradoxically for some, a bulwark *against* politicization. In a democracy, parties are elected to carry out their programme, and an effective government needs a politically committed team to drive it forward. Many civil servants had criticisms of special advisers—primarily of their sometimes excessive loyalty to an individual politician, or to either the Blairite or Brownite factions. If there was too much faction-fighting in New Labour, however, the main causes were Blair and Brown's dysfunctional relationship and the weakness, before 2005, of the opposition Conservative Party, rather than an excess of special advisers. As with the supposed downplaying of Cabinet government, one of the tests of this criticism is what the Coalition did next. While the number of special advisers rose from 38 under John Major to a peak of 84 under Gordon Brown, it then rose further, to 107, under the Coalition. Nick Clegg in particular felt forced by his situation to reverse his feisty pre-election rhetoric against New Labour's special advisers to hire 15 'spads' for his office of deputy prime minister alone.

Blair's decision to put a political chief of staff, Jonathan Powell, at the heart of the Downing Street operation with formal power to direct officials was an interesting one and something that took time to settle but eventually Powell worked well alongside the Civil Service linchpins, the principal private secretary and the Cabinet Secretary. This was reversed by Gordon Brown, who appointed Tom Scholar, a Treasury civil servant, to a joint chief of staff and PPS post. After seven months, however, he was replaced by a political chief of staff, Stephen Carter, alongside a civil servant PPS, Jeremy Heywood, who, after a further nine months, also took back the chief of staff role. Thereafter, the model of a political chief of staff alongside a civil servant PPS was resumed. David Cameron's chief of staff was Ed Llewellyn, and Theresa May for her first year had two, Fiona Hill and Nick Timothy, before they were despatched after the 2017 election and replaced by another special adviser, Gavin Barwell, a former MP.

As for the charge that New Labour was too reliant on spin and media manipulation, it contains its own refutation. For a government to acquire a reputation for spin—that is, for not being straight with people—is evidence that it is bad at the art of presentation. Indeed, the Labour government at an early stage, before 2000, found itself trapped in a cycle of trying to shake off this reputation, with each attempt being seized on by journalists as evidence of further manipulation. Thus Alastair Campbell put briefings of lobby journalists on the record and instituted frequent televised news conferences with Blair himself. But once the virus of the charge of spin had entered the bloodstream of the media–political complex, it could not be expelled. The allegation of spin was a tribute to Campbell's energy and discipline in opposition, but it was also, perhaps, the inevitable product of the scale of Blair's election victory in 1997, sustained in 2001, which raised expectations that would be impossible to fulfil.

Those high expectations, which were different and probably incompatible for different voters, were bound to be disappointed. As time went on and Blair's government took more and more decisions, the probability that one or more sections of the electorate would be offended grew. As people sought to rationalize their past enthusiasm for New Labour, the idea took hold that they had been taken in by the arts of slick presentation, or that decisions with which they disagreed—in some cases after the event—must have been arrived at by bad, politicized, or informal procedures.

We argue that such perceptions are ahistorical. We accept that the view in this book is slanted in Blair's favour. Most of the politicians, special advisers, and officials who came to our classes were proud of their collective record. However, in our opinion the prevailing view of Blair and New Labour is too negative, and it is one of the purposes of this volume to provide a counterweight, so that the independent-minded reader is better placed to reach a considered view.

Notes

PROLOGUE

1. Peter Hennessy, *The Hidden Wiring* (Gollancz, 1995); *The Prime Minister* (Penguin, 2000); and *The Secret State* (Allen Lane, 2002).
2. Peter Hennessy, *Whitehall* (Secker and Warburg, 1989).

INTRODUCTION

1. Ken Clarke, *Kind of Blue* (Macmillan, 2016), p. 460.
2. In addition, Jon Davis and his team of postgraduate researchers have worked with the prime minister's office, the Treasury, and other departments on projects aimed at improving their institutional memory, such as the history section of the 10 Downing Street website and a website based on interviews with the Cabinet Secretaries, called 'Men of Secrets'. See http://www.cabinetsecretaries.com.
3. Peggy Noonan, 'McClellan's book: More details, please', *Orange County Register*, 1 June 2008.
4. Gordon Brown, *My Life, Our Times* (Bodley Head, 2017 and Vintage, 2018).
5. Baroness Morgan, 'Blair Government' class, Queen Mary University of London, 26 January 2009. See chapter 5.
6. Polly Toynbee and David Walker, *The Verdict: Did Labour Change Britain?* (Granta Books, 2011).
7. Roy Jenkins, 'Churchill: The Government of 1951–1955', in R. Blake and W. R. Louis (eds), *Churchill* (Oxford University Press, 1993), p. 492.
8. Harold Wilson, radio and television broadcast, 19 November 1967.
9. Front-page editorial, 'Crisis? What Crisis?', *Sun*, 11 January 1979. Callaghan's actual words were: 'I don't think that other people in the world would share the view that there is mounting chaos.'
10. Labour's seats total is often given as 418, excluding the Speaker, Betty Boothroyd, originally elected as Labour MP for West Bromwich and then West Bromwich West. For the purposes of calculating the government's majority, however, hers counted as a Labour seat.

11. Neal Lawson, 'Dear Tony Blair, maybe it's your fault if the electorate hasn't shifted to the left', *Guardian*, 1 January 2015.

12. Jeremy Corbyn, *The Andrew Neil Interviews*, BBC One, 26 May 2017.

13. Jonathan Powell, *Great Hatred, Little Room* (Bodley Head, 2008); 'Blair Government' class, Queen Mary University, 9 February 2009.

14. John Appleby, 'How satisfied are we with the NHS?' *British Medical Journal* website, 22 March 2011. Available at: https://doi.org/10.1136/bmj.d1836.

15. Jonathan Powell, quoted in Lisa O'Carroll, 'Tony Blair knew immediately that 9/11 terror attacks "changed everything" ', *Guardian*, 10 September 2011.

16. Tony Blair, quoted in Alastair Campbell & Bill Hagerty (eds), *Alastair Campbell Diaries: Volume 4* (Hutchinson, 2012), 23 July 2002.

17. Private information.

18. John Major, *The Major Years*, BBC documentary, 11 August 1999.

19. Lord Wilson of Dinton, 'No. 10 Downing Street and the History of the Prime Minister' postgraduate class, King's College London, 14 October 2016.

CHAPTER 1

1. The idea of 'New Labour' had been suggested before, by Philip Gould, to Neil Kinnock, in 1989, and by Leslie Butterworth, advertising adviser to the Labour Party, to John Smith: see John Rentoul, *Tony Blair: Prime Minister* (Little, Brown & Co., 2001), p. 255.

2. Gordon Brown, *My Life, Our Times*, (Bodley Head, 2017 and Vintage, 2018) pp. 85–6; John Rentoul, *Tony Blair: Prime Minister*, pp. 180–5; Peter Mandelson, 'My handwritten argument for a Smith–Brown ticket for party leadership', in the enhanced e-book version of *The Third Man* (HarperCollins, 2011).

3. John Rentoul, *Tony Blair: Prime Minister*, p. 232.

4. John Rentoul, *Tony Blair: Prime Minister*, pp. 207–12.

5. Anji Hunter, 'Blair Government' class, King's College London, 23 January 2017.

6. Steve Richards, *Whatever it Takes: The real story of Gordon Brown and New Labour* (HarperCollins, 2010), p. 81.

7. Tony Blair, *A Journey* (Hutchinson, 2010), p. 63.

8. Michael White, 'The guarantee which came to dominate New Labour politics for a decade,' *Guardian*, 6 June 2003.

9. Peter Mandelson, *The Third Man*, p. 172.

10. Tony Blair, *A Journey*, p. 117.

11. Alastair Campbell & Bill Hagerty (eds), *Alistair Campbell Diaries: Volume 2* (Hutchinson, 2011), 21 October 1997.

12. *Alastair Campbell Diaries: Vol. 2.*, 14 November 1997.

13. Paul Routledge, *Gordon Brown: The Biography* (Simon & Schuster, 1998), p. 205.

14. Andrew Rawnsley, *Observer*, 18 January 1998.

15. *Alastair Campbell Diaries: Vol. 2.*, 16 January 1998.

16. *Private Eye*, 23 January 1998.

17. *Alastair Campbell Diaries: Vol. 2.*, 18 January 1998.

18. *Alastair Campbell Diaries: Vol. 2.*, 29 September to 2 October 1997.

19. Tony Blair, *A Journey*, p. 219.

20. Jonathan Powell, *The New Machiavelli: How to wield power in the modern world* (Random House, 2010), p. 117.

21. John Rentoul, *Tony Blair: Prime Minister*, pp. 359–62.

22. He said he was also 'happy to support' Blair's office as leader of the opposition: Geoffrey Robinson, *The Unconventional Minister: My life inside New Labour* (Michael Joseph, 2000), p. 7.

23. Jonathan Powell, *The New Machiavelli*, p. 109.

24. Peter Watt, *Inside Out: My story of betrayal and cowardice at the heart of New Labour* (Biteback, 2010), p. 105.

25. Baroness Jay, 'Blair Government', Queen Mary University of London, 6 October 2008.

26. Ed Balls, 'Blair Government', Queen Mary University, 4 April 2011.

27. Alastair Campbell & Bill Hagerty (eds), *Alastair Campbell Diaries: Volume 3* (Hutchinson, 2012), 6 June 2001.

28. Peter Mandelson, *The Third Man*, p. 276.

29. *Alastair Campbell Diaries: Vol. 3*, 11 April 2001.

30. Alastair Campbell & Bill Hagerty (eds), *Alastair Campbell Diaries: Volume 4* (Hutchinson, 2012), 26 September 2002.

31. *Alastair Campbell Diaries: Vol. 4*, 27 September 2002.

32. *Alastair Campbell Diaries: Vol. 4*, 7 January 2003.

33. Peter Mandelson, *The Third Man*, p. 369.

34. Tony Blair, 'Blair Government', Queen Mary University, 20 May 2011.

35. Robert Peston, *Brown's Britain* (Short Books, 2005), p. 335.

36. 'Blair and Brown make up after row over NEC place,' *Independent*, 8 November 2003.

37. John Prescott, *Prezza: My story* (Headline Review, 2008), p. 315.

38. Tony Blair, *A Journey*, p. 497.

39. Peter Mandelson, *The Third Man*, p. 373.

40. Tony Blair, *A Journey*, p. 496.

41. Ed Balls, 'Blair Government', Queen Mary University, 4 April 2011.

42. Baroness Morgan, 'Blair Government', Queen Mary University, 26 January 2009.

43. Baroness Morgan, 'Blair Government', Queen Mary University, 26 January 2009.

44. Robert Peston, *Brown's Britain*, p. 337.

45. Robert Peston, *Brown's Britain*, p. 338.

46. Alastair Campbell and Bill Hagerty (eds), *Alastair Campbell Diaries: Volume 5* (Biteback, 2016), 23 April and 4 May 2004.

47. Private information.

48. Andrew Marr, BBC Political Editor, Radio 4 *Today* programme, 10 July 2004; Tony Blair, *A Journey*, p. 508.

49. Tony Blair, *A Journey*, pp. 508–9.

50. Robert Peston, *Brown's Britain*, p. 343.

51. Alan Milburn, BBC Radio 4 *Today* programme, 9 September 2004.

52. Alan Milburn, 'Blair Government', Queen Mary University, 23 February 2009.

53. 'Milburn resigns from government', *Guardian*, 12 June 2003.

54. Alan Milburn, 'Blair Government', Queen Mary University, 23 February 2009.

55. Tony Blair, *A Journey*, p. 510.

56. Alan Milburn, 'Blair Government', Queen Mary University, 23 February 2009.

57. Robert Peston, *Brown's Britain*, p. 349.

58. Tony Blair, BBC *Breakfast with Frost* programme, 9 January 2005.

59. A YouGov poll for the *Mail on Sunday*, 9 May 2004, suggested a two-point swing to Labour if Brown were to replace Blair as leader; an ICM poll for the *Guardian*, 26 May 2004, showed the same; an ICM poll for the *Guardian*, 20 July 2004, suggested a three-point swing to Labour; an NOP poll for the *Independent*, 11 January 2005, showed a six-and-a-half-point swing; Communicate Research for the *Independent on Sunday*, 27 February 2005, showed a three-and-a-half-point swing, and another on 17 April 2005 showed a six-point swing. After the 2005 election, however, polls suggested that replacing Blair with Brown would worsen Labour's position.

60. Ipsos MORI, 'Most Capable Prime Minister—Trends' January and April 2005. Accessed at: https://www.ipsos.com/ipsos-mori/en-uk/most-capable-prime-minister-trends.

61. *Alastair Campbell Diaries: Vol. 5*, 18 March 2005.

62. Peter Mandelson, *The Third Man*, pp. 407–8.

63. *Alastair Campbell Diaries: Vol. 5*, 29 March 2005.
64. Alan Milburn, 'Blair Government', Queen Mary University, 23 February 2009.
65. *Alastair Campbell Diaries: Vol. 5*, 15 April 2005.
66. Gordon Brown, *My Life, Our Times*, pp. 260–1.
67. Alan Milburn, 'Blair Government', Queen Mary University, 23 February 2009.
68. Andrew Rawnsley, *The End of the Party* (Penguin Books, 2010), p. 398.
69. Gordon Brown, *My Life, Our Times*, p. 192.
70. Tessa Jowell, 'Blair Government', 7 Queen Mary University, March 2011.
71. Tony Blair, 'Blair Government', Queen Mary University, 20 May 2011.
72. Tony Blair, 'Blair Government', Queen Mary University, 20 May 2011.
73. Geoff Mulgan, 'Blair Government', Queen Mary University, 10 November 2008.
74. Jonathan Powell, *The New Machiavelli*, pp. 113–14.
75. Tony Blair, 'Blair Government', Queen Mary University, 20 May 2011.
76. Tony Blair, *A Journey*, p. 497.
77. Tony Blair, *A Journey*, p. 498. Ellipsis in original.
78. Peter Mandelson, *The Third Man*, p. 390.
79. *Alastair Campbell Diaries: Vol. 4,* 29 April 2003.

CHAPTER 2

1. 'Teflon Tony', *Economist*, 22 March 2001.
2. Tony Blair, *A Journey* (Hutchinson, 2010), p. xvii.
3. Jonathan Powell, *The New Machiavelli* (Bodley Head, 2010), p. 22.
4. Peter Hennessy, *Whitehall* (Victor Gollancz, 1995), pp. 56–7.
5. 9 May 1994 and 9 January 1995, both for Gallup/Telegraph, http://ukpollingreport.co.uk/historical-polls/voting-intention-1992-1997. Labour eventually won in 1997 with 44.4% of the vote compared to the Conservatives' 31.5% (Great Britain).
6. Peter Mandelson and Roger Liddle, *The Blair Revolution: Can New Labour Deliver?* (Faber and Faber, 1996), pp. 236–44.
7. Lord Wilson of Dinton, 'The Blair Government Revisited', Queen Mary University of London, 18 May 2004.
8. Peter Hennessy, *The Prime Minister* (Penguin Books, 2000), pp. 477–8.
9. Jonathan Powell, *The New Machiavelli*, p. 78.
10. Jonathan Powell, *The New Machiavelli*, p. 78.

11. Jon Davis interview with Sir Richard Mottram, 4 June 2014.

12. Peter Hennessy, 'The Cabinet Office: A magnificent piece of powerful bureaucratic machinery', *The Times*, 8 March 1976.

13. Stephen Roskill, *Hankey: Man of Secrets: Volume 1: 1877–1918* (Collins, 1970), *Volume 2: 1919–1931* (Collins, 1972), *Volume 3: 1931–1963* (Collins, 1974).

14. '100 Years of Cabinet Secretaries: Six in Conversation', seminar at Institute for Government, 30 November 2016.

15. Robert Hill, respondent to Peter Riddell, 'The Unfulfilled Prime Minister', Queen Mary University of London, 1 December 2005.

16. Michael Heseltine, 'When I knew I had to go', *Observer*, 12 January 1986.

17. Margaret Thatcher, *The Downing Street Years* (HarperCollins, 1993), p. 434.

18. Walter Bagehot, *The English Constitution* (Fontana, 1963), pp. 65–6.

19. Hennessy, *The Prime Minister*, p. 4.

20. Lord Falconer of Thoroton, 'The Blair Government' undergraduate special subject, Queen Mary University of London, 19 October 2009.

21. 'Men of Secrets' video history, Mile End Group, Queen Mary University of London, May 2013, http://www.cabinetsecretaries.com.

22. Quoted in Hennessy, *The Prime Minister*, p. 422.

23. Aaron Blake, 'Kellyanne Conway says Donald Trump's team has "alternative facts." Which pretty much says it all,' *The Washington Post*, 22 January 2017.

24. Peter Riddell, 'Cracks in the Cabinet cement', *The Times*, 10 November 1997.

25. 'Men of Secrets'.

26. Hennessy, *The Prime Minister*, p. 3.

27. Jon Davis interview with Sir Richard Mottram, 4 June 2014.

28. 'Men of Secrets'.

29. Tony Blair, *A Journey*, p. 17.

30. Alastair Campbell & Bill Hagerty (eds), *Alastair Campbell Diaries: Volume 2* (Hutchinson, 2011), 2 May 1997.

31. Quoted in Boris Johnson, 'How not to run a country', *The Spectator*, 11 December 2004.

32. 'Men of Secrets'.

33. 'Men of Secrets'.

34. Lord Mandelson, 'The Blair Government', Queen Mary University, 4 April 2011.

35. 'Men of Secrets'.

36. 'Men of Secrets'.

37. 'Men of Secrets'.

38. 'Men of Secrets'.

39. Nigel Lawson, *The View from No. 11* (Bantam Press, 1992), p. 126.

40. Edmund Dell and Lord Hunt, 'The Failings of Cabinet Government in Mid to Late 1970s', *Contemporary Record* 8(3), p. 461.

41. Lord Hunt of Tanworth, 'Cabinet Strategy and Management', paper delivered to CIPFA/RIPA conference, Eastbourne, 9 June 1983.

42. 'Men of Secrets'.

43. 'Men of Secrets': the agreement at Bretton Woods in New Hampshire in 1944 created the institutions of international post-war economic governance.

44. Jon Davis interview with Sir Richard Mottram, 4 June 2014.

45. *Alastair Campbell Diaries: Vol. 2*, 1 August 1997.

46. Sir Edward Bridges, 'Portrait of a Profession', Rede Lecture, University of Cambridge, 1950, printed by Cambridge University Press, 1950.

47. Kevin Theakston, *Leadership in Whitehall* (St Martin's Press, 1999), p. 83.

48. Richard Wilson, 'Portrait of a Profession Revisited', *Political Quarterly* 73(4), October 2002, p. 381.

49. 'Men of Secrets'.

50. 'Men of Secrets'.

51. Quoted in Boris Johnson, 'How not to run a country', *The Spectator*, 11 December 2004.

52. Lord Hennessy of Nympsfield, 'Number 10 Downing Street and the History of the Prime Minister', King's College London, 8 December 2017.

53. Peter Hennessy, 'The British Civil Service: The Condition of Mr Gladstone's Legacy as the Century Turns', *The Stakeholder*, July 1999.

54. Peter Hennessy, 'The Blair Centre: A Question of Command and Control?', *Public Management Foundation*, February 1999.

55. Lord Wilson of Dinton, 'The Blair Government Revisited', Queen Mary University, 18 May 2004.

56. Oonagh Gay, *Questions of Procedure for Ministers* (House of Commons Research Paper 96/53), 19 April 1996.

57. Quoted in Peter Hennessy, *The Hidden Wiring* (Victor Gollancz, 1995), p. 36.

58. House of Commons, *Official Report*, col. 1098, 13 July 2000.

59. 'Men of Secrets'.

60. 'Men of Secrets'.

61. Tony Blair, 'How Government Really Works', Queen Mary University, 28 October 2013.

62. Jon Davis interview with Sir Jeremy Heywood, 20 September 2016.

63. Jon Davis interview with Sir Richard Mottram, 4 June 2014.

64. Daniel Finkelstein, 'A nightmare, unless my memory deceives me,' *The Times*, 19 August 2003.

65. Report of a Committee of Privy Counsellors, *Review of Intelligence on Weapons of Mass Destruction*, HC 898, 14 July 2004, para. 611.

66. Sebastian Payne, ' "Yes, Minister" remains an unrivalled guide to British politics', *Financial Times*, 26 August 2016.

67. 'Basic Mandarin' available at: http://www.civilservant.org.uk/misc-humour-mandarin1-2.html.

68. Quoted in Jon Davis, *Prime Ministers and Whitehall* (Hambledon Continuum, 2007), p. 214, footnote 208.

69. Report of a Committee of Privy Counsellors, *Review of Intelligence on Weapons of Mass Destruction*, HC 898, 14 July 2004, para. 611.

70. Quoted in Sir Ivor Jennings, *Cabinet Government* (Cambridge University Press, 1936), p. 12.

71. Editorial, 'Chilcot has ended "whitewash" reports on Iraq war', *Financial Times*, 6 July 2016.

72. Letter from Sir John Chilcot to David Cameron, dated July 2016, contained within *The Report of the Iraq Inquiry*, Report of a Committee of Privy Counsellors, 6 July 2016.

73. *The Report of the Iraq Inquiry*, para. 392.

74. *The Report of the Iraq Inquiry*, para. 399.

75. *The Report of the Iraq Inquiry*, paras. 401–402.

76. *The Report of the Iraq Inquiry*, para. 409.

77. *The Report of the Iraq Inquiry*, para. 410.

78. John Cole, *As it Seemed to me* (Weidenfeld and Nicolson, 1995), p. 396.

79. Tony Blair, 'Blair Government', Queen Mary University, 20 May 2011.

80. Jonathan Powell, in an interview with Ian Katz, 'The inside man', *Guardian*, 15 March 2008.

81. Jonathan Powell, *The New Machiavelli*, pp. 57–8.

82. David Miliband used the phrase at the Lord Healey, 'Being Chancellor', Mile End Group seminar 70, 25 January 2011.

83. Peter Hennessy, *Whitehall* (Secker & Warburg, 1989), p. 76.

84. Jonathan Powell, *The New Machiavelli*, pp. 58–60.

85. Peter Hennessy, *Whitehall*, p. 238.

86. Jon Davis and John Rentoul interview with Sir John Holmes, 16 July 2014.

87. Jon Davis interview with Sir Jeremy Heywood, 20 September 2016.

88. Lord Butler of Brockwell, 'Number 10 Downing Street and the History of the Prime Minister', King's College London, 28 October 2016.

89. Jon Davis interview with Sir Nicholas Macpherson, 13 April 2011.

90. Alastair Campbell & Bill Hagerty (eds), *Alastair Campbell Diaries: Volume 3* (Hutchinson, 2011), 31 March 2000.

91. Alastair Campbell, 'Blair Government', Queen Mary University, 9 February 2009.

92. Lord Liverpool, Prime Minister 1812–27. Blair's majority was in fact the biggest since the National Government in 1935.

93. Lord Falconer of Thoroton, 'Blair Government', Queen Mary University, 19 October 2009.

94. Peter Mandelson, *The Third Man*, p. 213.

95. *Alastair Campbell Diaries: Vol. 3*, 19 May 2000; 20 May 2000; 25 July 2000.

96. Tony Blair, *A Journey*, p. 679.

97. 'Don't go that way', *Economist*, 30 December 2014.

98. Jon Davis interview with Sir Richard Mottram, 4 June 2014.

99. Lord Macpherson of Earl's Court, 'The Blair Years', King's College London, 13 February 2017.

100. Lord Mandelson, 'New Labour in Government', Queen Mary University of London, 4 April 11.

101. Andrew Rawnsley, 'The Chancellor and the Cabinet need to talk', *Observer*, 10 March 2002.

102. Jonathan Powell, *The New Machiavelli*, p. 113.

103. *Alastair Campbell Diaries: Vol. 3*, 29 March 2001.

104. *Alastair Campbell Diaries: Vol. 2*, 5 January 1999.

105. Gordon Brown, *My Life, Our Times* (Bodley Head, 2017), p. 208.

106. Gordon Brown, *My Life, Our Times*, pp. 224–6.

107. Peter Hennessy, 'Rulers and servants of the state: The Blair style of government, 1997–2004', lecture to OPM's Public Interest General Council, June 2004.

108. Ion Trewin (ed.), *The Hugo Young Papers* (Penguin, 2008), p. 596.

109. Tony Blair, 'How Government Really Works', Queen Mary University, 28 October 2013.

110. Lord O'Donnell, 'The Blair Years', King's College London, 6 February 2017.

111. Jon Davis interview with Sir Richard Mottram, 4 June 2014.

112. Hansard, House of Commons 6th series, vol. 258, cols. 655–6. Prime Minister's Questions, 25 April 1995.

113. Anthony Bevins, 'New sleaze row knocks at door of No 10', *Independent*, 2 June 1997.

114. *Alastair Campbell Diaries: Vol. 3*, 2 May 2000.

115. 'Men of Secrets'.

116. Peter Mandelson and Roger Liddle, *The Blair Revolution* (Faber & Faber, 1996), pp. 236–7.

117. Nigel Lawson, *The View from No. 11* (Bantam Press, 1992), pp. 561–85.

118. Ken Clarke, *Kind of Blue* (Macmillan, 2016), pp. 148, 252.

119. Peter Hennessy, *The Hidden Wiring*, p. 97.

120. Ken Clarke, *Kind of Blue*, p. 252.

121. Bagehot, 'Selling a New Spirit,' *The Economist*, 8 December 1990; Peter Hennessy *The Prime Minister*, p. 439.

122. Ken Clarke, *Kind of Blue*, pp. 252, 362–3.

123. Jon Davis interview with Sir Richard Mottram, 4 June 2014.

124. Lord Morgan, 'David Lloyd George and Clement Attlee as prime ministers', Downing Street History Seminar, 10 April 2014.

125. Peter Hennessy, *Cabinet* (Wiley-Blackwell, 1986), pp. 123–35.

126. John P. Mackintosh, *The British Cabinet* (University Paperback, 1968), p. 469.

127. Private information.

128. Clement Attlee to the House of Commons, Hansard *Official Report*, vol 520, col. 15, 3 November 1953.

129. Peter Hennessy, *The Prime Minister*, p. 199.

130. Lord Bancroft had been Private Secretary to R. A. Butler, Lord Privy Seal during Suez, and later, as Sir Ian, Head of the Home Civil Service, 1978–81: interviewed for *All The Prime Minister's Men*, 10 April 1986.

131. Peter Hennessy, *The Prime Minister*, pp. 210–11.

132. Peter Hennessy, *The Prime Minister*, p. 290; the National Archives, CAB 130/212, MISC 16, 1st meeting, 11 November 1964.

133. 'The New Britain', Labour Party Election Manifesto, 1964.

134. Jon Davis, *Prime Ministers and Whitehall*, pp. 129–30.

135. Margaret Thatcher, Conservative Party Conference, 10 October 1980.

136. Jon Davis, *Prime Ministers and Whitehall*, p. 144.

137. 'The IMF Crisis 40 Years on', King's College London, 26 October 2016.

138. Denis Healey, *The Time of My Life* (Michael Joseph, 1989), p. 431.

139. Quoted in Peter Hennessey, *The Prime Minister*, p. 388.

140. Edmund Dell and Lord Hunt of Tanworth, 'The Failings of Cabinet Government in Mid to Late 1970s', *Contemporary Record* 8(3) (winter 1994), p. 461.

141. Peter Hennessy, *Muddling Through* (Weidenfeld & Nicolson, 1996), p. 285.

142. Edmund Dell and Lord Hunt of Tanworth, 'The Failings of Cabinet Government in Mid to Late 1970s', *Contemporary Record*, 8(3) (winter 1994), p. 461.

143. Lord Barnett speaking at 'Learning the Lessons of Past Spending Reviews: The IMF Crisis 1976', Queen Mary University, in HM Treasury, 26 April 2013.

144. Phone conversation with Sir Kenneth Stowe, 6 December 2006; corroborated by Lord Donoughue, 8 December 2016.

145. Joshua Rozenberg, 'The Iraq war inquiry has left the door open for Tony Blair to be prosecuted', *Guardian*, 6 July 2016.

146. Ministerial Code, 2001 version.

147. Michael Everett, 'Collective Responsibility', *House of Commons Library Briefing Paper*, Number 7755, 14 November 2016.

148. Cabinet Office, *The Cabinet Manual: A guide to the laws, conventions and rules on the operation of government*, 2011, para 4.2.

149. See Hansard, HC Debate, 16 June 1977, vol. 933 col. 552.

150. James Forsyth and Fraser Nelson, 'Theresa May: "I get so frustrated with Whitehall,"' *The Spectator*, 10 December 2016.

151. Sam Coates, 'Big Brexit decisions delayed until next year amid cabinet squabbles,' *The Times*, 14 December 2016.

152. Henry Mance, 'Tory split on Heathrow exposed as critics attack decision,' *Financial Times*, 25 October 2016.

153. Oliver Wright, Francis Elliott, & Bruno Waterfield, 'Nick Timothy and Fiona Hill: How civil servants lived in fear of the terrible twins at No 10', *The Times*, 17 June 2017.

154. Francis Elliott, 'Theresa May splits up squabblers as Brexit customs deal eludes cabinet', *The Times*, 11 May 2018.

155. Michael Everett, 'Collective Responsibility', *House of Commons Library Briefing Paper*, Number 7755, 14 November 2016.

156. Nicholas Watt, 'Nick Clegg's "illegal" Iraq war gaffe prompts legal warning,' *Guardian*, 22 July 2010.

157. Peter Hennessy, *The Prime Minister*, pp. 319–26.

158. Peter Hennessy, '"Tony wants": The first Blair Premiership in historical perspective', The Colin Matthews Memorial Lecture for the Understanding of History, 7 November 2001.

159. *Alastair Campbell Diaries: Vol. 3*, 20 January 2000.

160. Baroness Morgan of Huyton, 'The Blair Government', Queen Mary University, 26 January 2009.

161. Jonathan Powell, *The New Machiavelli*, p. 43.

162. Tony Blair, *A Journey*, p. 294.

163. Jonathan Powell, *The New Machiavelli*, p. 43.

164. NA, PRO, PREM 15/1603, Robert Armstrong to Sir William Armstrong, 13 September 1972.

165. Private information.

166. Ian Blair recalls Campbell's words in *Policing Controversy* (Profile, 2009), p. 108.

167. Tony Blair, *A Journey*, p. 309.

168. Jonathan Powell, *The New Machiavelli*, p. 45.

169. *Alastair Campbell Diaries: Vol. 3*, 26 and 28 March 2001.

170. 'Blair praises Army's war on disease', BBC, 30 April 2001. Available at: http://news.bbc.co.uk/1/hi/uk/1303323.stm.

171. Nicholas Watt, 'Copy can-do army, Blair tells the Sir Humphreys', *Guardian*, 25 February 2004.

172. Peter Hennessy, *Whitehall*, p. 309.

173. Sir Kevin Tebbit, 'Blair Government', Queen Mary University, 3 March 2014.

174. Jon Davis interview with Sir Richard Mottram, 4 June 2014.

175. Ian Blair, *Policing Controversy*, pp. 108–11.

176. Lord O'Donnell, 'The Blair Years', King's College London, 6 February 2017.

177. 'Men of Secrets'.

178. Peter Hennessy, *The Prime Minister*, p. 6.

179. Hansard, House of Commons, vol. 444, col. 207, 11 November 1947.

CHAPTER 3

1. Alastair Campbell & Bill Hagerty (eds), *Alastair Campbell Diaries: Volume 1* (Hutchinson, 2010), 16 July 1994.

2. *Alastair Campbell Diaries: Vol. 1*, 25 July 1994.

3. Alastair Campbell, 'Campbell vs Campbell', *GQ*, September 2016.

4. Front page editorial, 'If Kinnock wins today will the last person to leave Britain please turn out the lights', *Sun*, 9 April 1992.

5. Front-page editorial, 'It's The Sun wot won it', *Sun*, 11 April 1992.

6. Tony Blair, interviewed by Peter Hennessy, *Reflections*, BBC Radio 4, 10 August 2017.

7. David Cannadine, *In Churchill's Shadow* (Allen Lane, 2002), p. 165.

8. See Charles Moore, *Margaret Thatcher: The Authorised Biography—Volume One: Not for Turning* (Allen Lane, 2013).

9. See Peter Hennessy, *Never Again* (Jonathan Cape, 1992) and *The Prime Minister* (Allen Lane, 2000), pp. 147–77.

10. See Ben Pimlott, *Harold Wilson* (HarperCollins, 1992), pp. 268–70.

11. 'Currie interview in full', BBC, 2 October 2002. Available at: http://news.bbc.co.uk/1/hi/uk_politics/2291467.stm.

12. *Alastair Campbell Diaries: Vol. 1*, 27 June 1995.

13. Blair speech at NewsCorp Conference, Australia, 17 July 1995. Available at: https://docs.google.com/open?id=0B5Ik-gKDMpozYnJaZldwbk43NmM.

14. Gordon Brown, *My Life, Our Times* (Bodley Head, 2017), p. 441.

15. Jon Davis and John Rentoul interview with Jonathan Powell, 10 June 2014.

16. The Report of the Committee on the Civil Service, Cmnd. 3638, 1968.

17. Committee on Standards in Public Life, Ninth Report, 'Defining the Boundaries within the Executive: Ministers, Special Advisers and the permanent Civil Service', April 2003.

18. *Special Advisers: Boon or Bane?*, Public Administration Select Committee, House of Commons, 28 February 2001.

19. Peter Hennessy, *Whitehall* (Secker and Warburg, 1989), p. 54.

20. See John Ramsden (ed.), *The Oxford Companion to Twentieth-Century British Politics* (Oxford University Press, 2002), p. 82.

21. Peter Hennessy, *Whitehall*, pp. 120–68.

22. Peter Hennessy, *Whitehall*, p. 189; and see Jon Davis, *Prime Ministers and Whitehall* (Hambledon Continuum, 2007); Andrew Blick, *People Who Live in the Dark* (Politico's Publishing, 2004).

23. Sir Charles Powell, interviewed by Michael Cockerell for the BBC2 documentary, *How to be Prime Minister*, 1996, quoted in Hennessy, *The Prime Minister*, p. 397.

24. Michael Everett and Edward Faulkner, 'Special Advisers', House of Commons Briefing Paper, Number 03813, 1 February 2017.

25. Jack Straw, *Last Man Standing* (Pan, 2012), p. 85.

26. David Hencke, 'Short flays Blair's "dark men"', *Guardian*, 8 August 1996.

27. Lord Patten, *House of Lords Hansard*, 13 July 2017.

28. *Special Advisers: Boon or Bane?* Public Administration Select Committee, House of Commons, 28 February 2001.

29. *Special Advisers: Boon or Bane?*, 28 February 2001.

30. Alastair Campbell & Bill Hagerty (eds), *Alastair Campbell Diaries: Volume 2* (Hutchinson, 2011), 13 May 1997.

31. *Alastair Campbell Diaries: Vol. 2*, 4 June 1997.

32. *Alastair Campbell Diaries: Vol. 2*, 28 July 1997.

33. *Alastair Campbell Diaries: Vol. 2*, 30 July 1997.

34. Tony Blair interviewed by Peter Hennessy, *Reflections*, BBC Radio 4, 10 August 2017.

35. Ed Balls, 'Blair Government', Queen Mary University of London, 4 April 2011.

36. Tony Blair, *A Journey* (Hutchinson, 2010), p. 17.

37. *Special Advisers: Boon or Bane?*, Public Administration Select Committee, House of Commons, 28 February 2001.

38. Tony Blair, 'Blair Government', Queen Mary University, 20 May 2011.
39. Lord O'Donnell, 'The Blair Years', King's College London, 6 February 2017.
40. John Campbell, *Roy Jenkins* (Jonathan Cape, 2014), location 6708.
41. Henry Fairlie, 'Political Commentary', *The Spectator*, 22 September 1955.
42. *Because Britain Deserves Better*, New Labour manifesto, 1997, p. 1.
43. Geoff Mulgan, 'Blair Government', Queen Mary University, 10 November 2008.
44. Sir Richard Wilson, 'Blair Government', Queen Mary University, 16 March 2009.
45. Tony Blair, *A Journey*, p. 17.
46. Jon Davis and John Rentoul interview with Jonathan Powell, 10 June 2014.
47. Quoted in *The Report of the Iraq Inquiry*, Report of a Committee of Privy Counsellors, House of Commons, 6 July 2016, p. 271.
48. Jonathan Powell, *The New Machiavelli* (Bodley Head, 2010), p. 21.
49. *Alastair Campbell Diaries: Vol. 2*, 30 July 1998.
50. Alastair Campbell & Bill Hagerty (eds), *Alastair Campbell Diaries: Volume 3* (Hutchinson, 2011), 12 March 2001.
51. Jon Davis and John Rentoul interview with Jonathan Powell, 10 June 2014.
52. Anji Hunter, 'The Blair Years', King's College London, 23 January 2017.
53. *Alastair Campbell Diaries: Vol. 3*, 7 June 2001.
54. Jon Davis and John Rentoul interview with Jonathan Powell, 10 June 2014.
55. Ed Balls, 'Blair Government', Queen Mary University, 4 April 2011.
56. Jon Davis interview with Ed Balls, 2 December 2015.
57. Jonathan Powell, *The New Machiavelli*, p. 21.
58. Jon Davis and John Rentoul interview with Jonathan Powell, 10 June 2014.
59. *Special Advisers: Boon or Bane?*, Public Administration Select Committee, House of Commons, 28 February 2001.
60. Jonathan Powell, *The New Machiavelli*, p. 21.
61. Gordon Brown, *My Life, Our Times*, p. 198.
62. *The Governance of Britain*, Green Paper, CM 7170, July 2007.
63. Gordon Brown, *My Life, Our Times*, pp. 225, 226.
64. Sir David Normington, 'The Blair Years', King's College London, 8 February 2016. At the time he was First Civil Service Commissioner, retiring from this position in April 2016.
65. *Special Advisers: Boon or Bane?*, Public Administration Select Committee, House of Commons, 28 February 2001.
66. Gordon Brown, *My Life, Our Times*, p. 199.
67. Jon Davis and John Rentoul interview with Jonathan Powell, 10 June 2014.

68. Ian Beesley, *The Official History of the Cabinet Secretaries* (Routledge, 2016), p. 585.
69. Jon Davis and John Rentoul interview with Jonathan Powell, 10 June 2014.
70. Anthony Bevins, 'New sleaze row knocks at door of No 10', *Independent*, 2 June 1997.
71. Richard Norton-Taylor and Ewen Macaskill, 'Whitehall blocks Blair over favourite aide's role', *Guardian*, 3 June 1997.
72. Nicholas Jones, *Sultans of Spin* (Weidenfeld & Nicolson, 1999).
73. Jon Davis and John Rentoul interview with Jonathan Powell, 10 June 2014.
74. Ian Beesley, *Official History of the Cabinet Secretaries*, p. 585.
75. Jon Davis and John Rentoul interview with Sir John Holmes, 16 July 2014.
76. Peter Hennessy, *The Prime Minister*, p. 347.
77. Jon Davis and John Rentoul interview with Sir John Holmes, 16 July 2014.
78. Jon Davis interview with Sir Jeremy Heywood, 20 September 2016.
79. Jon Davis and John Rentoul interview with Jonathan Powell, 10 June 2014.
80. Jon Davis interview with Sir Richard Mottram, 4 June 2014.
81. *Alastair Campbell Diaries: Vol. 2*, 12 March 1998; 16 March 1998; 1 June 1998; 8 March 1999.
82. *Alastair Campbell Diaries: Vol. 3*, 10 September 1999; 1 May 2000.
83. Peter Mandelson, *The Third Man* (HarperPress, 2010), p. 253.
84. Private information.
85. Jon Davis and John Rentoul interview with Jonathan Powell, 10 June 2014.
86. Ion Trewin (ed.), *The Hugo Young Papers* (Penguin, 2008), p. 576.
87. *Alastair Campbell Diaries: Vol. 2*, 11 April 1998.
88. See Jonathan Powell, *Great Hatred, Little Room* (Bodley Head, 2008).
89. Alan Parker (director), *The Commitments*, 20th Century Fox, 1991.
90. *Alastair Campbell Diaries: Vol. 2*, 2 August 1997.
91. *Alastair Campbell Diaries: Vol. 2*, 5–10 November 1998.
92. *Alastair Campbell Diaries: Vol. 2*, 27 July 1997; 2 November 1997.
93. *Alastair Campbell Diaries: Vol. 2*, 2 May 1997; 3 May 1997; 2 June 1997.
94. *Alastair Campbell Diaries: Vol. 2*, 3 June 1997; 6 June, 1997; 21 July 1997.
95. Mike Granatt interviewed by Ben Curtis for 'Blair Government', Queen Mary University, 25 February 2009.
96. *Alastair Campbell Diaries: Vol. 2*, 10 September 1997.
97. Alastair Campbell, 'The Blair Government', Queen Mary University, 9 February 2009.

98. *Report of the Working Group on the Government Information Service* known as The Mountfield Report, November 1997, para. 26. Available at: http://webarchive.nationalarchives.gov.uk/20090120211714/http://archive.cabinetoffice.gov.uk/gcreview/links/mountfield.pdf.

99. *Alastair Campbell Diaries: Vol. 2*, 21 August 1997.

100. *Alastair Campbell Diaries: Vol. 2*, 21 August 1997.

101. *Alastair Campbell Diaries: Vol. 2*, 5 June 1997.

102. *Alastair Campbell Diaries: Vol. 2*, 2 June 1997.

103. Alastair Campbell, 'Blair Government', Queen Mary University, 9 February 2009.

104. Jon Davis and John Rentoul interview with David Blunkett, 11 February 2009

105. *Alastair Campbell Diaries: Vol. 2*, 17 March 1999.

106. *Alastair Campbell Diaries: Vol. 2*, p. 236, 18 December 1997.

107. *Alastair Campbell Diaries: Vol. 2*, 22 February 1999.

108. *Alastair Campbell Diaries: Vol. 2*, 16 April 1999.

109. *Alastair Campbell Diaries: Vol. 3*, 15 October 2000.

110. *Alastair Campbell Diaries: Vol. 2*, 27 November 1997.

111. *Alastair Campbell Diaries: Vol. 3*, p. xiii.

112. *Alastair Campbell Diaries: Vol. 3*, 17 April 2000; 4 July 2000; 13 July 2000; 14 July 2000.

113. *Alastair Campbell Diaries: Vol. 3*, 24 July 2000.

114. Lord O'Donnell, 'The Blair Years', King's College London, 6 February 2017.

115. Broadcast by BBC2 on 15 July 2000.

116. *Alastair Campbell Diaries: Vol. 2*, p. xiii.

117. *Alastair Campbell Diaries: Vol. 2*, 22 March 1998.

118. *Alastair Campbell Diaries: Vol. 2*, 13 May 1998.

119. *Alastair Campbell Diaries: Vol. 2*, 3 January 1999.

120. *Alastair Campbell Diaries: Vol. 2*, 15 April 1999.

121. *Alastair Campbell Diaries: Vol. 3*, 9 June 1999.

122. Alastair Campbell, 'Labour and Manchester United: How two winning machines broke down', *Guardian*, 20 January 2016.

123. Tony Blair, *A Journey*, p. 459.

124. Tony Blair, *A Journey*, p. 166.

125. *Alastair Campbell Diaries: Vol. 3*, 29 June 2000.

126. *Alastair Campbell Diaries: Vol. 3*, 4 July 2000; 26 February 2001.

127. *Alastair Campbell Diaries: Vol. 3*, 16 March 2001; 22 March 2001.

128. Valentine Low, 'No 10 plotted to fight CND with photos of royal baby', *The Times*, 21 July 2016.

129. Private information.

130. The low of 36% came in 1957–8, *Public Spending under Labour*, 2010 Election Briefing Note No. 5 (IFS BN92).

131. Vyara Apostolova and Grahame Allen, *Civil Service Statistics*, House of Commons Library Briefing Paper, Number 2224, 12 January 2017.

132. Jon Davis and John Rentoul interview with Jonathan Powell, 10 June 2014.

133. Jon Davis interview with Sir Richard Mottram, 4 June 2014.

134. Jon Davis and John Rentoul interview with Jonathan Powell, 10 June 2014.

135. Jon Davis interview with Sir Richard Mottram, 4 June 2014.

136. Jon Davis and John Rentoul interview with Jonathan Powell, 10 June 2014.

137. Sir David Normington, 'The Blair Years', King's College London, 8 February 2016.

138. Geoff Mulgan, 'Blair Government', Queen Mary University, 10 November 2008.

139. *Report of the Machinery of Government Committee*, known as 'The Haldane Report', Ministry of Reconstruction, 1918, pp. 7–8.

140. See Jon Davis, *Prime Ministers and Whitehall*, p. 194, footnote 80.

141. Press Association, 'Blair wants to put an end to the "scandal" of homelessness', *Guardian*, 15 December 1999.

142. *Modernising Government*, Cm 4310, 1999.

143. Nick Assinder, 'Blair risks row over public sector', BBC, 7 July 1999. Available at: http://news.bbc.co.uk/1/hi/uk_politics/388528.stm.

144. Nicholas Watt, 'David Cameron calls civil servants "enemies of enterprise"', *Guardian*, 6 March 2011.

145. Jon Davis and John Rentoul interview with Jonathan Powell, 10 June 2014.

146. Dr Ian Beesley, 'The launch of the Official History of the Cabinet Secretaries', King's College London, 16 January 2017.

147. Lord Wilson of Dinton, 'The launch of the Official History of the Cabinet Secretaries', King's College London, 16 January 2017.

148. Private information.

149. Jon Davis and John Rentoul interview with Jonathan Powell, 10 June 2014.

150. Jonathan Powell, *The New Machiavelli*, pp. 80–1.

151. Jon Davis and John Rentoul interview with Jonathan Powell, 10 June 2014.

152. Tony Blair, Labour Party Conference keynote speech, 28 September 1999. Available at: http://news.bbc.co.uk/1/hi/uk_politics/460009.stm.

153. Tony Blair, *A Journey*, p. 255.

154. *Alastair Campbell Diaries: Vol. 2*, 11 February 1999.

155. NA, PRO, PREM 15/1603, Robert Armstrong to Sir William Armstrong, 13 September 1972.

156. See Jon Davis, *Prime Ministers and Whitehall*, pp. 83–156.

157. Michelle Clement, email, 5 September 2016.

158. 'Tony Blair's Victory Speech', *Guardian*, 8 June 2001.

159. Select Committee on Public Administration Minutes of Evidence, 1 November 2001.

160. Nehal Panchamia and Peter Thomas, *Public Service Agreements and the Prime Minister's Delivery Unit*, Institute for Government, n.d.

161. *On Target? Government by Measurement*, Public Administration Select Committee, House of Commons, July 2003.

162. Sir Michael Barber, Constitution Committee hearings, House of Lords, 8 July 2009.

163. Sir David Normington, 'The Blair Years', King's College London, 8 February 2016.

164. Tony Blair, *A Journey*, p. 338.

165. Michael Barber and Tony Blair, 'How to Run a Government', King's College London, 11 June 2015.

166. Ed Balls, *Speaking Out*, p. 135.

167. Quoted in Sian Cleary, 'The Prime Minister's Delivery Unit: 2005–7', unpublished undergraduate thesis, May 2011.

168. Private information.

169. 'Men of Secrets'.

170. Lord O'Donnell, 'The Blair Years' King's College London, 6 February 2017.

171. George Lucas, 'The New Statesman Profile—Gus O'Donnell', *New Statesman,* 27 November 1998.

172. Jonathan Powell, *The New Machiavelli*, p. 77.

173. Gus O'Donnell, 'Transforming Departments' Capability to Deliver', Letter to Prime Minister, 27 July 2005, quoted in http://www.instituteforgovernment.org.uk/sites/default/files/case%20study%20capabilities.pdf.

174. Uncorrected oral evidence to Public Administration Select Committee, 11 October 2005.

175. Sir David Normington, 'The Blair Years', King's College London, 8 February 2016.

176. Tony Blair, *A Journey*, pp. 574, 584, 589.

177. Sir David Normington, 'The Blair Years', King's College London, 8 February 2016.

178. Jon Davis interview with Sir Jeremy Heywood, 20 September 2016.

179. 'More spinned against than spinning': headline suggested by him, on article by Alastair Campbell in *The Times*, 31 January 2000.

180. Private information.

CHAPTER 4

1. Jon Davis interview with Ed Balls, 2 December 2015.
2. Ed Balls, speech to the Fabian Society, 14 January 2012.
3. Michael Heseltine speech to Conservative Party Conference, 12 October 1994.
4. Ed Balls, *Speaking Out* (Hutchinson, 2016); Gordon Brown, *My Life, Our Times* (Penguin, 2017).
5. William Keegan, *The Prudence of Mr Gordon Brown* (John Wiley & Sons, 2004), p. 156.
6. Nigel Lawson, 'The economic perils of thinking for the moment', *The Times*, 14 September 1978.
7. Anatole Kaletsky, 'Happy days are here again', *The Times*, 18 September 1992.
8. Martin Wolf, 'The post post-Thatcher era begins', *Financial Times*, 4 December 2009.
9. Ken Clarke, 'The Treasury and Economic History since 1945', King's College London, 7 December 2017.
10. Gordon Brown, *Maxton: A Biography* (Mainstream Publishing Co., 1986).
11. Geoffrey Robinson, *The Unconventional Minister* (Michael Joseph, 2000), p. 38.
12. Nigel Lawson, *The View from No. 11* (Bantam Press, 1992), pp. 868–70.
13. John Major, *The Autobiography* (HarperCollins, 1999), p. 137.
14. Norman Lamont, *In Office* (Little, Brown, 1999), pp. 322–7.
15. Gordon Brown, *My Life, Our Times*, p. 118.
16. Ken Clarke, 'The Treasury and Economic History since 1945', King's College London, 7 December 2017.
17. Tony Blair, *A Journey* (Hutchinson, 2010), p. 113.
18. Ed Balls, 'Blair Government', Queen Mary University of London, 4 April 2011.
19. Derek Scott, *Off Whitehall* (I. B. Tauris, 2004), p. 13.
20. Geoffrey Robinson, *The Unconventional Minister*, pp. 37–8.
21. Robert Peston, *Brown's Britain* (Short Books, 2005), pp. 124–6.
22. Robert Peston, *Brown's Britain*, p. 187.
23. Ed Balls, *Speaking Out*, pp. 146–7.
24. Geoffrey Robinson, *The Unconventional Minister*, p. 35.
25. William Keegan, *The Prudence of Mr Gordon Brown*, p. 163.
26. Sir Nicholas Macpherson, 'The Treasury and Economic History since 1945', King's College London, 20 November 2015.
27. Ken Clarke, 'Ministers Reflect' series, Institute for Government, 8 February 2016.

28. Gordon Brown, *My Life, Our Times*, p. 114.

29. Jon Davis interview with Sir Nicholas Macpherson, 18 March 2015.

30. Geoffrey Robinson, *The Unconventional Minister*, p. 36.

31. Geoffrey Robinson, *The Unconventional Minister*, p. 37.

32. Peter Hennessy, *Whitehall* (Secker & Warburg, 1989), p. 283.

33. William Keegan, *The Prudence of Mr Gordon Brown*, p. 174.

34. Lord Burns, 'The researchers meet the reviewers', HM Treasury & National Archives joint event, 24 April 2015.

35. Ed Balls, 'The Treasury and Economic History since 1945', King's College London, 20 November 2015.

36. Margaret Thatcher, first used on TV-AM, 24 October 1989.

37. Gordon Brown, *My Life, Our Times*, p. 113.

38. Ed Balls, *Speaking Out*, p. 139.

39. *New Labour Because Britain Deserves Better*, 1997 Labour Party Manifesto.

40. Peter Mandelson, *The Third Man: Enhanced Edition* (HarperCollins, 2011).

41. Ed Balls, *Speaking Out*, p. 139.

42. William Keegan, *The Prudence of Mr Gordon Brown*, p. 173.

43. Hugh Pym and Nick Kochan, *Gordon Brown: The First Year in Power* (Bloomsbury, 1998), p. 8.

44. Ed Balls, 'Blair Government', Queen Mary University, 4 April 2011.

45. Ed Balls, 'The Blair Years', King's College London, 25 January 2016.

46. Lord Burns, 'The researchers meet the reviewers', HM Treasury & National Archives joint event, 24 April 2015.

47. Jon Davis interview with Ed Balls, 2 December 2015.

48. *We Are the Treasury* (STV, 7 October 1997).

49. Gordon Brown, *My Life, Our Times*, pp. 116–17.

50. Ed Balls, 'Blair Government', Queen Mary University, 4 April 2011.

51. Ed Balls, 'The Treasury and Economic History since 1945', King's College London, 20 November 2015.

52. Anthony Seldon, *Blair* (The Free Press, 2005), p. 668.

53. Pym and Kochan, *Gordon Brown*, p. 11.

54. Paddy Ashdown, *The Ashdown Diaries: Volume Two, 1997–1999* (London: Penguin, 2001), p. 14.

55. Andrew Rawnsley, *Servants of the People* (Hamish Hamilton, 2000), p. 33.

56. Ed Balls, 'The Treasury and Economic History since 1945', King's College London, 20 November 2015.

57. Private information.

58. Gordon Brown, *My Life, Our Times*, p. 117.

59. Lord O'Donnell, 'The Blair Years', King's College London, 6 February 2017.

60. Robert Peston, *Brown's Britain*, p. 113.

61. Geoffrey Robinson, *The Unconventional Minister*, p. 45.
62. *We Are the Treasury* (STV, 1997).
63. 'Sarah Brown "didn't trust" mandarin Sir Gus O'Donnell', BBC, 3 March 2011. Available at: https://www.bbc.co.uk/news/uk-politics-12629496.
64. Peter Riddell, 'Brown must stick to his guns after bold opening shot', *The Times*, 7 May 1997.
65. Hugo Young, 'Abrogations of Sovereignty', *Guardian*, 8 May 1997.
66. Anatole Kaletsky, 'A steel cage for the Iron Chancellor', *The Times*, 7 May 1997.
67. William Keegan, 'Help! Labour's lost its monetary marbles', *Observer*, 11 May 1997.
68. Jill Sherman and Alasdair Murray, 'Independence for Bank of England', *The Times*, 7 May 1997.
69. Ed Balls, 'The Treasury and Economic History since 1945', King's College London, 20 November 2015.
70. Lord Adonis, 'Tony Blair & Europe: Shattering the Ming vase', lecture to Hertford College, Oxford, 10 November 2017.
71. Sir Nicholas Macpherson, 'The Treasury and Economic History since 1945', King's College London, 20 November 2015.
72. Robert Peston, *Brown's Britain*, p. 135.
73. Robert Peston, *Brown's Britain*, p. 136.
74. *We Are the Treasury*.
75. William Keegan, *The Prudence of Mr Gordon Brown*, p. 182.
76. Ed Balls, 'The Treasury and Economic History since 1945', King's College London, 20 November 2015.
77. Robert Peston, *Brown's Britain*, p. 139.
78. William Keegan, *The Prudence of Mr Gordon Brown*, p. 183.
79. Geoffrey Robinson, *The Unconventional Minister*, p. 41.
80. Geoffrey Robinson, *The Unconventional Minister*, p. 41.
81. Geoffrey Robinson, *The Unconventional Minister*, p. 42.
82. *We Are the Treasury*.
83. *We Are the Treasury*.
84. *We Are the Treasury*.
85. William Keegan, *The Prudence of Mr Gordon Brown*, p. 190.
86. William Keegan, *The Prudence of Mr Gordon Brown*, p. 189.
87. Robert Peston, 'Governor thought of quitting over Bank proposals', *Financial Times*, 22 May 1997.
88. Lord Burns, 'The researchers meet the reviewers', HM Treasury & National Archives joint event, 24 April 2015.
89. Gordon Brown, *My Life, Our Times*, p. 120.
90. Robert Peston, 'Governor thought of quitting over Bank proposals'.

91. Robert Peston, *Brown's Britain*, p. 141.
92. Geoffrey Robinson, *The Unconventional Minister*, p. 43.
93. Sir Nicholas Macpherson, 'The Treasury and Economic History since 1945', King's College London, 20 November 2015.
94. Jon Davis interview with Sir Nicholas Macpherson, 1 March 2013.
95. Andrew Rawnsley, *Servants of the People*, pp. 45–7.
96. Robert Peston, *Brown's Britain*, p. 107.
97. Ed Balls, 'The Blair Years', King's College London, 25 January 2016.
98. Peter Jay, quoted in Peter Hennessy, *Whitehall*, p. 191.
99. Ed Balls, *Speaking Out*, p. 129.
100. Sir Nicholas Macpherson, 'The Origins of Treasury Control', Queen Mary University, 16 January 2013.
101. Gordon Brown, *My Life, Our Times*, p. 113.
102. Ed Balls, *Speaking Out*, pp. 124, 126.
103. Jon Davis interview with Ed Balls, 2 December 2015.
104. Jon Davis interview with Sir Jeremy Heywood, 20 September 2016.
105. Jon Davis interview with Ed Balls, 2 December 2015.
106. Jon Davis interview with Sir Nicholas Macpherson, 18 March 2015.
107. Lord Macpherson of Earl's Court, 'The Blair Years', King's College London, 13 February 2017.
108. Jon Davis interview with Sir Nicholas Macpherson, 18 March 2015.
109. Ed Balls, *Speaking Out*, p. 263.
110. Lord Burns, 'The researchers meet the reviewers', HM Treasury & National Archives joint event, 24 April 2015.
111. Gordon Brown, *My Life, Our Times*, pp. 463–4.
112. Sir Nicholas Macpherson 'The Treasury and Economic History since 1945', King's College London, 20 November 2015.
113. Ed Balls, *Speaking Out*, pp. 127–8, 132.
114. Sir Nicholas Macpherson, 'The Treasury and Economic History since 1945', King's College London, 20 November 2015.
115. Tony Blair, *A Journey*, p. 114.
116. Lord Burns, 'The Treasury and Economic History since 1945', King's College London, 13 November 2015.
117. Jon Davis interview with Sir Nicholas Macpherson, 18 March 2015.
118. Ed Balls, *Speaking Out*, p. 61.
119. Robert Gray, 'Charlie Whelan, Press Secretary to Gordon Brown—Gordon Brown's fiercest ally: Behind the Iron Chancellor is a press secretary with balls of steel', *PR Week*, 17 October 1997.
120. Gordon Brown, *My Life, Our Times*, p. 91.
121. Ed Balls, *Speaking Out*, p. 140.

122. Lord Burns 'The researchers meet the reviewers', HM Treasury & National Archives joint event, 24 April 2015.

123. Tom Bower, *Gordon Brown* (HarperCollins, 2004), p. 246.

124. Lord Burns 'The researchers meet the reviewers', HM Treasury & National Archives joint event, 24 April 2015.

125. Stephen Wall, *A Stranger in Europe* (OUP, 2008), pp. 161–2.

126. George Pascoe-Watson, 'My love for Pound', *Sun*, 17 April 1997.

127. Andrew Adonis, 'Tony Blair & Europe: Shattering the Ming vase', lecture to Hertford College, Oxford, 10 November 2017.

128. Winston Churchill, *Great Contemporaries* (Readers Union, 1939), p. 72.

129. Ed Balls, 'The Blair Years', King's College London, 25 January 2016.

130. Robert Peston, 'Cabinet shifts towards EMU', *Financial Times*, 26 September 1997.

131. Gordon Brown, *My Life, Our Times*, p. 178.

132. Ed Balls, 'The Blair Years', King's College London, 17 March 2016.

133. Ed Balls, 'The Blair Years', King's College London, 17 March 2016.

134. Gordon Brown, *My Life, Our Times*, p. 179.

135. Robert Peston, *Brown's Britain*, p. 211.

136. Hansard, col. 584, 27 October 1997.

137. Gordon Brown, *My Life, Our Times*, p. 180.

138. Ed Balls, 'The Blair Years', King's College London, 17 March 2016.

139. Sir Dave Ramsden, 'The Blair Years', King's College London, 17 March 2016.

140. Stephen Wall, *A Stranger in Europe*, p. 169.

141. Gordon Brown, *My Life, Our Times*, p. 176.

142. Stephen Wall, *A Stranger in Europe*, p. 170.

143. George Brown, *In My Way* (Gollancz, 1971), p. 97.

144. Ed Balls, *Speaking Out*, p. 161.

145. Philip Webster, 'Blair and Brown unite to signal delay on the euro', *The Times*, 21 February 1997.

146. Ed Balls, 'The Blair Years', King's College London, 17 March 2016.

147. Stephen Wall, *A Stranger in Europe*, pp. 169–70.

148. Ed Balls, 'The Blair Years', King's College London, 17 March 2016.

149. Andrew Adonis, 'Tony Blair & Europe: Shattering the Ming vase', lecture at Hertford College, Oxford, 10 November 2017.

150. Andrew Adonis, 'Tony Blair & Europe: Shattering the Ming vase', lecture at Hertford College, Oxford, 10 November 2017.

151. Barrie Clement, 'TUC in Brighton: Cancelled Blair speech gave firm backing to euro', *Independent,* 11 September 2001.

152. Sir Dave Ramsden, 'The Blair Years', King's College London, 17 March 2016.

153. Robert Peston, *Brown's Britain*, p. 244.
154. Ed Balls, 'The Blair Years', King's College London, 17 March 2016.
155. Ed Balls, *Speaking Out*, pp. 155–6.
156. Ed Balls, 'The Blair Years', King's College London, 17 March 2016.
157. Ed Balls, *Speaking Out*, pp. 155–6.
158. Ed Balls, 'The Treasury and Economic History since 1945', King's College London, 17 November 2017.
159. Tony Blair, *A Journey*, p. 537.
160. Dave Ramsden, 'The Euro: 10th Anniversary of the Assessment of the Five Economic Tests', 25 June 2013.
161. Ed Balls, *Speaking Out*, p. 104.
162. Alastair Campbell and Bill Hagerty (eds), *Alastair Campbell Diaries: Volume 2* (Hutchinson, 2011), 3 January 1999.
163. *Alastair Campbell Diaries: Vol. 2*, 3 January 1999.
164. Polly Curtis, 'Charlie Whelan quits Unite union to write account of New Labour government', *Guardian*, 14 September 2010.
165. Patrick Hennessy, 'Charlie Whelan: The puppet master who "won it for Ed" ', *Daily Telegraph*, 3 October 2010.
166. Polly Curtis, 'Charlie Whelan quits Unite union to write account of New Labour government', *Guardian*, 14 September 2010.
167. Damian McBride, *Power Trip* (Biteback, 2013), pp. 114–17, 159–60, 226–7.
168. Damian McBride, *Power Trip*, pp. 165–9.
169. Tony Blair, *A Journey*, pp. 587, 682.
170. Hansard, 12 November 1992, col. 998.
171. Ed Balls, 'Blair Government', Queen Mary University, 4 April 2011.
172. Gordon Brown, *My Life, Our Times*, pp. 135–6.
172. Ed Balls, 'Blair Government', Queen Mary University, 4 April 2011.
173. Ed Balls, *Speaking Out*, p. 107.
174. HM Treasury, *A New Approach to Public Private Partnerships* (2012).
175. Peter Hennessy, *Whitehall*, p. 205.
176. James Callaghan, *Time and Chance* (Collins, 1987), p. 166.
177. Peter Riddell, *The Unfulfilled Prime Minister* (Politico's, 2005).
178. Tony Blair, Labour Party Conference speech, 1 October 2002.
179. Margaret Thatcher, speech at a Soviet official banquet, St George's Halls, the Kremlin, 30 March 1987.
180. Jackie Ashley, 'Brains at the heart of Brownland', *Guardian*, 4 November 2002.
181. Jon Davis interview with Ed Balls, 2 December 2015.
182. Jon Davis interview with Ed Balls, 2 December 2015.
183. John Kay, 'The left is still searching for a practical philosophy', *Financial Times*, 5 May 2010.

184. Gordon Brown, 'A Modern Agenda for Prosperity and Social Reform', speech at the Cass Business School, 3 February 2003.
185. Jon Davis interview with Ed Balls, 2 December 2015.
186. Tony Blair, *A Journey*, pp. 484–5.
187. Jon Davis interview with Ed Balls, 2 December 2015.
188. Lord Macpherson of Earl's Court, 'The Blair Years', King's College London, 13 February 2017.
189. BBC, 'Blair's legacy: Health', 10 May 2007. Available at: http://news. bbc.co.uk/1/hi/health/4555344.stm.
190. Ed Balls, 'The Blair Years', King's College London, 25 January 2016.
191. Tony Blair, *A Journey*, pp. 484.
192. Jon Davis interview with Ed Balls, 2 December 2015.
193. Alan Milburn, 'Blair Government', Queen Mary University of London, 23 February 2009.
194. Leader's speech, Labour Party Conference, Blackpool, 1 October 1996.
195. Jon Davis interview with Ed Balls, 2 December 2015.
196. Andrew Adonis, *Education, Education, Education* (Biteback Publishing, 2012), p. 116.
197. Jon Davis interview with Ed Balls, 2 December 2015.
198. Andrew Adonis, *Education, Education, Education*, p. 116.
199. Jon Davis interview with Ed Balls, 2 December 2015.
200. Jon Davis interview with Ed Balls, 2 December 2015.
201. Tony Blair, *A Journey*, pp. 484–7.
202. Alan Milburn, 'Blair Government', Queen Mary University, 23 February 2009.
203. Jon Davis, *Prime Ministers & Whitehall* (Hambeldon Continuum, 2007), pp. 23–49, 83–157.
204. Peter Hennessy, *Whitehall*, p. 266.
205. Alan Milburn, 'Blair Government', Queen Mary University, 23 February 2009.
206. Jon Davis interview with Sir Nicholas Macpherson, 18 March 2015.
207. Gordon Brown, *My Life, Our Times*, p. 226.
208. Ed Balls, *Speaking Out*, pp. 208–9.
209. Gordon Brown, *My Life, Our Times*, p. 226.
210. Gordon Brown, *My Life, Our Times*, pp. 352–3.
211. Gordon Brown, *My Life, Our Times*, p. 353.
212. Tim Shipman, *All Out War* (William Collins, 2017), p. 438.
213. Jon Davis interview with Sir Dave Ramsden, 5 June 2015.
214. Craig S. Hakkio, 'The Great Moderation: 1982–2007', Federal Reserve History available at: https://www.federalreservehistory.org/ essays/great_moderation.

215. Bruno Coric, 'The Sources of the Great Moderation: A Survey', Social Science Research Network, 2011, pp. 2–7.

216. Jon Davis interview with Sir Dave Ramsden, 5 June 2015.

217. Ed Balls, *Speaking Out*, p. 308.

218. Jon Davis interview with Sir Dave Ramsden, 5 June 2015.

219. *Securing Our Future Health: Taking a Long-Term View*, April 2002.

220. *Releasing Resources to the Front Line: Independent Review of Public Sector Efficiency*, July 2004.

221. *A New Pension Settlement for the Twenty-First Century: The Second Report of the Pensions Commission*, November 2005.

222. *Barker Review of Housing Supply*, March 2004.

223. *The UK Mortgage Market: Taking a longer-term view*, March 2004.

224. *Transport's role in sustaining the UK's productivity and competitiveness*, December 2006.

225. David Cameron, 'I'm on your side, not in your wallet', *News of the World*, 9 November 2008.

226. 'Tories attack Brown over economy', BBC, 11 January 2008. Available at: http://news.bbc.co.uk/1/hi/uk_politics/7182612.stm.

227. Mervyn King, Bank of England's Court Dinner, 12 October 2004.

228. Robert Peston, *Brown's Britain*, p. 167.

229. Ed Balls, 'The Treasury and Economic History since 1945', King's College London, 20 November 2015.

230. Sir Nicholas Macpherson. 'The Treasury and Economic History since 1945', King's College London, 20 November 2015.

231. Andrew Rawnsley, *Servants of the People*, pp. 337–8.

232. Ken Clarke, 'I left Gordon Brown a strong economy. He squandered it', *Guardian*, 25 April 2005.

233. Sir Nicholas Macpherson, 'The Treasury and Economic History since 1945', King's College London, 20 November 2015.

234. John Kingman, 'The Treasury and the Supply Side', King's College London, 20 October 2016.

235. Conversation with Jonathan Portes, 19 February 2015.

236. Jon Davis interview with Sir Nicholas Macpherson, 18 March 2015.

237. Tony Blair, *A Journey*, pp. 574–5, 681–2.

238. Ed Balls, 'The Blair Years', King's College London, 25 January 2016.

239. Jon Davis interview with Sir Nicholas Macpherson, 18 March 2013.

240. Sir Nicholas Macpherson, 'The Treasury and Economic History since 1945', King's College London, 20 November 2015.

241. Jon Davis interview with Sir Nicholas Macpherson, 18 March 2013.

242. 'Labour "must not lose its nerve"', BBC, 14 September 2009. Available at: http://news.bbc.co.uk/1/hi/uk_politics/8253816.stm

243. Jon Davis interview with Ed Balls, 2 December 2015.

244. Ed Balls, *Speaking Out*, pp. 65, 67.

245. Ed Balls, 'The Blair Years', King's College London, 25 January 2016.

246. Jon Davis interview with Ed Balls, 2 December 2015.

247. Ken Clarke, 'I left Gordon Brown a strong economy. He squandered it', *Guardian*, 25 April 2005.

248. Ed Balls, 'The Blair Years', King's College London, 25 January 2016.

249. George Osborne, 'The Treasury and Economic History since 1945', King's College London, 6 December 2016; David Cameron, 'No. 10 Downing Street and the History of the Prime Minister', King's College London, 30 March 2017.

CHAPTER 5

1. ICM for the *Guardian* interviewed 1,007 respondents, 16–18 July 2004: 'Do you yourself think Tony Blair lied over Iraq?' Yes 55 per cent; no 37 per cent. YouGov for the *Sunday Times* interviewed 1,699 respondents, 20–1 January 2011: 'Thinking about the war in Iraq, do you think Tony Blair, prime minister at the time of the war, deliberately set out to mislead the British public in the run-up to the war about whether Iraq possessed chemical and biological "weapons of mass destruction"?' Yes 52 per cent; no 32 per cent. YouGov for the *Sunday Times* interviewed 1,891 respondents, 22–3 July 2010: 'On Wednesday the Deputy Prime Minister Nick Clegg described the war in Iraq as "illegal". Leaving aside whether you personally supported or opposed the war in Iraq, from what you know, do you think it was legal or illegal?' Legal, 24 per cent; illegal 47 per cent.

2. ICM for the *Guardian* interviewed 1,002 respondents, 14–16 March 2003, just before the invasion on 20 March: 'Would you approve or disapprove of a military attack on Iraq to remove Saddam Hussein?' Approve 38 per cent; disapprove 44 per cent. ICM for the *Guardian* interviewed 1,002 respondents, 11–13 April 2003, after Saddam's statue was pulled down in Baghdad: 'Do you approve or disapprove of the military attack on Iraq to remove Saddam Hussein?' Approve 63 per cent; disapprove 23 per cent.

3. Kenneth Clarke, House of Commons, 13 July 2016.

4. Tony Blair, 'Blair Government', Queen Mary University of London, 20 May 2011.

5. Paddy Ashdown, *The Ashdown Diaries: Volume Two, 1997–1999* (Penguin, 2001), 15 November 1997.

6. Gordon Corera, *Shopping for Bombs* (C. Hurst & Co., 2006).

7. *The 9/11 Commission Report* (Barnes and Noble, 2005), p. 116.

8. *The 9/11 Commission Report*, p. 60.

9. *The Report of the Iraq Inquiry*, 1.1.190–1.

10. Charles Duelfer, *Hide and Seek: The search for truth in Iraq* (Public Affairs, US, 2009), pp. 107–16.

11. *The Report of the Iraq Inquiry*, 1.1.192.

12. Tony Blair, House of Commons, 19 November 1997.

13. See, for example, Margaret Thatcher, 'No Time to Go Wobbly', ch. XXVII in *The Downing Street Years* (HarperCollins, 1993), pp. 816–28.

14. John Rentoul, *Tony Blair: Prime Minister* (Little, Brown & Co., 2001), p. 516.

15. *The 9/11 Commission Report*, p. 70.

16. Michael Foot, interview, *New Statesman*, 8 January 1999.

17. Lance Price, *The Spin Doctor's Diary* (Hodder & Stoughton, Ltd, 2005).

18. *The 9/11 Commission Report*, pp. 116, 118.

19. George Robertson, BBC Radio 4, *The World This Weekend*, 23 August 1998.

20. Sir Kevin Tebbit, interviewed by Andrew Kennedy, 22 February 2011, undergraduate dissertation, 'Operation Desert Fox and Saddam Hussein: Tony Blair's First Excursion into Major Military Conflict', April 2011.

21. Tony Blair, House of Commons, 16 November 1998; see also John Rentoul, *Tony Blair: Prime Minister*, pp. 422–3, 512–13, 515–16.

22. Short accounts of both interventions are given in John Rentoul, *Tony Blair: Prime Minister*, chs 25 and 32. There are also chapters by Mike Jackson on Kosovo and David Richards on Sierra Leone in Jonathan Bailey, Richard Iron, and Hew Strachan, *British Generals in Blair's Wars* (Ashgate Publishing, 2013).

23. Tony Blair, 'Doctrine of the International Community', speech to the Chicago Economic Club, 24 April 1999.

24. Tony Blair, House of Commons, 24 September 2002. Blair may also have been aware of the lesson of Suez (which is mentioned once in his memoir) to beware of being on the opposite side to the US again—see Peter Hennessy, *The Prime Minister* (Penguin, 2000), p. 244.

25. Tony Blair, *A Journey*, p. 342.

26. See also John Rentoul, 'Afterword', *Tony Blair: Prime Minister* (Faber, 2013 edn).

27. Sir Christopher Meyer, UK Ambassador to the USA, talking about a meeting in Washington on 20 September 2001, PBS *Frontline*, 'Blair's War', 3 April 2003.

28. SIS 4, evidence to the Iraq Inquiry, published 20 January 2011: transcript part 1.

29. Sally Morgan, 'Blair Government', Queen Mary University, 26 January 2009.

30. *The Report of the Iraq Inquiry*, 3.2.11–13.

31. Tony Blair, *A Journey*, p. 405. (In Blair's text there is a 'not' after 'impossible', which we assume was a mistake, making a double negative a triple.)

32. Jonathan Powell, evidence to the Iraq Inquiry, 18 January 2010.

33. Stephen Byers, quoted in the Chris Mullin diaries, *A View from the Foothills* (Profile, 2009), 18 March 2002.

34. Donald Macintyre, *Independent*, 12 March 2002. In Alastair Campbell's diary, this was rendered as: 'I do want to assure you that the management has not gone crazy.'

35. Tony Blair, *A Journey*, p. 399.

36. George W. Bush, ITV *Tonight* interview with Trevor McDonald, 5 April 2002.

37. Bob Woodward, *Plan of Attack* (Simon & Schuster, 2004), p. 120.

38. *The Report of the Iraq Inquiry*, Executive Summary, paragraph 77.

39. Alastair Campbell and Bill Hagerty (eds), *Alastair Campbell Diaries: Volume 4* (Hutchinson, 2012), 23 July 2002.

40. Matthew Rycroft, minute to David Manning, 23 July 2002, 'Iraq: Prime Minister's Meeting, 23 July'. *The Report of the Iraq Inquiry*, 3.3.342.

41. *The Report of the Iraq Inquiry*, 3.3.348–61.

42. 'Report on the US Intelligence Community's Prewar Assessments on Iraq', 9 July 2004.

43. *The Report of the Iraq Inquiry*, Executive Summary, paragraphs 496 and 497.

44. Gordon Corera, *The Art of Betrayal* (Weidenfeld & Nicolson, 2011), p. 357.

45. *The Report of the Iraq Inquiry*, Executive Summary, paragraphs 565 and 566.

46. *The Report of the Iraq Inquiry*, Executive Summary, paragraph 806.

47. *The Report of the Iraq Inquiry*, Executive Summary, paragraph 533.

48. Lord Hutton, 'The Media Reaction to the Hutton Report', *Public Law* (Winter) 807, 2 November 2006.

49. 'The Review of Intelligence on Weapons of Mass Destruction', 4 July 2004.

50. Sir John Chilcot, BBC interview, 6 July 2017, available at: http://www.bbc.co.uk/news/uk-politics-40510539 referring to 'Minute Scarlett to Manning, 17 March 2003, "Iraqi WMD: Evidence of Possession",' quoted in *The Report of the Iraq Inquiry*, paragraph 463.

51. *Sun*, 7 July 2016.

52. George W. Bush, *Decision Points* (Ebury Publishing, 2010), p. 262.

53. *The Report of the Iraq Inquiry*, Executive Summary, paragraphs 94 and 95.

54. For example, Andrew Rawnsley, *The End of the Party* (Peguin Books, 2010), p. 155—Blair to Bush in a telephone conversation, 9 March 2003: 'I told you that I'm with you and I'm going to be with you' (from interviews with Andrew Card and Condoleezza Rice.).

55. *The Report of the Iraq Inquiry*, 3.3.443.

56. Tony Blair, evidence to the Iraq Inquiry, 21 January 2011, Report 5.0.334 and 335.

57. *The Report of the Iraq Inquiry*, Executive Summary, paragraph 801.

58. *The Report of the Iraq Inquiry*, Executive Summary, paragraph 507.

59. *The Report of the Iraq Inquiry*, 3.3.445.

60. *The Report of the Iraq Inquiry*, 6.5.1402.

61. *The Report of the Iraq Inquiry*, Executive Summary, paragraph 592.

62. *The Report of the Iraq Inquiry*, 6.5.1403.

63. *The Report of the Iraq Inquiry*, 3.6.656.

64. *The Report of the Iraq Inquiry*, Executive Summary, paragraphs 592 and 814.

65. *The Report of the Iraq Inquiry*, Executive Summary, paragraph 601.

66. Tony Blair, *A Journey*, p. 441.

67. Tony Blair statement in response to *The Report of the Iraq Inquiry*, 6 July 2016. Available at: https://www.independent.co.uk/news/uk/politics/chilcot-report-tony-blair-read-response-statement-in-full-iraq-war-inquiry-a7123251.html.

68. Tony Blair statement in response to *The Report of the Iraq Inquiry*, 6 July 2016.

69. Tony Blair, *A Journey*, p. 378.

70. Robin Cook, House of Commons, 17 March 2002.

71. 'The meeting that could have changed the history of Iraq,' *Independent on Sunday*, 17 October 2004.

72. John Rentoul, 'Chilcot: Implications for Blair and politicians', *Political Quarterly*, 87/4, October 2016.

73. Robin Cook, *Point of Departure* (Simon & Schuster, 2003), p. 116.

74. Jonathan Powell, 'Blair Government', Queen Mary University, 9 February 2009.

75. For example, the 'Cabinet Conclusions' of the meeting on 23 September 2002, followed by Campbell's account of the same meeting: *The Report of the Iraq Inquiry*, 3.5.147–50, and 3.5.153–5.

76. Jack Straw, evidence to the Iraq Inquiry, 2 February 2011. Available at: http://www.iraqinquiry.org.uk/media/95414/2011-02-02-Transcript-Straw-S1.pdf.

77. *The Report of the Iraq Inquiry*, Executive Summary, paragraph 422.

78. *The Report of the Iraq Inquiry*, Executive Summary, paragraphs 421, 424, 425, and 431–95.

79. Jonathan Powell, *The New Machiavelli* (Bodley Head, 2010), p. 60. And see chapter 2, this volume.

80. *The Report of the Iraq Inquiry*, Executive Summary, paragraph 407.

81. Tony Blair statement in response to *The Report of the Iraq Inquiry*, 6 July 2016.

82. *The Report of the Iraq Inquiry*, Executive Summary, paragraph 332.

83. Tony Blair, evidence, 29 January 2010, pages 228–9, quoted in *The Report of the Iraq Inquiry*, Executive Summary, paragraph 415.

84. Ed Balls, 'Blair Government', Queen Mary University, 4 April 2011.

85. Private conversation, November 2011.

86. *Mail on Sunday*, 21 April 2002.

87. Chris Mullin's diaries, *A View from the Foothills*.

88. Ed Balls, 'Blair Government', Queen Mary University, 4 April 2011.

89. BBC2 *Newsnight*, 12 March 2003.

90. Ed Balls, *Speaking Out* (Hutchinson, 2016), p. 181.

91. Robin Cook, *Point of Departure*, p. 320.

92. *The Report of the Iraq Inquiry*, 3.8.272 and 279.

93. *The Report of the Iraq Inquiry*, 3.8.278.

94. *The Report of the Iraq Inquiry*, Executive Summary, paragraph 469.

95. Alastair Campbell and Bill Hagerty (eds), *Alastair Campbell Diaries: Volume 4* (Hutchinson, 2012), 11 March 2003.

96. *The Report of the Iraq Inquiry*, Executive Summary, paragraph 726.

97. *The Report of the Iraq Inquiry*, Executive Summary, paragraphs 727 and 728.

98. Sally Morgan, 'Blair Government', Queen Mary University, 26 January 2009.

99. *The Report of the Iraq Inquiry*, Executive Summary, paragraphs 485 and 490.

100. Lord Goldsmith, Evidence to Iraq Inquiry, 27 January 2010. Available at: http://www.iraqinquiry.org.uk/media/235686/2010-01-27-transcript-goldsmith-s1.pdf.

101. *The Report of the Iraq Inquiry*, Executive Summary, paragraphs 435, 436 and 477.

102. *The Report of the Iraq Inquiry*, Executive Summary, paragraph 432.

103. *The Report of the Iraq Inquiry*, Executive Summary, paragraph 493.

104. The chiefs of staff also saw it: *The Report of the Iraq Inquiry*, Executive Summary, paragraph 465.

105. John Howard, 'Iraq 2003: A Retrospective', speech to Lowy Institute, 9 April 2013, and see note 8.

106. Tony Blair statement in response to *The Report of the Iraq Inquiry*, 6 July 2016.

107. *The Report of the Iraq Inquiry*, Executive Summary, paragraph 439.

108. Tony Blair statement in response to *The Report of the Iraq Inquiry*, 6 July 2016.

109. 'Iraq war illegal, says Annan', BBC, 16 September 2004. Available at: http://news.bbc.co.uk/1/hi/world/middle_east/3661134.stm.

110. Richard Norton-Taylor, 'Lawyers warned Eden that Suez invasion was illegal', *Guardian*, 1 December 2006.

111. *The Report of the Iraq Inquiry*, Executive Summary, paragraph 20.

112. Tony Blair statement in response to *The Report of the Iraq Inquiry*, 6 July 2016.

113. Seth Center, 'Policy Roundtable 1–1 on the Chilcot Inquiry', edited by Joshua Rovner and Diane Labrosse, International Security Studies Forum, 18 September 2016.

114. Sally Morgan, 'Blair Government', Queen Mary University, 26 January 2009.

115. Sir John Chilcot, BBC interview, 6 July 2017: 'Any prime minister taking a country into war has got to be straight with the nation and carry it, so far as possible, with him or her. I don't believe that was the case in the Iraq instance.' Available at: http://www.bbc.co.uk/news/uk-politics-40510539.

116. *The Report of the Iraq Inquiry*, Executive Summary, paragraph 807.

117. *The Report of the Iraq Inquiry*, 3.2.104–107.

118. *The Report of the Iraq Inquiry*, 3.2.104–107.

CONCLUSION

1. On average, 32 per cent said they were dissatisfied, and 61 per cent were dissatisfied, with Thatcher, Major, Blair, Brown, and Cameron in their last three months of office. Ipsos MORI Political Monitor Satisfaction Ratings: average of last three months before leaving office. Margaret Thatcher, satisfied 30 per cent: dissatisfied 65 per cent; John Major, 32:59; Tony Blair, 32:61; Gordon Brown, 35:59; David Cameron, 31:62. ('Are you satisfied or dissatisfied with the way X is doing his/her job as Prime Minister?')

2. Adam Drummond, 'Mixed reviews for former Tory PMs, poor marks for Labour ones', Opinium poll carried out 3–7 February 2017. The figures for Gordon Brown were: good job, 13 per cent, bad job, 48 per cent; while Margaret Thatcher was 40:35; John Major, 20:31; David Cameron, 26:42. Accessed at: https://www.opinium.co.uk/mixed-reviews-former-tory-pms-poor-marks-labour-ones/.

3. Robert Tombs, *The English and their History* (Penguin, 2014), pp. 830–3, 834–5, 845–6.

4. National Statistics statistical release: 'Provisional UK ODA tables 2015.' Accessed at: https://www.gov.uk/government/statistics/provisional-uk-official-development-assistance-as-a-proportion-of-gross-national-income-2015.

5. The US-led military action in Afghanistan was not specifically author-ized by the UN Security Council, as the US claimed to be acting in self-defence (after the 9/11 attack and the Afghanistan government's refusal to surrender Osama bin Laden and other al-Qaeda leaders), under Article Seven of the UN Charter. This was implicitly accepted by the UN Security Council when it adopted resolution 1386 in December 2001, setting up the International Security Assistance Force to help the interim Afghan government maintain security in Kabul and surrounding areas.

6. Dan Corry, Anna Valero, and John Van Reenen, 'UK Economic Performance since 1997', LSE Centre for Economic Performance, 15 November 2011.

7. Ed Balls, 'Blair Government', Queen Mary University, 25 January 2016.

8. ONS Digital, 'International migration: A recent history', 15 January 2015 http://visual.ons.gov.uk/uk-perspectives-a-recent-history-of-international-migration/.

9. Tony Blair, speech at the Corn Exchange, City of London, in which he expounded the 'third way' between a presumption in favour of either privatization or nationalization, 7 April 1997. Later institutionalized as the What Works Programme at the Home Office, for reduction of re-offending.

10. Nuffield Trust, 'A history of NHS spending in the UK'. Available at: https://www.nuffieldtrust.org.uk/chart/a-history-of-nhs-spending-in-the-uk.

11. Geoff Whitty and Jake Anders, '(How) did New Labour narrow the achievement and participation gap?' Institute of Education, University of London, 2014.

12. Paul Bolton, 'Participation in higher education in England and the UK', House of Commons Library, February 2017.

13. Jonathan Powell, 'Blair Government' course special lecture on the peace process in Northern Ireland, Queen Mary University of London, 9 February 2009.

14. Jonathan Powell, 'Blair Government' course special lecture, 9 February 2009.

15. See chapter 2.

16. David Laws was a member for the first 17 days of the Coalition before being replaced by Danny Alexander.

Publisher's Acknowledgements

From *The Alastair Campbell Diaries, Volume One: Prelude to Power* by Alastair Campbell, published by Hutchinson. Reproduced by permission of The Random House Group Ltd. © 2010.

From *The Alastair Campbell Diaries, Volume Two: Power and the People* by Alastair Campbell, published by Hutchinson. Reproduced by permission of The Random House Group Ltd. © 2011.

From *The Alastair Campbell Diaries, Volume Three: Power and Responsibility* by Alastair Campbell, published by Hutchinson. Reproduced by permission of The Random House Group Ltd. © 2011.

From *The Alastair Campbell Diaries, Volume Four: The Burden of Power: Countdown to Iraq* by Alastair Campbell, published by Hutchinson. Reproduced by permission of The Random House Group Ltd. © 2012.

From *Brown's Britain: How Gordon Runs the Show* by Robert Peston. Reproduced by permission of Short Books. © 2005.

From *A Journey* by Tony Blair, published by Hutchinson. Reproduced by permission of The Random House Group Ltd. © 2010.

From *My Life, Our Times* by Gordon Brown, published by Bodley Head. Reproduced by permission of The Random House Group Ltd. © 2017.

From *The New Machiavelli* by Jonathan Powell, published by Vintage. Reproduced by permission of Jonathan Powell. © 2010.

From *Speaking Out* by Ed Balls, published by Hutchinson. Reproduced by permission of The Random House Group Ltd. © 2016.

From *A Stranger in Europe: Britain and the EU from Thatcher to Blair* by Stephen Wall. Reproduced by permission of Oxford University Press. © 2008.

From *The Unconventional Minister* by Geoffrey Robinson, published by Michael Joseph. Reproduced by permission of The Random House Group Ltd. © 2000.

Anthony Bevins, 'New sleaze row knocks at door of No 10', *The Independent*, 2 June 1997.

Index